PATTERNS
OF
SOCIAL
ORGANIZATION

McGRAW-HILL SERIES IN SOCIOLOGY

Consulting Editor: Otto N. Larsen, University of Washington

McGRAW-HILL BOOK COMPANY

New York   San Francisco
St. Louis   Düsseldorf   Johannesburg
Kuala Lumpur   London
Mexico   Montreal
New Delhi   Panama
Rio de Janeiro   Singapore
Sydney   Toronto

JONATHAN H. TURNER

Department of Sociology
University of California, Riverside

PATTERNS

A
SURVEY
OF
SOCIAL
INSTITUTIONS

OF

SOCIAL

ORGANIZATION

This book was set in Baskerville by Applied Typographic Systems and printed on permanent paper and bound by The Maple Press Company. The designer was Janet Bollow; the chapter-opening illustrations were done by Susan Jaekel; the text illustrations were done by Judith McCarty. The editors were Ronald D. Kissack, Robert A. Fry, and Marge Woodhurst. Charles A. Goehring supervised production.

PATTERNS
OF
SOCIAL
ORGANIZATION

Printed in the United States of America.

Library of Congress catalog card number: 78-167498

1234567890 MAMM 798765432

07–065560–X

to
susan
for all your help
many thanks

contents

In the pages which follow I have attempted to provide an overview of six prominent institutions: economy, kinship, education, law, polity, and religion. While other institutions such as science, leisure, and medicine might properly be included, it seemed more useful to limit the scope of the book to the most universal and vital institutions.

Four major themes provide the organizing framework of the book. First, I am convinced that it is always necessary to examine social structures, particularly enduring and society-wide ones like social institutions, in a comparative perspective. In each chapter I have therefore offered a very general portrayal of the focal institution in both traditional and modern societies. In this way the features of American social institutions—and this is the second theme—can be placed in context and yet given added relief. After a general discussion of the traditional and modern profile of an institution is concluded, I then examine the general features of the American case, comparing it to profiles and trends of institutions in other types of societies.

A third theme concerns institutional change. It is obvious that basic institutions over the history of human societies and in the contemporary world have undergone and currently are undergoing profound change. I have therefore attempted to provide tentative answers to these questions: What kinds of transformations do institutions undergo as they move from a traditional to a modern profile? What kinds of changes are evident in the institutions of modern societies? And, what are some of the forces that have generated such changes?

Finally and most important, if the first three themes are to be explored adequately, I have placed tremendous emphasis on the interrelations among social institutions. Too often in previous analyses authors have tended to view each institution in a society as existing in a social vacuum. While for some purposes of exposition this is necessary and desirable, I have tried to trace—as fully as existing knowledge and my intellect will allow—the incredibly complex interrelations among institutions as they affect, alter, and circumscribe each other. To understand institutional change or the reasons for a particular institutional profile in a society requires that institutions be viewed as a web or network of mutual interaction.

The organization of the chapters will thus reflect an emphasis on four themes: the necessity for a comparative approach, the significance of institutional change, the importance of putting the American case in comparative perspective, and the need to view institutions as a complex web of interrelations.

A final note of gratitude should be addressed to those who have assisted me with the development of the manuscript. I would like to thank Robin M. Williams, Jr., Gerhard Lenski, Otto Larsen, Alvin Bertrand, Worth Summers, and John Foskett, who examined early drafts and made substantive, and in many instances, face-saving suggestions. A special thanks should go to Charles Ackerman, Robin M. Williams, Jr., and William Friedland, who introduced me to the study of social institutions.

JONATHAN H. TURNER

preface

the
analysis
of
SOCIAL INSTITUTIONS   1

INTRODUCTION

To examine the societies of the contemporary world or to delve into the history of past civilizations forces two apparently contradictory conclusions. On the one hand we must acknowledge the tremendous diversity in societies of the past and present. The exact way that societies have become structured around such fundamental problems as how to cope with the physical environment, how to regenerate the human species through birth, maturation, and socialization, how to distribute power and coordinate human endeavor, and how to deal with the inevitable emotional tensions and anxieties accompanying men's lives evidences no inflexible formula. However, under this enormous variability there appear to be certain structures common to all known societies. In varying forms and patterns, societies always display family and kinship, religion, economy, stratification, law, polity, education, and community. At least up to the present, these appear to be endemic to the organization of the human species into society.

The general intent of this book can be simply stated: to explore both the diversity and similarity in certain kinds of structures in human societies. Specifically, we will examine those fundamental structures called social institutions. It is within these structures that many of the most basic activities necessary for the survival of society occur. In the chapters to follow, we will describe, analyze, and compare the features of those six institutions which come close to being universal in all societies: law, polity, economy, kinship, education, and religion. As we will discover, some types of societies reveal only the bare rudiments of some of these institutions, while others display elaborate and complex institutional forms.

The notion of institutions has been central to sociological thought for a long time. It would appear that a concept of such long standing would have a clear and precise meaning for all sociologists, but unfortunately such is not the case. Just what constitutes a social institution has not been fully agreed upon; and in fact, many sociologists are even hesitant to acknowledge the existence of social institutions (Homans, 1964). Rather, institutions are conceived of as reifications or conceptual fictions in the minds of sociologists. Obviously a book with *Social Institutions* as part of the title does not hold to this latter perspective. Yet asserting the existence of real and concrete structures called institutions immediately presents us with the problem of delineating just what they are. Because of the ambiguity surrounding the notion of institutions, we will spend the better part of this first chapter outlining one definition and general framework for the analysis of social institutions.[1]

---

[1] Even though the reader may disagree with this viewpoint the concrete descriptions and analysis of various institutions are presented in a manner compatible with other perspectives on social institutions.

SYSTEMS

One of the most useful ways to approach the study of any phenomenon is with an eye to its *systemic* qualities. For example, more complete understanding of the solar system came when scientists began to unravel its systemic features, such as the relations of the planets to the sun and to each other. Comprehension of the human anatomy and physiology came when early physicians began to explore the body as a system of interconnected, functioning parts. Understanding of the nature of matter and energy was greatly expanded when scientists theorized about the systemic interrelations among the ultimate components of matter. Perhaps the most recent example of new insights stemming from considering the systemic qualities of a phenomenon is in the field of ecology where increasingly the total world is being viewed as an ecosystem. From this perspective new understanding of processes and problems is emerging. Similar advances in knowledge in all spheres of human inquiry have tended to follow once analysts became attuned to the systemic nature of the phenomena under study. Such is also the case with the study of society.

basic elements of systems

Thus, crucial to understanding of society from an institutional standpoint is the notion of system (Bertalanffy, 1956; Hall and Fagen, 1956; Chin, 1964; Buckley, 1967). At the most general level, a system can be defined as a complex of *interrelated parts*, surrounded by a *boundary*, and existing in an environment. The parts of a system can be virtually anything, including cells, atoms, stars, springs, gears, groups, organizations, and institutions. Just what the parts of a system are depends upon the nature of the system under study—whether a solar system, society, or human body. But they are also dependent upon the *analytical purposes* of the investigator. What are parts for one may not be parts for another investigator, even though they are analyzing the same system. For example, depending upon our analytical purposes, we could consider the basic parts of the same human body to be neutrons and protons, atoms, cells, organs, tissues, and so forth. To consider a particular system unit a part of a larger, more inclusive system can thus be a somewhat arbitrary matter. The same is true of a sociological analysis of society, since for different purposes groups, crowds, social strata, large-scale organizations, communities, or social institutions can be considered system parts.

In order to constitute a system, parts must be interrelated so that a change in one part will have consequences for other parts comprising that system. In a body system, it is safe to say that a change in that part called the heart will have consequences for other parts. Or in the system we call the family, a change in the father's status will have consequences for the other parts of that system. If we are analyzing a whole society, a drastic change in the economy such as a depression will have a profound impact on the family, polity, and educational institutions of that society. This is true because the parts of a system are related. The more interrelated the parts, the more we may be confident in calling something a system.

Systems to varying degrees are also *bounded,* which means that they can be distinguished or separated from other systems and their general environment. Sometimes boundaries are permeable and sometimes they are closed, allowing little in or out. Skin is the obvious boundary for the body systems and a guarded border the boundary for a social system. Most system boundaries are permeable and constantly penetrated by the surrounding environment. In such "open" systems boundaries are sometimes difficult to identify because of their high degree of permeability. For example, the boundaries of the solar system or of a family are not easily discernible although the parts of these systems display such a high degree of interrelatedness that they constitute a system.

Many of the parts of a larger system can also be considered as systems in their own right, since they display constituent parts bearing interrelations as well as a boundary. An organ of the body can be considered a system in and of itself, and a particular family, group, organization, or social institution can also be viewed as a separate system. Where this is done, system parts are analyzed as *subsystems* of the larger, more inclusive system. When parts are viewed as subsystems, analysis is greatly expanded, since attention must now be drawn not only to external relations among subsystems but also to relations within subsystems as they affect these external relations.

basic elements of social systems

Like any system, a society is composed of parts or subsystems which are interrelated, bounded, and exist in an environment. The most basic parts of a social system are *status positions*, *roles*, and *norms*. Out of these basic parts are built the various subsystems of society. Status is a position in the social system indicating the location of a person. Norms are rules or sets of expectations specifying the appropriate behavior for individuals in status positions. Role is adjustive behavior of people trying to conform to norms.[2]

[2] With respect to these concepts, especially status and role, divergent interpretations are evident in the literature: Role can often refer to "total behavior" (hence meaning the same thing as norm), to an actor's "perception" of norms and how he should behave, or to clusters of status positions. Following Williams (1970:43), our analysis will emphasize role performance or enactment as actors in status positions attempt to conform to norms. Status position is a less ambiguous concept, but Goode (1960) has

The degree of "fit" or correspondence among statuses, roles, and norms is rarely perfect. Norms often conflict or are ambiguous. An actor can often occupy two or more different status positions at the same time that are guided by divergent, changing, and conflicting norms. Therefore role behavior usually reflects an adjustment process as people attempt to interpret ambiguous or changing norms and to reconcile conflicting norms of different statuses. Furthermore, individual personality differences inevitably affect the style of role behavior and the way actors adjust to norms. While these considerations greatly complicate analysis, we can at the most basic level still hold to these definitions: statuses constitute a map or grid of positions in a system, norms represent the obligations attendant on those positions, and roles are the adjustive behaviors of actors in status positions.

Isolating out statuses, roles, and norms as basic system parts should point to the fact that they often exhibit an interrelatedness with other statuses, roles, and norms. These parts are rarely found in isolation from one another, but rather they cluster into highly complex networks or webs of interrelations. In an ultimate sense a total society can be viewed as an incredibly complex clustering of different statuses, roles, and norms. However, to identify, count, code, keep track of, map, and record role adjustments among the billions of interrelationships among different statuses, roles, and norms in larger societies is impossible. And this complexity is compounded by the fact that every individual actor in a society occupies multiple statuses and plays multiple roles. Fortunately these basic system parts cluster into larger system parts or subsystems that are easier to see, record, and analyze. Such a clustering of these system parts into larger subsystems greatly facilitates analysis, since it allows for the examination of system units larger than each particular status, norm, or role enactment and adjustment. The analysis of societal subsystems constitutes much of the subject matter of soiology. Individual actors are rarely studied by themselves but in larger social contexts such as families, work groups, peer groups, classrooms, complex organizations, political parties, and the like. In turn some of these larger units cluster together or with other social units to form even larger societal subsystems: individual families into a kinship subsystem, work groups into a factory, factories into an economy, classrooms into a school, schools into the institution of education, or political parties into a polity.

Thus the subsystems ultimately comprising a society can be of

5

---

attempted to redefine status to denote only those role behaviors which are highly circumscribed by norms. For our purposes, however, we will maintain that status is simply a locational concept without reference to the degree of clarity and compulsion of norms. Again, we might add, the unfortunate lack of consensus over long-term, basic concepts in sociology forces ponderous definitions as a necessary prelude to any analytical activity.

different size and complexity. Conspicuous types of societal subsystems that have come under particular scrutiny by sociologists include groups, communities, complex organizations, stratification, and social institutions. Within each of these general types are encompassed a wide variety of specific kinds of structure: rural and urban communities, economic and governmental bureaucracies, open and closed stratification systems, or large and small groups. As will become increasingly evident in this book, many variations in different social institutions are evident in the world's societies, since social institutions as one general type of societal subsystem display tremendous diversity.

Societal subsystems overlap with one another. Their boundaries are not closed but are highly permeable, and frequently the components of one are also components of another. For example, the polity of a society would include certain components of various communities such as the local government. The economy of a society would ultimately be composed of factories, companies, and corporations which are also part of local communities. Or, the kinship system of a society is constituted of specific family groups residing in local communities. Such overlap underscores the interrelatedness of the parts of the social system. Often the interrelatedness involves so much structural overlap that distinguishing separate and discrete subsystems becomes difficult. Yet we can usually distinguish the statuses, norms, and roles of different subsystems, even though one person may enact roles in several different subsystems.

Such differentiation of subsystems is possible not only because of clear differences in the nature of statuses and the content of norms but also because actors usually engage in role behavior at different times and places. For instance, an adult male in a modern society will occupy statuses, conform to norms, and enact roles in at least the economic, familial, community, and political subsystems of a society. Many such statuses and the norms attendant upon them allow role performance to be separated in time and space. However, this is not always the case. Often convenient segregation of statuses, norms, and roles is not possible, with the result that actors experience "role conflict." Much of everyday life is rife with people's incapacity to segregate effectively the normative demands of different positions that they occupy. For our purposes it is most crucial that we recognize one of the basic reasons for role conflicts: Societal subsystems overlap and most actors occupy statuses, conform to norms, and enact roles in several different subsystems.

In sum, then, societies are ultimately composed of statuses, roles, and norms. In turn these cluster into larger types of subsystems, which vary in size and complexity. Social systems can be viewed as the organization of myriad interrelations among large and small subsystems. Many of these cut across each other's boundaries and display structural overlap. Depending upon the purposes of analysis, the interrelations with, among, or between different subsystems are explored by sociologists. In this book analysis will focus on the interrelations within that general type of subsystem called social institutions. During the course of this analysis interrelations among economy, kinship, education, law, polity, and religion, as well as between any two of these institutions, will be examined. Naturally, to the extent that this analysis focuses only on social institutions, it is incomplete. Many other societal parts—from small groups to stratification—would have to be analyzed to gain a complete picture of the structure and processes of social systems.

SOCIAL INSTITUTIONS

Like any societal subsystem social institutions are ultimately composed of statuses, norms, and roles. Unlike many system parts, however, institutions cut across whole societies. This means that specific institutions overlap with and encompass many other segments of a society, including groups, collectivities, strata, organizations, and communities. Thus, social institutions are extremely large units that are highly conspicuous features of any society. In virtually every society the institutions of economy, kinship, education, law, polity, and religion are important societal subsystems.

To determine the nature of these large societal subsystems it is necessary to understand the kinds of statuses, norms, and roles out of which they are constructed.[3] As already noted, the status positions and roles which make up institutions often are located in smaller social units, such as a family, factory, school, political party, organization, or community. Of the incredibly vast number and variety of status roles in all societal subsystems only some can be considered as part of a social institution. Furthermore, of the myriad of norms attached to the diversity of statuses in all societal subsystems only some are institutional. In order for these basic system components to be parts of larger institutional subsystems they must be: pervasive and general in a society; relatively stable over time; and have broad consequences for the larger society.

7

[3] The scheme presented here deviates somewhat from other prominent conceptualizations of institutions, particularly those of Martin (1968) and Bertrand (1968). It comes closest to the scheme presented by Williams (1970:36–45) and Eisenstadt (1968). Again, it should be emphasized that even though the reader might disagree with this conceptualization, the subject matter of the book is presented in a manner compatible with other conceptualizations of social institutions.

Statuses, roles, and norms that are relatively pervasive and conspicuous in a society are likely to be institutional. The positions of mother, father, son, daughter, political leader, worker, teacher, student, clergyman, and worshipper are institutional because they are widespread in social systems. Only the general norms guiding role behavior in these widespread positions can be considered institutional. There are many highly specific norms attendant upon institutional statuses, but they are not part of the institutional subsystem of a society. Rather, just the more general norms applying to a whole class or category of pervasive statuses are institutional. Thus the general norms attendant upon positions such as those listed above are the "building blocks" of institutional subsystems. Related to their generality and pervasiveness, norms guiding institutional role behavior possess some additional features (Williams, 1970:37):

1 Institutional norms are consistently conformed to by status incumbents.
2 Institutional norms tend to be widely known by the members of a society.
3 Institutional norms tend to be learned early in life.

This listing should not obscure the fact that institutional norms for certain individuals and segments of a society are often violated, unknown, ambiguous, not sanctioned negatively, and never learned. Deviance, defiance, rebellion, ignorance, and alienation exist in all societies and make the fit between what is normatively prescribed and what is actually done imperfect. Lack of clarity in and conformity to institutional norms of a society is particularly likely when societies are undergoing rapid change in their basic institutions and other subsystems. Under these conditions old norms conflict with the new and emerging statuses are devoid of clear-cut norms to guide role behavior. The result is that ignorance or uncertainty about how to behave becomes widespread and it becomes difficult to apply strong sanctions for violations as well as to socialize the young into a coherent body of institutional norms. For example, in the United States certain institutional norms concerning the role of women in the family and the economy have been undergoing rapid change with the result that considerable conflict, ambiguity, and variance in the way women behave as mothers, wives, and workers has become conspicuous. The expansion of the Women's Liberation movement in the late 1960s marked the increasing codification and perhaps socialization of the young and old into a new set of norms deviating noticeably from the more traditional norms of women as homemakers. This kind of conflict and variation of institutional norms is inevitable in virtually all societies and underscores the fact that while institutional norms tend to be general and pervasive they never are completely free of ambiguities, contradictions, and conflicts, nor are they always conformed to by individuals and subgroups.

RELATIVE STABILITY

Institutional statuses tend to be relatively stable. The emphasis here is on relative stability, for rarely are institutional statuses and norms fixed and unchanging. New statuses, norms, and roles emerge, some cease to exist, others change; thus it is critical that we not view institutions as unchanging or static. Yet some degree of stability over time is necessary for us to call an interrelated set of statuses an institution. For example, the basic statuses of kinship have existed over a long period of time and this allows us to call the family subsystem institutional. However, role behaviors of family members have changed in recent years, as have familial norms and the number of positions included in the family nucleus. At one time grandparents, aunts, and uncles were an intimate part of the family unit, but these status positions are less and less an intimate part of the family in modern societies. Also, the norms governing behavior of family members have changed so that children are now expected to be more independent, parents more permissive, fathers less authoritarian and stern, and so on. Yet we should not lose sight of the stable characteristics of the family: The interrelated status positions of mother, father, son, and daughter still exist and certain general norms concerning child rearing, feeding, sheltering, and obeying parents have persisted over time. It is this kind of stability that allows us to call the family a social institution.

SOCIETAL CONSEQUENCES

Almost any system part has consequences for other parts. This is inevitable given the interrelated nature of systems. Many crucial subsystems not only have consequences for other system parts but also for the maintenance, change, or destruction of the broader society in which they are located. Social institutions are such a subsystem. Societies face many problems of survival from within and outside their boundaries, such as resource scarcity, natural disaster, political incompetence, alienation, demoralization, revolution, and external conquest. As we will see, institutions are rarely unimportant or irrelevant to these problems of survival. Usually institutions partially resolve these problems, although they can also aggravate them or make system survival problematic. The specific consequences of a particular institution for these problems will always vary from system to system in terms of a society's degree of modernity, size, history, geography, and present social conditions. Despite this variability our analysis will be able to delineate at least some common consequences of institutions in all types of societies. For example, in all societies family and kinship have far-reaching consequences for the persistence of a society, since it is in the family that each new generation is born, biologically supported, and socialized. To illustrate further, it can be noted that the primitive economy of the Australian aborigines revolving around the gathering of roots, plants, and wildlife with crude tools differs considerably from a modern industrial economy operating with vast complexes of machines and factories. Yet at the most basic level, the overall consequences of these two types of economies for their respective societies are much the same: Each provides insulation from the vicissitudes of the physical environment and each supplies the material subsistence, such as food, shelter, and clothing, on which human life and society depend.

However, at a more specific level of analysis, we must also draw attention to the divergent and changing consequences of institutions in different types of societies. Many of the specific consequences of institutions change with alterations of and developments in the institutions themselves, in the broader society, or in the environment of a society. For example, as we will examine in subsequent chapters, kinship and family in primitive and traditional societies have many society-wide consequences extending beyond reproduction and socialization. In these traditional systems, kinship is the actual place where economic, political, and religious roles are enacted. Kinship is thus a dominant institution that structures, regulates, and pervades almost all spheres of a society's functioning. On the other hand, kinship and family in modern societies do not have these extensive consequences. Economic, political, and religious activity is carried out primarily in other structures, such as churches, factories, and governmental bureaucracies, which are clearly separated and insulated from the family. Even the socialization of the young is removed from the exclusive purview of the family as schools and other educational structures assume a prominent place in modern societies. Thus, we must remain constantly alert to the diversity of consequences that institutions can have for the survival of different types of societies.

In sum, then, we can offer a general definition of social institutions as clusters of interrelated statuses, roles, and norms, which are pervasive and general, relatively stable, and significant for system survival. Six institutions that appear related to the survival of all human societies are economy, kinship, education, law, polity, and religion. The degree to which these institutions have consequences for survival problems facing social systems varies greatly from society to society—as we will explore extensively. Not only this, but as we will also see, the structure of these institutions can be vastly different from system to system. Furthermore, many modern societies display other institutions not to be treated extensively in our analysis. For example, institutions such as health care or medicine, psychiatry, social work, and leisure are highly relevant to the survival problems of modern social systems. But these are not institutions in primitive or even more advanced traditional societies. They remain recessive, being neither pervasive, general, stable, nor very relevant to system survival. As will become abundantly clear, one of the principal concerns of the analysis in the following chapters is the comparison of the structure and consequences of institutions in a wide variety of societies from the simplest to the most complex. For this reason we have chosen those six institutions that are most likely to be evident in both simple and complex societies. In the analysis of these institutions, we will examine their emergence early in societal development, while focusing on their changing structure and importance for system survival during all stages of modernization.

the web of institutional subsystems in societies

Since social institutions are societal subsystems, they exhibit interrelatedness with each other. Were this not the case, it would be difficult to view them as parts of a larger, more inclusive social system. These interrelations constitute a fantastically complex web or network. To comprehend the totality of this web is presently impossible, but in the following chapters we will begin to sort out at least its more conspicuous strands and fibers.

Institutions display mutual, direct, indirect, weak, and strong influences on each other. The economy, for example, directly influences the structure and functioning of all other institutions, and vice versa. Furthermore, the economy can have an indirect influence on other institutions, such as is the case when the economy affects the polity, which in turn influences all other institutions. Similar indirect influences can be traced among other institutions. Because of these connections among institutions, a change in the structure and functioning of one will have repercussions for the others. Just how extensive these multiple repercussions will be varies from society to society and from institution to institution. For example, in a primitive society changes in the institution of religion would have profound consequences for all other institutions, whereas in modern societies this would not be the case. But changes in some institutions such as the economy reverberate throughout the rest of a society, whether very simple or exceedingly complex. Thus we cannot view any institution as existing in a social vacuum. Such an assumption would prevent analysis of the full dynamics in the structure and functioning of social systems. For this reason analysis in the following chapters will focus on the mutual and multiple influences of institutions on one another.

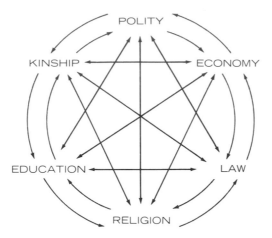

Figure 1–1 The complexity of the institutional web.

In Figure 1–1 some of these interrelations among institutions are plotted in order to provide a picture of the complexity in the web of institutional subsystems. Each line and arrow in Figure 1–1 represents the influence of one institution upon another. By tracing the arrows among several institutions it is possible to visualize the direct, indirect, and multiple interrelations among institutions. Yet the diagram does not delineate the relative strength of the interrelations, nor does it communicate the number of different types of interconnections. Even without these latter elements, which would greatly complicate the figure's appearance, it is easy to visualize the interrelations as a complex web. The exact way this web is spun for any particular society is always a reflection of many unique historical and contemporary forces. However, one major theme of this book is that despite the many unique and varied relationships among different institutions in the world's societies, certain common patterns of influence among the institutions of different types of societies are evident.

12

PERSONALITY, CULTURE, AND INSTITUTIONS

personality

While society, in the framework outlined above, is a complex network of statuses, roles, and norms, it is people who occupy statuses, enact roles, and conform to (or deviate from) norms. This fact necessitates the examination of personality. Just as society can be considered a system, so can personality; and as we will examine later, the personality system affects and is affected by institutional structures and processes in a society. From an institutional perspective personality involves a whole set of attributes or traits which affect a status incumbent's capacity and motivation to interpret and conform to norms and enact roles. Many institutional structures could not persist unless actors evidenced the ability and willingness to play institutional roles. It is not surprising, then, that many institutional structures have consequences for generating personality systems with the capabilities and desire to become incumbent in institutional statuses, interpret norms, and enact appropriate behaviors. Of course this process is never completely successful since deviance, alienation, rebellion, disaffection, and incompetence of personalities are ubiquitous human conditions. The fact that these conditions also influence the structure and functioning of institutions makes the treatment of personality even more necessary in an institutional analysis of societies.

culture

Every society has a culture consisting of knowledge, values, beliefs, ideologies, and a host of artifacts from freeways and nuclear bombs to bows and arrows. Like personality, culture also may be considered a system. Cultural systems are composed of two basic types of parts: material artifacts and nonmaterial, symbolic components such as values and beliefs. Culture circumscribes institutional processes while at the same time being maintained and created by these institutional processes. From an institutional perspective, the nonmaterial components of culture as they affect and are affected by institutional structures and processes are most critical to our analysis. Many institutional norms are reflections of basic beliefs, values, ideologies, and the level of knowledge in the cultural system of a society. Conversely, certain institutions, such as kinship, preserve culture and pass it on through socialization from one generation to the next. And virtually all institutional structures expand and alter cultural components, whether knowledge, beliefs, or values. The inclusion of culture in an institutional analysis of society is therefore indispensable, as we will see throughout this book.

Just as institutions do not exist in a vacuum, neither do social systems. The clusterings of statuses, norms, and roles making up a social system are constantly affected and penetrated by two other systems—culture and personality. In turn culture and personality are greatly influenced by social systems, especially institutions. It may seem strange to describe culture and personality as systems distinguishable from the social system since they are so intimately involved in social life. But for precisely this reason it is necessary to separate them analytically. Were this not done it would be impossible to make sense out of complex structures and processes in society. The utility of these distinctions will become clear as we turn to the analysis of specific social institutions.

SUMMARY

Society has been portrayed as one kind of system. It has also been emphasized that the boundaries and parts of social systems are open and often overlapping. We have emphasized that the basic units of the social system are not people per se, but statuses, roles, and norms. Out of these basic parts are constructed the larger subsystems of a society, which can be a wide variety of units, including groups, organizations, communities, social strata, and institutions. Institutions as one kind of societal subsystem have been viewed as composed of interrelated clusters of status norms which are general, pervasive, relatively stable, and significant for social system survival. Institutional subsystems are seen as displaying very complex interrelationships. To understand the structure and functioning of any institutions, the nature of these relationships must be examined. Furthermore, the necessity of accounting for certain components of culture and personality in the study of institutions has been emphasized.

Finally, we should pause on a point made earlier. An institutional analysis of society is only one way to look at society. It is incomplete and ignores much of what goes on in society. Many structures and processes in society are noninstitutional and subinstitutional, and this fact must always be kept in mind.

SUGGESTED READINGS

Alvin L. Bertrand, "A Structural Analysis of Differential Patterns of Social Relations," *Rural Sociology*, 33, 4, December 1968, pp. 411–423.

Talcott Parsons, *The Social System*, New York: The Free Press, 1951, pp. 1–85.

Pitirim Sorokin, *Society, Culture, and Personality*, New York: Harper & Row, Publishers, Incorporated, 1947, pp. 1–91.

Martin W. Thomas, "Social Institutions: A Reformulation of the Concept," *Pacific Sociological Review*, 2, 2, Fall 1968, pp. 100–109.

Robin M. Williams, Jr., *American Society*, 3d ed., New York: Alfred A. Knopf, Inc., 1970, pp. 36–45.

the
analysis
of
SOCIAL
    INSTITUTIONS

ECONOMY 2

From the beginning of human societies economic problems of how to secure enough food and insulation from the natural environment have persisted. Today in many modern societies actual subsistence is no longer in question, but what is perceived as "necessary" for human survival has escalated to new levels (Moore, 1967:79). Men in these societies now desire television sets, cars, elaborate homes, and a host of material comforts. Karl Marx noted this fact long ago in his dictum that as soon as one need is satisfied, new ones will emerge. Thus for both an Australian aborigine gathering roots and other plant life to fulfill his basic needs for food and a worker in a modern factory earning money to provide for his subsistence and escalating material needs, economic activity is a driving and consuming concern. Because of its centrality to human life, economic activity usually becomes institutionalized and displays a particular pattern and profile in every society. Understanding the various profiles of the economy is one of the most important tasks for a sociologist since the structure and functioning of any society are profoundly shaped by the way the economy has become institutionalized.

BASIC ELEMENTS OF ECONOMY

"Classical" economists (Cole, 1969) initially isolated three basic elements in describing economic processes: *land, labor,* and *capital.* Later a fourth was included: *entrepreneurship.* And sociologists added a fifth: *technology* (Marx and Engels, 1848).

Land refers to natural resources such as oil, timber, coal, uranium, gas, and agricultural acreage. Obviously the natural resources available to a society's economy can vary—some social systems have a plentiful supply, others very few. However, more important than the level or abundance of indigenous resources is the degree of access a society has to natural resources, whether its own or another society's. Many social systems have an abundance of natural resources but cannot get at or utilize them. Conversely, many societies have few indigenous resources but have high access to the resources of other systems. Labor concerns the level and kind of human effort put into economic processes. Labor can be viewed in both quantitative and qualitative senses. The number of people who can participate in the economy (quantity) always affects economic processes. But more important, the level of skill, knowledge, expertise, and motivation (quality) is an equally significant influence on the economy. Capital pertains to the level and kind of tools used in conjunction with labor in an economy. In gathering resources and then converting them into goods for consumption in a society, tools and equipment must be used. Sometimes tools are simple and uncomplicated, as is the case with the bow and arrow, stone chisel, hoe, or ox-drawn plow. At other times capital is extremely complicated and includes sophisticated machinery located in large factories. In addition to the actual tools and machines of the economy, financial and other resources available for buying or acquiring tools can be considered capital.

For a long time economists assumed that land, labor, and capital would automatically become organized. This was an unfortunate oversight, for in practice the organization of these elements into an economy is highly problematic. A growing recognition of this fact led analysts to the concept of *entrepreneurship*. While the notion of entrepreneurship is somewhat illusive,[1] it has come to refer to those structures and processes in a society that promote the organization and integration of other basic elements into an economy.

With the notable exception of Marx and Engels, early economic theorists ignored the importance of technology to economic processes. In an age when there is much sensitivity to the technological revolution this may seem incredible, but it is only recently that technology has been added to the list of basic economic elements (Moore, 1967). Technology is knowledge or verified understanding about the world and environment contained within the culture of a society. Knowledge that is applied in an attempt to alter or manipulate both the social and physical environment can be considered technological.[2]

---

[1] Some analysts, such as Schumpeter (1934, 1950), are willing to include other behaviors under the term *entrepreneurship:* Entrepreneurs, in one portrayal, are often viewed as the risk takers and gamblers of an economy who invest their money in the pursuit of profit and gain. Another portrayal revolves around the "innovator" concept of entrepreneurship. Here entrepreneurs are those individuals who make startling new discoveries which revolutionize and change the tide of economic production. A third version of the entrepreneur depicts him as the great man of industry, such as Ford, Rockefeller, Kaiser, Carnegie et al. All these conceptions of entrepreneurship operate under an "individualistic" premise that is wholly inadequate in explaining economic processes. Rather than viewing entrepreneurship as an individual character trait we should focus on more neutral mechanisms—from individuals to groups, organizations, and so forth—that are responsible for organizing basic elements into an economy.

[2] This definition may appear to run counter to common-sense understandings of technology. Frequently, we are accustomed to thinking about technology as the machines and gadgets involved in progress and the better life. And so we talk about the wonders of medical technology, industrial technology, space technology, and the like. Such notions are not incorrect; they are just imprecise and incomplete. For example, medical technology refers to that knowledge about the human body which is applied to cure and prevent disease. It just so happens that much of that knowledge when applied manifests itself in the form of complicated machinery and gadgets (heart pacers, kidney machines, etc.). These machines are not technology; rather, the knowledge which generated them is the technology. The same is true of industrial technology. And since the results of this technology—machines—are visible, we come to think of the machines, rather than knowledge, as the technology. However, sometimes technology does not have such visible consequences. The knowledge in the hands of a sociologist, social worker, psychiatrist, or counselor is also technology.

19

As will become evident, the level of technology in a society influences and is influenced by the level of skill in the labor force, the amount and degree of sophistication in capital, the principles of entrepreneurship, and the resulting access to land or natural resources.

In sum, then, these five basic economic elements — land, labor, capital, entrepreneurship, and technology — are central to the analysis of the economy. In the following portrayal of the economy as an institution they will be crucial in determining its structure and functioning.

ECONOMY AND SOCIETY

Societies are open systems and therefore engage in interchanges with the social and nonsocial environment. If an open system is to adapt to its environment it must have some way of controlling and regulating what is taken in from that environment. A plant must regulate the intake of water and sunlight or it will die. A body must control the kind and amount of food, air, and sunlight it absorbs. A personality (this can be considered a system) has defenses that control the amount of hostility experienced in the environment. Open systems thus must be *selectively* open, taking in only certain aspects of the environment and excluding unessential and harmful aspects of the environment. In most systems intakes from the environment are converted into usable commodities or substances. Air and food in a body system are transformed into useful substances and then transmitted to various parts or subsystems. Similarly, natural resources such as iron, rubber, oil, and others are first converted or transformed into commodities and then distributed.

In open systems specific structures or subsystems having these adaptive consequences for the broader system can usually be isolated. The mouth, skin, stomach, heart, lungs, and blood vessels are among such structures in a body system. In a plant system there are roots, leaves, and other structures having these adaptive consequences. In social systems the economy is the primary structure involved in adaptive processes. Specifically, we can delineate four of these processes found in all social systems: gathering, producing, distributing, and servicing.

GATHERING

Social systems extract natural resources from the environment. What and how much is gathered from the environment is a reflection of the level of technology, the degree of capital formation, the nature of labor, and the ability of a society to organize these elements. Societies low in these elements and their organization will be capable of taking in only limited resources from the environment. Furthermore, such societies will be poorly insulated from the environment and easily subject to floods, drought, disease, and famine. Conversely, societies high in all the economic elements will gather a wide variety and large quantity of resources as well as being insulated from the vicissitudes of the environment.

PRODUCTION

Once resources, whether in large or small quantities, are gathered they usually must be converted into goods and commodities usable by other system units. This process is called production. Again the extent of such production depends upon the level of technology, capital, labor, and entrepreneurship existent in a society. Societies high in all these factors will display an elaborate productive apparatus, whereas the reverse will be true of societies low in these basic economic elements.

DISTRIBUTING

Once commodities are produced they are distributed to other system units. Since other societal subsystems are not always engaged in resolving the adaptive problem they rely on the distributive process of the economy. When such distributive processes fail, an economic or adaptive crisis is generated. As with other economic processes, the level of the five basic economic elements is crucial in determining the extensiveness of such distribution.

SERVICING

The economy thus gathers and converts natural resources into commodities and then distributes them. Economies produce and distribute another kind of product, however, which does not have the natural environment as its origin. This product can be referred to as *services;* it becomes a vital product in large and complex economies with high levels of technology, capital, labor, and their organization, and hence a high rate and volume of gathering, producing, and distributing. A service is not easy to visualize, but we can begin by saying that it is the organization of basic economic elements that does not result in the production of a thing or commodity but that nevertheless facilitates the operation of other economic processes. For example, in the United States economy, banks, insurance firms, title and holding companies, stock brokerages, data processing facilities, and accounting firms do not generate goods but provide services which make possible the functioning of other economic organizations engaged in gathering, producing, and distributing.

Economic structures involved in these four processes are necessary for the maintenance of social systems. Unless gathering, producing, distributing, and servicing can occur, the survival of a society can only be tenuous. However, despite the centrality of the economy to system survival, we should not assume that economies always promote a society's adaptation to the environment. As is the case with many Third World nations, such as India, rapid population growth has outstripped the capacity of the economy to support the population. Similarly, the history of many extinct primitive societies would point to failures in their economies to support the population. Even where economies display a tremendous productive capacity, such as in the United States, the present modes of gathering, producing, distributing, and servicing are sufficiently disruptive and polluting to the ecosystem so as to create long-run problems of survival. More immediately, current patterns of distributing economic goods and services in Third World nations and among certain racial and ethnic minorities in the United States are so blatantly discriminatory and unequal that considerable domestic turmoil, perhaps even revolution, is inevitable.

These examples reveal that the consequences of an institution can be both functional and dysfunctional with respect to system survival. To have consequences for resolving one set of problems never guarantees that an institution will not create other problems of survival. Just how extensive the functional or dysfunctional consequences of an institution such as the economy are for a society is a reflection of the structure of the economy itself as well as many historical and current conditions unique to each particular society in the world.

DEFINITION OF ECONOMY

Despite this variability in the structure and consequences of economies, we can offer a broad definition of the economy as an institution. From an institutional perspective the economy must be defined in terms of the ways in which statuses, norms, and roles are organized around the processes of gathering, producing, distributing, and servicing. Without *some degree* of such economic organization the maintenance and persistence of society is unlikely. With these facts in mind, we can draw upon our general discussion in Chapter 1 and define the institution of the economy in this way:

> The economy is that interrelated, pervasive, relatively stable cluster of statuses, general norms, and role behaviors revolving around the gathering of resources and the producing and distributing of goods and services. In doing so, the economy has far-reaching consequences for the survival of a society.

TYPES OF ECONOMIES

It seems obvious that the structure of the economy varies from one society to another. Economies can be very simple or exceedingly complex. Analytically, even the most simple and primitive economy is involved in the four economic processes of gathering, producing, distributing, and servicing. However, different economies tend to display statuses revolving more around some of these economic processes than others. For example, some primitive societies are concerned more with merely gathering natural resources than with their conversion or production into commodities, with their distribution, or with servicing. Other economies, such as the United States or the Soviet Union, have a high proportion of their statuses, norms, and roles involved in the production and distribution of services and a lesser proportion concerned with gathering natural resources or production of goods and commodities. And many societies lie somewhere between these two. In reality there is enormous variation in the way roles are organized around basic economic processes. With respect to the economy we can isolate out at least four general types of economic organization: hunting and gathering economies, agricultural economies, industrial economies, and postindustrial economies. Naturally, few actual economies can be so neatly categorized; and yet it is necessary to begin to categorize if we are to make sense out of our topic.[3]

hunting and gathering economies[4]

Hunting and gathering societies have little insulation from the environment (Nash, 1966; Lenski, 1966:97). They are at the mercy of natural and sometimes social elements—famine, drought, scarcity, imperialism, and natural catastrophies. Technology or knowledge about how to manipulate and control the environment is low. Capital —bows, arrows, chisels, hoes—available for gathering resources and converting them into commodities also is low (Spier, 1970). Under these conditions the penetration and intrusion of the natural and social environment is a constant fact of life. Men often live in a state of submission, awe, and fear of the powers and vicissitudes of the natural environment. Labor is unspecialized, encompassing general abilities of how to hunt wild animals and gather indigenous plant life.

23

[3] For more extensive typologies with considerable descriptive data and an ethnographic bibliography, see: Goldschmidt (1959) and Lenski (1966).

[4] Goldschmidt (1959) correctly documents several different types of hunting and gathering societies in terms of their degree of mobility, kinship and community structure, and level of technology. Furthermore, the type of hunting and gathering of a society can vary greatly from the fishing activities of the Trobriand Islanders of the South Seas to the hunting of game by African bands. The brief description offered in this volume cannot possibly encompass or touch upon all this diversity. It represents a crude attempt to abstract out crucial elements of this type of economy. For a more detailed analysis the reader is directed to the references in the preceding footnote.

The organization of technology, capital, and labor in the pursuit of resources is simple, with family heads and various high-prestige leaders directing economic action.

The net result of this is a society which must "live off the land" — frequently in only a most tenuous way. There is little if any agricultural acreage, for farming as a means of gathering and converting resources is not a capacity possessed by such societies. Nor is there extensive domestication or herding of animals. By necessity, economic life revolves around and within a family unit such as a tribe or band, which wanders and roams a delimited territory in a semicyclical pattern in search of resources. When these wandering families exhaust the plant and animal life of one area they move on in order to let resources replenish themselves. Should these resources not be regenerated upon their return, as is often the case, the society faces a crisis of survival. Because of this mobility, hunting and gathering societies are usually small, composed of variously connected family units possessing their own internal organization. As resources are gathered they are minimally converted into basic commodities (food, clothing, shelter) and then distributed within the family.

Hunting and gathering societies thus possess a precarious adaptive capacity because of low levels of technology, capital, human skill, and entrepreneurship with which to extract natural resources from the environment. Because such extraction is problematic, it is inevitable that economic roles should focus on the basic processes of gathering and not on the comparatively insignificant processes of production, distribution, and servicing. When social systems can barely extract resources and insulate themselves, their economies must be organized primarily around gathering.

Hunting and gathering economies were the first type to emerge in human societies and have dominated most of man's history. It is only recently, over the last 10,000 to 12,000 years, that other types of economies have replaced hunting and gathering as the basic means of environmental adaptation. However, even today many economies such as those among the Australian aborigines, the Pygmies and bushmen of Africa, and various South American tribes remain basically a hunting and gathering type, despite the massive economic changes associated with industrialization in the contemporary world. In the long run, of course, it is unlikely that these tribal societies wandering over delimited territories can remain isolated or persist in the face of world economic development. For example, the Yic Yoront aborigines of the Cape York Peninsula in Australia effectively resisted contact with and influence by Western society from 1623 when the Dutch first made contact until the mid-1940s (Sharp, 1952). Even more recently, the Yic Yoront maintained their basic form of economic organization. Technology had been raised little above limited knowledge about hunting animals, gathering plants, and making crude tools. The stone ax, and later the steel ax, remained the basic capital resource of these aborigines. Though recent contacts with Western society have greatly altered the Yic Yoront group, some other aboriginal societies still survive in their habitat primarily on the basis of a hunting and gathering economy.

agricultural economies[5]

Agrarian economies display a considerably higher level of insulation from the environment than hunting and gathering economies. Advances in technology have greatly increased the capacity of these economies to control and manipulate the natural environment. Technology or knowledge in spheres such as planting, cultivation of land, harvesting, domestication of animals, and irrigation, coupled with higher levels of capital (tools and equipment), enable agrarian economies to stabilize a relationship with the environment. Human abilities now go beyond simple gathering and hunting techniques so that labor also possesses skills in crafts, tilling the land, harvesting, domestication and herding of animals. Along with these developments there is increased specialization of labor. These increases in technology, capital, and human skill enable agrarian economies to accumulate a surplus from the environment which can be used during periods of hardship and scarcity. Such surplus further insulates agrarian systems from their environment, thereby raising their level of adaptation (Lenski, 1966).

Because there is a more stable adaptive relationship with the environment, agrarian societies are less mobile, occupying a delimited territory. As the society becomes stable it urbanizes and grows larger, since small size is no longer advantageous as it was in a nomadic hunting and gathering economy. In fact the larger the society, the more manpower available for tilling, cultivating, harvesting, milling, and herding. A large manpower pool is especially important in societies where machines and other capital resources of modern societies do not exist. Since men and animals are the major sources of energy, the larger their numbers, the more productive the economy.

With a farm technology and capital, gathering resources is not as problematic as in hunting and gathering economies. This enables

[5] More so than with hunting and gathering societies, we are encompassing a tremendous diversity of economies under this type. Many economies display both hunting and gathering as well as agricultural activities. Many engage in herding, hunting, gathering, and agricultural activities. Some are small, organized into villages. Others are large and display high degrees of urbanism. The description offered here thus is only a rough and very blurred picture of agrarianism. For references to a more thorough analysis, see footnote 3, page 23.

families to concentrate more on the process of production—converting these resources into goods and commodities. While most gathering, production, and distribution still occurs within the family, sometimes nonfamilial economic units, such as mills, craft guilds, and blacksmithing, become involved in basic economic processes. The family then transfers its economic surplus to these productive units in exchange for finished goods. Once this occurs the process of distribution also becomes more complicated since it is no longer the exclusive domain of the family.

When a social system can generate a surplus it has a problem of what to do with it. In societies with low insulation from the environment, surplus is usually stored for times of hardship and scarcity. But economic units—usually the farms—in more advanced agrarian economies with large surpluses and high insulation do something else: They sell it for money or exchange it for other needed or desired goods and products. The place where all this takes place is called a market. A market is not so much a geographical location as a domain where transactions, negotiations, and prices are determined. Some markets are based on barter, where only goods are exchanged; other markets use money as a measuring stick to set the value of a commodity; and many markets are a combination of the two. Although markets often exist in hunting and gathering economies, the emergence of an extensive and stable market, whether barter or money, usually occurs only in relatively stable agrarian economies and marks a major advance in the economy. Markets are concerned with the economic process of distribution and thus as the market increases in pervasiveness, so do distributive statuses. Moreover, large and complex markets require specialists—merchants, salesmen, wholesalers, and retailers who facilitate transactions. Once money emerges as the medium of exchange, so do many service roles: financing, insuring, banking, and lending. But these processes are only in their incipiency in most agrarian economies. While many distributive and servicing statuses exist in advanced agrarian economies, a larger number revolve around gathering and producing. It is only with industrialization and the production of even higher levels of surplus that distributive and servicing statuses become prevalent and begin to dominate the economy.

Both very simple agrarian (sometimes referred to as *horticultural*) and advanced agrarian economies are a comparatively recent phenomenon in the history of human societies. Approximately ten thousand years ago, planting and cultivating technology coupled with crude hoes allowed men to grow for themselves certain plant foods (Lenski, 1966:117). From this beginning crude hoes eventually were replaced by animal-drawn plows around six thousand years ago. It is impossible to trace completely the paths of diffusion of this agrarian technology from region to region over the last several thousand years. Nor is it possible to sort out the processes of diffusion from independent discoveries and use of agrarian technology and capital in different regions. Yet by the fifteenth century agrarian economies were evident in most regions of the world. Today, despite the world trend toward industrialization, both simple and advanced agrarian economies persist in the world's societies. For example, much of Latin America, Indonesia, Indochina, and Africa display basically an agrarian form of adaptation to the natural environment.

industrial economies

Industrial economies are highly insulated from the natural environment (Lenski, 1966:297–389). The level of technology or knowledge about how to manipulate the environment is exceedingly great — so great that increasingly the products of such technology such as machines and other devices begin to assume the burden of gathering resources from the environment. Along with this occurs a diversification of the kinds of resources that can be gathered by industrial economies. These changes generate demands for new kinds of specialized human skill. As a result of these increases in technology, the specialization of human skill, and the resulting efficiency in gathering resources, surplus becomes a common feature of industrial economies. Although such surplus can be drawn upon in periods of scarcity, it is more likely in industrial economies to be reinserted into the economy and hence further economic growth and adjustment to the environment. Capital surplus thus is no longer a stagnant force, but a highly dynamic force accelerating the expansion of certain economic processes.

With increased adaptive capacity, especially in gathering resources from the environment, a high proportion of now diversified economic roles revolves around the process of production — converting the ever-increasing quantity and variety of natural resources into commodities. In fact a greater proportion of the status network of the economy centers on this process than on gathering resources. This expansion of the productive process eventually results in distributive problems, which tend to focus on how the myriad of goods being produced are to be disseminated throughout the society. Extensive markets with a money medium of exchange now emerge — increasing the proportion and diversity of distributive roles in the economy. Sales and marketing thus become prominent features of the economy. Increases in these activities usually stimulate the growth and expansion of the service sector of the economy: banking, insurance, accounting, advertising, and managing. And so industrial economies begin to produce and distribute services as well as products.

Industrialization began around two centuries ago in Western Europe. By 1900 industrialization was evident in Eastern Europe, Asia (Japan), and North America (United States). This century has seen the rapid diffusion of industrial technology and capital to all continents. However, a large number of areas in Africa, Indochina, Indonesia, and South America are just currently undergoing industrialization. As we will examine throughout this book, industrialization of the economy usually has extensive consequences for reorganizing nearly every segment of social life in a society (Hoselitz and Moore, 1963). Many of the trends evident today in the world's societies are to a great extent a reflection of the massive changes in the economy ushered in by industrialization.

postindustrial economies

As machines are increasingly applied to the processes of gathering resources and converting them into commodities, distributive problems intensify. Partially in response to these increased distributive problems, economies usually expand the production and distribution of services. Not only this, but serious problems in integrating and coordinating the activities of workers with each other or with machines, machines with machines, or factories with factories also emerge as industrial production expands (Smelser, 1964). Here too the economy must utilize services that can resolve these problems. Thus, after a certain stage of industrialization, the status network of the economy begins to revolve not so much around the production of commodities as around the production and distribution of services (Mills, 1951). When a greater proportion of economic statuses focus on these latter processes we can speak of a postindustrial economic system.

The word *post* is not intended to deny the continuing and accelerating use of machines in gathering resources and producing goods. Indeed this appears to be endemic to industrialization, for once it is initiated the use of machines tends to expand. This results from the fact that surplus capital is continuously poured back into the economy (rather than stored) and the fact that technological innovations provide a knowledge base from which new innovations spring. Such new innovations further expand the potential use and application of machines. This is especially true when human labor possesses high degrees of skill and knowledge and certain motives and drives which push them to use and expand their skills and knowledge. The result of these processes is the expansion of the economy, both in size and complexity.

Several economies are approaching a postindustrial form. The most notable of these is the American economy, where more than one-

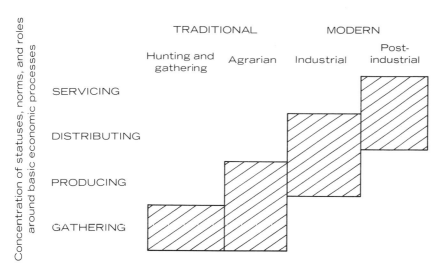

Figure 2–1 Variations in the institution of the economy.

half of the work force is employed in nonmanual occupations. However, postindustrialization is more of a future inevitability than a current fact, even in the United States. The above description of such a postindustrial economy can represent only a conservative extrapolation of present trends. To go much further than this would put analysis in the realm of social science fiction.

These brief descriptions of various types of economies are incredibly crude and imprecise. However, they do provide some clues about how and why different economies are structured the way they are. We have emphasized the institutional aspects of this structure— i.e., the nature and organization of statuses, norms, and roles as they revolve around basic economic processes. This organization as it is reflected in different types of economies is summarized in Figure 2–1.

Figure 2–1 diagrams the proportion of the total statuses in a society allocated to the four basic economic processes: gathering, producing, distributing, and servicing. For convenience we can designate as *traditional* those economies where the highest proportion of economic positions revolves around gathering natural resources and production of goods. As soon as an economy begins to allocate a high proportion of statuses to distribution and servicing we can designate the economy as *modern* (Moore, 1967:109). Thus hunting and gathering as well as agrarian economies are traditional, while industrial and postindustrial economies are modern. In this way we are provided with institutional criteria (the organization of statuses, roles, and norms) for distinguishing traditional from modern economies.

WORLD TRENDS IN ECONOMY

Traditional economies are disappearing because economic systems throughout the world are becoming—or trying to become—modern. They are attempting to approximate current industrial and post-industrial systems like Russia, England, the United States, and in some instances, China. To say that economies are modernizing means that they are altering the levels of basic economic elements: land, labor, capital, technology, and entrepreneurship. This in turn has profound consequences for the reorganization of roles around basic economic processes: gathering, producing, distributing, and servicing. During this reorganization, several trends, which are discussed below, sweep across the economy.

industrialization

In hunting and gathering as well as agrarian economies the level of technology is low, allowing only for the use of crude capital such as tools and weapons by human and animal sources of power. Resource extraction and conversion is highly limited by the lack of knowledge with respect to gathering and producing. Hunters and gatherers with a knowledge capable of generating only capital resources such as bows and arrows, spears, fish nets, knives, fire, bone needles, and the like cannot gather or convert resources in a very comprehensive way. Similarly, in agrarian economies technology allows for only crude capital formation—animal-drawn plows, hoes, irrigation systems, wells, and so on. More advanced agrarian systems might be typified as possessing domesticated animals, money, and other more sophisticated capital resources. But traditional economies still are greatly restricted by the inability of technology to generate a capital base capable of expanding resource gathering and conversion.

Since for hundreds of thousands of years these restrictions on economic development existed, it seems something of a miracle that they were finally broken. They were broken with industrialization, which involved (and involves today) the application of new sources of power to economic processes. As long as human, animal, and water are the only sources of power, an economy will remain traditional, since these yield only small amounts of energy relative to that needed for industrialization. Although a precise date is impossible to pinpoint, the application of steam to gathering and producing processes initiated the Industrial Revolution in Europe around two hundred years ago.[6] While knowledge about steam had existed for hundreds of years, the additional knowledge or technology necessary for its

[6]Many authors consider the Industrial Revolution to have begun long before the extensive application of steam power. See for example, Duncan (1964).

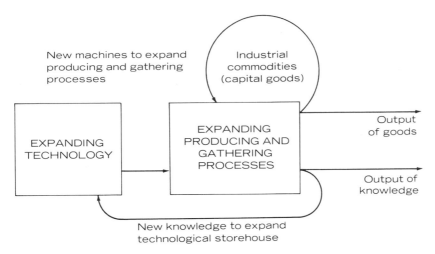

Figure 2-2 Technological and industrial expansion of the economy.

widespread application as well as man's interest in such application emerged only recently in the history of human societies. Yet the consequences of steam technology for generating a capital base that could expand gathering and producing processes were immense. Steam eliminated the exclusive reliance on crude and inefficient sources of human and animal power. Steam enabled the construction of powerful pumps and drilling shafts in mines—thus generating high access to resources such as coal and iron ore. Steam power also enabled the development and operation of blast furnaces, automatic hammers, and rollers for converting iron ore into more refined metals. With these advances in conversion of resources new and more efficient machines for expanding resource extraction and conversion could be built (Phillips, 1969:254–256). A machine capital base not only produces goods at a rapid rate but also generates new knowledge or technology about how to make more extensive and efficient machinery—thereby expanding further the processes of gathering and conversion. For example, the original blast furnaces provided for the large-scale conversion of iron ore into metal, but they also generated a legacy of knowledge and experience which could improve production—hence the bessemer converter and open-hearth process. Similarly, through trial and error, other sources of power such as oil, electricity, uranium, and hydrolysis were discovered and applied to the revolution ushered in by the application of steam and resulting mechanization of gathering and producing. Furthermore, when men are emancipated from subsistence toil by the emergence of new gathering and productive techniques they have the time to create new innovations which further emancipate them. Analytically this process is represented diagramatically in Figure 2–2.

31

In Figure 2–2 two kinds of outputs—goods and knowledge—occur with industrialization. Portions of these two outputs can be reinserted back into the economy in such a way that they expand the economy's gathering and producing potential. This process of re-inserting a segment of output can be referred to as *feedback* (Wiener, 1950). When feedback accelerates an existing tendency, such as industrialization, it is termed *positive feedback*. And when reinserted output inhibits a tendency, it is called *negative feedback*. Knowledge and capital goods as diagramed above represent positive feedback because they can potentially expand the economic processes of gathering and producing. Many commodity outputs of an industrializing economy are machines which, when fed back into the economy, increase the resources available and the capacity of converting them. The same is true of knowledge. Experience in machine producing and gathering can generate new knowledge about how to expand these processes. A technological storehouse is thus created by machine production.

These same processes are occurring today in underdeveloped nations of Asia, Indonesia, Latin America, and Africa. Technology and capital are borrowed from modern nations such as the United States, Russia, England, and China. The capital and knowledge then increase the borrowing nation's access to natural resources as well as its capacity to convert them into commodities not only for consumption, but also for further capital accumulation (and hence greater gathering and producing). Very rapid development can potentially occur in these nations because they can expand technology and its application not only from internal feedback but also from borrowing.

The expansion of gathering and producing processes with the application of new technologies and new forms of capital usually results in centralization of the economy, especially its capital base—machines and money. Machines and other capital resources increasingly become located near sources of fuel, resources, transportation, and commerce. And as capital becomes centralized, so must the labor force. Work can no longer be organized in the family unit; it must be concentrated near the machines of an industrial economy. Hence work becomes organized in large urban centers where gathering and productive units—called factories—are emerging. Work in central factories is organized differently than work in traditional economies. An extensive division of labor develops, with workers specializing. No longer do laborers possess the skill or knowledge to be "general-ists" capable of performing all economic tasks, since a machine-based economy is too large and complex. Under these conditions work norms change because large concentrations of men must now schedule, pace, and standardize their work with that of machines. Large numbers of workers concentrated in factories with each performing specialized tasks must also coordinate more precisely than before

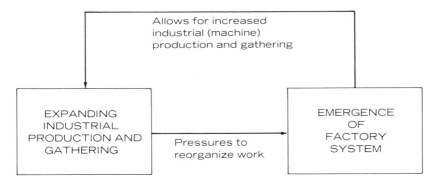

Figure 2-3 The factory and industrial expansion.

their activities with each other — thus furthering the salience of norms that emphasize scheduling, pacing, and standardizing of work (Moore, 1951, 1964). Work that must be highly coordinated tends to become hierarchically organized, with work at one level being supervised and coordinated by work at higher levels, resulting in the proliferation of foremen, supervisory, and managerial roles in the factory system.

The factory system allows for the organization of vast numbers of employees around an extensive network of machines. Once this system is established it allows for the concentration of even more men around even bigger machines, resulting in expansion of the factory system. Larger machines are usually cheaper to run, while increasing productivity and profits. Enlarging the factory also has other advantages in obtaining resources and other materials. Hence the factory system makes possible greater industrial productivity, and in doing so it can generate positive feedback which often encourages its own expansion. This feedback process is represented diagramatically in Figure 2-3.

In sum, then, industrialization is endemic to economic development. It involves the increasing application of new technology and capital to gathering and producing processes. With the accumulation of capital, economic production becomes centralized with the result that the labor force becomes concentrated into urban centers. Many of the entrepreneurial problems of coordinating masses of labor with large concentrations of machines are resolved through the emergence of the factory system. In turn the factory system encourages even more centralization and urbanization, leading to greater industrialization of a society's economy.

33

market modernization
When machine power is applied to gathering and producing, a distributive crisis revolving around how to distribute the increasing

number, variety, and volume of goods of an industrializing economy is often generated. The reasons for this crisis lie in the fact that markets in traditional economies display at least three features which can inhibit rapid and efficient distribution of the increasing volume of industrial goods.

1. There is always an element of *barter* in the markets of traditional economies. Commodities are often exchanged for other commodities rather than money.

2. *Bargaining* is central to traditional markets. Buyers and sellers initially state prices much different from what they intend to pay or receive. They then "haggle" or bargain on a compromise price.

3. *Credit* is usually difficult to obtain in the markets of traditional economies. Because there is inevitable uncertainty about the borrower's capacity to repay (because of poor insulation from the environment), interest is high and often prohibitive (Bazelon, 1959).

A market with these features cannot easily handle the volume of commodities generated by an industrial economy because barter and bargaining are cumbersome and slow and because the inability to readily form credit suppresses exchange. An economy using machines to rapidly produce an ever-increasing variety of standardized goods can become hopelessly bottlenecked in this type of market, since rapid and efficient exchange are usually necessary to keep pace with industrial production (Belshaw, 1965). Although far from inevitable, these economic conditions frequently encourage the virtual disappearance of barter in lieu of money as a standard medium of exchange (Moore, 1967:307). Bargaining also decreases for it hinders the rapid flow of standardized goods, and credit becomes more easily formed, since greater insulation from the environment creates greater security and regularity (Moore, 1951:226–230). Once these changes in distributive processes occur, further expansion of industrial production can occur. The easy exchange of commodities represents positive feedback to productive economic units because it encourages more production. When goods can be distributed easily and rapidly, industrial production and the factory system expand. In turn increased industrial production creates greater pressures for rapid distribution, which can accelerate market modernization and expansion. In Figure 2–4 this spiraling feedback process is diagramatically represented.

One of the most dramatic illustrations of how a modern market can facilitate industrialization is found in Africa. While the wisdom of many colonial policies can be questioned, colonial powers in Africa tended to impose a modern market on the hunting and gathering or

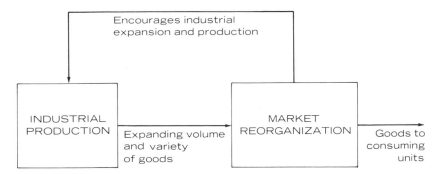

Figure 2–4 Market expansion and economic growth.

agrarian economies of this continent (Bohannan, 1964:218). Although such imposition was premature and often disruptive to the host society, it can now greatly facilitate the current push toward industrialization in many newly independent African societies. Because both internal and international exchange can occur efficiently and rapidly in these markets, they can potentially accommodate the increased volume of transactions inevitable with industrialization. However, initiating industrialization has often proved problematic in African nations because of several factors (Moore, 1967:153), including the inability of many nations to accumulate capital; racial antagonisms and discrimination; and traditional skills and motives in the labor force. Until these problems can be overcome, the African market system will remain only a potential encouragement to economic development.

Figure 2–4 indicates that as industrial production expands, so do statuses, norms, and roles revolving around distribution. Furthermore, expansion of distributive roles also results in productive increases, which create further pressures for the expansion of distribution. And these increases take place by virtue of the expanded use of machines, instead of human labor, in gathering and producing. Thus with industrialization there is a trend for the proportion of statuses revolving around gathering and production to decrease, while the proportion of statuses focusing on distributive processes increases. In industrial systems vast networks of sales, advertising, financing, marketing, merchandising, and promotional positions emerge. People tend to become incumbents in what one sociologist called the "Great Salesroom" (Mills, 1951).

the servicing revolution
Expansion of industry and markets creates a wide variety of pressures for services. These services are necessary to facilitate the operation of

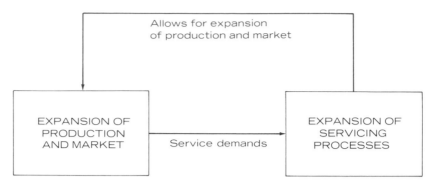

Figure 2-5 Servicing and economic growth.

large factories and market facilities. Thus as the production capacities of factories expands and as the volume of transactions in a modernized market increases, services such as banking, insuring, financing, titling, accounting, copying, and mortgaging become prominent. When these service occupations do not emerge, as is often the case in societies lacking educational facilities to train labor in the necessary skills, producing and marketing can become bogged down. When the demands for services can be met the emergence of the service sector allows for further economic growth, since it can facilitate the operation of complex economic structures and processes (Moore, 1967:95–96). The positive feedback processes of economies capable of generating economic services is represented diagramatically in Figure 2–5.

bureaucratization

Economic development greatly increases the size, scope, and complexity of the economy. When development can proceed it eventually generates a "crisis of administration" revolving around how to organize gathering, producing, distributing, and servicing. Controlling, regulating, managing, allocating, communicating, keeping track of, and making decisions intensify exponentially in all sectors of an economy with increases in size and complexity. Though the exact processes vary from society to society in terms of a wide variety of historical and present conditions, one typical response to this crisis is the proliferation of an endless array of managing, executive, business agent, public relations, labor relations, and accounting roles in economic organizations. These statuses are added on to those revolving around actual gathering and producing. And as several studies (Haire, 1959) clearly document, staff or administrative roles tend to increase dramatically with the initial growth of any productive economic organization. Conversely, bench workers, machine operators, and assembly-line workers decrease as a proportion of the total work force within any particular organization or throughout the economy as a whole. This latter trend is accelerated when distributing and servicing sectors are expanded during economic growth. In these sectors most statuses require considerably more administrative role behavior. For example, salesmen, manufacturers, representatives, wholesalers, retailers, bankers, insurance agents, loan consultants, and the like all administer in that they direct, regulate, control, manage, and supervise various types of economic activities. One consequence of these processes is that work in the modernizing economy becomes removed from gathering and producing, which can be more efficiently handled by machines in the factory system. Increasingly occupations revolve around the administration of gathering, producing, distributing, and servicing. Everyday phrases such as the organization man, the managerial revolution, the professionalization of work, and white collarism denote the proliferation of these new administrative roles which come to dominate advanced industrial and postindustrial economies.

These expanding administrative statuses typically become organized bureaucratically (Moore, 1967:113). Bureaucratization is thus one of the most prominent ways administrative positions of modern economy are organized (Weber, 1946; Blau, 1956; Presthus, 1962). Although the rate of and exact route to bureaucratization can vary with respect to unique conditions in each society some form of bureaucracy appears to be endemic to economic development. The general features of bureaucracies include (Blau, 1956):

1. Work is guided by a formal set of norms for each status, although informal arrangements usually emerge to supplement these formal norms.

2. Specialized training is required for each incumbent. Such training tends to emphasize expertise in a narrow rather than in a broad sphere.

3. Work is to be performed neutrally and unemotionally. Although this is never completely possible, bureaucratic norms attempt to regulate the expression of intense emotion.

4. Work is mental rather than physical, with most employees expending cognitive energy.

5. Work is organized into subsystems called offices where it is coordinated and regulated. Within each office there are norms indicating a hierarchy of supervision and control.

6. For each office there is a higher office to regulate its overall activities. Bureaucracies can be visualized as hierarchies of offices.

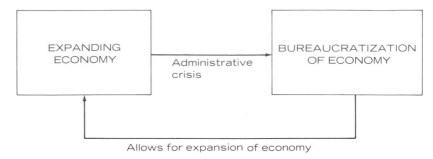

Figure 2–6 Bureaucratization and economic growth.

7. Norms emphasize the opportunities to make a career of moving up within an office or through the organizational hierarchy of offices.

8. Recruitment and promotion in bureaucracies is to be based upon the incumbent's proficiency of role performance and expertise.

Bureaucracies can often be inefficient and rife with "red tape." Despite these indictments, bureaucracy has the consequence of organizing a large number of administrative roles in a way that can cope with the volume and complexity of tasks in a modern economy. Well-coordinated masses of specialists organized into offices, which in turn are arranged into hierarchies of offices, appears to be the only way these tasks can presently be performed. As long as the economy is small with low productivity, limited market facilities, and few servicing requirements, large bureaucracies are unnecessary. But when the economy modernizes it becomes large and complex, which eventually stimulates bureaucratization. Once large-scale bureaucratization occurs it can feed back and allow for the further expansion of the factory system, markets, and service organizations. In this way bureaucratization, when occurring along the lines listed above, actually provides the structural base for growth and development in an economy. Diagramatically this process is portrayed in Figure 2–6.

38

automation

Most generally automation refers to the increasing capacity of machines to replace human labor in all economic sectors. Initial industrialization is a form of automation, since machines driven by new sources of power engage in tasks formerly performed by labor. But in the short run, such automation does not displace labor as a basic economic element because it creates many new jobs requiring skilled workers. But eventually machines assume an increasing burden of the gathering and producing tasks of an economy. In the long run the factory system as a place where large concentrations of men and machines work together will probably give way to vast networks of machines working with each other. Yet presently the expansion of the administrative as well as the market and service sectors of a modern economy is so great that labor can be absorbed into the growing number of giant administrative bureaucracies. This is reflected in the very definition of a modern economy where the proportion of status norms revolving around gathering and producing decreases (see Figure 2–1). Yet there is some possibility that in the distant future bureaucracies will also come under the impact of automation. It appears that fifth-, sixth-, and seventh-generation computers may become more efficient bureaucrats than men. In fact computers are currently displacing extremely simple and routine tasks formerly performed by low-level bureaucrats. How much of a future trend this represents is at present difficult to determine precisely.

trends and prospects in economies: an overview

Economic development in any society can be visualized as a reflection of crucial feedback processes outlined in Figures 2–2 through 2–6. Through diffusion and innovation technology reaches a level allowing for the harnessing of machine power to gathering and producing. The application of machines to economic processes often creates new knowledge or technology, which can be used to increase the application of machines and hence economic production. More production can encourage the development and application of new technologies. In turn large-scale production can be more efficiently carried out in a factory system. When efficient, the factory system can facilitate even more production. Machine production in factories generates a high volume of new and standardized products, which stimulates the reorganization of the market. These changes in the market encourage even more production. Modernization of the market and expansion of production rely on new and varied services. If these services develop they allow for further expansion of the economy. Ultimately the growth of production, the factory system, the market, and service organizations results in the development of large-scale bureaucracies. When reasonably efficient, bureaucracies enable the expansion of all economic processes.

The rate of this growth is dependent upon the extent to which the emerging factories, markets, service units, and bureaucracies can represent positive feedback—encouraging expansion of the process which generated them. The application of new technology is often resisted, even though it could result in more material comfort and insulation from the environment. For example, in 1913 Lee De Forest was almost convicted of mail fraud for selling shares in a strange thing called the audion tube—the predecessor of many modern electronic devices (Chinoy, 1967:220–230). Arab villagers resisted vehemently the installation of a village pump because it would destroy the traditional female task of carrying water. And Cuban sugar workers resisted the introduction of machines because "cane needs the human touch to grow." Farmers in this country resisted the implementation of the cast-iron plow because "it would poison the soil." Labor unions resist much new technology since it will "put men out of work." Even the ubiquitous automobile was at one time resisted. English workers during the early part of the Industrial Revolution often attacked and destroyed the machines that were changing their lives, and so on. Thus the application of new knowledge to gathering and producing is often resisted since it can conflict with traditional values and customs, existing institutional patterns, and powerful vested interests.

The application of machine power has far-reaching consequences for the institutional organization of society. We have already seen some of its consequences for the economy. And we will see in subsequent chapters the drastic changes it effects in the institutions of the family, religion, law, polity, and education. It is inevitable that to some extent technological application and accumulation are often resisted since institutions are relatively stable and change only under the impact of powerful forces.

Another crucial process affecting the rate of economic growth lies in the nature of the feedback from the emerging factory system of a developing economy. Since the factory revolutionizes gathering and producing, its norms can require new labor attributes which the familial and educational institutions of many developing systems cannot yet instill. Work norms requiring the capacity to schedule, pace, standardize, or even to show up for work on time or work steadily can be alien to a labor force. Norms requiring specialization, routinization, and neutrality at work can be equally difficult for labor in a developing economy. And to the extent that a labor force cannot display these and other traits demanded by the norms of the factory system or other units in a modern economy, productivity will be inhibited.

Another essential feedback process affecting the rate of economic growth can be seen in the relationship between the market and the productive sector of a developing economy. Since industrial production requires a money-based market, the persistence of bargaining and barter, along with poor credit facilities in the market, will bottleneck economic growth. Bargaining and barter are often well institutionalized in an economy and are therefore difficult to eliminate. To bargain is considered in most developing countries an inalienable right. To have fixed prices on standardized goods would violate a well established normative pattern. Nor is credit easily formed in developing countries, for it requires large capital reserves and secure banks which are scarce in a developing nation. Economic and political instability typical of most developing nations can aggravate this situation. And when prices are not fixed and subject to bargaining, establishing interest rates and collateral becomes extremely difficult. A market that is congested and cumbersome will inhibit industrial production (and ultimately technological accumulation).[7]

The nature of bureaucratization also greatly circumscribes the rate of economic growth in a society. Although bureaucratization of the economy can allow for the growth and enlargement of economic organizations, it is often inefficient and serves as a drag on economic growth. To the extent that bureaucracies do not meet the characteristics outlined above they tend toward inefficiency. The literature on bureaucratic inefficiency is vast, but two principal sources of inefficiency appear particularly important: lack of expertise appropriate to the normative requirements of positions within the bureaucracy; and recruitment, promotion, and advancement in the bureaucracy based on criteria other than expertise. Because educational institutions in developing countries often lag behind job requirements of certain economic positions, actors do not display the proper attributes necessary for their specialized jobs. They often do not possess the mental skills or level of knowledge necessary for effective role performance. This problem is often compounded because workers possess inappropriate orientations, values, motives, and interpersonal styles (these will be discussed in the next chapter). This problem can be amplified even more when recruitment and promotion within and between bureaucratic offices are based on criteria other than expertise or role-performance capacities. In bureaucracies of developing economies (and sometimes in modern economies), recruitment and promotion are based on "irrelevant criteria" such as race, sex, family background, and social-class origin. In order for rapid and sustained economic growth to occur, these bases of recruitment and promotion must be partially displaced by the single criterion of expertise. This is especially true when low numbers of qualified incumbents are being socialized in the lagging educational institutions of the society. This is a difficult transition for developing economies to effect and it represents a serious blockage to sustained economic growth.

These are illustrative of some of the forces affecting the *rate* of

41

[7] In this vein it is relevant to note that the easy-term loan, the ubiquitous charge account, and the endless array of credit cards typical of the American economy represent the ultimate expansion of the market, which in turn greatly accelerates production. Thus the significance of these so-called conveniences on economic development is far from minor.

economic growth. It is rare that these forces halt growth altogether, for the pressures generated by the application of machine power to basic economic processes—especially gathering and producing—are great. Eventually these sources of blockage are overcome, but they can seriously thwart economic development.

THE AMERICAN ECONOMIC SYSTEM

We can say that the American economy is approaching a postindustrial stage because it displays extremely high levels of technology, capital, labor skill, and entrepreneurship. While the American economy is involved in mass gathering and producing, the actual gathering and producing increasingly are performed by machines rather than by laborers. Service roles allowing such gathering and producing to occur have thus proliferated, and it is becoming common for them to outnumber those revolving around actual gathering and producing. The front office, filled with sales manager, accountants, vice-presidents, personnel managers, market liaisons, advertising executives, and researchers, is frequently as big as the assembly line. With mass production, mass distribution occurs and the number of statuses focusing on this economic process is large. America is indeed the land of the salesman, wholesaler, retailer, and manufacturer's representative. Mass distribution requires mass servicing and so the economy increasingly is the locus of banking, titling, insuring, financing, mortgaging, holding, accounting, and advertising.

The American economy is complex, requiring many trained specialists, from the assembly-line worker to the advertising executive. Because of its size and specialization, entrepeneurial problems are intense. These problems are partially resolved through the dominance of the large corporation (Williams, 1970:179). The economic statuses in the American economy are organized corporately, with gathering, producing, distributing, and servicing rapidly becoming dominated by a few hundred large corporations. To understand the American economy is thus to comprehend "America, Inc." (Mills, 1951).

the corporation

The corporation is basically a mechanism for amassing wealth. Through the issuance of stock to many dispersed individuals, money capital can be generated for various economic goals. It is in this way that financial resources are pooled, but with an interesting extra feature: The individual stockholder is protected from liability. Once formed, the corporation operates as a separate entity apart from its individual stockholders and its many employees. The corporation thus becomes a legal unit possessing the rights to hold property, enter contracts, sue and be sued, and conduct economic activity in its own name (Williams, 1970:193). Also, stock can be transferred and exchanged, thus providing a stable level of financial capital despite changes in specific investors.

The control of corporations in the United States is increasingly displaying a complicated pattern. Most corporate stocks are held by a large number of individuals—20 million in 1965 (Williams, 1970:195). And most shareholders own only a few shares of stock for any one corporation. Those who own more than a few shares can therefore yield power disproportionate to their holdings, since no resisting counter power block is likely to exist. These block shareholders usually sit on a board of directors elected by all the smaller, individual stockholders. They are in a sense entrusted with the responsibility of making general policy decisions for the whole corporation. However, much control of corporations has also moved to top management. Often managers own significant—though still small—blocks of stock and thus have dual sources of power and control. But even when top executives own no stock their power is considerable, since they make the day-to-day decisions. The board of directors and these top executives thus share the control of the corporation. Often top executives actually sit on the board of directors.

From these top decision-making positions a corporation proliferates into a vast hierarchy of decision making. The statuses, norms, and roles of this hierarchy are organized into various functional units concerned with the operation of certain specific aspects of the corporation—accounting, advertising, sales, manufacturing, public relations, research, and development. Within these units are specific hierarchies of offices and within the offices specific hierarchies of authority and decision making. To put it simply, the corporate structure is the form that bureaucratization takes in the American economy. In other economies, especially those displaying a nationalized or socialized profile, bureaucratization takes a somewhat different form. However, the general features are the same, for bureaucratization appears to be endemic to resolving the administrative problems generated by size and specialization (Williams, 1970:204).

Corporate bureaucracies pervade all economic processes— gathering, producing, distributing, and servicing. This means that corporations can be purely administrative (servicing and distributing) or a combination of administration and manufacturing. These latter can be involved in all economic processes, gathering their own resources and converting them, distributing their products, and providing their own services. Major oil companies in the United States are examples of corporations coming closest to being involved in all four basic economic processes. But even these companies utilize the services of separate accounting and advertising corporations. Furthermore, distribution is frequently allocated to separate businesses and/

or corporations (e.g., franchised gasoline). Even though many large corporations are involved in all economic processes, we can still distinguish four types of corporations in terms of their primary process: gathering corporations; producing or manufacturing corporations; distributing corporations; and servicing corporations.[8]

GATHERING CORPORATIONS

The activities of these corporations revolve around resource extraction from the natural environment. Because of this fact, many of the statuses of these corporations are occupied by manual labor working in conjunction with machines. But as these corporations increase in size, nonmanual administrative statuses become equally prevalent (Haire, 1959), for at least four reasons. (1) Large gathering corporations tend to be geographically dispersed, nationally and internationally. Such dispersion increases problems of coordinating, controlling, and financing. These conditions often force the proliferation of administrative roles. (2) Since resources in a region eventually become depleted, men and machine capital must be moved and this requires extensive administrative support. (3) Once resources are extracted they must be distributed either to manufacturing divisions within the corporation or to other, strictly manufacturing corporations. In either case distributive processes can cause the proliferation of administrative roles. (4) Automation or mechanization tends to occur in large-scale corporations. This means that the number of laborers needed decreases as machines become more efficient. It also means that extensive research and development, servicing, and other administrative supports are required to facilitate the operation of highly mechanized gathering processes. Thus, gathering corporations are extensively bureaucratized around what during early industrialization is a machine-labor enterprise. The trend toward an increasing proportion of administrative and related statuses in the overall corporate structure is a direct reflection of increases in corporate size and machine capital.

44

MANUFACTURING CORPORATIONS

Manufacturing means producing—converting resources into goods and commodities. These corporations have the factory system as a prominent feature, with stable capital machinery and manual labor coming under unified direction and control. The assembly line becomes its conspicuous feature. Yet as the factories of a manufacturing corporation grow in size, administrative and service roles become an equally conspicuous feature of the corporate structure, because

---

[8] Naturally, such a classification represents a gross oversimplification. However, one of the four basic economic processes tends to dominate in most American corporations.

coordination of the factory system with resource supplies and markets must occur. Administering the complex web of men and machines in the factory system becomes ever more problematic, especially in a competitive market where research and development become necessary services.

DISTRIBUTING CORPORATIONS

While many manufacturing corporations also engage in distribution (thereby increasing the number of administrative statuses), the American economy displays a large number of strictly distributive corporations. They acquire goods and commodities from various manufacturing corporations and distribute them through a wide variety of retail stores. These range from chain grocery stores to all-purpose department stores. These corporations are vast networks of clerk, accountant, buyer, local and regional managers, and sales statuses, norms, and roles. As the gathering and manufacturing capacities of the American economy increase, these distributive corporations will increase and account for a growing proportion of the overall economic status-norms network. These corporations greatly facilitate the movement of goods and commodities in the market by supplying manufacturing corporations with large, nationwide, and stable outlets. Furthermore, they relieve many manufacturing corporations of the necessity for engaging in extensive market operations, which could prove an expensive administrative burden and drain capital needed for manufacturing. Distributing corporations also facilitate the movement of commodities in the market by providing consumers with easy access to goods and commodities through chain stores and with readily available credit. Probably more than any other economic system the United States has developed the process of rapid distribution.

SERVICING CORPORATIONS

Many gathering, manufacturing, and distributing corporations provide most of their own services. But as they expand in size it often becomes more economical and practical to contract out services such as crediting, banking, accounting, computerizing, advertising, and copying to specialized service corporations. The fact that many of the "high flyers" on the New York Stock Exchange are essentially service corporations attests to this growing form of incorporation. Like other corporations, service corporations are bureaucracies, but with a very high proportion of workers possessing extensive mental skill. Aside from various administrative and managerial personnel, the product of these corporations — accounting, banking, information processing, and advertising — by virtue of being a service is also a skill. Furthermore these corporations must also constantly engage in research and development to improve the level of services offered, especially in a competitive market. This in turn furthers the proportion of skilled employees in the corporate bureaucracy.

In sum, we can say that the American economy is dominated by the corporation. Ownership of the corporations is diverse and dispersed, but virtually complete control rests in the hands of a few key stockholders, the board of directors, and high administrative or management positions.[9] The corporation is simply the American manifestation of economic bureaucratization. The nature of the bureaucratic structure for any corporation is to some extent reflective of the major focus of economic activity—whether gathering, producing, distributing, or servicing. But in general there is a tendency for norms of bureaucratic statuses to require nonmanual, administrative, and service personnel.

Corporations are endemic to the American economy. But more importantly, *large* corporations are increasingly assuming dominance. While small businesses and corporations outnumber large ones (and by quite a bit), large corporations account for a disproportionate share of revenues, power, and influence. Large corporations dictate the conditions under which smaller businesses and corporations must operate. For example, independent car dealers are franchised and controlled by the large automobile manufacturers; service stations are dependent upon the large oil companies; small retail stores must compete with large retail chains; small suppliers of resources are dominated by the large manufacturers' need for resources; and so on. Large corporate domination in all economic processes is becoming an economic fact of life in America (Mills, 1951; Williams, 1970: 182–183).

*Inter*corporate control of certain economic processes is also becoming common. Through various alliances, linkages, and agreements, several corporations are increasingly becoming centrally coordinated. A number of mechanisms are used to effect such linkage and coordination. These include interlocking directorships, intercorporate stockholdings, and trade associations (Williams, 1960: 183–188).

Interlocking directorships. An interlocking directorship exists whenever several corporations have at least some of their board of

---

[9] Some have argued that the total stockholdings of managers and the directors on the corporate board can be considered to amount to *both* ownership and control. There is no doubt that the stockholdings of top level management and the board of directors are considerable for most corporations. This is what gives them control and whether or not this also amounts to actual ownership varies from corporation to corporation. The latter would appear to be almost a moot question, given the control exercised by just a few key persons.

director incumbents in common. Presumably this situation allows these directors to coordinate and control several companies in harmonious ways. While interlocking directorships among *competing* companies are illegal under the antitrust legislation, violations still occur. However, even when the companies linked through interlocking directorships are not directly competitive, their alliance still furthers economic domination by large corporations across a wider economic spectrum than would otherwise be the case.

Intercorporate stockholdings. Corporations can buy the stock of other corporations with the result that large corporations can own a controlling interest in smaller ones. While antitrust legislation prevents large corporations from buying out all of their smaller competitors (and thus establishing a monopoly), they can obtain a controlling interest in allied—but not directly competitive—smaller corporations. And recently the conglomerate corporation holding a controlling interest in a wide variety of unrelated smaller companies has become a feature of the economy.

Trade associations. The trade association disseminates information and sets standards and guidelines for economic activity in certain areas. Such associations exist in banking, insuring, railroads, and small or large business. Typical among these associations are the National Association of Manufacturers, the Chamber of Commerce, and the National Railroad Association. At most trade associations can fix prices, while at the least they can merely disseminate trade information. It is not clear how much these associations contribute to corporate dominance of the economy, but it appears that large corporations within these associations can greatly control activities of smaller corporations, if only by controlling the distribution of information. This in turn furthers the dominance of large corporations in the American economy.

It is clear that corporations are getting larger and/or increasing their capacity to manipulate other smaller businesses and corporations. When we refer to big business and the business establishment, we are confirming from everyday experience what appears to be a universal trend—the dominance of the economy by large corporations. In many ways this runs counter to American economic ideologies stressing laisse faire among small independent businessmen (Mills, 1951) and small family corporations. But the inescapable conclusion is that long ago this ideology ceased to represent actual practice.

capitalism, american style

Laissez faire ideology posits that units of the American economy are supposed to be in free competition with each other in pursuit of profit. The "profit motive" is assumed to be the central dynamic of the economy, as each economic unit risks its capital (machines, money) in a competitive search for profit and gain. Competition among such units is assumed to maximize efficiency within each economic organization while generating rapid economic growth (and general prosperity for all). Such a conception of the economy has a very limited utility. It is singularly inappropriate in analyzing hunting and gathering, agrarian, or any modern nationalized or socialized economy. But more importantly it does not come close to describing actual processes in the American economy (Williams, 1970:208–209; Moore, 1962; Mills, 1951): (1) Large corporations in the American economy usually do not have to take excessive risks. Because of their size and centrality to the economy, the political subsystem has a vested interest in their continuance. Should a major corporation fail, economic and political instability could result. Though not always, major corporations are often subsidized, protected legally, and awarded lucrative government contracts at appropriate times. Small corporations and businesses are more likely to face extreme competitive risks. (2) The competition in the American economy is far from free or laissez faire. Through government subsidies and noncompetitive contracts, interlocking directorates, trade associations, and intercorporate stockholdings and conglomerates, competition is greatly mitigated, especially among large corporations. (3) As Williams (1970:209) points out, the notion of a "profit motive" anthropomorphizes a nonhuman entity—an economic organization. Organizations have overall goals but they are not motivated. Individual employees in the organizational bureaucracy may have motives, but such motives for most employees are not likely to be a profit motive. More likely these are motives for power, increased wages, security, promotion, and the like. High-level managers are probably concerned with profits but this is not true for the salaried rank and file.

Capitalism is thus more of an economic ideology than a fact. American corporations compete but the competition is not "all out" or free. It is regulated, bounded, and controlled from within the economy itself or from without by the federal government. And as the dominance of large corporations increases competition is likely to decrease, since the failure of a very large, conglomerate corporation involves many other related corporations. For example, if General Motors were to fold, so would those corporations supplying its resources and services and marketing its goods and commodities. This might result in high unemployment in whole communities. With unemployment, buying power is decreased. As buying power decreases, other corporations—and those connected to them—begin to fail, and so on. Thus, once large concentrations of capital and manpower become invested in the survival of one large corporation, the consequences of failure become far reaching. As this occurs competition decreases to reduce the possibility of failure.

the organization of labor in american society

As we know, basic economic elements—land, labor, capital, technology, and their organization—center around the corporation in the American economy. And corporations can be of several types, depending upon which economic process they utilize. In all modern or modernizing systems the integration of labor with other basic economic elements in corporations is highly problematic. Labor does not automatically become or stay employed in the factories and bureaucracies of a particular corporation. Much of the history and current controversy in the American economy—or any modern economy—revolves around the problem of organizing and integrating labor into various economic structures. In this section we will explore two aspects of this problem in the American economic subsystem: blue-collar unionism and white-collar unionism. In doing so we will first examine how manual labor becomes an integral element in the factory system and then how white-collar and nonmanual labor adjusts to participation in the ever-expanding bureaucratic structures of the American economy.

BLUE-COLLAR UNIONISM

In the United States the emerging factory system of the late nineteenth century represented a fundamental new form of economic organization. Laborers now had to work away from the family around vast concentrations of machines in a factory. They became compartmentalized and specialized, performing specified tasks in a specified way at a specified tempo. Workers no longer needed to be generalists, capable of performing a wide variety of agricultural tasks. With scheduling, specialization, and compartmentalization, work was now performed neutrally and impersonally. And laborers now worked for a wage. Human effort was exchanged in the marketplace for money that could be used in the same market to buy those things needed for survival.

In the United States the adjustment of labor to these new work conditions was somewhat unique. Like all labor first confronting the emerging factory system its origins were rural, but with a difference: There was more racial and ethnic heterogeneity in the emerging labor force in the United States than in other industrializing

49

systems. This heterogeneity increased during the early twentieth century with the vast migrations from Europe. And perhaps more than other systems there was a powerful ideology stressing individual achievement guiding workers' actions. Workers believed that through individual effort and hard work a better life would be possible. Racial and ethnic heterogeneity, plus this powerful individualistic ideology, perhaps helps account for the slowness with which unionism developed in the American economy. Workers from diverse cultural backgrounds, speaking different languages, and guided by a strong sense of individualism did not organize collectively.

The consequences of the above facts for the organization of work in the emerging American factory were far reaching. Not checked by organized labor, management possessed a tremendous amount of power within the factory and in the wider political system. Laborers were often subjected to arbitrary action on the part of management—being hired and fired at the will of management. This resulted in tremendous insecurity and uncertainty for the early American labor force. Although it is difficult to determine, this uncertainty coupled with the new neutrality, impersonality, compartmentalization, and specialization of the factory probably had degrading consequences for self-esteem and respect among early workers.

As these conditions persisted and as the sons and grandsons of the first industrial workers became incumbents in the now developed factory system, the heterogeneity of the work force decreased. An urban proletariat with common interests and grievances began to press for better working conditions and wages. Initially these protests from labor were resisted because the American judiciary was sympathetic to the interests of management. But eventually labor became organized into effective unions which successively won the right to bargain collectively. With this development, union demands for better wages and working conditions could be effectively leveled. Unlike many other industrializing societies, no nationwide, political labor movement emerged in the United States. There has never been a nationwide strike of all industrial workers, nor have labor-oriented political parties been conspicuous (Williams, 1970:215). However, labor union activity including walkouts, slowdowns, strikes, and violent confrontations with management and police have not been mitigated by these facts.

Today there are a wide variety of union organizations in the American economy. These include (Williams, 1970:214): *craft unions* of workers in particular trades or occupations; *industrial unions* of all workers in a particular industry (steel, automobile manufacturing, mining, etc.); and emerging *geographical unions*, where manual workers from a wide variety of occupations in an area or region are organized into one union. Yet the goals of these various types of unions remain essentially the same: the right to bargain collectively and thereby control wages and working conditions.

Recent trends, however, indicate a fundamental change in unionism in the American economy. First, under the impact of automation where machines increasingly can perform the work of men, the proportion of the total work force employed in industrial jobs has decreased. Consequently the proportion of the work force involved in unions also has decreased. Second, unions have become increasingly involved not only in the economic welfare but in the social welfare of their members as well. Recreational, health, social, and educational programs are becoming as central to the union as the strike fund. Third, unions are becoming business corporations in their own right, investing money in certain profit-making enterprises. Fourth, unions, with their large size and diverse programs, are becoming bureaucratized with vast administrative hierarchies. This allows for better organization and control of activities but can place rank and file union members in the grips of two giant bureaucracies: the corporation for which they work and the union that is supposed to "protect" them. And finally, there is a trend toward unionization of nonmanual, white-collar workers in large administrative bureaucracies. As these workers become subject to the same kinds of occupational uncertainty as their manual counterparts in industry, union activity can be expected to increase.

In sum, unionization in the United States and in other industrializing systems represents an initial response to a severe entrepreneurial problem of integrating labor into the factory system. In the American economy unionization was slow in coming, which perhaps accounts for its nonpolitical character (although this should not underemphasize the violent confrontations that did occur between labor and enforcement agents of the state). Today unions represent an effective entrepreneurial mechanism for coordinating, controlling, and integrating a mass labor force into a mass economy.

WHITE-COLLAR UNIONISM

The history of white-collar organization and integration into the economy has been less visible and spectacular. Without much open and violent conflict (as of yet) labor has made the transition from an economy dominated by the factory to an economy dominated by bureaucracy. One reason for this is that the differences between bureaucratic and factory forms of economic organization are not so great as those between factory and agrarian forms of organization. The required changes in labor were thus less extreme than those in the transition from an agrarian economy. Like the factory system, bureaucracies require specialization, compartmentalization, neutrality, scheduling and pacing, and a wage nexus between employee and employer. The only real differences between the factory and bureaucracy are in the trade skills of workers. Participation in bureaucracies tends to require more education and less physical effort than employment in factories.

Another reason for the smooth transition to a bureaucratized economy is that an established, cosmopolitan, and educated urban work force developed before extensive economic bureaucratization. Employment in bureaucracies thus represented less of a "cultural shock" than was the case with the transition from an agrarian to a factory form of economic organization. A third reason is that professionalism emerged early in the American economy, with the result that many white-collar workers had professional organizations regulating the kinds of bureaucratic demands that could be made on them. And fourthly the higher levels of education and expertise of bureaucrats offered more job prestige and security than their blue-collar counterparts. Such a situation exposed them to less job insecurity than that of the early industrial workers.

But increasing problems of integrating white-collar employees into the giant corporate bureaucracies of the American economy are becoming evident. There are several reasons for this: (1) Many clerical jobs can now be mechanized, and this process is likely to increase with expansion of information-processing machines. The result is that job insecurity in the face of automation has emerged. (2) Incomes for many bureaucrats now lag behind those of factory workers, thus creating a sense of economic deprivation. (3) The fact that many clerical jobs are as routine as industrial jobs (or even more routine) is beginning to cause job dissatisfaction, especially under conditions of low pay and declining occupational prestige. The result of these forces is that white-collar workers are becoming receptive to unionization (Williams, 1970:222). This is evidenced by the fact that the Retail Clerks International Association (a white-collar union), with many members in large distributing corporations, is now one of the ten largest unions in the economy (Harrington, 1962). But unionization of other white-collar occupations encounters severe resistance where professional associations are strong. Furthermore, many white-collar employees resist unionization because of anticipated losses in prestige associated with what traditionally has been a working- or lower-class phenomenon. In fact the conflict between unionism and professionalism and white-collar prestige appears to be intensifying. We can predict that it will be resolved in favor of unionization under these conditions:

1 When automation generates high levels of job insecurity in white-collar occupations

2 When salaries and wages lag considerably behind those of industrial workers
3 When professionalism ceases to maintain high salaries and occupational prestige

Just how extensive and tranquil white-collar unionism will be in the future is difficult to determine. What is clear, however, is that new relationships between white-collar employees and large corporate bureaucracies are emerging. This fact may signal the formation of new mechanisms of white-collar organization and integration into corporate bureaucracies.

the american economy: an overview

The American economy is approaching a postindustrial stage of development. This means that economic statuses, norms, and roles are increasingly involved in the economic processes of distributing and servicing. In the American economic subsystem roles are becoming ever more organized within large, interrelated corporations. Corporations are simply the American form of integrating the factory system with administrative bureaucracies. As a postindustrial stage is reached many corporations will not have the factory system as one of their components. They will be totally administrative structures, engaging only in distributing and servicing.

One of the major problems encountered during economic development is integrating great masses of labor into factories and bureaucracies. Unionization is the principal mechanism for coordinating machines and labor in the factory system. As problems of integrating white-collar labor into giant corporate bureaucracies increase with postindustrialization, unionization can be expected to expand into this sphere. Industrial relations problems will give way to administrative relations problems. Whether these problems will involve a white-collar political movement or violence is at present unclear.

SUMMARY

This chapter has outlined some of the basic institutional structures, processes, and trends in different types of economies. We began analysis by isolating five basic economic elements: land, labor, capital, technology, and entrepreneurship. The level of these elements was seen as affecting and being affected by structures involved in basic economic processes: gathering, producing, distributing, and servicing. Depending upon how roles clustered around these processes, four general types of economies were briefly described: hunting and gathering, agrarian, industrial, and postindustrial.

Next some of the more conspicuous trends during economic change and development were analyzed. Emphasis was placed upon industrialization and the factory system, market modernization, the servicing revolution, bureaucratization, and automation. In this analysis, attention was drawn to certain key feedback processes as affected by the rate of economic development. Finally, we turned to a description of the American economy. In this description, we focused on the corporation as the basic economic structure and on the processes integrating labor into this structure.

54

the
institutional
environment
of
ECONOMY 3

It is difficult to overstate the complexity of interrelations among institutions in even the simplest society. This fact rings especially true for the economy, since this pivotal institution touches and affects virtually every segment of society. For example, a hunting and gathering economy like that among the Australian aborigines or African bushmen greatly circumscribes the profile of kinship, law, polity, and religion in those societies. Furthermore, should a hunting and gathering economy change or undergo development to an agrarian or industrial form we can expect massive changes in these other institutions. Throughout the remaining chapters of this book we explore some of the more visible ways change in the economy influences kinship, polity, law, education, and religion. However, in this chapter we will explore some of the influences these other institutions have on the economy. No institution, even one as influential as the economy, remains completely isolated from the institutions surrounding it. Like any societal subsystem, the economy is embedded in a network of interrelationships comprising a fantastically elaborate social web. Our present task is to begin the long process of untangling and scrutinizing some of the strands and fibers in this web.

KINSHIP AND ECONOMY

In all traditional societies kinship is a dominant institution, for virtually all social activity is circumscribed by kinship norms. Kinship is thus a pivotal structure around which and within which social roles are enacted. While we will reserve analysis of kinship for the next chapter, we can list just a few salient features of this dominant subsystem in traditional societies.

1. The family is large or *extended*, with several generations and a wide range of relatives intimately connected to the family unit, including grandparents, aunts, uncles, and cousins, as well as children and parents.

2. Within the extended family there are clear-cut authority relations among family members. Elders tend to have high authority and often relatives have as much or more authority over a child than his parents.

3. The division of labor within the family is clear. Just who does *what, when*, and *where* is clearly specified by norms.

4. There is a strong sense of loyalty among family members, with norms stressing involvement in and commitment to the family unit.

    In traditional societies much economic activity occurs within this kind of kinship structure. Economic role behavior is enacted by family members within particular kinds of family units—from a small kinship band or tribe wandering over a territory in search of food to a large family farming a tract of land handed down from generation to generation. Thus the kinship subsystem is often the *structural locus* of economic activity, as well as the *principal entrepreneurial structure* organizing economic activity. Depending upon the kinship norms each family member is allocated specific economic responsibilities or tasks. These are usually allocated on the basis of age, sex, and birth order of the various family members. Kinship norms thus circumscribe just who enacts what economic roles.

These consequences of the family for organizing economic activity are illustrated by the Tikopia (Firth, 1965). Tikopia is a small and until recently isolated island in the Pacific inhabited by fewer than 2000 Polynesians. Social organization in Tikopia is profoundly circumscribed by kinship norms which divide up the society and place members of families into four major clans. However, actual economic activity is organized and carried out in smaller families and households. Economic subsistence in Tikopia revolves around horticulture and fishing. In agriculture each household has a plot of land on which are grown those foods and materials necessary for survival. Economic role behavior on these plots is clearly specified by kinship norms. If the family is extended, with a living grandfather, the land is usually divided up into several plots with each son and his family working a separate plot. In working the land a clear division of family labor between men and women exists, with men performing the tasks of breaking the ground and clearing off brushwood and women doing the weeding and tending of the crops. In times of emergency or when large economic tasks such as house building are required each household can summon labor from the larger kinship grouping in accordance with certain kinship rules. With respect to the fishing activities of the Tikopia, only males engage in the dangerous deep-sea pursuit of bonita, shark, and other large fish. Women are only allowed to fish around the reefs with hand nets. Sometimes fishing activity organized by kinship norms occurs. But more frequently it is organized on a local community or village level, with family units engaged only in consumption of the fish.

The Tikopia illustrate two facts of economic life in traditional societies: (a) A great deal of economic activity is organized and carried out within kinship; (b) however, kinship is not the only principle of organization. Sometimes other societal subsystems such as the community can also be the locus and principal entrepreneurial structure organizing economic roles.

Because of the frequent overlap of the economy and kinship, it is often difficult to determine empirically where familial roles become economic roles, and vice versa. This partial fusion of economic and familial roles inevitably means that kinship is also the principal source of labor for traditional economies. Since kinship is usually the only major socialization structure in traditional systems it instills those attributes necessary for participation in the economy. Such socialization involves the instillation of basic motives, knowledge, and skills necessary for enacting economic roles. Much of this socialization is the unconscious by-product of growing up in the large kinship subsystem of traditional societies. However, with respect to crucial economic skills and knowledge, designated family members usually offer explicit instruction to the appropriate young. Such instruction tends to take a kind of familial master-apprentice form with certain elders designated by kinship norms instructing similarly designated young. It might be noted that frequently these designated relationships do not involve mother-daughter or father-son tutelage but rather relationships between other older kinsmen and the young — such as a mother's brother and her son. Kinship norms thus vary with respect to who is to instill crucial labor attributes in the young.

One of these attributes is knowledge or technology about how to manipulate the environment. In highly traditional societies without a written language, technology must be stored in the minds of men. While in some advanced agrarian systems a written language and schools exist to store technology, the technology needed for most economic tasks is cerebral (Parsons, 1966). Such technology is thus made available to the economy through family socialization of the young by older kinsmen. Just as the family imparts other cultural components such as values, beliefs, religious dogmas, and traditions, so it imparts to children basic knowledge about the environment. By the time the young are ready to become full-fledged participants in the economy, much of the knowledge about manipulation of the environment has been implanted in their minds and is therefore available to the economy. In more advanced traditional economies some children will be partially socialized in another way: in school structures outside the family. In these schools knowledge is disseminated by reading books and other manuscripts. However, much knowledge acquired in this way in these societies is not technological. It is more likely to be religious or historical, for only in modern economies do these new structures and methods of knowledge retrieval revolve primarily around technology. In societies where most technology is stored in people's minds and transmitted through family socialization, technological expansion is limited. Because kinship norms specify what knowledge is to be transmitted by whom and how, innovation becomes difficult since norms do not encourage people to discover new ways to manipulate the environment. Rather, emphasis is on the transmission of existing knowledge. Aside from stifling technological innovation, such an emphasis can discourage acceptance of new knowledge from other systems because diffusion can "threaten" kinship norms and traditional ways of carrying out economic activity. Thus while traditional kinship systems are a major institutional source of technology in traditional societies, they can often inhibit the expansion and discovery of new technologies. Not until new nonkinship structures evolve in societies to provide technology for the economy will the technology of a society expand rapidly.

In sum, kinship can be considered as a central institution in traditional societies. With respect to the economy, it is intimately involved in all economic processes in that it provides the structural locus, principles of entrepreneurship, labor pool, and technology underlying these processes.

With the modernization of a society, the economy becomes more clearly differentiated from kinship, with the result that the consequences of kinship for the economy change drastically. Kinship ceases to provide the structural locus, principles of entrepreneurship, or technology sustaining the economy. These economic elements are maintained either by internal economic structures and processes such as factories or by other emerging institutions such as education and law (see following chapters). Even with respect to instilling labor with attributes necessary for participation in the economy, the functions of kinship decrease. Increasingly, as will be examined later, educational structures begin to assume much of the socialization burden in modern societies, especially in instilling the attributes of labor.

The dramatic transformation of kinship from a dominant to recessive institution with respect to the economy is the result not only of the differentiation of the economy from kinship but also of the structural changes within both kinship and economy. A modern industrial economy is a vastly complex and ever-expanding web of statuses requiring attributes of workers which the family cannot instill. These attributes include new kinds of *trade skills*; new *interpersonal styles*; and new forms of highly *specialized knowledge*.

Trade skills. Skills are both mental and manual in all economic statuses. In modern economies some norms require extensive manual skills (skilled machine operatives, mechanics, repairmen, etc.). Yet, trade skills in modern economies are increasingly mental and embody the ability to gather, sort, and evaluate information and make decisions. Instead of physical dexterity, mental dexterity is crucial to meeting the norms of a modern economy. This is true because the economic processes of gathering and production become relatively unproblematic in modern economies and are better handled by technology and its byproduct, the machine. Furthermore occupations involved in the processes of distributing and servicing are distinctly mental in character, requiring expanded mental skills of the work force.

Interpersonal styles.   Economic statuses, whether the factory assembly line or administrative bureaucracy, rely on a host of interpersonal skills, or styles, that usually cannot be acquired within kinship. Such interpersonal styles include (Parsons, 1951)[1]: (a) neutrality and (b) specificity. (a) Norms in modern economic structures require labor to interact comparatively neutrally, unemotionally, and dispassionately. This does not mean that labor is unemotional but only that norms emphasize inhibiting and controlling the expression of emotion.[2] A factory or bureaucracy is a complex web of specialized statuses, and coordinating this web of specialized jobs poses a continual problem for modern economic organizations. If employees could freely vent frustrations, depressions, hates, loves, and jealousies their efficiency would decline, for the capacity to pace, schedule, time, or standardize work would be disrupted by emotional strains. Under these conditions temperament rather than expertise would be more likely to dominate the work place. When this happens, coordinating activities in both factories and bureaucracies becomes difficult since the regularity and predictability of work output necessary for effective coordination would break down. Norms thus increasingly must emphasize neutrality and workers must increasingly become capable of interacting in such neutral situations. (b) Interaction on the job in a factory or bureaucracy tends to be highly compartmentalized, for others are not whole or total persons but specialized functionaries to whom only delimited and job-related obligations are owed. This situation forces employees in modern economic organizations to display at least some capacity to interact only segmentally with their fellow workers. This interpersonal capacity is sometimes termed *specificity.*

Knowledge.   Norms in modern economies frequently require that the knowledge of workers be specialized, with each displaying ex-

62

---

[1] Although we cite Parsons' classic work *The Social System* and employ two of his "pattern variables," our usage obviously differs somewhat from his. Rather than focusing on the value orientations underlying certain norms of status roles we are focusing on the personality attributes necessary to conform to value orientations emphasizing neutrality and specificity.

[2] This emphasis on neutrality does not deny that informal cliques and groups among workers emerge in the modern work place. Indeed the literature documenting this emergence is extensive. But compared to the "diffuse" relations of the extended family the modern economy is comparatively neutral.

pertise in only a delimited area. Acquiring such narrow expertise involves a period of technical and specialized training and instruction.

Kinship systems are not structured in ways conducive to instilling these three labor attributes upon which modern economies rely. However, this fact does not mean that kinship is not a crucial institutional source of labor attributes in modern societies. On the contrary, many basic motives determining whether or not an actor will release and sustain energy and commitment within a modern economy are acquired within the kinship subsystem (Parsons, 1964). Furthermore, by being instrumental in the formation of basic motivation, kinship influences the young's acquisition of crucial labor attributes elsewhere, such as in schools. Without basic commitment acquired through family socialization students will be unwilling to participate in the schools which instill attributes necessary for effective role performance in the economy. Yet compared to traditional kinship systems, the modern family's consequences for the economy appear greatly diminished. Kinship is no longer the locus, means of organization,[3] source of technology, or exclusive source of labor.

EDUCATION AND ECONOMY

In most traditional societies education is a recessive institution; and where visible, it has little impact on the economy. Instead educational structures tend to store, preserve, and transmit nontechnological cultural components as well as impart skills for noneconomic statuses such as those necessary for becoming a religious or political elite. Educational structures are therefore conservative and elitist, having consequences primarily for the religious and political subsystems (see Chapters 5 and 6 for details).

Partly under the influence of changes in the economy and other institutions, education undergoes alteration with modernization. It comes to have far-reaching significance as the principal institutional source of labor and technology.

63

[3] In many modern societies kinship often does have major consequences for the organization of the economy. In Japan many of the major corporations, particularly in electronics, are owned and run by quasi-extended families. The members of these families often hold a majority of the top management positions and are thus responsible for much economic organization. Kinship control of the economy also existed during early industrialization in the United States, where families owned and controlled industries and hence were responsible for the organization of much of the economy. Even today corporations like DuPont maintain a large number of family members in top management positions.

In modern societies educational structures assume a large share of a society's socialization burden, especially with respect to interpersonal styles, knowledge, and trade skills. A quick overview of the general structural features of modern educational systems can reveal why this is so (Halsey, 1967): (a) Educational structures are separated from the home and usually operate independent of its direct influence. (b) They are formal structures with incumbents' duties explicitly defined. (c) They pursue highly delimited goals — to impart skills and knowledge. (d) They require impartial evaluation of performance in terms of objective standards and criteria (test performance). (e) Advancement and promotion in the school system are based on expertise and performance. Such a structure requires the development in children of interpersonal styles of neutrality and specificity. When forced to participate in a formal, goal-oriented, delimited structure where their performance is judged objectively in accordance with established standards, children usually develop these interpersonal styles. Were these interpersonal styles not present, considerable disruption of the educational system could occur. To interact other than neutrally disrupts the objective evaluation of performance as well as undermines the formality of modern educational systems. And to interact with other than specificity can undermine the narrow obligations of teachers to implement delimited educational goals of imparting knowledge and skills. Although schools also teach manual skills, they are more instrumental in imparting mental skills to children. Children must learn to gather, process, and evaluate information — all important skills of participants in a modern economy. Finally schools transmit both the general and specialized knowledge necessary for incumbency in a modern economy. These various labor attributes can be implanted in children only by formal educational structures. Since the organization of education approximates the bureaucratic organization of the modern economy, it serves not only as a building ground but also as an arena for rehearsal of all the attributes necessary in a modern labor force. Schools thus represent a "halfway house" between the family and economy. Schools impart what the family cannot; and in doing so, they become the principal institutional source of labor in modern societies.

Aside from imparting labor attributes, modern educational structures affect the placement of labor in the economy. Since schools socialize the skills crucial to participation in the economy, just *what* and how *extensive* the skills imparted to students determines where in the economy they will eventually end up. How far a student goes in the educational hierarchy — from first grade to graduate and professional school — becomes a crucial variable determining his placement as labor in the economy. To regulate the passage of students through the educational hierarchy and hence eventually into the economy, modern educational subsystems evolve a whole series of evaluating mechanisms, such as grades, tests, and counseling facilities. Thus as educational structures increasingly assume the burden of providing labor with attributes and traits necessary for effective role behavior in the economy they also become a conspicuous entrepreneurial mechanism for inserting and placing labor in the economy of modern societies.

EDUCATION AND TECHNOLOGY

The technology of modern economies is complex and extensive. No single person can store much of this technology in his mind. Because of these limitations in human intellect, complex networks of storehouses for technology exist in modern societies. Books, journals, and computer banks supplement the human mind as the basic storage units for technology. In turn these storage units are consolidated in even larger storehouses such as schools, libraries, research organizations, patent offices, government files, and various economic organizations.

These elaborate storage facilities generate severe problems of retrieval revolving around how the technology in this vast cultural storehouse is to be made available to the economy. The institution of the family is inadequate to the task, for the combined level of knowledge of all family members is very small in comparison to the vastness of technology in modern social systems. Although considerable educational development often occurs for reasons unrelated to technology, educational structures in modern societies come to have major consequences for the economy not only as a cultural storehouse (libraries, computer banks, research files) but also as a retrieval structure that makes technology available to the economy. Just how this transformation of education from a training ground for religious and political elites to a principal source of technology occurs is highly variable from society to society. Sometimes political elites, such as in Russia and China, deliberately initiate technical schools and institutes to store and retrieve technology. At other times, as in the United States and England, the process occurs more by trial and error as school curricula and facilities slowly and sporadically adjust under pressures from the economy or polity. Whatever the exact historical process, educational structures in modern societies eventually develop close connections with the economy and come to store and provide its technology.

Universities are particularly crucial in this interchange between the economy and education. When the graduates of undergraduate, graduate, and professional schools of all the colleges and universities of a modern society are viewed in the aggregate as a "knowledge mass" to be inserted into the economy, it is easy to picture one way in which socialization processes within the institution of education have retrieval consequences for the economy. No one graduate may possess large amounts or a wide scope of technological knowledge; but when we look at the total knowledge of the thousands upon thousands of graduates injected each year into the economy, the extensive retrieval function performed by education becomes apparent. Moreover, there are also specific clusters of statuses within the university making technology directly available to the economy. Researchers and consultants often infuse knowledge directly into specific organizations and structures in the economy. Whether indirectly through socialization of students or through direct consultation and contact with the economy, higher education is constantly engaged in the retrieval of technology from the vast and complex cultural storehouses of modern societies.

We know that the level of technology is constantly increasing in modern societies. The reasons for this lie in structures and processes of two institutions—economy and education—as well as in a new, emerging institution—science. Within the economy there are many roles (scientists, researchers, consultants, etc.) concerned with the expansion and application of new knowledge to basic economic processes. Indeed these positions in the economy—usually termed *research and development*—are increasingly becoming essential to the organization of a modern economy. Their explicit function is technological innovation. Similarly, within the institution of education, many such innovative statuses exist. But there is a new institution that is becoming increasingly distinguishable from other institutions: science. Science might be considered a separate institution, but for our purposes it will be viewed only as an emerging institution that is a major subsystem of the educational subsystem of modern societies. Science is that increasingly widespread, interrelated, and stable cluster of statuses within education (and other institutions) concerned explicitly with the acquisition and systemization of knowledge about the world (Hirsch, 1966). One primary consequence of this structure is to generate technology. As the positions of scientists become increasingly widespread and interrelated in modern societies, so do the general norms guiding conduct in these positions. One author (Merton, 1957:574–606) has isolated four such norms: (1) universalism, (2) communism, (3) disinterestedness, and (4) organized skepticism. Universalism refers to the norms emphasizing that data about the world are to be judged by preestablished, agreed upon, and objective criteria; communism concerns the scientist's obligation to communicate findings and discoveries to other scientists. The norm of disinterestedness holds that scientists are concerned most with truth rather than glory and personal gain; and organized skepticism is that norm requiring that no idea or finding is sacred and above re-examination and formulation. Only in modern systems do these norms and the status position of scientists become highly interrelated, widespread, and stabilized.

However, these norms represent normative ideals and are often violated. Only within education are they perhaps frequently conformed to, but within private industry and government, norms of communism are clearly irrelevant, as scientists engage in secret and applied research. Even within education, where government and military research is often performed, norms of secretiveness are dominant and begin to displace those of communism. In fact it might be safe to hypothesize that as scientists become more widely distributed within various institutional spheres in modern societies and as they increasingly become engaged in applied research, many of the norms of pure science will break down. Even in the face of long traditions revolving around academic freedom, free inquiry, and a concern for pure science, applied military, governmental, and business research may well subvert scientific ideals. This projection rings true for education in the United States and other countries with long traditions of higher education.

However disruptive applied research within educational structures may be to the norms of science, one fact is inescapable: The amount of technology flowing from educational structures to the economy and other institutional spheres such as government is increasing. Despite the clear dangers to pure (as opposed to applied) scientific research, educational structures will continue to be a major institutional source of technology for the economy.

In conclusion, we can note the shifting impact of kinship and educational structures for the economy during societal modernization. In traditional societies, education is a highly recessive institution, with kinship as a major institutional source of labor, entrepreneurship, and technology. In modern systems the situation is reversed. Kinship has comparatively few consequences for the economy, while education becomes a major source of labor, entrepreneurship, and technology.

RELIGION AND ECONOMY

Religion concerns beliefs and rituals directed at a supernatural realm of forces, powers, and deities (see Chapter 12). Religion deals with many of the nonempirical, cosmic parameters of social life. However, religious beliefs and rituals can have profound impact on everyday occurrences in social systems. This is particularly evident in traditional societies, where religious beliefs and rituals have far-reaching entrepreneurial consequences for the economy. In such economies religion mobilizes actors to perform crucial economic roles and reinforces economic norms guiding role behavior. Religious beliefs mobilize actors to engage in economic roles by reducing the anxiety often associated with economic behavior. By providing actors with a recourse to rituals designed to invoke the benevolence, or at least suspend the malevolence, of supernatural beings and/or forces, they become willing to engage in uncertain and hazardous economic activity. One of the best illustrations of this comes from Malinowski's (1955) account of the Trobriand Islanders' use of extensive magic rites before participating in dangerous deep-sea fishing expeditions. Such rituals alleviated anxiety and thus mobilized actors to pursue deep-sea fishing.[4] Religious beliefs and rituals also have entrepreneurial consequences for the economy by reinforcing crucial economic norms, as illustrated by Firth's (1936) account of Tikopian fishing rituals. One of the more elaborate rituals among the Tikopians revolved around preparation of fishing equipment — especially canoes — for expeditions into the open sea. Such preparation was an obvious economic necessity but it was considered particularly necessary because it was a religious ritual having significance for the supernatural. Hence overhauling and preparing canoes for fishing was just one part of an elaborate ritual concerning the Tikopians' obligations to secure food offerings for the gods. Under these conditions economic tasks were performed more rapidly, efficiently, and with greater harmony. In a very real sense, then, religious rituals in "sacredizing" crucial economic norms increase normative conformity. Such religious reinforcement of norms, coupled with the mobilizing consequence of religious rituals, represents a major institutional source of entrepreneurship in traditional societies since religion secures the involvement of labor in economic statuses and makes more efficient and harmonious economic role behavior in these statuses.

Perhaps one of the most dramatic documentations of the entrepreneurial influence of religion on the economy is contained in Weber's (1904) seminal essay on the impact of the Protestant Reformation on the emergence of modern industrial capitalism. Weber hypothesized that the worldly ascetic elements of Protestant beliefs and the forms of ritual behavior (such as individualism, acquisitiveness, thrift, and good works) they condoned accelerated the accumulation and organization of basic economic elements into an early industrial economy. The thesis did not engage in a one-sided asser-

[4]This is not to deny Radcliff-Brown's (1938) contention that these rituals may also arouse anxiety by creating a sense of danger and insecurity. This is probably true but the important point is that the magic rites also alleviate the anxiety they arouse. And in this whole process of anxiety arousal (whether from the ritual or perceived economic danger) and then alleviation, actors have been mobilized.

tion that these religious beliefs and the behavior they initiated were the sole cause of economic development in Europe. On the contrary, the thesis emphasized that given a certain level of capital, labor, technolgy, and other economic elements, Protestantism encouraged their organization into an industrial economy. Weber was thus pointing to Protestantism as a major institutional source of entrepreneurship during early industrialization.

However, current industrialization in the modernizing Third World is comparatively uninfluenced by religious beliefs and rituals. And in highly modern economies religion has virtually no impact, since religious beliefs and ritual concerning the supernatural are simply incompatible with the rational and secular norms of factories and bureaucracies. Notions of divine intervention in economic processes become difficult to maintain in the face of massive accumulations of technology (secular knowledge) and capital organized into factories and bureaucracies with clear-cut goals, schedules, and norms. Thus in modern economies religion becomes segregated from a sphere for which in traditional economies it has profound entrepreneurial consequences (for further discussion see Chapter 13).

LAW AND ECONOMY

Through a wide variety of processes and historical paths, law tends to become a major institutional source of entrepreneurship during economic development. While in many respects legal evolution often occurs independently of economy under pressures from other societal spheres, its consequences for the economy expand as a society modernizes. In traditional economies kinship and religion are major sources of entrepreneurship. Kinship norms and religious rituals guide, coordinate, and direct economic activity as well as mobilize commitment and willingness of actors to play economic roles. Such entrepreneurial mechanisms are adequate in economies with low levels of all economic elements (land, labor, capital, and technology) and very simple gathering, producing, distributing, and servicing processes. However, as the economy expands and becomes more clearly separated from kinship and religion these entrepreneurial mechanisms increasingly prove inadequate. Through political edict and/or a long process of trial and error as conflicts in the economy intensify, law begins to exert an influence on the organization of economic activity.

Probably the initial economic sphere in which law exerts a visible influence in traditional societies is the marketplace. As soon as economies can generate a surplus, exchange of goods and commodities occurs and such exchanges usually become regularized through laws and their enforcement. For example, if a native of the Trobriand

Islands in the Pacific fails to meet exchange obligations he has incurred with others, laws prescribe that others in the community refuse to engage in further exchanges with him. The result is that the defaulter is isolated and economically helpless. In economies with more developed markets, laws tend to expand their consequences for regulating exchange. This process is not always deliberate or intended but rather it occurs sporadically as men attempt to deal with conflicts, default, bad faith, and dishonesty in market transactions. This is best illustrated by the legal systems of feudal, preindustrial Europe. In the societies and territories comprising this area, laws tended to be tied to local urban centers and were established by common-law precedents as local court judges attempted to deal with disputes as they emerged. In the marketplace a whole series of "merchant laws" similarly developed as merchants attempted to regularize market exchange. Although binding and enforced these merchant laws were frequently not incorporated into the formal legal system until long after they had become institutionalized.

As economic activity becomes clearly differentiated from kinship with further modernization, entrepreneurial problems expand beyond those evident in the marketplace. The reason for this is that once kinship and religion cease being the primary sources for organizing, gathering, producing, and servicing, nonkinship principles of entrepreneurship begin to organize technology, capital, and labor. Just as when distributive or market processes move outside the exclusive purview of kinship and are assumed by new principles of organization, so gathering, producing, and servicing tend to be gradually organized in new ways. Two of these new forms of economic organization are the factory system and giant administrative bureaucracies of modern economies. While these structures have far-reaching entrepreneurial consequences for the economy, they never completely resolve problems concerning the organization of land, labor, capital, and technology. By various routes, with varying degrees of success, and under different historical and current conditions, the legal system in most modern societies comes to have entrepreneurial consequences for these remaining problems, as well as for a whole cluster of problems created by the emergence of factories and bureaucracies. The history of economic development in the United States provides a vivid illustration of how law has increased its entrepreneurial functions over the last 150 years.

LAW AND CAPITAL ACCUMULATION IN AMERICA

One of the contradictions inherent in a free-enterprise or capitalist system is that some corporations tend to gain a market advantage and then attempt to restrict and limit competition or enterprise. The end result of this process is that monopolies are likely to be formed, with the result that a few companies possess or control disproportionate amounts of the capital resources in a particular economic sphere. Monopoly is an endemic tendency in competitive market economies such as the United States. During early industrialization, capital—money, machines, and other resources—became increasingly owned by a few companies in key productive areas, particularly steel, oil, lumber, and sugar. Once this occurred competition in the market decreased because a few corporations could fix prices, control distribution, and force suppliers of raw materials to sell exclusively to them. Beginning in 1890 a series of antimonopoly laws was initiated to cope with this problem. The Sherman Antitrust Act of 1890 and later the Clayton Act of 1917 began to regulate the degree of monopolization possible in the economy. Since then this trend has been buttressed by many laws—Robinson-Putnam Act, McGuire Act, Public Utility Holding Company Act, Miller-Tydings Act, Federal Reserve Act, and a host of others—restricting and regulating the formation of capital by a single corporation.

LAW AND LABOR IN AMERICA

Violence has always been typical of the labor movement of the United States. The early 1800s, the 1870s, and the 1920s and 1920s were rife with violent conflict between labor and management of the developing industrial economy. The issues over which the conflict occurred revolved around child labor, minimum wages, eight-hour working days, overtime pay, retirement benefits, workman's compensation, and collective bargaining. As the American economy moved from an agrarian to industrial basis of organization, the traditional ways of securing, organizing, and maintaining a labor force became increasingly inadequate. Although some laws pertaining to labor-management conflicts existed as early as 1915 (for example, the Adamson Act provided for an eight-hour day in some jobs), a massive legal system response to the problem occurred only in the 1930s with the passage of a series of laws specifying some of the conditions of labor's participation in the economy. The titles of these laws best describe their entrepreneurial consequences: National Labor Relations Act, Labor-Management Reporting and Disclosure Act, Federal Mediation and Conciliation Service Act, Fair Labor Standards Act, and the Social Security Act. Less descriptive labor-management laws (for example, the La Guardia Act and Taft-Hartley Act) also began to regulate the processes of securing and maintaining a labor force in the economy.

LAW AND LAND IN AMERICA

Modern economies possess high levels of technology generating heavy concentrations of capital, which can be used to extract enormous quantities and varieties of natural resources from the environment. Since many crucial resources such as oil, coal, natural gas, copper, magnesium, and other minerals are not replenishable, large-scale extraction could eventually generate serious shortages. And even many replenishable resources—lumber, soil, wildlife—under the impact of massive applications of capital can be diminished. These processes pose a potentially serious problem—the depletion of all essential resources. Modern economies have typically heightened the process of depletion in at least these ways: (a) wasteful but inexpensive and rapid means of extraction are usually employed; (b) often little care has been taken to replenish extracted resources; and (c) increasingly the practices of gathering resources and converting them result in the depletion through pollution, erosion, and waste of other resources. Although the impact of depletion has yet to be felt, analysts predict serious shortages in the near future of many resources—especially copper, coal, iron, oil, lumber, soil, water, and air. The reasons for this lie in the fact that modern economies possess almost total access to the natural resources of the environment. Hunting and gathering economies have low access, as do agrarian systems. But with industrialization and the ever-expanding levels of technology and capital formation, access becomes virtually unlimited and yet problematic. It is a curious irony that low access and high access to resources may generate similar problems of resource scarcity. As yet a major resource or land crisis has not emerged, for two reasons: (a) while rapidly declining, modern economies have not yet exhausted most crucial resources; and (b) as shortages emerge, modern economies can extract the resources of less modern countries which do not need them. But as these underdeveloped countries become modern they will be less willing to lend or sell resources to modern systems. They will increasingly extract them for their own developing economies. The recent appropriations of American oil, agricultural, and mining industries in Latin America attest to this inevitability. Also some experts predict that by 1980 many indigenous resources such as copper and tungsten in the United States will be depleted. While alternatives to these and other depleted resources currently exist or possibly can be discovered, there seems to be a potential crisis. To the extent that this is true it could be expected that legal systems of modern societies such as the United States would begin controlling and regulating resource extraction. As of 1968 there were approximately seven hundred federal laws concerning the mining of minerals in the United States (Federal Code, Title 30). While seemingly a vast number, most are not concerned with limiting resource extraction. But the laws are clearly entrepreneurial in that they set guidelines and procedures for resource extraction. They do not, however, in any comprehensive way—as with labor or capital—deal with limiting resource depletion. Or if we look at the 1136 conservation laws in the United States, we find that most of the laws are not directly or indirectly concerned with resource depletion (Federal Code, Title 16). Of those that are, most deal with water and forest reserves; few concern conservation of more primarily industrial resources. Many laws establish commissions and boards which in principle could regulate resource extraction, although the power of these boards seems negligible. It can be pondered why the legal system in the United States (and other modern systems) is not responding in a direct or comprehensive way to the potential crisis. One answer lies in the fact that laws tend to be passed only when a crisis reaches serious proportions. For instance, comprehensive labor and antitrust laws only emerged after successive and extreme crises. Also there are pressures from the powerful vested interests in the economy preventing such legislation.

LAW AND TECHNOLOGY IN AMERICA
Since the beginnings of the United States as a nation system, technological expansion has been encouraged by law. Even the Constitution specifies that inventors should be protected. In his inaugural address of 1789 George Washington noted the importance of ". . . giving effective encouragement as well as the introduction of new and useful inventions" (Dynes et al., 1964:195). As early as 1790 the first patent law was implemented to protect and regulate the discovery of applied knowledge. In 1836 this law was revised to outline the legal procedures for verifying inventions. In 1862 the Morrill Act established guidelines for founding and maintaining colleges "where the leading object shall be . . . to teach such branches of learning as are related to agriculture and mechanic arts."

The American legal system has thus traditionally had entrepreneurial consequences for generating and organizing technology for the economy. Once law encourages, tolerates, and specifies procedures for the cataloging and storing of technology, knowledge expands and proliferates at a rapid rate. Knowledge that can be efficiently stored and retrieved provides a base upon which knowledge can be expanded. Currently the legal system in the United States and other modern systems has yet to set many restrictions on such expansion—except with respect to military technology. Rather it has tended to encourage and organize its accumulation. But perhaps there is a potential crisis emerging under these conditions, since technological knowledge may reach proportions where resource extraction and production become completely capitalized or mechanized. Such automation could possibly reach a level where

the
institutional
environment
of
ECONOMY

extraction of all resources could be accomplished in a short period of time. Just as with the current military technology, when industrial technology reaches this level we can expect the legal system to become more restrictive, regulating more carefully the processes of gathering and production. Because of the increasing penetration of vast technological knowledge into all institutional spheres of society—economic, educational, and political—we can expect that law will increasingly assume new entrepreneurial functions in regard to technology, just as it did with capital, labor, and, to a lesser extent with land.

POLITY AND ECONOMY

The political subsystem of a society is always involved in mobilizing, allocating, and distributing a society's human and material resources toward achieving certain goals and political policies. In doing so the polity has far-reaching consequences for many economic processes, since ultimately the economy supplies many of the resources necessary for implementation of political policies and decisions. The most direct of these consequences is the capacity of the polity to regulate the flow and accumulation of capital in the economy. In turn such regulation of capital flows and accumulation can affect access to natural resources, the distribution of labor, the way technology is used, and the way economy becomes organized.

In highly traditional societies with a hunting and gathering economy and where little capital exists beyond the bow and arrow, spears, sticks, and chisels, a polity is comparatively inconspicuous. The reason for this (to be explored in Chapter 10) is that the economy cannot generate sufficient economic surplus to support an elaborate political subsystem. This is clearly illustrated by such geographically dispersed societies as the Inland Eskimos and the !Kung Bushmen of Africa. Among the Eskimos leaders arise and recede in terms of how successful they are in basic economic activities (Fried, 1968: 86–87). For example, a successful hunter will be followed by others and his advice will be sought, but he has no power to compel conformity to his wishes. Should he cease being successful, he also ceases to be a leader. Among the !Kung Bushmen leadership is more stable, with an established chief directing certain crucial economic activities and tribal migrations. But the chief has no real power to sanction nonconformity to his wishes and directives (Schapera, 1956). These two illustrations document probably the simplest kind of political subsystem (Fried, 1968:28–101). Yet, even in these societies political leaders have some capacity to regulate how capital such as spears, bows and arrows, and other crude tools are used for hunting and gathering. But clearly these leaders' capacity to regulate capital flows is not great and represents only the rudiments of the political power that becomes so evident in more developed societies.

In more advanced agrarian societies, which are capable of generating an economic surplus and hence supporting an autonomous political subsystem, the polity comes to have the power to *appropriate* economic surplus and then redistribute it. The typical pattern involves certain kin groups in a society acquiring more territory and power than other kin groupings and utilizing that power to appropriate the economic surplus of other familial-economic units. In more advanced systems with a clear-cut state army and administrative staff, appropriation becomes institutionalized into norms allowing the polity to tax economic surplus in accordance with some formula. Much of this surplus simply goes to increase and consolidate the wealth and privilege of an elite ruling class but some is allocated to system goals, such as war, conquest, and public works, which have been established by the polity. The dual processes of appropriation-redistribution and allocation profoundly affect the level of capital available to the economy because just how much economic surplus is appropriated determines how much capital is available to expand the economy. And just how much of the appropriated capital is reallocated to which economic processes determines the basic profile of the economy. In traditional societies of the Third World, where a major system goal is economic development, these appropriation-allocation processes influence the rate and sphere of industrialization. Frequently to control more precisely the accumulation of capital in the economy these polities assume ownership or nationalize major concentrations of capital in the economy. Nationalization allows the polity to regulate directly the flow of appropriated capital into various economic processes. The polity can now control more directly the ratio of consumer to capital goods, the amount of money capital devoted to technological expansion, the distribution of labor, the kinds and levels of goods to be placed in the market, and so on.

In order for extensive appropriation by the polity to occur, the polity must possess the power to coerce compliance of other system units. But more important for the long run is the capacity of the polity to cultivate legitimacy. Legitimacy is simply the population's perception and belief in the right of the polity to wield power and establish system goals. With legitimacy the capacity of the polity to control the accumulation of capital in the economy is greatly expanded. Furthermore, the various components of a society's culture such as values, beliefs, religious dogmas, and customs that the polity may use to legitimatize itself can also be used to manipulate the population into accepting certain forms of appropriation and allocation of capital. Because the polity has control over many communication processes in a society, it can manipulate these symbolic aspects of culture to achieve certain goals. When capital is accumulated for the production of weapons for war, it can be done much more effectively in the name of a "holy crusade," "national integrity and prestige," "to preserve cherished traditions," "in the name of God," or "to save face." By such *symbolic manipulation* the polity can pacify other system units and make endurable the accumulation of capital in areas not to their immediate interests. Inserting capital into the economy requires justification, since it places hardships on other system units. To do this the polity must utilize symbolic manipulation. The power of such manipulation was very evident in the Holy Crusades or today in many African and Latin nations where nationalistic ideologies such as that of Cuba are a major political tool. In all such systems, better food, housing, and other material comforts are foregone in the name of nationalism while capital resources are accumulated in the economy for long-range economic goals.

Thus in traditional societies the related mechanisms of appropriation and symbolic manipulation increasingly are utilized by the polity to regulate the accumulation and flow of capital in the economy. In modern societies these are supplemented by the extensive use of additional mechanisms for regulating capital formation, including tariffs and subsidies. *Tariffs* are limitations or bans imposed by the polity on the importation of certain goods and commodities in order to protect internal gathering and productive processes. Such limitations and bans enable the economy to accumulate capital in areas which would not develop if imports were allowed. By changing and altering such tariff restrictions the polity can regulate the degree to which capital is accumulated around various productive processes. *Subsidies* are "gifts" of capital bestowed upon certain economic units that the polity wishes to develop. Such gifts allow for the establishment of an initial capital base. Subsidy has meaning only in a capitalistic economy where most capital accumulations are not owned or nationalized by the polity, since in these latter economies *all* capital accumulation represents a subsidy from the polity.

Modern polities utilize a wide variety of mechanisms to regulate capital accumulation. All modern polities appropriate surplus, symbolically manipulate the population, and impose tariffs. In enterprise economies, subsidy becomes the principal mechanism for direct infusions from the polity into private enterprises. To illustrate the utilization of these mechanisms by the polity we can turn to a brief examination of capital-formation processes in the United States.

We are accustomed to thinking of the United States as a capitalistic or free-enterprise economy, although many an embattled capitalist has noted the increasing intervention of government in economic affairs. Such intervention reveals the extensiveness of the polity's regulation of capital formation, even in a supposedly free-enterprise system. Appropriation powers of the federal government are immense. Through taxation of the economic surplus of individuals, corporations, and businesses, the government can control the amount of capital in the economy since most of this economic surplus ultimately becomes economic capital (Reagan, 1963; Lowi, 1969). For example, when a commodity or service is bought with economic surplus in the American economy there is usually a profit which becomes capital and is reinvested into the company supplying the good or service. If surplus money is deposited in a bank it is often loaned out as capital to some enterprise. Or if surplus money is invested in the stock market, this supplies capital for a corporation. By taxing this surplus the polity indirectly controls the amount of capital available to the economy. Some appropriated monies are not reinserted directly into the economy: some of it goes to welfare, some goes to education, health programs, science, space, and so on. Of course indirectly this becomes economic capital because it creates income that becomes capital for the economy when spent on goods and services. More directly the polity can use its monies as subsidy for creating capital bases in various spheres in the economy, the railroads and airlines being prominent examples in the United States.

Another form of direct infusion of capital into the economy by the polity derives from the fact that government is a big buyer for certain goods in the marketplace. The polity in the United States spends much money on national defense and this in turn becomes capital for defense-related enterprises. When we speak of the military-industrial complex, we are talking about the processes by which capital is channeled through the market by the polity to certain kinds of productive processes. When the channeling of appropriated capital resources is extensive it is indicative that their destination is toward major political goals and policies. Of all societal goals in the United States, defense is given the highest priority. Other goals—elimination of poverty, education, welfare, space exploration—are important, but in terms of the allocation of capital, defense clearly is the most important societal goal. Until very recently this priority has had considerable consensus within the system. Such consensus has been maintained through symbolic manipulation whereby defense is made to seem as essential to preserving certain traditions, values, and beliefs from contamination or subversion.

Finally, modern societies typically impose restrictions on the importation of goods and commodities that could undermine domestic economic production. In the United States, tariffs have existed since initial industrialization and have been revised in response to a series of perceived threats to the domestic economy. In reality tariffs are often established for multiple reasons—some economic, others political. Political ideology of elites as well as pressure from powerful economic interests has often had more to do with tariff restrictions than economic realities, with the result that tariffs often protect obsolete industries maintaining an inefficient and archaic capital base for lack of foreign competition.

SUMMARY

In this chapter, we have attempted to unravel some of the complexity of the institutional web of the economy. In doing so, attention has been drawn to the one-way influence of kinship, education, law, religion, and polity on the economy. The other side of this relationship between the economy and other institutions will be examined in subsequent chapters. We began by analyzing how the kinship system in traditional and modern societies influences the economy. In traditional societies, kinship is a major institutional source of labor, entrepreneurship, and technology, whereas in modern systems it represents only a source of labor. Analysis then shifted to the impact of education on the economy. In traditional societies, education is a recessive institution and has few consequences for the economy. But with economic development, education becomes the major institutional source of labor and technology for the economy. Next, religion and the economy were examined. For traditional economies, religion has many entrepreneurial consequences, such as mobilizing actors and reinforcing crucial economic norms. Initial economic development, as revealed in the Weber thesis, was viewed as greatly accelerated by the entrepreneurial consequences of early Protestantism. However, with further economic development, religion becomes segregated from economic processes. In its place, law increasingly assumes major entrepreneurial consequences for a modern economy. This was illustrated by examining the American case. Finally, the extensive consequences of the polity for capital accumulation in the economy were examined. With increasing economic development, the mechanisms employed by the polity to regulate capital flows expand, as was illustrated with respect to the American polity.

78

SUGGESTED READINGS

Peter Blau, *Bureaucracy in Modern Society,* New York: Random House, Inc., 1956.

Charles Cole, *The Economic Fabric of Society,* New York: Harcourt Brace Jovanovich, Inc., 1969.

C. Wright Mills, *White Collar,* New York: Oxford University Press, 1951.

Wilbert E. Moore, "Economic and Professional Institutions," in N.J. Smelser (ed.), *Society*, New York: John Wiley & Sons, Inc., 1967.

Wilbert E. Moore, *Order and Change: Essays in Comparative Sociology*, New York: John Wiley & Sons, Inc., 1967.

Wilbert E. Moore, "Social Aspects of Economic Development," in E. L. Faris (ed.), *Handbook of Modern Sociology*, Chicago: Rand McNally & Company, 1964.

Robert A. Mundell, *Man and Economics*, New York: McGraw-Hill Book Company, 1968.

Manning Nash, *Primitive and Peasant Economic Systems*, San Francisco: Chandler Publishing Company, 1966.

Robert Presthus, *The Organizational Society*, New York: Random House, Inc., 1962.

Max Weber, *The Theory of Social and Economic Organization*, New York: The Free Press, 1964.

Clair Wilcox et al., *Economies of the World Today*, 2d ed., New York: Harcourt Brace Jovanovich, Inc., 1966.

Robin M. Williams, Jr., "American Economic Institutions," in *American Society*, 3d ed., New York: Alfred A. Knopf, Inc., 1970.

79

the
institutional
environment
of
ECONOMY

KINSHIP   4

One of the most pervasive and visible groups in human societies is the family. Within this basic group sexual relations among adults are regularized, the incapacitated cared for, children born and socialized, and subsistence realized. Just how these activities are carried out varies enormously from society to society, but the fact remains that family groupings are the hub of much social life in virtually all societies (Stephens, 1963:19–31).

In light of these facts it may appear strange to reveal that family groupings per se are not to be the principal focus of this chapter. Rather our attention will be drawn to the more general *kinship* subsystem of a society. The immediate family group is only a part or subsystem of kinship. To emphasize kinship, however, does not mean that the family will be ignored. On the contrary, analysis of the family will be placed into the broader institutional context of kinship.

BASIC ELEMENTS OF KINSHIP

Kinship is a vast web of relationships among familial statuses. In all societies there are certain general norms specifying just what is familial and just how familial relationships should be organized. These norms resolve such questions as who lives together, who is the family head or boss, who marries whom, how mates are selected, which relatives in and between specific family groups are more important, and how children are to be raised and by whom. These general norms determine the definition as well as the pattern, profile, and form of familial statuses and roles in a society. For this reason we can consider such norms as the basic elements of the kinship subsystem of a society. Despite tremendous diversity in these norms and the resulting kinship system of a society, we can isolate certain general types of norms that ultimately determine the organization of familial statuses and performance of roles (Stephens, 1963, 1967; Nimkoff, 1965; Murdock, 1949).

NORMS OF FAMILY SIZE AND COMPOSITION

If one maps out the genealogy or family chart of kinsmen on both sides of his family, the potential size and composition of the family becomes immense. And in some societies where just about everyone is related in some way a few large kinship groupings would be virtually coextensive with the total society. Many Polynesian societies come close to doing just this. Kin ties can be traced for just about everyone in a village, district, or even the total society. As Firth notes in his description of the Tikopia, virtually everyone can trace his kin relationships in a community numbering well over a thousand so that "the whole land is a single body of kinfolk" (Firth, 1936:234). However, kinship ties are rarely this extensive, for there tend to be specific norms which limit the scope of family and kinship. One set of such norms are those that regulate the size and composition of family groupings in a society. Ignoring much complexity, variations in these norms result in three general forms of family groupings: (a) extended, (b) polygamous, and (c) conjugal. (a) The *extended* family is large and includes many relatives within the household unit. Parents, children, grandparents, great-grandparents, aunts, cousins, and other statuses are usually part of the family. The degree of extendedness of such families can vary greatly, with family members living within one house or a compound of houses. Yet regardless of how concentrated their residence, the members of the family perceive themselves as a discrete unit that must control and coordinate activities. Such perception is often bolstered by the fact that extended families as a unit own and work property upon which their subsistence depends. (b) A *polygamous* family unit is one in which plural marriage and residence is allowed. The most common form of polygamy is *polygyny*, where norms permit inclusion of several wife statuses with just one husband status. The husband and his wives (and their children) live in a single house, or each co-wife occupies a dwelling of her own. These dwellings are then clustered together within a family compound or homestead. Where polygyny exists families tend to be large. However, even in societies that permit polygamous families, monogamous marriages are often more common, because women and their children are expensive and most males in societies allowing polygamy cannot afford multiple wives. (c) The *conjugal* family is small and contains only father, mother, and their children. Immediate relatives are excluded from the household or living unit. This conjugal form is the dominant type of family in the United States and other industrial countries (we will explore the reasons for this in the next chapter). Yet the conjugal family is a comparatively rare form of family structure in the world's societies. Extended and polygamous far outnumber conjugal families (Goode, 1964; Murdock, 1949).

NORMS OF RESIDENCE

Once two people get married, they confront the problem of where they are going to live. There are three logical possibilities: (a) alone and where they wish; (b) with the groom's family or in their community; or (c) with the bride's family or community. Respectively, these three possibilities are labeled *neolocal*, *patrilocal*, and *matrilocal* residence norms.[1] Societies tend to be dominated by one of the three.

[1] These definitions differ somewhat from those commonly employed by anthropologists. Frequently when a newly married couple does not move into one of their parents' family compounds, but still within the same community, this is referred to as a neolocal residence pattern. In the definitions offered here this would be either a matri- or

The residence norms of the United States are neolocal. However, most societies in the world evidence either a matri- or patrilocal pattern. For example, if a kinship system is composed of extended families and has a patrilocal residence norm, then the married couple lives not only in the groom's community but most likely in his parents' home, compound, or village. The reverse would be the case for a matrilocal residence rule in a kinship system composed of extended families. And in systems with a polygamous family unit, residence norms also tend to be either matrilocal or patrilocal.

NORMS OF FAMILY ACTIVITY

Most kinship systems display clusters of norms concerning family activities. These rules revolve around three major concerns: (a) household tasks, (b) child care, and (c) socialization of the young. (a) Just what the task obligations of males and females are within the family is usually spelled out by norms, although the specific norms vary from society to society. Frequently males are required to engage in economic activity, with females involved in household or domestic tasks. But often females engage in as much or more economic activity than males. Children in most kinship systems assume the status of student apprentice, acquiring the skills of their parents. In extended or polygamous systems the division of labor becomes much more complex and difficult to analyze. In general males perform the economic, females the domestic, and children the apprentice activities. (b) There are numerous ways to bring up a child, and rarely is this decision left up to his parents (or other kin). Just how a child is to be fed, clothed, and sheltered is usually specified by kinship rules, which establish minimum standards for child care. Should the adults responsible for this care—usually the parents, but not always—not meet these standards, child care then becomes the responsibility of designated kin. (c) Parents often socialize the young, but in many kinship systems one parent is excluded from socialization. For example a mother's brother (or child's uncle) may be more responsible for a young male's socialization than the biological father. And other arrangements excluding a parent from socialization exist in the world's kinship systems. Furthermore, in all societies there are at least some general norms indicating how children are to be socialized. The ways love, affection, discipline, and instruction are administered by adults are greatly circumscribed by kinship norms, although these display great diversity from system to system.

84

patrilocal pattern. For us neolocality pertains to norms allowing for the free choice of residency by married couples.

NORMS OF DISSOLUTION

People sometimes do not get along even when there are clear and powerful kinship rules. When a marriage becomes unstable, all societies provide ways for its dissolution. In general there are three types of rules in kinship systems governing dissolution: (a) conditional rules, (b) procedural rules, and (c) rules of dependence. (a) Conditional rules indicate the conditions under which dissolution is possible. The conditions appropriate for dissolution differ greatly from society to society; among them are lack of female fertility, mutual incompatibility, criminal offense, and mental cruelty. Conditional rules can be either broad or narrow and encouraging or discouraging. (b) Procedural rules indicate how dissolution should occur. They can be simple (moving belongings out of your spouse's house) or exceedingly complex (going to court, pleading a case, and establishing guilt). (c) Dissolution usually involves children (and sometimes other dependent members, such as old people). Kinship rules tend to insure that these dependents are cared for and/or socialized.

NORMS OF DESCENT

With birth one inherits two separate bloodlines and this raises the question of whose bloodline—the mother's or the father's—is to be more important. In the United States this is not an issue since discrimination between families (except in the assignment of surnames) does not occur. But it is not a moot issue in most societies. The vast majority of societies have explicit rules indicating which side of the family is to be more important. These are called *rules of descent* and there are three general types: *patrilineal*, *matrilineal*, and *bilateral*. For example, in a patrilineal descent system a person belongs at birth to a special group of kin on the father's side of the family. This group includes siblings (brothers and sisters), father, father's siblings, father's father and his siblings, and father's brother's children. These and others represent the male kin who are important to the newborn. Mother's kin are not important. It is to this special group of male kin that an individual owes allegiance and loyalty, and it is these kin who will protect, socialize, and eventually place into society an individual. And it is from these kin that the succession of authority and inheritance of property and wealth will pass. In a matrilineal system the mother's instead of the father's kin would assume this important place in the life of the young. Bilateral descent systems assign considerable influence and power to both sides of the family. But they are comparatively rare because working out a division of power and influence between family lines is awkward. Where bilineal descent exists it is frequently truncated so that both mother's and father's kin are equally recognized and respected but neither kin group exerts much influence or power over the children.

Unilineal descent rules (that is, patri- or matrilineal norms) divide up a particular residential unit, since one member of the family (either wife or husband) must be an "outsider" (Stephens, 1963: 105). For example, in a patrilineal descent system, father and children belong to the same descent grouping, with the mother as an outsider. Aside from dividing up a particular family group or household, descent norms also divide societies into "segments" (Murdock, 1949). In a unilineal society one belongs to a patrilineal residential unit and then to other patrilineally reckoned units in the village, community, and perhaps territory. In this way various residential units within some geographical territory are linked together through a patrilineal descent system or the male bloodline. Such linkages are usually referred to as *lineages*. Frequently they own property and can be considered a kind of "corporation" which can be engaged in wars, feuds, economic competition, and be subject to legal liability. When several lineages are connected by a descent norm, a *clan* can be said to exist. And when clans are linked together by descent norms, a *moiety* is formed and represents the largest kind of unilineal kin grouping. Many societies are divided into a couple of moieties, each with their constituent clans, lineages, and residential family units. Just how extensive, clear, and far reaching such descent groupings can be varies tremendously from society to society. Yet in many societies they represent one of the principal bases of societal organization and integration. Furthermore, the existence of such extensive descent norms underscores the fact that a particular family group or residential unit is only a subsystem of a larger and more inclusive kinship system.

NORMS OF AUTHORITY

In all kinship systems there are rules of authority. These rules concern who makes the important and ultimate decisions affecting the welfare of a particular family or larger kin group such as a lineage or clan. But even where rules clearly specify authority, others in the family may still exert considerable decision-making powers in less important or more trivial (actually these are often quite important) areas. Yet the rules of a kinship system usually endow specific statuses with authority. These rules can be of three general types: (1) *patriarchal*, (2) *matriarchal*, and (3) *egalitarian*. In patriarchal kinship systems, the father makes major decisions for his family or residential unit. Eldest and/or most-able males make decisions governing the larger kin grouping embodying all kin wherever their residence may be. In a matriarchal system the reverse is true, although these are less common than patriarchal systems. Egalitarian systems are even rarer. In these systems ultimate decision-making power is invested in neither males nor females. There is usually a division of labor in decision making, with males making major decisions in some areas and females in others.

NORMS OF MARRIAGE

Almost all societies require a mother to be married. Marriage sets up a series of mutual obligations between husband and wife concerning domestic duties, child rearing, and sex, while at the same time it perpetuates the kin grouping. Aside from the general rule requiring marriage of all mothers, most kinship systems have norms concerning whom one may and may not marry. The three most prominent types of marriage rules are (a) incest taboos, (b) norms of exogamy, and (c) norms of endogamy. *Incest taboos* are norms prohibiting sex and marriage among close kin. Some of these are universal or nearly so—mothers and sons, fathers and daughters, and siblings may not have sex or marry. Usually more distant kin (aunts, uncles, cousins, nieces, and nephews, etc.) are also covered by an incest taboo. The effect of such rules is that they force people out of their immediate residential kin group in search of partners. Often marriage rules are also *exogamous* and prohibit marriage to members of one's community or larger kin grouping—thus forcing marriage with partners from other communities, regions, clans, moieties, or lineages. Sometimes rules are *endogamous*, requiring marriage within certain groups—usually a social class, kin group, caste, or village. Coupled with incest (and perhaps exogamy) rules, endogamous norms severely restrict the pool of potential mates. However, some kinship systems—such as that in the United States—have few rules of marriage. Mothers are "encouraged" to be married. Incest rules apply only to close blood kin, and explicit norms of exogamy do not exist.

In sum, then, these seven types of kinship norms can be considered the basic elements of *kinship as an institution*. They define and organize familial statuses and roles into a variety of kinship groupings. Many more highly specific norms also regulate familial role behavior, but for present analytical purposes these have been ignored.[2]

[2] Aside from these specific norms, some authors have isolated other general types of norms which define and organize kinship systems. For example, Stephens (1963:78) has viewed "comportment" norms pertaining to patterns of deference, avoidance, joking, address, and informality as central to an understanding of a kinship system. For the purposes of this volume, however, these types of norms are considered extraneous to an institutional analysis.

KINSHIP AND SOCIETY

The consequences of kinship for the broader society of which it is a subsystem are highly variable. For example in Tikopia, where the whole society is "a single body of kinfolk," the specific consequences of kinship will be vastly different from those in the United States, where kinship tends to be hazy and ambiguous beyond two generations and first cousins. Yet despite this diversity kinship can still be viewed as having certain general consequences for both simple and complex societies.

REGULARIZING SEX AND MATING

Sex drives pervade the human species. All species must reproduce themselves and sex drives are one of those convenient mechanisms of nature assuring that the appropriate parties get together. Without sex drives it seems unlikely that societies could regenerate themselves. If we look at any society, sex is regulated and controlled by norms. These norms specify "appropriate" persons, times, places, ways, ages, and circumstances where sex can occur—although the specific content of norms naturally varies from society to society (Davis, 1949: Murdock, 1949). The exact historical processes leading to this situation are buried in the history of early social evolution. However, sufficient empirical and analytical work on norm formation now exists so that we can block out at least the generalities of this process (see, for example, Thibault and Kelly, 1959; Warriner, 1970). Sex drives can lead to competition among individuals for certain sex objects. Out of such competition can arise jealousies, anger, and perhaps murder. Furthermore, since males tend to be physically stronger than females, sexual dominance and exploitation of females by males can occur. This fact can also lead to anger, frustration, and hostility. Such a situation can create tremendous personal anxieties as well as threaten the survival of the human species, since newborn children are apparently dependent upon physical and emotional support from parents (or surrogates). Through trial and error as early men had to cope with these facts, they probably developed implicit "understandings" about how competition for sex objects was to be mitigated and how enduring physical relations among adults were to be established. Initially these understandings were probably not consciously or deliberately instituted, but over time, because of their success in mitigating sexual conflict and in establishing enduring sexual relations, they persisted. As they persisted, implicit understandings became translated into binding norms that combined with other norms arising out of similar processes to form a kinship system. Once established, these kinship norms rarely remain static but change as social conditions dictate. For example, societies now often deliberately pass laws concerning sex and mating. Furthermore, norms concerning sexual relations can undergo profound changes in the absence or defiance of laws, as is currently the case in the United States. But for our purposes the important conclusion is that all kinship systems evolve norms regulating and regularizing sexual relations.

BIOLOGICAL SUPPORT

The newborn are biologically helpless, for a baby cannot feed, cloth, shelter, or protect itself. (And for brief periods, neither can the mother, especially if she must care for the infant.) Through processes similar to those delineated above, powerful norms originally emerged in human societies which insured the protection of biologically helpless members of the species. Though greatly embellished by thousands of years of history and evolution, kinship systems still evidence norms requiring the able bodied to care for the biological needs of infants (and mothers during periods of incapacitation). These persons insulate and protect the infant (and mother) from the environment. Societies have different kinship norms regarding which and how many people are to protect the infant. With some exceptions, at least the biological father and mother are the two prominent statuses so designated—although the cast of protectors is much more extensive in most societies. However, the biological support functions of kinship are more encompassing than this because in most societies the family also protects adults from ill health, tension and anxiety, and other sources of destruction. The incapacitated, aged, and diseased, as well as the young, thus derive biological support from the family.

SOCIAL REPRODUCTION

Social systems regenerate themselves not only through biological reproduction of the species but also through social reproduction. Such social reproduction occurs through the process of socialization whereby the newborn, over a number of years, acquires through interaction with others those personality traits necessary for participation in many social positions in society. All known societies have evolved structures having consequences for social reproduction. The most prominent (and nearly universal) of these structures is the family. The father and mother are usually intimately involved but sometimes, aunts, uncles, grandparents, and other relatives do as much or more to assure social reproduction. As with biological support of the infant, the specific familial statuses focusing on this important process of socialization vary from society to society.

SOCIAL SUPPORT

Humans of all ages experience a wide range of potentially disruptive emotions such as fear, frustration, uncertainty, anger, and jealousy.

These emotions can generate tremendous anxiety and tension, which can immobilize individuals and disrupt social relations. It appears that the human species requires at least some social relations providing emotional support and affection to mitigate the many sources of fear, anxiety, and uncertainty that social life inevitably breeds. While the exact evolutionary processes can never be known, family groupings in all societies have far-reaching consequences for providing the social and emotional support that humans seemingly need to perform social roles effectively.

SOCIAL PLACEMENT

After years of biological and social support as well as socialization of the young, the issue of how and where to insert the young adult into the wider society appears. This issue is one of the most fundamental for all social systems and involves questions such as how the status transition from child to adult is to be made, where the young adult will go in a society, how this decision will be made, and what criteria will be employed in making it. Finding the proper niche in society for the biologically and socially matured youth is a crucial problem. Through varied historical and evolutionary processes social systems currently display two basic ways of resolving it and the family is intimately involved in both (Davis, 1949; Stephens, 1967; Parsons, 1953). (1) Some systems insert youth into the wider society network on the basis of *ascription*, where a child's adult status in the society is determined at birth by the place (usually social class or caste) of his family. A child assumes the occupational, religious, political, and legal status of his family. Because social placement is determined at birth, family support and socialization are directed toward preparing youth for this predetermined slot in the wider society. (2) Less common in the world's societies is the process of inserting youth into the larger society on the basis of *performance.* Such a placement mechanism emphasizes the role-performing capacity as the criteria by which one is inserted into various statuses. In turn such capacity is a reflection of inherited and socialized or acquired personality traits. Because kinship circumscribes both biological inheritance and socialization, it has far-reaching consequences for social placement in nonascriptive, performance-oriented societies.

SOCIAL COORDINATION

In societies exhibiting certain elements of kinship, such as an extended family or descent norms leading to the formation of lineages and clans, the kinship subsystem can have far-reaching consequences for organizing and coordinating many segments of society. Under such conditions much role behavior in a society is carried out within the context of kinship. For example, we have already noted in Chapter 3 that because the family or larger kinship grouping (such as a lineage or clan) is the locus of economic activity its norms have entrepreneurial consequences for the economy. Or, as will be examined in Chapter 10, certain types of political subsystems are organized around and within kinship, with elder kinsmen serving as elite decision makers. In societies with extended family or household units formed into lineages and with lineages grouped into clans, and clans into moieties, every member of the society can locate himself precisely and understand his obligations to all other members of his kin group and the total society. Such a situation represents the ultimate in societal integration along kinship lines. In reality, however, kinship norms rarely categorize incumbents this clearly. Yet even if norms are only clear at the extended family and lineage level, considerable societal integration and coordination still occurs because of kinship norms. As will be analyzed shortly, kinship tends to have these extensive consequences for only traditional societies. In modern societies where extended or polygamous families and protracted unilineal descent are absent, kinship has little direct impact on overall societal coordination. For instance we have already seen how factories, bureaucracies, and laws replace kinship as the major sources of entrepreneurship in modern economies. In Chapter 10 we will examine how a highly bureaucratized state replaces kinship as the organizational form of a modern polity. Thus, only in more traditional societies where kinship dominates and intrudes into all institutional spheres does it have major coordinating functions.

defining kinship as an institution

From the above discussion, it should be evident that kinship is the normative patterning of familial statuses that are related to one another by blood or heredity and by marriage. While the profile of these familial statuses can vary from society to society, as can their functions, a general definition of kinship as a social institution is still possible:

> Kinship is composed of those interrelated, pervasive, general, and relatively stable norms which organize familial statuses and regulate familial role behaviors, while having primary consequences for regularizing sexual mating, biological support, socialization, social support, social placement, and in some societies, societal coordination.

TYPES OF KINSHIP SYSTEMS

Kinship displays structural diversity. This can be best appreciated by visualizing all the possible combinations and permutations of the various types of kinship norms outlined earlier. However, not all these possible combinations and permutations are evident in the world's kinship systems. In reality certain kinship rules typically appear in relation to other rules, for kinship norms (and statuses) are not randomly clustered but systematically related to one another. If this were not the case, some rather awkward kinship structures would exist. For example a kinship system with extended, exogamous, patrilocal, patrilineal, and matriarchal norms would generate enormous chaos, conflict, and strain. In such a system a young man would go out and bring into his parents' house a wife who would then have authority over him and certain in-laws. And the children in a patrilocal and patrilineal system with an imported matriarch would be a bit confused, if not schizophrenic, about their loyalties. Hence many kinship rules are blatantly incompatible with each other, although the incompatibility may not be so severe as in this example. Furthermore the conditions under which kinship rules are compatible or incompatible also vary. For instance a patriarchal, patrilocal, patrilineal, exogamous, and extended set of kinship rules would be viable in most societies, except those with industrial or postindustrial economies where they would inhibit the mobility and independence of a modern labor force (this will be explored in the next chapter).

These kinds of incompatibilities reduce somewhat the diversity and variation in kinship systems (Murdock, 1949; Stephens, 1963). This fact facilitates the difficult task of classifying kinship systems into discrete types. One crude way of classifying kinship systems is in terms of modernity and traditionalism. Such a classification necessarily ignores much of the diversity in the real world and thus does it an injustice. Yet, for present analytical purposes, it is necessary to ascertain some of the *general* features which differentiate traditional from modern kinship systems.

traditional kinship systems

Because most of the world's people live in underdeveloped or traditional societies there are more incumbents in traditional than modern kinship systems. Utilizing the basic types of kinship norms delineated earlier, some of the general features of traditional kinship systems are listed below (Goode, 1963; Nimkoff, 1965; Stephens, 1963; Murdock, 1949; Kluckhohn, 1960; Queen and Habenstein, 1967).

1. Family residence units tend to be extended or polygamous. Often the family will be a combination of an extended family composed of polygamous families. Only a minority of traditional kinship systems evidence a conjugal residential unit.

2. Residence rules are either matrilocal or patrilocal. In traditional societies people do not have much choice about where and with whom they will live. Although there are matrilocal systems, patrilocal is the more dominant pattern. A few traditional societies have a neo-local pattern.

3. Descent—or which side of the family is important—is usually unilineal, with patrilineal the dominant type. Some systems are bi-lateral but they are a distinct minority.

4. All societies have incest rules concerning intimate kin. Traditional systems tend to have incest rules encompassing a broad range of kin. In part this results from the fact that incumbents keep track of these distant kin. Furthermore traditional kinship systems almost always have rules of exogamy, if not endogamy.

5. Traditional kinship systems are authoritarian. Lines of authority are clear and hierarchically arranged. Most systems are patriarchal, but a significant number are matriarchal. Egalitarian authority relations are uncommon.

6. Rules concerning family activity are unambiguous. Members of the family know the duties and tasks appropriate to their status position. Labor is clearly divided. And the ways in which children are to be cared for and socialized are also clear. Parents do not agonize over whether or not they are raising their children correctly.

7. Rules of dissolution are usually explicit. But traditional systems vary greatly in the degree of restrictiveness in their conditional rules. Traditional systems display widely divergent rates of family dissolution—some have extremely high rates, others very low ones. The distinguishing feature of these systems is that conditional, procedural, and dependency rules are clear. Dissolution is not as messy or confusing as in modern systems.

From this description we can derive a general picture. Traditional kinship systems are extensive and encompassing; home is not just parents and siblings but a host of kin; one knows who important kin are and where loyalties belong; authority is clear; each family member knows his role; one knows where to live when married; where to go look for a marriage partner is clear; and couples know when and how to dissolve marriage. Traditional kinship systems are restrictive but they display stability, continuity, and a comparative lack of ambiguity.

It should be emphasized again that this portrayal of the traditional kinship system can only be approximate. Many concrete kinship systems in traditional societies will deviate considerably from this portrayal.

modern kinship systems

Like the word *traditional, modern* encompasses an enormous range and diversity of actual kinship systems. In listing the general features of a modern kinship system below, only a modal approximation of this range and diversity is possible (Goode, 1964; Cavan, 1969, Williams, 1970; Stephens, 1967; Parsons and Bales, 1955).

1. The family residential unit is conjugal. The family is small, usually composed of mother, father, and one or two children. Other kin are excluded from the family unit and it is considered unfortunate if other relatives must live in the family.

2. Residence is neolocal. The family is not required to live with or near either the wife's or husband's kin. Although this does occur, there are no kinship rules indicating that this is imperative. The family is comparatively free to live where it desires.

3. Descent is truncated and bilateral, except for surnames. Loyalties and attachments to kin of either side of the family are not strong and become progressively weaker over time. Children are relatively uninvolved in family structures beyond the immediate conjugal residence unit. And involvement—if any—is divided equally between mother's and father's kin.

4. Incest rules apply to members of the conjugal unit as well as to close kin (usually not much further than first or second cousin). There are no explicit kinship rules of exogamy or endogamy. Kinship rules emphasize a free choice of marriage partners on the basis of love and mutual compatibility.

5. The modern kinship system tends toward egalitarian authority patterns. Kin outside the conjugal residence unit exert little control over family activities. Within the conjugal family, authority is divided more or less equally between mother and father. Often children have considerable voice and influence in decisions affecting the family.

6. Rules concerning family activity are ambiguous. Just how labor is to be divided is not clearly specified by kinship rules. Rules of child care are relatively clear but rules concerning socialization are unclear. Just how children are to be raised is often a mystery with several conflicting and ever changing sets of rules dominant.

7. Family dissolution is high; but unlike traditional systems with high rates, the conditional, procedural, and dependency rules are

TABLE 4-1 A summary of traditional and modern kinship systems

KINSHIP NORMS	TRADITIONAL SYSTEMS	MODERN SYSTEMS
Family size and composition	Extended and/or polygamous	Conjugal
Residence	Patri- or matrilocal	Neolocal
Descent	Unilineal	Bilateral truncated
Marriage	Incest, exogamy (sometimes endogamy)	Incest; few rules of exogamy and endogamy
Authority	Authoritarian, usually patriarchal	Tends toward egalitarianism
Family activity	Comparatively unambiguous	Ambiguous norms of socialization and division of labor
Dissolution	Comparatively clear norms	Ambiguous norms

unclear, variable, and subject to contest in courts of law. Although there seems to be a trend toward clarifying norms of dissolution, only a few modern societies have yet to succeed in this effort.

Overall we can see that modern kinship systems allow for a tremendous amount of freedom. The family unit is autonomous; it is free to live where it wants; it is unencumbered by descent and kin loyalties; it is democratic, with authority more or less equally distributed; marriage is relatively unregulated; and socialization is a matter of choice, as is working out the division of labor. Yet aside from great autonomy and freedom, modern kinship systems display ambiguity. Little is spelled out. Much uncertainty accompanies family life. Questions revolving around who to marry, where to live, how to raise children, and how to divide up household labor can make the modern family system a hotbed of insecurity, worry, concern, and anxiety. Modern kinship systems are not as restrictive as traditional systems, but neither are they as stable, continuous, and unambiguous.

While these two portrayals of traditional and modern kinship systems are idealized and represent analytical artifacts, they are useful in that they cut through at least some of the complexity in the real world. Table 4–1 summarizes the salient features of and differences between traditional and modern kinship systems.

the consequences of kinship in traditional and modern societies

Traditional kinship systems have extensive consequences for the broader society. Because much institutional activity occurs within the kinship system in traditional societies, kinship norms have consequences for ordering relations among statuses and circumscribing role behavior. This is particularly evident in a kinship system with an extended family structure and unilineal descent culminating in lineages, clans, or moieties. Under these conditions a whole society becomes integrated within kinship groupings. In all except the more advanced traditional systems education is not a dominant institution. If only by default, this means that virtually all socialization must occur within the kinship. Although all traditional societies exhibit a religious subsystem which has consequences for alleviating uncertainty and anxiety, most of the day-to-day social support necessary for emotional well-being occurs within the family unit. Thus, as was alluded to earlier, kinship is a pivotal institution in traditional societies for it pervades and embraces much of the institutional life of a society.

The features of modern kinship systems point to an inevitable decrease of its functions in modern societies. Because the family is conjugal and displays truncated descent, it has few major consequences for societal integration. It is simply too small and isolated to integrate a modern society. Instead structures and processes within other institutions, such as factories and bureaucracies in the economy or the state in the polity, assume a major integrative burden performed by kinship in traditional societies. Furthermore, panintegrative institutions such as law begin to assure society-wide coordination in modern societies. With respect to social reproduction, much socialization is assumed by educational and media structures in modern systems, while many social support problems are resolved by proliferating mental health organizations. Yet the consequences of kinship systems for regularizing mating, biological support, social reproduction, and support remain far reaching in modern societies.

THE AMERICAN FAMILY SUBSYSTEM

Since the institution of kinship is a subsystem of a more inclusive society, we should be alerted to both its consequences for the broader society and its internal systematic qualities. This has already been done for general types of families in traditional and modern societies. Now we turn to a familiar case—the American kinship system—and examine it in more detail. As with any institutional subsystem we are concerned with the basic parts (statuses, norms, and roles), their interrelations, and their boundaries.

boundaries of the american family

We have already examined some general norms typical of kinship systems in modern societies (see Table 4–1 above). Three of these types of norms—composition and size, residence, and descent—are most useful in defining the boundaries of the American kinship sub-system. The nature of these three norms reveals just what the general parameters of each family grouping are. With respect to composition and size, American kinship norms emphasize the conjugal family composed of only two generations of kin—mother, father, and their children. Other kin statuses—grandparents, aunts, uncles, and cousins—are not prominent within the family. Residence norms in the American kinship system are neolocal, requiring residence with neither the wife's nor husband's kin. This norm reinforces the conjugal family because it emphasizes the residential autonomy of the husband, wife, and their children from other kin. The truncated bilateral descent norms of American kinship further supports these boundaries. Kin on neither side of the family are favored, nor are great loyalties or commitments to kin outside the conjugal family required. This does not mean that love and affection for kin do not exist, nor does it indicate that kin do not influence some family decisions. Rather, truncated descent rules emphasize the potential for autonomy, if chosen. In the American system actual practice is various: dependence, intimacy, autonomy, rebellion from kin, and negative relations with kin. Despite an emerging literature on the subject (Litwak, 1960), no clear conclusions are evident as to how much influence kin exert on the conjugal family. This fact itself indicates the lack of a clear and binding descent norm.

These three kinship norms—conjugal, neolocal, and truncated bilateral—give a good indication of family boundaries. They reveal that it is most important to focus on the structure of parent and children statuses for further understanding of American kinship.

internal structure of the american family

The basic parts of the American family are thus the statuses of father, mother, child, and the norms guiding role behavior which accompany these statuses. The interrelations among them can be revealed by examining the general norms attendant on each of these three statuses, since contained within such norms are requirements about how family members should behave relative to one another.[3]

ADULT MALES

Compared to those for females and children, adult male norms are relatively unambiguous (Williams, 1970:69–75). One norm requires

---

[3] This examination will necessarily be highly abstract and very crude. The diversity in the internal structure of the American family by region of the country, ethnicity, social class, and degree of urbanization is great and precludes a single detailed portrayal. Therefore the following discussion is an attempt to isolate the modal features of the American family without delving into its diverse forms. For more detailed accounts of the American family, see Williams (1970) and Cavan (1969).

husband-fathers to work as steadily as possible. Income should be sufficient to support all family members in an above-subsistence manner—the more above subsistence the better. Secondly, all American husband-fathers are to give love, affection, and kindness to both wives and children. Over a third kinship norm there appears to be tremendous ambiguity in the American kinship system: To what extent should fathers be involved in the daily activities of home-making and child rearing? Much of the confusion over the division of labor in the American family can be traced to ambiguity in this sphere. In traditional kinship systems, such confusion is less likely to exist. But unlike men in most traditional systems, American males are given no clear-cut guidelines about household activities: Just who should change diapers, discipline children, wash dishes, shop, take care of the yard, transport children, and perform other duties is left for American males (and females) to work out after marriage (Cavan, 1969).[4]

With respect to decision making in the family, males have somewhat clearer—though highly variable in different segments of the society—normative guidelines (Williams, 1970). Husbands make decisions about their own economic (job) activities. Wives are allowed only a minor say in this sphere (but the reverse is not true). American husbands also have the right to make major decisions on durable and expensive purchases—the car, the house, and so forth (wives are usually consulted but men make the final decision).[5]

ADULT FEMALES

Norms attendant on the status of females are in flux in the American kinship system. One reason for this lies in the increasing emancipation of women in modern societies. Women have been able to "leave the home" and involve themselves in educational, political, recreational, and economic spheres closed to them in traditional societies. Perhaps the last of these is the most significant: Women now have jobs and make money. Thus many families have two breadwinners and this forces new internal family arrangements. But just what kinds of new arrangements are to occur is unspecified by kinship norms because questions such as these inevitably emerge: Who takes care of the kids? Who decides on a budget? Who is boss, with females also supporting the family? How many of the domestic tasks should women

[4]Some of this ambiguity stems from changes occurring in adult females norms in American kinship (see below).
[5]These norms are perhaps becoming more ambiguous under the impact of female "liberation" in American society. Yet currently even when women in the family work, males appear to make major family decisions, even with respect to the females' jobs. Much of the supposed impact of Women's Liberation on present family relations has been exaggerated, although more fundamental changes appear inevitable in the next decades.

do if they are also breadwinners? There are no unambiguous norms providing answers to these and similar questions. Rather, there tend to be three divergent normative clusters surrounding the status of adult females. This situation would be expected in light of the fundamental changes in the status of women in the larger institutional framework of society (more of this in the next chapter). These three roles for women can be labeled: (1) the wife and mother, (2) the companion, and (3) the partner (Kirkpatrick, 1935; Parsons, 1942).

(1) *The wife and mother role.* Norms require the mother to concentrate on the bearing and rearing of children. Also, she must perform most of the housekeeping tasks. And she is required to always subordinate her economic interests to her husband's, thus remaining economically dependent upon him. Women are to limit the number and range of their outside interests and activities.

(2) *The companion role.* The woman must bear children (there is no alternative here), but she can relinquish and delegate much of the rearing responsibilities to the father and other agencies (child-care centers, schools, etc.). The wife is entitled to demand romantic and emotional responses as well as admiration from her husband. She is entitled to her own leisure for social and recreational activities. She must make herself an object of pride for her husband by cultivating social contacts to his occupational advantage.

(3) *The partner role.* The wife bears children, but she defers much of the rearing to the father and other agencies. She works and is economically independent. She must contribute to the financial support of the home and children. And she has equal authority in finances. She performs only her fair share of household tasks, relegating the rest to her husband or others outside the family. She shares equal social and moral liberty with her husband.

These are modal types and various combinations of them certainly exist. Yet one of them probably dominates a particular family. Although data are scarce we can safely say that American kinship norms requiring wife-mother role behavior are decreasing in prevalence. Currently the American kinship system is dominated by norms emphasizing the companion role. But there are signs that the partner role is prevalent and increasing. It is probably true that the trend over the last 100 years in the American kinship system has been away from the wife-mother role to the partner role (Cavan, 1969).

This signifies a growing equality between husbands and wives in all family spheres—household tasks and responsibilities, child care, and socialization.

NORMS OF CHILD SOCIALIZATION

Modern kinship systems usually possess diverse and often confusing clusters of child-rearing norms (Bronfenbrenner, 1968; Parsons and Bales, 1955; Cavan, 1969; Miller and Swanson, 1958; Rosen and D'Andre, 1959). In the United States there appear to be two general sets or clusters of such norms attendant on the status of parent: (1) norms of permissiveness; and (2) restrictive norms.

(1) *Permissive norms.* These norms stress the importance of letting children do things on their own, being independent and responsible. Parents are to encourage achievement, trying hard, and doing well on the part of their children. They are also required to be more tolerant of a child's needs, impulses, and mental lapses. And they are to allow the child's expression of emotion. Discipline involves the withdrawal of love and manipulation of guilt ("See how you hurt mommy's feelings," "How could you do this to your father?" etc.) rather than physical punishment.

(2) *Restrictive norms.* These norms emphasize control and regulation of the child's activities by parents. Children are taught by parents how to get along rather than how to be independent and achievement oriented. The expression of emotion is restricted. Parents display impatience with children's impulses and lapses. And punishment tends to be physical (slapping, spanking, etc.).

This portrayal of child-rearing norms is greatly oversimplified. But there are clear divergences in the way children are reared in American families and this is a reasonable—if somewhat simplified—way to represent them. While trends are difficult to establish firmly, the permissive normative cluster is increasing and becoming dominant in the American kinship system.

NORMS OF NONADULTS

As children grow up they occupy different statuses and play different roles. This fact poses an analytical problem of how to isolate kinship norms if they vary and change with a child's age. The best solution to this kind of dilemma is to separate out major stages or periods in the life cycle of nonadults and look at the general norms attendant on these. In the American family we can isolate out three such stages (Williams, 1970; Cavan, 1969; Nimkoff, 1965): (1) childhood; (2) youth; and (3) adolescence.

(*1*) *Norms of childhood.* This period lasts from infancy to the first years in school. In it, the child is to be dependent upon his parents for love, affection, approval, and guidance (as well as biological maintenance). Seeking these outside the family is discouraged. Children are to respect elders as possessing superior levels of knowledge and "wisdom." They are to gather from parents as much of this knowledge and wisdom as possible. What is good, bad, proper, and improper is to be a matter of parental definition. Children are also expected to begin imitating basic parental role behaviors ("playing house" or "daddy" and "mommy" being the most encouraged).

(*2*) *Norms of youth.* With advancement in school much of a child's attention is shifted away from the home and parents. Youth norms reflect this fact. Youth are expected to acquire much knowledge and wisdom outside the home and independent of it. Yet basic ties of loyalty and affection are to remain with parents. And parents are to be respected as the most important positions of authority. But youth are required to perform and become involved in many nonfamilial statuses, including school and peer groups. In peer groups youth are expected to expand their imitation of adult roles to include a larger cast of characters. And in school a child's level of knowledge is to expand, as is his capacity to function in nonfamilial and impersonal statuses ("teacher's pets" and "apple polishing" are considered deviant forms of school behavior). Thus youth are expected to display independence from parents (in school and with peers) and yet remain emotionally tied and dependent upon them. In this way, youth can experiment, practice, and be frustrated by new and quasi-adult roles while having an emotionally secure retreat in the family.

(*3*) *Norms of adolescence.* After seven or eight years of schooling and with the onset of biological maturity a new nonadult status is reached. Adolescence in most kinship systems is normatively explicit, short, and a prelude to full adult status (including the right to marry and have a family). This is not so in the American kinship system. Adolescence is a normatively ambiguous, prolonged, and unclear prelude to full adult status (Williams, 1970; Stephens, 1967; Parsons, 1949; Davis, 1940). Biologically, adolescents are adults, but socially they are "immature." They do not yet possess all the necessary traits—knowledge, skill, and interpersonal styles—necessary for full-fledged participation in adult statuses, especially in the occupational sphere of a modern, postindustrial economy. Adolescent norms stress this fact and thus force biologically mature actors to prolong their stay within the family. While norms require these (socially) nonadults to acquire those traits necessary for adult roles, they do not specify clearly the adolescent's relationship with parents. The adolescent is expected to be independent and involved in non-familial structures (school, peer groups, organizations) and yet financially and emotionally dependent upon parents. And this is compounded by truncated descent rules and a neolocal residence rule stressing independence from parents and other kin. American kinship norms thus generate a powerful independence-dependence conflict among adolescents. This conflict creates many tensions and conflicts for both individual family members and the family as a whole. Such tensions are compounded even more by the way sex is regulated in these biologically mature nonadults. Norms require heterosexual interaction but noninvolvement until social maturity (this is usually when the adolescent is about to take a job). Thus adolescents are to interact with but not marry representatives of the opposite sex for a prolonged period, often lasting ten years. And this is to take place within the family and under parental supervision. Yet there are no clear-cut norms telling adolescents (or their parents) how all this is to occur.

THE GENESIS OF NEW FAMILIES: NORMS OF COURTSHIP AND MARRIAGE IN THE UNITED STATES

Because the American family is comparatively isolated from extensive kinship ties, the selection of marriage partners is less influenced by kin than in more traditional systems. In traditional systems, not only do rules of exogamy prevail but marriages are often arranged by parents and other kin for economic and political reasons. But in a system with truncated bilateral descent, neolocal, and conjugal kinship norms, marriages are less likely to be arranged for at least these reasons: (1) Truncated and bilateral descent makes inheritance of wealth and succession of power and property less salient, thus decreasing pressures for marriage control by kin. (2) Neolocal residence rules in conjunction with a conjugal family norm reduce the need for marital control by kin, since the new family is not incorporated into the existing household unit. (3) Socialization outside the family in schools inevitably generates some differences in marriage preferences between parents and children (a "generation gap"). Potential conflict is avoided by formal exclusion of parental authority in matters of mate selection. (4) Finally, since the newly married couple must live alone and away from kin, selection of a marriage partner by these excluded kin could result in colossal mismatches which the isolated couple—not kindred—would have to endure.

For at least four reasons, then, kin are excluded from the *direct* selection of marriage partners in the American kinship system. But *indirectly* these kin are highly influential. Despite the generation gap and other kinds of discontinuities between parents and their children, a youth's general values, beliefs, and tastes are more often similar than dissimilar to those of parents. Furthermore eligible youth are likely to seek out mates of the same social class as their parents because of the similarity of interests and educational background, as well as sheer propinquity (middle-class youth do not interact much with ghetto residents). Thus, while not directly constrained by parents, the family has a subtle and yet powerful influence on mate selection in the American kinship system. This might best be termed *de facto endogamy.*

Aside from these subtle and indirect family influences, there are more explicit kinship norms governing marriage. One of the most powerful clusters of marriage norms is that concerning "romantic love." This is the most dominant cluster of norms in the American kinship system guiding the selection of marriage partners (Goode, 1963). As an adolescent approaches the status of "eligible and available," these norms begin to guide conduct (Goode, 1963; Cavan, 1969):

1. The decision about whom to marry is made by the young. A partner is to be judged in terms of personal traits and qualities rather than in utilitarian terms. Little importance is to be placed upon the partner's wealth and social position (to do this is considered gold digging or calculating). Evaluation is made on the basis of the other's personality.

2. There will be complete attraction and compatibility between partners. Life together should be an unbroken sequence of mutual compatibility. Because of this, conflicts and troubles will be easily ironed out.

3. Thus love should involve a feeling of "oneness" between two people. The solitary couple should be separated and divorced from the world and its corrupting influences. Love should not be contaminated by outside influences.

4. Under these conditions, sexual bliss should be inevitable. Complete sexual attraction and compatibility should ensue.

These kinds of norms guide mate selection in the American kinship system. They may appear idealistic or naive; but even masked by an emphasis on rationality and sophistication, these norms still underlie most mate selection in the United States. Although their origin is not clear, they display a high degree of compatibility with the rest of the American kinship system. In a society where mobility is prevalent (more on this later) and where neolocal, truncated descent, conjugality, and egalitarian authority norms dominate, "romantic love" norms provide that mate selection will be made by the partners since it is they who must live and move together, separated from their kin. However, "romantic love" norms have negative consequences for the stability of marriage. Lovers tend to be unrealistic about many of the "grubby details" of a day-to-day, working marriage. "Romantic love" norms do not guide the young in this area. In traditional kinship systems potential couples must seriously consider their less romantic qualities such as strength, ability to do housework, bear children, and perform labor. Also, "romantic love" can establish false expectations about the sexual bliss (which rarely is automatically forthcoming) and capacity to remain compatible and isolated from the world (a difficult chore) as a devoted dyad of oneness (also difficult). Thus, while promoting autonomy from kin, "romantic love" norms fail to guide the young in many crucial areas of mate selection. This is compounded by the ambiguity of American kinship norms guiding the couple once they form a separate family and household.

NORMS OF FAMILY DISSOLUTION IN THE UNITED STATES

A functioning marriage in the United States can be terminated in four general ways: desertion, legal separation, annulment, or divorce. Only the first of these is not regulated or condoned by kinship norms. However, the norms regulating the latter three are far from clear and vary from state to state (Cavan, 1969:422–452). Since divorce is the major form of marriage dissolution this section will focus only on it. We could predict high divorce rates in kinship systems like the United States, because in so many crucial areas such as division of parental labor, child rearing, authority relations, decision making, and marriage, norms are ambiguous. But we should not think that the United States has the highest divorce rate. It does not, and in fact many traditional systems with more explicit kinship rules have higher rates of divorce. Yet divorce is common in the United States (Murdock, 1949; Stephens, 1967). Logically we might predict that a kinship system with strains toward dissolution and high rates of dissolution would have explicit norms concerning the conditions and procedures of divorce as well as care of dependents. However, such is not the case, although in recent years conditional and procedural laws have become less ambiguous. In most states conditional rules of divorce require that guilt of one marriage partner be established in a court of law. Only a few states (Cavan, 1969) allow for divorce on the basis of mere "incompatibility." Procedural rules are more explicit, but cumbersome. Both parties must obtain lawyers, present a case in court, establish guilt, assign alimony, and then haggle over division of property. Even in states with community property laws, partners are likely to contest in court what constitutes community property. Until recently norms concerning care of dependents were explicit, with judicial precedent favoring the mother in child custody while requiring the father to pay child support. Recently the precedent has been reversed occasionally, with fathers granted custody of children. Thus care of dependents is often contested in the courts.

The lack of clear-cut divorce laws and the fact that each phase of divorce must be contested in court appears inefficient compared to the explicit rules of other kinship systems. This apparent inefficiency might be predicted in a kinship system where the family is autonomous and where each partner's contributions in and needs after the marriage vary—oftentimes greatly. "Justice" in dissolution has to be established in each case since each marriage has unique elements. In systems where the role behaviors of all family members are more clearly specified by kinship norms (though not always practiced), rules of dissolution can be more explicit and standard since each partner's contributions to and needs after the marriage are known and hence do not need to be established. Thus in traditional systems with extended families, descent, authority, residence rules, and clear norms of family activity, dissolution is not so problematic because kinship rules specify when a partner has not met the norms. And how property and dependents are to be divided is established by descent and residence rules. But in a system where these kinds of kinship rules do not exist, dissolution is inevitably going to be more ambiguous. Such is the case in the United States.

consequences of the american family for society

As already noted, kinship in modern systems has few society-wide coordinating and integrating functions. Even in modern societies, however, kinship has these five basic consequences: social reproduction or socialization, social support, social placement, biological support, and regularization of sex and mating. Kinship is always involved in these but not always equally. In some societies, such as the United States, other institutions besides the family also perform many of these functions. In this section we will assess the degree of involvement displayed by the American family in each of these five processes.

SOCIAL REPRODUCTION

Without socialization, systems cannot reproduce themselves. Just where socialization occurs varies from society to society. Traditional systems rely almost exclusively on the kinship structure, whereas in modern societies such as the United States other institutions have emerged to share the burden. One such institution is education; it has taken over many aspects of socialization in American society, with the result that social reproduction is divided between two major institutions: the family and education.

SOCIAL SUPPORT

Modern societies generate large amounts of tension and stress in people. The reasons for this are not fully understood but part of the answer lies in the nature of the institutional structure of modern systems, which requires impersonality, performance, neutrality, specificity, scheduling, and rationality. Such normative requirements force actors to suspend and inhibit considerable emotion, especially in the factories and bureaucracies of the occupational sphere. One consequence of this situation is for emotions to accumulate and in some cases create personality disorders. In response to the emotional problems of actors in contemporary societies mental health structures are rapidly proliferating. However, the day-to-day repository of accumulated emotions in modern societies is the family. In fact many sociologists have argued that this has become the major function of the modern American family. As it has lost many of its socialization functions it has increased its social support functions (Parsons and Bales, 1955). The reason for this is that kinship is one of the few institutions "geared up" for providing warmth, affection, and support in modern systems. The economy is guided by norms requiring neutrality and specificity, and education is a formal structure designed more for socialization than social support. The American family thus offers an emotional haven from the impersonality, specificity, and scheduling typical of other major institutions in which people must participate. The frustrations, anger, and anxieties that are accumulated but are unexpressible because of neutrality norms in the economy and elsewhere can be vented and mollified in a supportive family structure. This generalization applies to both adults and children, since children at an early age begin to participate in structures such as schools—increasingly dominated by neutrality, specificity, and scheduling.

From the high divorce rates in the United States it is clear that sometimes the family is far from an emotional haven. This is partially caused by ambiguous kinship norms, but there is perhaps another force promoting American family instability: emotional overload. The increased emotional load on the family is often too great, creating an emotionally tense set of relations among its members. This situation is compounded by the fact that the American family is small and isolated from kindred, which forces absorption of an increased emotional burden on a small social unit. In more extensive kin networks emotions can be displaced on a large number of kin, whereas in the neolocal, truncated, and conjugal kinship system a few must absorb most emotions. Tensions become centered on three or four people, which often makes the American family rife with strain and tension. We could predict that in kinship systems such as that of the United States, where the social support function of the family is greatly increased, family dissolution rates will be high.

SOCIAL PLACEMENT

While considerable racial and ethnic ascription exists, social placement into the wider society occurs primarily on the basis of *performance* criteria. From socialization experiences of the young, many of those traits determining eventual social class and occupational position are acquired. Since the family still engages in considerable socialization in modern societies it greatly circumscribes social placement both directly and indirectly. Family socialization directly affects social placement by imparting those crucial personality traits in the young, such as motives, values, beliefs, aspirations, and self-concept, that determine how well the young as adults can perform at a job. Indirectly, in instilling these same personality traits the family affects how well and how far a child will go in school. In turn the level of education can eventually determine occupational and social-class position in the broader society. Furthermore, the financial resources of a family are also a crucial factor in social placement, since those families with ample resources are obviously in a better position than those without them to help their offspring find high-paying jobs or acquire the education leading to a high-paying job. A series of studies by Sewell and various associates (1965, 1968) and by Blau and Duncan (1967) provide a wealth of empirical data and analytical clarity to how parental economic status, along with their treatment of children, influences educational and occupational aspirations as well as attainment and success in these spheres. Their studies clearly reveal that in the United States the financial resources of parents and their encouragement of educational and occupational success for offspring create aspirations which apparently determine their children's performance in both the educational and occupational spheres. In sum, then, we can conclude that the social placement functions of the American family remain extensive.

BIOLOGICAL SUPPORT

Kinship norms require the biological support of the young in American society. And they tend to be strongly enforced with severe penalties for parents who violate them. Also, in many respects American kinship norms of biological support are more demanding than in traditional systems, because a well-above subsistence level of existence is possible. If dependents are forced to live at a subsistence level, strong legal sanctions can be invoked.

REGULARIZING SEX

Kinship norms regulate premarital sex. These norms are neither restrictive nor permissive but semirestrictive, allowing for premarital sex as long as it is more or less secretive (Cavan, 1969:350–375). As with many kinship systems, American sex norms are formally strict but only loosely and erratically enforced. Actual role behavior deviates considerably from kinship norms. However, American sex norms are not permissive. Sex play at early ages is still deviant; sex still has many moral implications; and it is not yet considered normal, natural, or justifiable for pure physical pleasure. But role behavior is increasingly violating those semipermissive norms and it is clear that they are in transition to a more permissive profile. There are strong norms against extramarital sex, although these apply more to women than to men. Penalties for deviation are high (divorce, high alimony, and in some states criminal prosecution), but much deviant behavior still occurs.

SUMMARY

This chapter has examined the structure and functioning of kinship in both traditional and modern societies, especially in the United States. We began by distinguishing the larger, more inclusive notion of kinship from family. Family was viewed as a group that is a basic subsystem of kinship. Then we delineated the basic elements of kinship systems. These involved a series of general norms concerning family size, residence, activity, dissolution, descent, authority, and marriage. It is out of these norms that the kinship system of a society is constructed.

Next attention was drawn to some of the general consequences of kinship for the broader society. We isolated out six major functions of kinship systems:

1 Regularizing sex and mating
2 Biological support
3 Social reproduction
4 Social support
5 Social placement
6 Social coordination

Analysis then shifted to a comparison of the structure and function of kinship in traditional and modern societies. Traditional kinship systems were seen as most likely to display norms of extendedness or polygamy, parti- or matrilocal residence, unilineal descent, strong and extensive marriage rules, strict authority patterns (usually along patriarchal lines), unambiguous family-activity norms, and clear dissolution rules. On the other hand, modern kinship systems were viewed as most probably displaying a conjugal family, neolocal residence, truncated and bilateral descent, incest taboos governing marriage (but no exogamy or endogamy), egalitarian family authority, ambiguous norms of family activity and dissolution. It was emphasized, however, that these two portrayals of traditional and modern kinship systems are idealized and represent only a kind of modal approximation of the enormous variation in the real world.

Finally a description and analysis of the American kinship system was undertaken. In this analysis, we focused on the norms governing role behaviors of and among members in the conjugal family—mother, father, children. It became clear that tremendous ambiguity, and frequently conflict, exists in American kinship norms. Much of the uncertainty and instability of American family life can be attributed to this fact.

the
institutional
environment
of
KINSHIP   5

In this chapter we will examine how the institutional environment of kinship influences its structure and functioning in different types of societies. A guiding theme will revolve around the changes and trends occurring in kinship systems during broader societal modernization. To the extent that any trends are discernible, kinship systems will be seen as moving toward the modern profile outlined in the previous chapter. However, kinship modernization cannot be viewed as inevitable. Nor does it necessarily result in a perfect approximation of a modern profile, since modernization of kinship will always represent an uneasy accommodation with its traditional predecessor. Yet during societal development and change, powerful institutional pressures force alterations in traditional kinship patterns. The degree to which alterations approximate a modern form will vary in terms of the intensity of institutional pressures for change and the rigidity of traditional systems. While we cannot begin to delineate the numerous variations and paths of kinship modernization, we will explore some of the general institutional conditions and pressures that are most likely to generate changes in the profile of kinship in a society.

ECONOMY AND KINSHIP

Perhaps more than any other institution the economy influences the structure of the family and wider kinship system. Major alterations in the economy almost always result in profound changes in kinship. To understand kinship modernization it is therefore necessary to focus on its relations with the economy. We try to do this by first examining the economic basis of traditional and then the basis of the modern kinship systems (Goode, 1964). In doing so we will see why economic development can lead to at least some changes in kinship (Ogburn and Nimkoff, 1955).

traditional economies and kinship

Basic to any economy are the elements of labor, capital, technology, entrepreneurship, and access to resources (land). The profile of kinship in a traditional society is greatly circumscribed by these basic economic elements. Traditional economies display low levels of technology, capital, and access to natural resources (Lenski, 1966). To compensate for these deficiencies, a traditional economy must have a large and coordinated pool of human labor. Only in this way can the economy gain sufficient access to resources and insulation from the environment to persist. The organization of this labor pool occurs within the kinship subsystem of most traditional societies. Economic and familial roles overlap because kinship organizes economic behaviors around crude technology and capital. It is in this sense that in Chapter 3 we considered kinship to be the structural locus of and hence have entrepreneurial consequences for the economy.

However, just as the organization of the economy is influenced by kinship, economic realities of a society with low levels of technology, capital, and access to resources probably have much to do with the organization of kinship. In fact human societies emerged thousands of years ago as small groupings of advanced primates who stabilized relationships in response not only to sexual and reproductive matters but also to economic exigencies. Even in the more recent past or today in highly traditional societies, kinship norms in a society appear to represent one way of coping with the problem of amassing and organizing a labor pool around low levels of technology, capital, and access to resources. For example, we can note that norms of extendedness or polygamy result in large family groups which can perform necessary labor. Rules of residence insure that the family will remain large by requiring either the daughter or son to bring his spouse (who will perform labor) into the family residence. Norms of exogamy force the incorporation of new members from outside the community into the family labor pool. Unilineal descent rules insure that the labor pool will remain loyal and tied to the familial economic unit. They also insure that capital will remain tied to and concentrated in a particular kin grouping, whether an extended family, lineage, clan, or moiety. Rules of authority, whether patriarchal or matriarchal, allow for the coordination and control of the family labor pool and capital. This process is facilitated by unambiguous norms concerning family activity, especially rules concerning the division of household tasks (which often shade into economic role behaviors). Clear norms of dissolution keep the labor force intact by spelling out where dependents (future labor) are to reside (Service, 1966).

It is difficult to indicate exactly how much influence economic conditions have on the emergence of traditional kinship norms. Yet, the influence appears to be great, judging from the compatibility of kinship norms with the conditions inherent in a traditional economy. To have a kinship system deviating too far from the traditional pattern would endanger the resolution of economic problems. But we can expect that as the structure of the economy changes with increases in technology and capital formation, so does the structure of the kinship system.

113

modern economies and kinship

With economic development kinship becomes inadequate to store and retrieve technology, to accumulate capital, to generate labor, and to organize these around basic economic processes. This transformation is reflected in the fact that the economy becomes structurally differentiated from kinship with the result that kinship ceases to be the structural locus of economic activity. Such differentiation or separation of kinship and economic roles is both a reflection and a cause of the emergence of new entrepreneurial mechanisms for pooling and organizing labor around capital and technology. These changes in the relationship between economy and kinship are inevitably reflected in the norms of the kinship subsystem.[1] More specific changes in the economy as they can affect kinship norms are now discussed below.

DIFFERENTIATION OF ECONOMY FROM KINSHIP

With modernization, economic and familial roles are clearly separated in time and space. Work is performed away from the home for designated periods of time in the factories and bureaucracies of a modern economy. Not only are these statuses separated but also the number of workers coming to the economy from the family changes. Now only one family member has to participate in the economy, for other family members usually do not, out of necessity, have to become employed in the economy. Once as little as one kin need participate in the economy to assure survival, a breakdown of extended family norms can occur without disasterous economic consequences. Furthermore economic conditions promoting clear norms of family authority, residence, and descent can become less salient, since the regulation, coordination, and control of a family labor pool around low levels of capital and technology is no longer a function of the family.[2]

NEW MECHANISMS FOR POOLING LABOR

Human labor is not the major energy source of a modern economy, nor is animal power. As outlined in Chapter 2, industrialization begins with the utilization of sources of energy other than man or

[1] It should be emphasized that changes in the economy do not always completely reorganize kinship. All that is intended in this section is to document some of the forces in modern economies which might lead to changes in kinship norms. Furthermore, this delineation does not preclude the possibility of these changes occurring long before industrialization of the economy. If such were the case, as it appears to have been in the United States (Furstenberg, 1968), economic development would be accelerated by these prior changes in kinship.

[2] It should be noted here that kinship may remain involved as a major source of entrepreneurship in a modern economy. For example, many major Japanese corporations are owned and run by extended family structures. Similarly certain German cartels and American corporations were—and are—owned and managed by kinsmen. In India major capital resources in industry remain in the hands of extended families or even lineage-like structures. It is not inconceivable, then, that fairly large kin groupings can prove a viable source of capital as well as provide a managerial labor pool in a modern economy.

animal. In traditional economies kinship systems are a major mechanism insuring the concentration of human energy necessary for economic activity, especially gathering and producing. But with advanced technology and its by-product, the machine, larger concentrations of labor with new skills and attributes become necessary. And so the family becomes inadequate as a means for concentrating and coordinating human power. In its place modern economies evolve factories and bureaucracies to concentrate and coordinate the vast numbers of needed workers. Once this pooling consequence of traditional kinship systems is eliminated a major economic force promoting extended residence, unilineal descent, and marriage rules also is eliminated. Strict authority and family-activity rules allowing for the coordination of the family labor pool likewise become irrelevant. Thus traditional kinship rules can begin to lose their economic significance in modern economies, where new ways of pooling labor emerge.

EMERGENCE OF A WAGE INCOME

We are so accustomed to wages and salaries that we often fail to realize what an economic revolution they represent. Besides enabling a money market to emerge and function, a wage (or salary) income greatly alters the structure of kinship. A wage income encourages a conjugal family unit by placing financial limits on how many persons can be supported per family unit. With a wage income system, children and relatives become liabilities rather than economic assets (as labor). As long as a large labor pool is necessary to generate food, shelter, and clothing, extended families are likely. But once an individual can generate enough income in the form of a wage to support himself and his immediate family (wife and children), the economic necessity for an extended family (and the large labor pool it provides) is diminished. Wages can also reduce the need for residence and unilineal descent rules, for when it becomes possible to earn a sufficient wage to support themselves, young adults can leave the home and survive independently of their kin. With this the salience of descent and residence rules tying people economically to various kindred decreases.

SOCIAL MOBILITY

Modern economic organizations tend to become located where resources, markets, and transportation facilities are best. Since resource supplies, markets, and transportation facilities often change, organizations are constantly moving in a modern economy. This situation makes patterns of location and relocation typical of large economic enterprises. Such organizational movement depends upon and at the same time stimulates the geographical mobility of the labor force. Once such mobility patterns are established in a society they have several potential consequences for kinship. First, geographical mobility encourages small, conjugal families, because large and extended families are difficult and expensive to move. Second, mobility makes neolocal residence norms almost an economic necessity. Where people are tied to extended families, mobility is impaired. And third, these norms of neolocality and conjugality weaken descent rules, since a small and mobile family is unlikely to bind and tie itself to a particular set of kindred.

Modern economic organizations eventually begin to recruit and promote workers on the basis of their performance. A bureaucracy that does not to some extent utilize criteria of worker proficiency and expertise will become and remain stagnant and inefficient, as will the entire economy (see Chapter 2). As specific economic organizations recruit and then promote on performance, vertical mobility in a society increases. With promotions in economic organizations come rises in a worker's income as well as prestige. Such vertical mobility can have a profound effect on kinship, for it may widen the social distance among kindred. A son who has risen to become an executive in a large corporation can come to feel alien and strange in the world of his parents and kin (a kind of generation and social-class gap), and vice versa. This reinforces neolocal, truncated descent and conjugal family norms. In systems where vertical mobility is common (in most societies in the world it is very uncommon) such norms free the mobile family unit from kin ties that would inhibit movement to a new social class.

Finally, both horizontal and vertical mobility encourage "romantic-love" norms (Goode, 1964). Because the conjugal family may move far away—both geographically and socially—from kin, the normative exclusion of parents and kin from mate selection is a likely result. In systems where kin have no vested interest, such as having to live and work with the mate of a kinsman, marriage rules can more easily emphasize free choice of mates in terms of criteria stressing love and mutual compatibility. Such criteria allow for flexible and varied patterns of accommodation among members of the autonomous and mobile conjugal family, for these members must be capable of adjusting and readjusting *to each other* as the family environment changes. This fact also helps explain much of the ambiguity of activity norms in modern families. To have hard and inflexible rules would make the conjugal family less capable of accommodating itself to new physical and social environments.

FAMILY AND FORMAL EDUCATION

A modern economy requires certain attributes of workers that cannot be acquired in the family. Trade skills and interpersonal styles of neutrality and specificity are more readily acquired in the educational subsystem of modern society, with the result that much of a child's waking hours are spent in schools away from the family. One consequence of this fact is that school attendance allows children at an early age and increasingly over a long period of years to become independent of the family. And eventually, when the time comes to move away from the family (in accordance with neolocal residence rules), little difficulty is experienced by the young, since a lifetime of daily departures has preceded the final move. This is particularly true in systems where youth leave home for extended periods to attend college.

Aside from reinforcing neolocality, participation in school structures undermines authoritarian family patterns. With participation in the educational system a child's level of knowledge as well as mental and interpersonal skills become sophisticated at a comparatively early age. Often by adolescence children surpass the parents' level. And yet adolescents must remain in the household unit under parental supervision. This situation is amplified because the young participate in so many nonfamilial organizations, such as peer groups, for most of their waking hours. Just how parents and other kin are to regulate and control strictly their sophisticated offspring, who are both tied to them financially and emotionally and yet independent of them, becomes highly problematic. One typical family adjustment to this problem is for parental authoritarianism to give way to more egalitarian relations between kin generations. As this occurs other kinship norms also become less salient. Rules of endogamy and exogamy become difficult to enforce, as do rules of residence and descent. Thus economic conditions requiring the young to participate in school structures disrupts traditional kinship norms. However, such disruption generates a series of new problems: How much freedom should the young have? How egalitarian should relations be? How should parents and children interact? What socialization practices should parents employ? How is the generation gap to be handled? The isolated, conjugal family has few clear-cut kinship norms guiding its members in these areas. And perhaps it never can, since the changing economy and educational system generate new gaps between each generation of parents and young. Societies with rapidly changing economies requiring prolonged participation of the young in schools will always face ambiguity in kinship norms concerning family activity, especially socialization.

EMERGENCE OF AN EGALITARIAN LABOR FORCE

In traditional economies women perform labor of a very physical and demanding nature (Blisten, 1963). And in some traditional systems women do more economic labor than men. But rarely are men and women regarded as equals in the labor force, for women usually perform jobs that are considered inferior to men's. In general this is still true in even the most advanced postindustrial systems. Yet once brain power becomes more important than muscle power as a requisite for employment and once recruitment and promotion become based upon expertise and performance, a trend for the employment of women in economic positions equal to those of men becomes evident. This trend is accelerated in modern systems because women have access to the educational structures that can instill those traits necessary for equal participation in the economy. Discrimination against women still persists and is widespread, but in the long run economic conditions operate against it. With increasing female involvement in the economy on a level approaching equality with men the kinship structure is inevitably altered (Blood and Hamblin, 1960). With both adults working in the family and providing economic support in the form of wages and salary, family-activity norms change. This trend is intensified by the fact that women earn wages that have a precise value in the marketplace. As long as women's labor and its resulting contribution to economic survival remained vague and unmeasurable, demands for women's equality were difficult, especially in a patriarchal kinship system. Once their contribution can be measured precisely in "dollars and cents" there is a strain toward greater equality in the family between men and women. Increasingly women move away from the wife-mother role to the partner role. As women and men become equals, descent and residence rules become less viable since a patrilineal descent norm or patrilocal rule would generate powerful conflicts between the emancipated wife and her in-laws. The reverse would be true for men in a matrilineal and matrilocal system. With the females becoming men's equals and emancipated from kin, smaller conjugal families are likely, since too many children can force the mother out of the labor force and into the mother-wife role.

economy and the changing consequences of the family for society

Before closing this section we should explore the impact of a modernizing economy on the functions of kinship. In the previous chapter it has been emphasized that the modern family releases many of its socialization functions while intensifying its social support functions (Parsons and Bales, 1955). The reasons for this change in emphasis can be partially traced to forces within the economy. An economy organizing statuses in a factory or bureaucracy generates certain normative demands for neutrality, specificity, scheduling, expertise, performance, and pacing on the part of workers. Each employee has a specialized job where he interacts somewhat dispassionately and where he must schedule and pace role behavior. To have status posi-

the
institutional
environment
of
KINSHIP

tions organized differently would generate confusion and chaos, for coordination of the myriad of economic statuses typical of modern societies would break down. But such normative requirements make the work place somewhat "cold and impersonal." Emotions must be suppressed in the name of efficiency, performance, and the ubiquitous schedule. And thus emotions arising out of frustrations, anxiety, and repression accumulate. The personality system of man has a limited capacity for storing emotion, and sometime, somewhere it must be released. As noted earlier, the family is the most frequent repository of such emotions accumulated by workers in a modern economy, with the result that the social support consequences of the modern family increase.

There are also other sources of tension which the family must resolve. Modern economies require formal education of workers, and thus the institution of education emerges in modern systems (see Chapter 6 for details). As we know, these educational structures assume much of the socialization burden in modern systems, especially of job-related traits and attributes. This fact reveals that the family is less comprehensively involved in socialization. Educational structures are also arenas of rehearsal for future economic status incumbents, since norms require some degree of neutrality, specificity, scheduling, performance under pressure, and pacing. Yet the young student can be susceptible to stress, anxiety, and strain which the family must mitigate.

The mobility demanded of the conjugal family by modern economies also generates strains and tensions. Adjustment to new social and physical environments is often difficult for all family members. Yet with mobility the family is isolated and must absorb and manage alone these tensions. This further increases the social support consequences of the modern family.

POLITY AND KINSHIP

All societies face problems of establishing goal priorities and then allocating resources toward the attainment of these goals. These problems eventually result in the emergence of statuses charged with society-wide decision making. These statuses eventually become translated into clear leadership roles, lines of authority and power, and coordinated action in pursuit of society-wide goals. Eventually leadership positions and lines of authority and power culminate in the emergence of a state in modern societies. However, in traditional societies where a state may not exist, leadership and decision making are often embodied within kinship. In both societies with a clear-cut state and those without a state, political problems of leadership and decision making greatly circumscribe the organization of kinship.

the
institutional
environment
of
KINSHIP

polity and kinship in traditional societies

In highly traditional systems with only a hunting and gathering or simple agrarian economy, system goals are not elaborate and usually involve attainment of sufficient insulation from the environment and subsistence. In these systems a government or state is not clearly differentiated or distinct from other institutions, particularly kinship (Fried, 1967). The reasons for this include: System goals are not sufficiently complex to justify a state. Traditional systems usually do not have the economic surplus to support the luxury of full-time leaders occupying separate and discrete political statuses. The smaller size of many traditional systems usually does not necessitate the formation of the state. In Chapters 10 and 11, we will examine other institutional processes leading to the emergence of the polity and state as a separate institution. But for the moment we can say that most traditional systems are too small, poor, or simple to have an elaborate polity. Yet these societies face decision-making questions, such as: How is economic activity to be carried out? Where? Who gets the most economic goods and commodities? What is going to be done about depleting resources? Where will the tribe move next? What is to be done about the drought? These are typical problems facing either hunting and gathering or simple agrarian systems. As with any set of problems concerning the goals of a society, they set up a series of pressures for leadership, decision making, lines of authority, and coordination of social action. In the absence of a state with a military and administrative bureaucracy the kinship subsystem organizes much necessary political decision making. While such organization varies tremendously in the world's societies of both the past and present, we will outline below ways in which kinship norms accommodate political exigencies faced by highly traditional social systems.

Descent norms often have the consequence of establishing lines of decision making. Such rules, especially in unilineal systems, designate certain kin as decision makers for the kin grouping—usually the eldest and/or ablest male of a descent grouping in a patrilineal system. When such a grouping extends into a clan or moiety, descent norms can have far-reaching consequences for ordering decision making and lines of authority across a whole society. These norms also delineate and delimit the decision-making spheres of various decision makers in a society. Family-authority norms also can prove an efficient way to delegate authority or establish a chain of command in a society without a governmental bureaucracy and administrative staff. Such rules can resolve administrative problems by indicating which adults in each family unit will possess ultimate authority, and when combined with descent norms, family-authority norms indicate just who the "chief executive" and his "lieutenants" are. Extended or polygamous family norms also promote clarity in decision making by specifying the sphere of authority possessed by each decision maker within the larger descent grouping. If families were not extended (or polygamous and extended) there would be too many chiefs and not enough followers. This can be visualized by imagining what would happen if each family unit in a stateless society were conjugal, with each patriarch (or matriarch) making goal-priority decisions for his own family unit while attempting to coordinate his decisions with the decisions of other patriarchs, plus the head of the wider kin group. Under such conditions coordinated pursuit of goals would be difficult. Rules of extendedness remove traditional systems from this danger. They aggregate large numbers of kin under a patriarch (or matriarch)—thus limiting the number of family units to be coordinated by the head of the larger kin group.

Residence norms in indicating where kin are to live enclose kin within various geographical areas. Such enclosure facilitates coordinated decision making by cutting down on geographical dispersion. Dispersion would inhibit decision making, especially when systems of transportation and communication are cumbersome and cannot effectively unite large territories. Residence rules also stabilize the boundaries and numbers of those in a political sphere by regularizing and keeping in balance immigrants and emigrants. For each daughter who leaves a territory, a new daughter-in-law comes in (assuming patrilocal residence rules). The reverse is true in a matrilocal system. Marriage rules such as exogamy force actors outside their kin group or village in search of partners. In gathering partners from other kin groups (or villages) a system of allegiances and alliances emerges among kin groupings and communities. Exogamy in conjunction with rules of residence forces kin to exchange kindred with other kin groups and/or villages. To be at war or have strained relations with these other groups or communities would make life miserable for transplanted kin. And so these cross-cutting kin ties promote allegiances and some degree of political stability in societies lacking a well-articulated state and military apparatus.

In traditional societies such as a feudal monarchy, where certain kin groupings dominate over other groupings, marriage rules are particularly crucial in promoting political allegiance and stability. In these systems intermarriage of sons and daughters of leaders in powerful kin groupings creates a system of allegiances which can cut across vast territories, as was the case in feudal Europe and precolonial Africa. Frequently rules of endogamy among powerful clans and moieties can develop, with the young of leaders in one kin group marrying only certain specified others in another kin group. Such a pattern strengthens the power of elites by promoting some degree of political stability among potentially competing rulers. It can also allow for political coordination and control over large geographical areas in the absence of an elaborate and centralized state bureaucracy and military organization.

It should be emphasized that political processes are not always intimately tied to kinship in traditional societies. For example, decision making can become organized at the community level and bear little relationship to kin groupings. The important point is that to the extent that political processes in highly traditional societies are embodied within kinship, they are likely to reinforce a traditional profile of kinship. In more advanced traditional systems with an economy capable of generating a surplus, political action can be accommodated by an autonomous state that can undermine and destroy the very kin groupings from which it originally evolved. The reason for this is that larger kin groupings can appear as a threat to the power of elites within the state. Frequently, during the initial emergence of a state, a kin-based polity can be said to exist. Such a polity is formed primarily of kinsmen from a larger kin group that has been able to subordinate other kin groupings. But eventually, as the administrative and military tasks of this polity expand, it loses its kinship profile and increasingly approximates a modern state bureaucracy. Such state bureaucracies are rarely willing to share power with large clans and moieties.

polity and kinship in modern societies

Political structures and processes are elaborate in modern societies, for there are many society-wide goals, and processes for allocating men and resources toward their achievement are complex. Some goals in modern systems are directed outward—conquest, war, national defense, landing on the moon. Other goals are directed inward—domestic tranquility, full employment, equal opportunity, and better living conditions. Yet whatever the direction, the implementation of these goals usually has consequences for the modernization of kinship.

THE WELFARE POLITY AND KINSHIP

One of the major goals of a modern system is to improve the living conditions of the population. These goals stem from genuine humanitarian concern to attempts to placate a restless population. Whatever the political motivation, welfare programs alter family structure. Although welfare programs vary greatly from society to society, we will look at the consequences of two typical programs. (1) Most modern polities provide welfare for the aged. Once the capacity to work is terminated, support of the aged becomes problematic. In traditional sytems this is not the case, since older kin can be supported by the extended family. But in systems where the conjugal family is increasingly necessary (for at least economic reasons), support of the aged is often assumed by the polity. Such a trend reinforces conjugal, truncated descent, and neolocal residence rules because it frees the family from the burden of caring for the aged. As long as older kin must be maintained within the kinship system, families tend to be large (in order to provide support), stable and immobile (large familites are difficult to move), and authoritarian (so that decision-making disputes between generations are minimal). The welfare polity removes this burden from kinship—thus furthering modernization of the family. (2) Many modern systems—and those attempting to modernize—seek to limit family size through birth-control programs. It is a curious irony that those systems least able to support large families have them, partially because old kinship norms appropriate to an agrarian system where a large labor pool was necessary persist. But in a modern and urban economy large populations pose a problem; they drain the polity's capital away from the economy into welfare programs. And this problem escalates and magnifies, since the economy has been deprived of capital needed for growth and the population has probably increased even more—thus creating a greater welfare burden. This vicious cycle is acute in many systems. Polities attempt to counteract it by various birth-control programs: dissemination of literature, propaganda, distribution of pills, legalized abortions, and sterilization. Where successful, as in Japan, the size of the family is reduced. With decreased size many of the reasons for norms of extendedness, residence, descent, and authoritarianism are removed, with the result that modernization of the family is furthered.

These are two examples of how welfare programs typical of modern polities promote a modern kinship system. Welfare programs vary from society to soceity; and if their impact on a particular kinship system is to be fully understood, each program of each polity would have to be assessed. Aside from research on the effects of birth-control programs, little data are available on just how welfare influences kinship.

POLITY AND SOCIALIZATION

The polity has a vested interest in socialization, since it depends upon biologically and socially mature citizens to be loyal and committed to the existing political system. In all modern societies the polity therefore becomes involved in socialization. Sometimes this includes direct intervention into the family, while at other times it involves supporting and requiring formal education outside the home. In either case, the polity affects socialization, and in doing so it alters the structure and function of the family.

(*a*) *Direct intervention of the polity into socialization.*   In some societies the polity intervenes directly into the family. In Russia, for example, the state rather than the family often dominates the socialization of children. The Soviet "kindergarten" can take children from infancy up to seven years. After this children begin regular school. In these kindergartens, children are fed, medically cared for, and given instruction for up to twelve hours each day. Parents drop children off in the morning and pick them up in the evening. Similarly in the Israeli kibbutz (Spiro, 1956), socialization comes under the control of the polity, with children spending the majority of their waking hours from an early age in schools. The consequences of such intervention in the family is that it removes almost completely from the family early socialization, biological support, and social placement functions. Perhaps it increases the social support consequences of the family, although many Soviet kindergartens have professional conselors to provide necessary emotional guidance.[3]

A major consequence of state control of socialization is that it furthers modernization of the family. With state socialization, both parents can work—thus promoting egalitarianism. And with the abandonment of many socialization functions one of the major forces promoting the persistence of descent, residence, and marriage rules is eliminated.

Only rarely does the political subsystem directly assume functions usually performed by the family. In the Israeli kibbutz, workers in fields as well as defenders of borders were needed. Because of manpower shortages both male and female adults had to become involved in these duties. In Russia after the revolution, rapid economic development along with the development of the new "Soviet Citizen" were major system goals leading to the state's assuming major socialization functions.

These facts permit a few generalizations about the conditions under which the polity will most likely take on the socialization burden: (1) when a major system goal such as economic development requires a new kind of incumbent with traits radically different from those of the previous generation; (2) when manpower shortages exist and all adults must work and when elders in the traditional kinship system cannot assume the socialization burden; (3) when the polity must

124

---

[3] Perhaps such usurpation of family functions is unsettling to us who live in a society where family is considered so important and somewhat encompassing. But Soviet and Israeli children seem to grow up physically and emotionally healthy under the system (Bronfenbrenner, 1968:57–65). It should be noted, however, that a majority of Soviet and Israeli children do not undergo state socialization. And the family still performs the early socialization of even those young who go into kindergarten.

create a generation of incumbents loyal to a new political system; (4) when the polity needs to engage in excessive social control and manipulation. But more often than not, even under these conditions, the polity refrains from direct involvement in family affairs, because state socialization is expensive and because people strongly resist intrusion into the family. The family is a conservative institution having an almost "sacred" quality which prevents its direct and visible manipulation.

(b) *Indirect involvement of the polity in socialization.* In all modern systems the polity provides public education. In fact the extensiveness of public schools is one good indicator of societal modernity. The reasons for this correlation between modernity and education reside in the fact that most major goals of modern systems—economic development, social equality, eliminating poverty, national defense, world dominance, etc.—require that citizens have personality traits that can only be acquired in educational structures. For example, to develop economically requires certain mental skills, levels of cognitive knowledge, and interpersonal skills in workers. Achieving economic development thus requires the polity to provide those socialization structures (i.e., formal education) where necessary personality traits can be acquired by future workers. The same is true of many other societal goals in modern systems. To the extent that the polity cannot achieve major goals, its long-run legitimacy and survival are undermined. Hence because of the centrality of education to goal achievement, the polity often must promote education in order to persist.

In systems attempting to modernize, education is often viewed as the symbol of and key to modernization. Polities are therefore likely to encourage the development of educational structures, per se, even though there are no statuses—especially economic—to absorb graduates. For example, in India educational structures have proliferated and expanded beyond the capacity of the economy or other institutions to absorb the emerging educated work force. This has led to bizarre situations where people with engineering degrees drive taxi cabs or buses. Such systems also suffer from a severe "brain drain," since their students studying abroad are reluctant to return to an economy that cannot place them (Coombs, 1968). One major consequence of extensive educational development is that polities divert potential economic capital to education and thereby impede economic development and the emergence of those economic positions where the educated actor could become employed. The solution to this problem may appear easy—to strike a better balance in the allocation of resources between the economy and education. However, the populations of developing countries often define education as welfare—something that polity *must* do for the people to make their lives better. Educational structures are highly visible and offer impoverished people hope that things are getting better. Should the polity not invest in education the population might withdraw its legitimacy and approval from the polity. In essence the polity is forced to concentrate on education in developing systems, even if it does not want to or is aware of the long-run consequences. These facts lead to an important conclusion: Economic and political pressures on the emergence of education as an institution are often separate. Polities can accelerate or retard the emergence of education somewhat independently of economic conditions.

In some modern systems such as the United States, where the polity supports extensive preschool educational programs as well as primary, secondary, and higher education, the impact of the polity on kinship can be profound. In other societies where only primary and secondary education are heavily financed by the polity, the effect on kinship will be lessened. But in the long run the polity's support of education tends to expand; and once the polity supports preschool through graduate education, kinship is usually altered. In these systems the family releases to the schools many of its social reproduction, social placement, and social support functions. Children at an early age leave the home for significant periods of their waking hours and participate in formal education structures. Preschool and kindergarten are less formal, emphasizing social support functions for the student. But as a student progresses in the educational system, social placement and socialization functions come to dominate. Students learn those traits that will greatly determine where they become incumbent in the wider society—especially the economy.

As a kinship system loses significant portions of its socialization and placement consequences for a society, traditional kinship norms begin to break down. Norms of parental authority are difficult to enforce as adolescence is reached, since the dependent's level of knowledge, mental skills, and interpersonal styles approach or surpass those of his parents. Residence rules become less salient as the child participates more and more away from home in school structures or other peer organizations. In systems where universities are dominant structures and where adolescents must leave the home for long periods of time, residence rules begin to disappear. Marriage rules also change under these conditions. When heterosexual activity can occur in a setting geographically separated from the home, marriage rules lose their impact. Once residence, authority, and marriage rules break down, extendedness of the family unit is difficult to maintain. When the young feel no obligation to live near parents, question the authority of elder kin, and choose their own mates, maintaining a large and stable family unit with several generations of kin becomes highly problematic. And with all these changes, descent necessarily becomes truncated, especially since social placement is now as much an educational as a familial function.

And so as the extensiveness of the educational subsystem supported by the polity increases, the descent, size and composition, residence, authority, and marriage rules of traditional kinship systems break down. In their place at least some norms of a modern kinship are likely to emerge, as kin groupings attempt to cope with the conditions generated by an advanced educational system. Neolocal residence makes separation from home in order to participate in educational statuses unproblematic. Egalitarian family norms make the authority (and generation gap) problems generated by schools less severe. "Romantic love" norms are more compatible with mate selection away from home. And truncated descent rules remove the young student from troublesome problems concerning loyalty and involvement with kin.

RELIGION AND KINSHIP

In traditional societies religion has many consequences for coordination and control in the family, since religious beliefs and rituals often reinforce and maintain the norms of the existing kinship system. One of the principal ways such integration occurs is through religious observances of major status transitions or *rites de passage* within the family. As children grow they assume new statuses within their family and larger kin grouping. The new normative obligations accompanying these statuses require a whole new set of attitudes, dispositions, and self-identity on the part of the incumbent. Religious rituals surrounding such major status transitions generate particular awareness of these new obligations by bringing to bear supernatural forces; and in doing so, the young are admonished under the threat of supernatural intervention to display the dispositions and behavior appropriate to their newly acquired station in life. The puberty rites of many traditional societies are a conspicuous example of how religious rituals solemnly inform the adolescent that he is now close to assuming adult status. The rituals also mark emphatically the new relationship between the new adult and his fellow kinsmen. In this way internal family reorganization occurs with a minimal amount of internal role strain and conflict among kinsmen. Marriage is another major status transition, for it marks the creation of a new family or the incorporation of new members into an existing extended family. In either case a reorganization of the kinship system must occur. By marking such reorganization with religious or sacred significance, the new obligations attendant on both the marrying partners and their kinsmen are made explicit, if not emphatic. The birth of a child confers another cluster of obligations on parents and surrounding kinsmen and is therefore marked by religious rituals in many traditional systems. Since birth is the beginning of social reproduction and ultimately a society's persistence these rituals are often very elaborate, as in the case among the Zuñi. In delivering her child, a mother calls upon a Zuñi priest to enact the appropriate rituals. At birth, the child is placed in a bed of hot stones covered with sand and then appropriate prayers are offered for a long life and good health. Four days later the child and mother must be brought to the Sun Father at dawn to be ritually washed and offer more prayers.

Probably the most dramatic status transition experienced by members of a kinship system is death. A death profoundly reorganizes family and kinship relations, since a person for whom strong attachments and emotions existed is simply removed from the daily life of the kin group. When a kinship leader dies reorganization of the larger kin grouping must ensue. It is therefore not surprising that elaborate rituals surround death, since the removal of a kinsman generates both intrapersonal anxiety and the need for structural reorganization of the family. Death rituals thus provide for the alleviation of anxiety and grief, as well as ritually reintegrating the disrupted kinship group.

Aside from the ritual embellishment of major status transitions, traditional religion also integrates the kinship subsystem by making sacred crucial norms. To violate certain kinship norms thus invites divine intervention and punishment. Since it is within kinship that such beliefs about intervention are instilled, they become a strong institutional source of conformity to kinship norms.

Another form of religious integration of kinship in traditional societies comes through ancestor worship. Prominent ancestors become part of the supernatural realm and are worshipped as quasigods. In some societies elaborate rituals performed in specially designated temples emerge to guide ancestor worship. For example, among the Tikopia the houses of important ancestors are maintained as temples where rituals to ancestors and gods are enacted. This constant ritual observance of the past maintains descent norms by reffirming as sacred the continuity of the kin group over long periods of time. In turn the maintenance of unilineal descent norms has the result of reinforcing other kinship norms.

These are only some of the ways religion has coordinating and integrating consequences for kinship in traditional societies. With modernization, religion ceases to be a major integrative institution as other institutions develop their own internal sources of coordination and integration and as new panintegrative institutions such as law and polity become dominant. This transformation is clearly manifested within the family, where religious rituals lose much of their significance in marking major status transitions. While birth, marriage, and death are still observed ritually, they have little significance in maintaining the social organization of kinship. Part of the reason for this may lie in the small size of the family unit and in the lack of powerful descent norms in a modern kinship system. The very lack of an extensive kin organization perhaps diminishes the necessity for religious integration. Coordination and control in a small, isolated, and conjugal family may come more from interpersonal adjustment and accommodations of members than from the implied threat of divine intervention and sanction. Furthermore, crucial kinship norms in modern societies increasingly become reinforced by law and the threat of *secular* sanctions.

LAW AND KINSHIP

Broadly speaking, legal subsystems contain four basic elements (Lloyd, 1964; Hoebel, 1954): (1) a body of rules or laws; (2) statuses involved in the enforcement of these rules; (3) a cluster of roles concerning the interpretation and application of rules; and (4) statuses revolving around the alteration and addition of laws. In some societies, the legal subsystem is an elaborate cluster of interrelated statuses and norms including a constitution, penal law, civil law, courts, police, legislatures, and administrative agencies, while in other societies, these elements can be found only in rudimentary form. Whether in simple or complex form, a legal system has far-reaching consequences for coordinating, controlling, and regulating relationships among individuals, groups, and organizations in a society. The influence of law thus extends into virtually all spheres of human activity, including kinship.

law and kinship in traditional societies

Only in more advanced traditional societies do separate and discrete rules (written constitutions and laws) as well as enforcement (police), interpretive (courts), and additive (legislatures or assemblies) statuses exist, for in most traditional systems only some of these components are clearly differentiated from the kinship and other institutions. However, even though the legal system is immersed in kinship it can be identified and some of its general consequences for kinship can be assessed. The rules of a traditional legal system are unwritten but they are nevertheless indelibly imprinted in people's minds. Because of this strategic location, they control role behavior in kinship

the
institutional
environment
of
KINSHIP

statuses. Laws are also customary or traditional, for they have the weight of time behind them. And laws are infused with religious overtones — with what the gods and cosmos prescribe. Laws are thus powerful forces of social control in traditional societies.

Laws concerning kinship roles are often fused with kinship norms. This fact poses an analytical problem of how to discover which kinship norms are also a part of the legal system in a society. One way is to examine those kinship norms which if violated are *enforced* by specific statuses, and around which interpretive statuses (or courts) exist. Some kinship norms can be violated and not much happens, but some norms when violated automatically lead to punishment by specific kin statuses. For example, to desert one's family in some systems automatically gives the adult male kin of the deserted party the right to punish the deserter. These kin constitute a police force of a modern society. They do not have precinct headquarters or a radio dispatcher but these kin temporarily occupy the status of policemen. And there may be other kin, perhaps elders, who when family desertion occurs assume the status of court judges and decide on appropriate punishments. Most of the time they are just elderly kin, but with certain violations of norms, they assume the legal position of judge and their behavior is guided by a set of norms evoked specifically for their temporary status. This is how legal systems function where economic resources and social needs do not allow or justify a separate system of laws, police, and courts (Hoebel, 1954).

We can ask whether or not there is any consistency from society to society concerning which kinship norms are also a part of the legal system. Unfortunately there is little information on the topic, but some tentative hypotheses follow. Kinship systems have several major consequences for society, including regulating sex, biological support, social reproduction, social support, and social placement. Since these functions are performed exclusively in the family in traditional systems and since their neglect would pose serious survival problems for the society, we might expect those general kinship rules concerning the minimal performance of these activities by kin to be incorporated into the legal system. Naturally the content of these laws would be as varied as the profile of kinship in human societies. Yet over time, as systems cope with the disruptions and conflicts generated by violations of crucial kinship norms, these same norms become incorporated into a special body of rules which carry with them specific sanctions by designated members of a society. Because so much human activity in traditional societies is organized and carried out within kinship, many of these laws as well as their mediation and enforcement focus on the "correct" performance of kinship roles. Only in this way can a traditional society evince that minimal degree of coordination and control necessary for its persistence.

law and kinship in modern societies

Modern legal systems are complex networks of laws, police, courts, agencies, and law-enacting bodies. Not only is law clearly differentiated from other institutions such as kinship, but it also displays considerable internal differentiation and specialization. One differentiated area of specialization is "family law," for in most modern societies there exist separate laws, courts, and agencies concerned with sources of disruption, conflict, and deviance in family relations. While many aspects of family law tend to be anachronistic and/or reflective of the moral biases of legislators and enforcement agencies, some of these specialized family laws can have consequences for regulating those family processes necessary for the persistence and survival of a society. While much social activity occurs outside the purview of kinship in modern societies, many crucial processes such as birth, socialization, and child maintenance are still carried out within the family. Yet kinship norms guiding family activity are often vague and ambiguous in modern systems, with the results that confusion in and dissolution of the family is frequent. Such normative ambiguity coupled with the centrality of the family for the survival of modern societies makes inevitable the existence of a wide variety of formal laws and agencies to cope with malintegration of the modern family. Some of the areas where the legal system is most likely to intrude into family processes are examined below.

Law and premarital sex. Premarital sex relations occur in all systems — even those prohibiting them. In modern systems there is a trend toward removing both legal and informal rules and restrictions against sex, heterosexual or otherwise. But even with "the pill," pregnancy occurs out of wedlock. It is in this area that the rules, courts, and agencies of a modern legal system intervene, because babies must be socialized and cared for if a society is to persist. Despite enormous variability in laws applying to childbirth out of wedlock, almost all modern legal systems require the father to support his child financially. In some instances the father must also support the mother, but these laws are less frequently enforced.

Law and marriage. In modern societies marriage becomes a *legal contract.* Even where no official marriage ceremony is performed, common-law marriages are usually considered legally binding after a specified period of time. While marriage is perhaps one of the most frequently violated contracts, it is still both a reflection of and a stimulus to kinship modernization. On the one hand, the decreasing regulation of marriage by religion,[4] kindred, and community in modern societies, coupled with high dissolution rates, forces legal intervention into the modernizing kinship system. On the other hand, such legal intervention encourages the exclusion of kindred, community, and even religion from intervening in marriage, since marriage and its dissolution become legal questions.

One consequence of this situation is that family units created by marriage can be conjugal and neolocal, as well as less conscious of unilineal descent, because laws rather than kindred regulate the general obligations of marriage partners. Thus legal intervention in marriage becomes likely when the breakdown of traditional sources of social control such as kinship, religion, and community begins to occur. At the same time legal intervention accelerates the dissipation of these sources of social control, and in doing so it encourages a more modern kinship system.

Law and socialization. Societies cannot persist without the socialization of new generations to replace the old. In modern societies much of this socialization occurs outside the family in schools because many economic norms require skills that the family cannot impart and/or because the polity often encourages formal education in order to indoctrinate the young or placate the old with visible evidence of progress toward a more modern society. Under these conditions compulsory-education laws are likely to be enacted for assuring the socialization of the young in schools. As outlined earlier, such legal intervention into socialization can have multiple consequences for kinship modernization: (1) Compulsory-education laws remove from the exclusive purview of family one of its traditional functions—socialization. (2) By forcing children to participate in formal structures requiring specificity and neutrality, these laws increase the social support consequences of the family. (3) Forced education away from the family creates a sense of independence and a cosmopolitan outlook in the young which decreases the salience of norms of residence, extendedness, and a unilineal descent. (4) Socialization in structures outside the family also makes strict authority patterns difficult to maintain for sophisticated and cosmopolitan children. Thus, while compulsory-education laws are probably enacted for economic, political, and humanitarian reasons, they

132

[4]Obviously religion exerts considerable influence on marriage. Most people are married in churches and many still ponder the religious sanctions against marriage dissolution. However, the long-run trend, as will be outlined in Chapters 12 and 13, operates against the extensive intrusion of religion into marriage.

usually have the consequence—usually unanticipated—of reinforcing modernization of kinship.

Law and child care. Aside from socialization, essential family activities include the biological support and care of infants. The legal system in all modern societies establishes minimal criteria for biological maintenance of infants and the young. These laws usually concern neglect and brutality. In systems with an isolated conjugal family structure where kin are excluded from family life, child-care laws become essential because there are no kindred to control and inhibit neglect of the young in the isolated conjugal unit. These laws can support the exclusion of kin from the household (as well as other features of a modern kinship system) by removing extended kin from the obligation of overseeing child care and support.

Law and family authority. Modern families become egalitarian. While there are several economic pressures contributing to this trend, there are also supports from the legal system. Women in modern systems have general legal rights not typical of women in patriarchal traditional societies (Williams, 1960:60–61). These include the right to make contracts, vote, own property, make wills, sue and be sued, and rights for equal employment, education, and recreation. Before the law, men and women are usually equals in modern systems. These general rights, which are codified in a myriad of laws from civil rights to business contracts, give women an equality in the wider society which inevitably spills over into family relations. When the legal system supports the rights of women to engage in economic, legal, and recreational activities outside the home, kinship norms of male authoritarianism no longer receive the institutional support from law evident in traditional systems. Once this authoritarianism is undermined by the legal system other kinship rules can become less viable: Descent rules to the male's side of the family are weakened; family socialization changes; residence becomes a joint decision made by both adults; and extendedness becomes difficult to maintain.

Law and divorce in modern systems. Family dissolution represents a problem in all social systems because it raises questions of what is to be done with dependents, especially children. In traditional systems residence, descent, and authority rules, plus the existence of a large and extended family unit, make these problems less difficult. Children are allocated to the kin deemed appropriate by these kinship rules. And so even high divorce rates do not seriously threaten the performance of biological support and socialization in traditional societies. But in systems with an isolated conjugal family, truncated descent, neolocal, and egalitarian kinship norms, a high dissolution rate poses a more serious problem, because kinship rules do not offer guidelines as to how children are to be allocated or cared for. Under these conditions laws and various family service agencies attached to courts tend to emerge to cope with these problems (Bohannan and Hickleberry, 1967). Extensive divorce laws, courts, and agencies dealing with family dissolution thus become a prominent feature of modern legal systems. Yet surprisingly the legal agencies revolving around family dissolution—especially divorce —do not always facilitate or ease or regularize family breakup. They often inhibit as much as facilitate family dissolution. One reason for this situation is that laws are often anachronistic and reflective of moral biases appropriate to previous times and are changed only under strong public pressure. Yet as the susceptibility of the family for breakup increases under economic and other pressures, laws inhibiting family dissolution increasingly become self-defeating since they encourage desertions and unregulated separation. Desertions and separations can generate even more serious problems, because under these circumstances it is unclear how the child is to be cared for and socialized.

Modern legal systems are now in transition. As the inevitability of family breakup in modern societies is recognized, laws, courts, police, and agencies are being restructured to cope with this inevitability. Rather than being prohibitive, legal systems are becoming restructured to either correct the sources of dissolution and/or facilitate it by providing clear procedural guidelines for such dissolution. Increasingly the conditions for divorce are liberalized, the court proceedings simplified, and the processes for allocating property and dependents clarified.[5] Currently or in the near future, the legal systems of modern societies will display these features:

1 Divorce can be obtained through mutual consent.
2 Property will be divided equally between adults.

[5] For example, in several European countries, "marriage Continental style" may soon involve compulsory "marriage insurance." West Germany and Sweden currently are preparing programs making it mandatory for the bridegroom to insure the bride against divorce in advance of the wedding ceremony. In the event of divorce such insurance would provide the female with enough income to support herself and dependents (should she be awarded them)—thus maintaining an economically (and emotionally) secure family unit. Such laws are unlikely in most modern systems for a while, but legal systems are increasingly becoming involved in easing the emotional and economic burden of divorce.

3 Alimony and child support will be assumed by insurance—perhaps subsidized by the state.
4 Dependents will be allocated to the adult best qualified to support and socialize the child as determined by court agencies.
5 Therapeutic agencies will be attached to the court to resolve marital conflicts.

Some, but rarely all, of these are basic parts of many current legal systems. In the future they will probably be typical of all modern legal systems.

KINSHIP IN THE FUTURE

If we extrapolate from current worldwide trends, we can wonder whether or not there will be a family in the future. Kinship has become less extensive and encompassing. It is becoming small, isolated, truncated, and it has fewer consequences for social reproduction, social placement, and even biological support. It is difficult to tell if these trends will continue, because there are forces both facilitating and inhibiting the dissipation of kinship as a social institution (Nimkoff, 1965:357–369).

the dissipation of kinship?

Theoretically, it is possible to conceive of alternative structures which could replace the family. For example, infants could be taken out of the family and medically, emotionally, and intellectually cared for by a staff of highly trained professionals in large "school" structures. In these schools, professional parent surrogates could perform many of the social support functions now performed by parents. Biological maintenance functions would be performed by a medical staff. Social placement into the wider society would be a natural consequence of the child's performance in the social and intellectual life of the school. The fact that those Soviet children who participate in state kindergartens do not suffer and that children in other societies are frequently shuffled off to boarding schools without apparent harm indicates the potential viability of these nonfamilial structures. In fact they might well eliminate many of the rigors of growing up in a modern kinship system. For example, the transition from the warmth of the home to the impersonality of the wider society would be less severe, since a school and home as one unit could more easily integrate the two. The generation gap would be lessened, since the staff of these schools could be trained to stay abreast of the times. The dependence-independence conflict typically resulting from prolonged adolescence in the modern family could be mitigated since the demands of home and school would be coordinated and integrated into one structure staffed by professionals. The ambiguity over appropriate role behavior typical of the young in modern kinship systems could be eliminated by clear-cut norms and regularized status transitions from infant, to child, to adolescent, to adult. Socialization would more easily be made relevant to what the child will encounter as an adult (this is often not the case with family socialization). And parents could forego the financial and emotional burden (and, of course, the pleasure) of raising children.

Although possible (whether desirable or undesirable is a separate issue), it is difficult to determine if such structures are probable. To a great extent they already exist, for increasingly the young are incumbent in school structures—often from age three to age twenty-six. Internally the schools are becoming restructured to cope with the emotional (counselors, special programs, escalated teacher credentials, etc.) needs of students. The same is true of biological needs (school lunch programs, school nurses, dental programs, etc.). And the modern family encourages these trends, especially when both parents work and are away from home during most of the child's waking hours (and often television "baby-sits" during the rest of the time). The polity also encourages these school programs as it attempts to use educational structures to realize system goals, such as economic development, political stability, and social equality. As it escalates the work requirements for employees the economy encourages further proliferation of educational structures. Yet whether or not these forces will lead to the dissipation of the family subsystem is impossible to predict.

the persistence of kinship?

There are also countervailing forces sustaining kinship in modern societies. While these do not assure or guarantee the persistence of kinship as a major social institution, they inhibit its dissipation in the near future.

Although we can rationally construct alternative structures to the family, we can seriously ask whether or not these would be more efficient than the family. There is some evidence indicating that perhaps kinship is better suited than any conceivable alternative structures in performing certain functions, such as those listed below.

(1) *Companionship.* People require companionship to remain emotionally stable. The modern family provides the personality system with this necessary kind of relationship. To conceive, finance, and implement politically an alternative companionship structure would perhaps be very difficult, although far from impossible.

(2) *Emotional security.* Children—especially the very young—need an emotionally secure social environment, as do mature adults. The family is one of the few structures in modern societies providing this kind of environment.

(3) *Sex.* The family provides adults with a stable environment for sexual intercourse. It provides privacy, emotional security, insulation from competition, and regularity for this most basic of human acts. While sexual bliss is not always automatic or inevitable within the family, it would be difficult to structure another means for stabilizing sexual relations.

(4) *Birth and early socialization.* Babies can be taken out of homes and socialized in agencies without generating major personality disorders. To do this on a wide scale, however, might tax the financial and manpower resources of even the most modern society. Because the family is already existent (and hence cheap) and is a reasonably efficient structure for performing these functions, the utility of conceiving, financing, and implementing alternative structures can be questioned.

The performance of these basic functions by the family is perhaps sufficient to insure its persistence in the future. While other functions—social placement, biological support, and the latter part of socialization—may be exclusively taken over by other institutions in the future, these four may remain within the province of the family.

the future structure of kinship

Assuming some form of family will persist in the future, we can now ponder just what its structure will be like. To do this, it is necessary to know what will occur in the environment of the family. In this section we will briefly examine three of these environmental influences: (1) the economy, (2) mass transit and communications, and (3) education.

137

1. Perhaps the most significant outside influence on the family will be the economy of the future. We already know how economic development (industrialization) has consequences for the modernization of kinship. But in forecasting the future it must be determined just what will be the impact of automation in the economy on kinship. As machines do the work of men, a "leisure" as opposed to "labor" force is likely to emerge in the future. The consequences of this on the family are twofold: (a) economic pressures for a small, isolated, and mobile family subsystem will be removed; and (b) adults will no longer

have to leave the home in order to procure an income. These will lead to a fundamentally new basis of integration in the family. Family has always revolved around economic tasks—from procuring a mere subsistence living in traditional systems to extensive consumption orientations in modern systems. But in the future the family will depend more and more on leisure tasks for its integration (Nimkoff, 1965:366).

2. There is another major force in society affecting kinship: the communications and transportation revolution. Instant communications and rapid transportation already exist and are likely to expand in the future. Several current studies offer tentative answers to the consequences for kinship of this expansion; it will increase the interaction and solidarity of family units in a kinship subsystem. Even though families may remain geographically dispersed, kinship ties will be strengthened through constant visiting and communication of kin with one another (Litwak, 1960).

3. The nature of education will also profoundly affect the future structure of kinship. Judging from current trends, educational structures will probably expand into these areas: providing leisure-time activities for both children and adults; child socialization; adult socialization; biological maintenance; and social placement. This means that both children and adults will be out of the home in educational structures for significant periods of time. Participation of all family members in educational structures can either bring together or divide the family. Involvement of each family member in education may diminish family interaction and hence relations. But it could also unite the family, since with all members in schools the traditional separation of adults' and children's activities will be diminished.

By projecting some of these outside influences on kinship, we might venture a list of the structural features of future kinship systems.

(1) *Family size and composition.*   The family unit will remain conjugal and small. Other kin will frequently be involved in family activities (through extensive visiting and communications) but living units will remain conjugal. Also, the childless family will become more common, with couples living for emotional support and companionship. Such "mini" families may be temporary, lasting as long as is convenient for the two members.

(2) *Residence.*   Residence will remain neolocal but frequent interaction among kinsmen will occur. Several family units may live together for short periods of time and then disperse. Mobility of

the family unit will become more and more a way of life (as a result of inexpensive and readily available mass transit systems).

(3) *Descent.* Descent will remain bilateral since both husband's and wife's kin groups will frequently be involved in family relations. However, truncated descent will be less likely to persist with frequent visits and communications from kin. Expanded ties of loyalty, warmth, and affection will emerge, but strong authority relations among family units will not reemerge.

(4) *Family activities.* These will be flexible but not ambiguous. Child care and late socialization will be assumed by educational structures—thus removing a major source of ambiguity from the kinship structure. The family division of labor will revolve around leisure interests of its members. There will be a vast array and diversity of leisure-time pursuits from which to choose.

(5) *Authority.* Egalitarianism will increase. With the schools performing many family functions much authority will be transferred to these structures. With all family members involved in leisure strict authority relations become difficult, if not detrimental to creative leisure.

(6) *Marriage.* This will be almost exclusively in terms of "love," but the romantic component will be lessened. Potential marriage partners will be able to realistically assess their compatibility and chances for an enduring social relationship. This new sophistication in mate selection will come from an increased focus of schools on sex and marriage education.

(7) *Dissolution.* Divorce will be easy to obtain, but rates will decline as mate selection becomes more realistic and the ambiguity of family activities is lessened.

139

SUMMARY

This chapter has briefly explored the institutional environment of kinship in both traditional and modern systems. While much institutional activity occurs within the kinship structure of traditional systems, its structure is nevertheless formed and maintained by outside institutional processes and forces. We have examined how economic pressures for a large and coordinated labor pool to work around low levels of technology and capital create conditions favoring the formation of a traditional kinship system. We have also noted how political processes of decision making, authority, and coordination generate political pressures partially resolved by traditional kinship. And finally we have noted how religion and law provide integrative supports for traditional kinship systems.

In modern systems, economic and political processes undermine traditional kinship patterns. Economic conditions requiring an educated, mobile, and skilled labor force greatly alter the socialization and social placement functions of kinship. The size and complexity of a modern economy also precludes kinship as a major integrative force in the economy. Such functional changes necessitated by the economy are reflected in the restructuring of kinship along a modern profile. Political pressures for state socialization and/or indoctrination in schools similarly undermine the structure and function of traditional kinship. With the growing institutional exclusion of religion from kinship, law increasingly assumes the necessary integrative functions for kinship. Law provides for the integration of modern kinship with its institutional environment, especially education, while sanctioning crucial intrakinship norms.

Finally we speculated on the profile of kinship in future societies. While many trends evident in modern systems will continue to erode certain functions of kinship, it appears that kinship has certain key consequences for society which preclude its total dissipation in the future.

SUGGESTED READINGS

Norman W. Bell and Ezra F. Vogel (eds.), *A Modern Introduction to the Family*, New York: The Free Press, 1968.

Ruth Shonle Cavan, *The American Family*, New York: Thomas Y. Crowell Company, 1969.

George P. Murdock, *Social Structure*, New York: The Macmillan Company, 1949.

M. F. Nimkoff (ed.), *Comparative Family Systems*, Boston: Houghton Mifflin Company, 1965.

Talcott Parsons and Robert F. Bales (eds.), *Family, Socialization and Interaction Process*, New York: The Free Press, 1955.

Stuart A. Queen and Robert W. Habenstein, *The Family in Various Cultures*, Philadelphia: J. B. Lippincott Company, 1967.

David M. Schneider, *American Kinship: A Cultural Account*, Englewood Cliffs, N.J.: Prentice-Hall, Inc., 1968.

William N. Stephens, *The Family in Cross-Cultural Perspective*, New York: Holt, Rinehart and Winston, Inc., 1963.

Robin M. Williams, Jr., "Kinship and Family in the United States," in *American Society*, New York: Alfred A. Knopf, Inc., 1970.

the

institutional

environment

of

KINSHIP

EDUCATION   6

In highly traditional societies education is fused with kinship, religion, and community. It is difficult in these societies to isolate empirically or analytically educational roles from the routine activities of community life. On the other hand, education is a highly visible and controversial structure in modern societies. In fact, in virtually all societies of the contemporary world education occupies an almost venerated place in people's minds. In traditional societies initiating the arduous task of economic development, political and economic policies inevitably focus on educational development. In highly modern industrial and postindustrial societies, education is perceived as the key to greater social equality and the necessary condition for material comfort and security. The *institution* of education, which became conspicuous only recently in the history of human societies but which is now a driving force in almost all the contemporary world, is thus a crucial link in the institutional web of society.

EDUCATION AND SOCIETY

The impact of education on society is varied. In some societies the consequences of education are extensive, while in others they are more limited. Cutting across much of this variability we can isolate six general consequences of education in social systems: cultural preservation and storage; cultural retrieval and dissemination; cultural expansion; socialization; social placement; and social transformation.

cultural preservation and storage

In Chapter 1 the brief discussion of the cultural system noted that culture is a complex system of interrelated parts and subsystems with material and nonmaterial components. We emphasized that it was the nonmaterial components, such as language, beliefs, values, ideologies, knowledge, lore, tradition, customs, mythologies, dogmas, and technology, that are most important in an institutional analysis of society. One way of viewing culture is as a giant "storehouse" which is filled with a symbolic inventory. Some of this inventory is active and constantly penetrates role behavior, while much remains buried and obscure. For example, values, beliefs, ideologies, scientific knowledge, and technology are intimately involved in what goes on in modern societies, whereas history, lore, and much religious dogma become less relevant to processes in contemporary societies. Societies thus preserve and store culture—sometimes out of respect for the past or as "museum" pieces, but always out of necessity.

The fact that societies preserve some cultural components

raises the question of how it is done. In primitive hunting and gathering systems of the past, or today in isolated parts of the world, cultural storage usually occurs within the family, but sometimes shamans, magicians, and other special persons are also charged with maintaining certain sacred aspects of culture. In these societies culture is unwritten and stored in the minds of men. For the most part, it is preserved through family socialization but sometimes through instruction by religious practitioners. Such a system for cultural preservation greatly limits the symbolic inventory of a society, since without a written language only an oral tradition is possible. Under these conditions only very simple technologies, limited historical accounts, and fundamentalistic dogmas, beliefs, and values can be stored. More advanced traditional societies of the past and present that display a written language as a cultural component can begin to store more complex and extensive technologies, dogmas, beliefs, histories, customs, and values, because the limitations of memory, time, and intellect are eliminated. At this stage of societal development cultural storage is increasingly removed from the purview of the family and tribal practitioners. Specialized statuses such as elite literati and religious scholars become charged with preserving components of culture.

Thus at its incipiency in the past or in the contemporary world, educational roles revolve around storing and preserving culture. Currently in more modern systems these roles have proliferated and become incorporated in highly complex structures of cultural preservation such as libraries, museums, files, computer banks, and universities, as well as trade, professional, and graduate schools. In these structures culture is written, coded, cataloged, cross-tabulated, and processed.

cultural retrieval and dissemination

Societies always evidence means for retrieving nonmaterial components of the cultural inventory and then disseminating them to the members of a society (Halsey, 1967). Through most of the history of human societies and in various places in the contemporary world, cultural retrieval and dissemination occur primarily within kinship. Yet the long-run trend with modernization is for the cultural storehouse to become so complex as to necessitate the appearance of discrete educational structures to assume much of the retrieval and dissemination burden. Today in the most modern societies, the family disseminates only general values, beliefs, histories, and dogmas, while the institution of education imparts an increasing proportion of the knowledge, history, and technology of a society's culture.

cultural expansion and innovation

At some point in a society's development, education begins to have consequences for not only preserving but also adding to and expanding the inventory of the cultural storehouse (Clark, 1962; Halsey, 1967). The expansion and innovation consequences of education are most apparent in societies with large universities that are staffed by researchers, technicians, graduate students, and scientists who are explicitly charged with the task of cultural expansion. Usually these positions are concerned with generating new technologies for the economic, military, and governmental structures of society. However, other researchers such as the social scientist, artist, literary scholar, and philosopher in educational systems are charged with expansion of other nonmaterial components, including music, literature, and social technologies.

socialization

Socialization is the process whereby the personality system becomes structured and formed. Much of this structuring is what enables people to participate in the broader society, for through socialization individuals become *committed* (i.e., motivated, oriented, and willing) to enact roles of major institutional statuses. They also learn the specific *skills* necessary to fulfill the normative demands of these statuses. In traditional systems, acquiring commitment and skills is an unconscious by-product of living and interacting in the family. However, as the institutional environment of the family modernizes, family socialization becomes inadequate to impart all the skills and commitment necessary for participation in the growing number of nonfamilial roles in a society (Parsons, 1955). New values, orientations, interpersonal styles, trade skills, and levels of knowledge are required. Under these conditions, modernizing societies usually evolve new statuses such as student, teacher, school administrator, counselor, and a host of related norms to carry out the increasingly complex task of socialization (Drucker, 1959:144). As societies become modern socialization thus becomes one of the major tasks of the constantly expanding institution of education.

146

social placement and allocation

Social systems have ways for inserting members into society. We know from Chapter 4 that there are two general mechanisms for doing this: *ascription* and *performance*. Ascription is the process of placing people into various economic, political, legal, and class positions on the basis of characteristics inherited at birth. In traditional societies family background is the most important of these ascribed characteristics. Where a child ends up in the economic, political, class, religious, and legal spheres is a direct reflection of where the heads of his family are currently located. And depending upon other ascribed characteristics such as sex and birth order, more specific allocation to statuses occurs: women occupy different positions from men; oldest sons and daughters hold different positions from youngest; and so on. Thus in traditional systems social placement and allocation are processes intimately connected to kinship. However, as societies modernize, the normative requirements on people become more varied and complex and require greater ability as well as prolonged and extensive training. Ascription becomes inadequate for allocation, since at birth it is impossible to match a person's qualifications to the requirements of various statuses. In the long run and through a variety of historical routes, new mechanisms for allocating actors emerge in modern systems and these revolve around performance criteria. From birth to young adulthood becomes a period in which performance is judged and evaluated. Later, on the basis of performance, initial allocation and placement of a person in the wider society occurs. In this way a somewhat more efficient, though imperfect, way of matching up the normative requirements of various statuses with people's capacity to meet these requirements is possible. As the difficulties of matching individuals' qualifications with the normative demands of certain statuses increase, systems tend to develop extensive school structures to identify, channel, and certify (with a diploma) ability. Schools become arenas for "proving" one's ability to assume and perform in certain positions (Clark, 1962; Goslin, 1965). And as we will see, schools display elaborate mechanisms, such as testing, counseling, and tracking, for identifying and developing the young's capacities (Halsey, Floud, and Anderson, 1961:183–268). Thus in modern systems the allocation or social placement consequences of education become extensive.

social transformation and reform

Education develops as a clearly discrete institution under the impetus of change in other institutional spheres. As the economic, political, religious, legal, and family subsystems are transformed, education emerges and has profound consequences in resolving problems associated with such transformation. Initially educational development is often sporadic, unplanned, and resisted. Yet once education becomes a dominant institution it is often used as a deliberate vehicle for social change and reform. Because of its importance for storing, disseminating, and expanding culture, as well as for socialization and placement, education can be an effective means for implementing desired social change. The nature of the changes and the extent to which education is viewed as the means for their implementation varies from one society to another. In Third World nations education is seen as the key to economic development. In Russia after the revolution, education was considered crucial not only for economic development but also for creating a new "Soviet Citizen." In the United States education has become one of the principal means for creating equality and opportunity for racial and ethnic minorities. Thus, once the centrality of education in social change becomes recognized by the polity and various pressure and reform groups in a society, it comes to have far-reaching consequences for planned social change.

defining the institution of education

Education is a somewhat unique institution. Unlike the economy it is difficult to differentiate empirically *and* analytically from the kinship subsystem in highly traditional societies. But early in the process of societal modernization it begins to differentiate and display a few separate statuses. And with further development these multiply and proliferate and come to form what is a conspicuous institution in modern systems. As this occurs, the consequences of education for society become more extensive. In defining education we must therefore remember that it is a developing institution displaying some degree of stability and yet constantly extending its impact on society:

> Education is that interrelated, general, pervasive, and relatively stable cluster of nonkinship statuses, roles, and norms which increasingly come to have consequences for: (1) cultural storage and preservation; (2) cultural retrieval and dissemination; (3) cultural expansion; (4) socialization; (5) social placement; and (6) social transformation.

EDUCATION IN DIFFERENT SOCIETIES

education in traditional societies

Some traditional societies have the rudiments of an educational subsystem. While vastly different from a modern educational system, the institution of education in traditional societies can still be differentiated or distinguished from other institutions such as the economy and family. In traditional societies of the past or present which display only the rudiments of education, just two statuses are clearly differentiated from kinship: teacher and student. Teachers, who usually are practitioners of certain crucial activities in a society, impart their skills and knowledge to select and small groups of students. Because teachers are active practitioners of what they teach, the relationship between student and teacher is one of master and apprentice with students learning by watching and assisting (Williams,

1970:306). Probably the first explicit teachers in human societies were religious elites such as shamans, and witch doctors who guarded and preserved the sacred dogmas, lores, customs, rituals, and traditions of the cultural storehouse. By virtue of ascribed characteristics (usually family rank and birth order), certain students were selected to become the future guardians of the cultural storehouse. But early in the development of most traditional societies other kinds of teachers emerged, especially in the economic spheres. Certain highly skilled craftsmen possessing vital technologies and skills became teachers to student apprentices selected on the basis of ascription. These teachers usually had special expertise in the hunting, gathering, domesticating, fishing, horticultural, and other activities in the economic subsystem of traditional societies. Yet even in these societies education was still carried out in the routine activities of kinship for the vast majority.

In more advanced traditional societies of the past and present the structure of education is (and was) more complex, involving more statuses clustered into more complex structures. Furthermore, formal education occurs in a diversity of spheres, reaches more students, and is of longer duration than in highly traditional systems. The positions of student and teacher probably first became extensively differentiated from other societal subsystems by being incorporated into new, revolutionary structures called schools. The emergence of school structures was highly significant to educational evolution for at least these reasons: (1) Schools are geographically separated from familial, economic, and religious activities. Such separation clearly marks the structural differentiation of education from other institutions. (2) Teachers in schools are often not actual practitioners of what they teach. Under these conditions, instruction begins to emphasize ideas, concepts, and knowledge rather than actual practical skills. Teaching is *about* activities rather than their demonstration (Williams, 1970: 306). (3) With the grouping of teachers and students in schools, administrative problems arise, for teachers, students, courses, and other aspects of the curriculum have to be coordinated, school facilities have to be maintained, and teachers have to be remunerated. These and related problems led to the emergence of administrative roles and marked the crude beginnings of educational bureaucratization (more on this later). (4) After the intital emergence of schools and specialized roles in them, more complex educational structures could develop. Schools could become specialized in certain areas—usually religion, humanities, and only rarely in science and technology. Schools could become hierarchically arranged into primary, secondary, and university levels. Thus with initial differentiation of education from other institutions and with the internal differentiation of educational statuses, the conditions for further educational development are established.

The history of past societies reveals that the initial emergence and later development of education was a slow, unconscious, and somewhat sporadic process. However, in modern Third World nations educational development is a conscious and deliberate political policy. Under these conditions extensive educational structures are imposed upon highly traditional communities and territories, with the result that compared to the initial emergence of education in human societies, educational development can be greatly accelerated. For example, in most Third World nations universal primary education for all members of the society was implemented as a major political goal in the last three decades. What took hundreds of years of gradual and sporadic change in the Old World has been accomplished within a comparatively short period of time in most societies currently undergoing modernization (Coombs, 1968). In these societies state and sometimes church schools are imposed upon the traditional tribal, caste, village, and territorial patterns of elite education. In itself such educational imposition has many consequences, not only for disrupting primitive educational processes but also for drastically altering traditional patterns of social organization. Coupled with the fact that the rapid extension of universal education usually involves *deliberate* attempts to politically indoctrinate young students and to upgrade technologically depressed areas, the rapid social transformation ushered in by the current educational "revolution" in the Third World surpasses those changes created by more gradual educational "evolution" in Western societies over the last 200 years.

education in modern societies

Educational statuses, norms, and roles found in traditional societies —student, teacher, administrator—have undergone profound changes in modern societies. They have proliferated in number, degree of specialization, and structural location. The number of student statuses has expanded and in the most modern systems everybody at some point becomes a student, for education now reaches the nonelite masses. The number of teachers and administrators has also expanded to cope with the instructional and administrative problems of mass education. Student, teacher, and administrative roles become more specialized as the normative requirements attendant upon each status become narrow and circumscribed. These statuses become clustered into different kinds of schools, including primary, secondary, and higher, as well as peripheral structures, such as adult education, trade schools, schools for retarded and handicapped, extension services, business colleges, and secretarial schools. These schools are usually ranked hierarchically with higher educational structures at the pinnacle, followed by peripheral, secondary, and primary schools. This hierarchy furthers specialization since students, teachers, and administrators engage in specialized role behavior appropriate to a particular type of school.

Aside from the expansion and reorganization of these educational statuses, new roles evolve and become a prominent feature of the educational subsystem. The most prominent of these emergent statuses are the counselor, researcher and scientist, and support positions. In modern education the counselor is a conspicuous position in all school structures. Norms require counselors to engage in a variety of role behaviors, including testing, guiding, administering therapy, and advising (Cicourel and Kitsuse, 1963). As the educational subsystem becomes structured for cultural expansion, the roles of researcher and scientist become prevalent—especially in higher education. Of less analytical significance than counselors or researchers is the proliferation of support statuses. These statuses revolve around the secretarial, maintenance, dining services, and other tasks necessary to maintain the more complex structures of modern educational subsystems.

These are the general structural features of a modern educational subsystem. We can now visualize a general picture of student, teacher, administrator, counselor, researcher-scientist, and a host of support statuses clustering into different types of school structures. In turn these various types of schools possess interrelations which form the complex web of statuses, roles, and norms of a modern educational subsystem. In modern societies education thus becomes a dominant institution which touches almost every member of a society at some time, consumes a large portion of a society's financial resources, and becomes one of the largest employers of the work force.

One way to analyze this large and complex institution is to examine the various types of schools forming the educational hierarchy of a modern society. This kind of analysis involves not only delineating the broad structural features of schools but also assessing in general crucial statuses such as students, teachers, counselors, administrators, and researchers within university, secondary, primary, and peripheral schools. In this way a profile of the institution of education is possible.

THE PRIMARY SCHOOL

The primary school is the first formal organization in which the young must participate. Because the obligations of teachers, administrators, and counselors are narrowly and formally defined, as well as being neutrally implemented, students must become adjusted to a structure that differs greatly from all their previous kinship experiences. Furthermore, since the primary school is the first nonfamilial structure in which the child must participate for an extended period of time, adjustment to prolonged separation from kin must also be made. Finally students soon learn that teachers expect regularized performance from them and that their behaviors are evaluated objectively in terms of established grading procedures. This new emphasis on achievement and on the objective evaluation of achievement forces additional adjustments on the part of students.

Probably the most interesting form of accommodation by young students to the classroom and formal school structure is the emergence of peer solidarity. Increasingly as a child moves up in the primary school system, student norms emphasize peer solidarity, companionship, and *esprit de corps.* The reason for this can probably be traced to the impersonal and formal school environment, for as students must accept distance, impartiality, objectivity, and authoritarianism from the school structure, as well as an emphasis on achievement and performance from the teacher, they retreat into their own subculture to mitigate the severity of this newly encountered formality and concern for performance. Frequently by the time students are ready to leave the primary school, peer solidarity begins to conflict with classroom norms emphasizing achievement and performance. In some systems, such as in the United States, this conflict is severe with student pranks subverting classroom activities, while in other societies, such as the Soviet Union, where the peer group and peer achievement have been utilized in meeting classroom norms, the conflict is mitigated. But in both types of systems, the peer classroom conflict increases in secondary school structures (Coleman, 1961).

THE SECONDARY SCHOOL

In most modern societies secondary schools become specialized. After completion of primary school, students are shunted into different types of secondary schools. These schools represent tracks or lanes, preparing students for different careers. For example, one school can lead to higher university education, another to teacher training, and still another to vocational training (Havighurst and Neugarten, 1967). In some societies, such as the United States, tracking occurs within *one* type of secondary school. This is called a *single-track* system. But most societies have *multiple-track* secondary systems with separate schools representing different career lines for students. These two types of systems are represented diagramatically in Figure 6−1 (Havighurst and Neugarten, 1967:90).

In both the single- and multiple-track secondary schools, specialization occurs. In the multiple-track system students become specialists by virtue of which secondary school they attend. In the single-track system students have majors or minors and are either

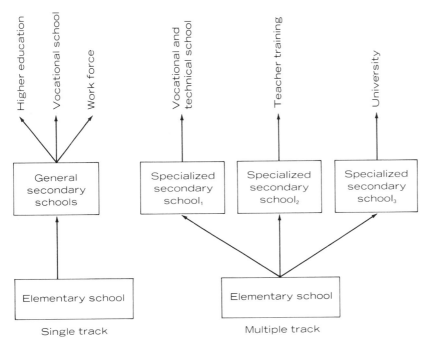

Figure 6–1 Types of secondary systems.

college preparatory or vocational. This means teachers also become specialists who instruct a delimited amount of material for a limited time. Once student and teacher specialization occurs, problems of coordination, control, and integration intensify, leading to the proliferation of administrative roles. Whether coordinating the various lanes in the single-track system or the different schools in the multiple-track system, administrators assume a dominant place in secondary education. Furthermore the whole notion of multiple tracking or of acquiring majors and minors points to the increasing significance of counselors who guide, channel and allocate students into different programs and tracks.

Norms of performance, coupled with the increased impersonality and specialization in secondary schools, often reinforce and extend peer solidarity norms with the result that students can become alienated from classroom activities. As an impartial, objective, authoritarian, specialized, and neutral teacher-student relationship increases, students may retreat into their own supportive subculture with its unique norms. From one perspective, peer norms mitigate the transition from home to school and later to job by providing

153

social support and companionship. Because the young in modern industrial societies must eventually move from supportive kinship relations to impersonal work roles outside the purview of kinship, they must acquire the capacity in schools to interact in situations where neutrality, specificity, scheduling, and performance are required. For most persons this transition occurs over a number of years of participation in primary and secondary schools. Apparently to mitigate this transition, students form peer groups which can provide some degree of support within the formal and specialized requirements of secondary schools (Eisenstadt, 1956).

HIGHER EDUCATION

All modern societies have extensive higher education structures. The internal organization of higher education is much more complex than lower education. There is a high degree of specialization of teacher, counselor, administrator, and even student roles. And the requirements of training, competence, and expertise of the incumbents are considerably higher than in lower education.

Probably the most unique feature of higher education is the emergence of a new status: the researcher. Researchers are specifically charged with cultural expansion. They are to question, inquire, reason, and discover new knowledge or expand the old. And they are to communicate findings and discoveries. Frequently researchers are also teachers engaging in dual role behaviors. But as higher education in a society expands and comes to have extensive cultural expansion consequences for the total society, researcher roles can be clearly differentiated from teacher roles although they frequently remain fused.

Another prominent feature of higher education is the emergence of distinct types of student subcultures. At the most general level we can distinguish four such types: (a) collegiate; (b) vocational; (c) academic; and (d) activist (Clark and Trow, 1966).

(a) *Collegiate subculture.* The norms of this subculture stress non-involvement with the intellectual ideas and life of a college structure. Academic roles are played just enough to remain in the status of student. Norms stress involvement in extra-curricular activities including social, recreational, leisure, and "fun" behaviors. In many ways these are uniquely American norms; and they have lost salience in American higher education only recently. While collegiate student roles are typical of many higher educational structures in other societies, they dominate the American system to an unusual degree.

(b) *Vocational subculture.* In this subculture roles revolve around taking and passing specific courses leading to a diploma in an area that will bring employment. Education is viewed as a means to a vocation, with the result that students often remain uninvolved in either social or intellectual activity not necessary for vocational training.

(*c*) *Academic subculture.* Students in this subculture are seriously concerned with intellectual ideas and are likely to pursue knowledge for its own sake rather than as a direct means to a job. The norms of this subculture require involvement in course work beyond the minimum required to pass or graduate.

(*d*) *Activist subculture.* Norms in this group require the student role to be relevant and germane to "vital" social issues and problems. Students tend to be deeply concerned with intellectual ideas only as they relate to resolving social problems. The student's role is political and involves eradicating injustices and inequalities within and outside of the college structure.

Overall, we can view the educational hierarchy in modern societies as displaying several distinct transformations from lower to higher education:

1 The degree of formality, social distance, and neutrality between students and other statuses increases.
2 There is increased pressure for achievement and performance on the part of students as they move up the educational hierarchy.
3 The degree of specialization of student and other roles increases from the primary and secondary to university level.
4 Administrative roles, including those of counselors, proliferate in order to cope with the problems of increased specialization.
5 With increased formality, specialization, and concern for performance from lower to higher education, distinct types of student subcultures emerge to cope with the increasing severity of the school environment.

THE CONSEQUENCES OF EDUCATION IN TRADITIONAL AND MODERN SOCIETIES

education in primitive societies

In primitive societies of the past or in isolated spots in the contemporary world, the consequences of the rudimentary educational subsystem tend to be confined to the preservation of selected cultural components, such as religious dogmas, rituals, and myths; their select dissemination; and formal socialization of a select few. In these systems, certain cultural components have special, if not sacred, significance and are preserved by elite religious practitioners.

These components include important dogmas, lore, and histories, but only rarely technological and other kinds of purely cognitive knowledge. Religious elite, such as shamans, witch doctors, and high priests, become teachers disseminating these special components to students who are selected on the basis of family ascription and who will become the next generation preserving these important and sacred cultural components. In this way cultures without a written language in their inventory can be preserved and stored over many generations. But many other cultural components, such as technologies, basic values, beliefs and orientations, are stored in the minds of ordinary incumbents and disseminated within kinship. Thus the preservation and dissemination functions of education tend to be limited to only certain kinds of cultural components in highly traditional societies. The socialization consequences of education are even more limited, with certain skills appropriate to elite religious, economic, and perhaps warrior statuses being demonstrated to students of high-ranking families by a few highly skilled practitioners in these spheres. Sometimes these teachers are of the same kinship group as their students, but often such education cuts across kin groups. To the extent that it does, it marks the emergence of formal education outside family and kinship. But almost all socialization of commitment and skills still occurs within a child's immediate kinship grouping.

education in the traditional old world

In advanced traditional or agrarian systems of the past with an emerging school system, the functions of education were greatly expanded: (1) Less select and sacred cultural components such as technology were added to the growing and secularizing cultural storehouses; (2) dissemination of more components to a larger number of students occurred; (3) socialization of more complex skills became typical; and (4) for the first time, education per se began to have social placement consequences—thus removing allocation from the exclusive purview of kinship. These more advanced traditional systems had a written language as a cultural component. A written language allows for storage of additional cultural components in places other than the human mind and therefore marks a major revolution in a society, for now the quantity and complexity of the cultural inventory can be expanded. Under these conditions educational structures began to preserve in greater detail not only histories, dogmas, and lore, but also cultural items related to secular roles. Economic, political, warfare, and other experiences could be written down, codified, and stored not only in the minds of teachers and students but also in a growing body of books and manuscripts. However, such storage was limited by a simple fact: what was stored had to be slowly written down by hand and few actors were capable of doing this. Until the typed and printed word as well as higher levels of literacy became prevalent, the educational subsystem of these historic societies could preserve only a small cultural storehouse with a limited inventory. But for the first time in the history of human societies, this inventory included components other than quasi-sacred histories, dogmas, and lores. With school structures, dissemination of an expanded cultural inventory could reach a larger number of students. Depending on the extensiveness of the emerging school structures, young from nonelite families began to participate in at least the lower schools. Usually only basic components such as the written language and the rudiments of technologies were disseminated to these nonelite students, since they would typically not go on to higher school levels. A few with exceptional performance may have continued in the school hierarchy but this was rare, for it was to students from elite families that the broader and more complex cultural inventory was most likely to be disseminated.

Socialization of specific skills and more diffuse commitment to engage in certain role behaviors in the emerging schools of the Old World increased with societal development. More students from both elite and nonelite families acquired skills necessary for participation in the broader institutional structure of society. This is especially true of nonelites who underwent training for administrative statuses in the economy, polity, military, and even the expanding school structure. On the other hand, students from elite families were more likely to undergo socialization involving dissemination of general cultural components such as history, philosophy, lore, and religion, since these elites were to assume leadership of those administrative structures increasingly staffed by the educated nonelites. But the fact that a few nonelites became involved in the educational system and on the basis of exceptional performance could acquire skills enabling them to assume administrative positions marked an increase in the allocative and social placement consequences of education. Criteria of performance in school rather than family ascription now became a basis for placement of a few nonelite individuals into the wider society. This development marked the incipiency of what became a major educational function in the contemporary world (Parsons, 1955).

Education even in advanced traditional systems of the past had few consequences for *cultural expansion* and *social transformation*. To a limited extent cultural innovation occurred with the accumulation of more secular components in educational structures. But since higher education preserved and disseminated the more esoteric and sacred aspects of culture, innovations affecting what goes on in the wider social system were rare. Until educational structures—especially higher education—became specifically structured in the eighteen and nineteen centuries to generate new knowledge, the cultural expansion consequences of education remained negligible. Innovations in these systems were more likely to occur in other spheres of society. The social transformation and reform consequences of education in these historic systems were also imperceptible. Education did not yet occupy a sufficiently dominant place in the institutional structure for it to be recognized as a potential tool for social reform.

education in the traditional third world

Today in traditional societies of the Third World the social transformation consequences of education are clearly recognized by political leaders. Because of this fact mass lower education has been extended to all segments of the population. An educated population is now viewed as the key to: political stability through educational indoctrination; economic development through socialization of work skills in the masses, as well as research and development of industrial technologies; and national prestige as a "progressive" and "modern" society. Yet even in these modernizing Third World nations higher education often remains elitist (Halsey, 1967), because the young from traditionally high-ranking families constitute the majority of university students. In the long run, however, mass lower education creates expectations and demands from the general population that nonelites be allowed to go on to higher educational levels. Coupled with economic and political demands for skilled manpower and new technologies, the elitist profile of higher education in Third World nations is currently being transformed.

The recognition of education as a means to social transformation and its subsequent expansion has also greatly expanded its consequences for society. Much of the technology as well as political history and lore of the cultural storehouse is now stored within education rather than kinship. Cultural expansion of industrial technologies has now become one of the major functions of higher education as Third World nations embark on programs of economic development. Many of the skills and commitment for participation in these changing societies are now acquired in education instead of kinship. As these retrieval and socialization consequences of education become prominent the social placement functions of education expand, for now the amount of formal education acquired by a student begins to influence eventual incumbency in the broader society.

education in modern societies

In modern societies almost everyone at some time becomes a student. And this means that other educational statuses must expand to keep pace. As education expands it becomes a dominant institution having manifold consequences for the social system. Education is the principal cultural storage, dissemination, and expansion structure, while having major consequences for socialization, social placement, and social transformation.

Cultural storage. The libraries, files, computer banks, and other facilities of educational structures store a tremendous amount of a society's cultural inventory. This is particularly true with higher education where many of the most complex cultural components are preserved. But we should not forget that much culture—especially technologies—is stored in other institutional structures, including military, governmental, and economic. The secret files of the military, business corporations, and government are involved in cultural storage, but these tend to be limited and involved only in storing those components useful for specific purposes, such as war, making money, or international diplomacy. The rest of the cultural inventory—philosophy, history, lore, technology, knowledge—is preserved in educational structures. Aside from the physical facilities of education, the minds of teachers and researchers are also a major locus of cultural preservation. Although any one human mind can maintain only a small inventory, the collective storage capacity of all teachers and researchers becomes incredibly immense.

Cultural dissemination. In terms of imparting the cultural inventory, the teacher-student dyad in modern societies becomes more important than the parent-child relationship. Except for basic beliefs, ideologies, and values, teachers disseminate a tremendous amount of the cultural inventory to the young. Customs, history, philosophies, symbol systems, cognitive knowledge, and technologies are disseminated by teachers in schools rather than by parents in the home. When we realize the amount of time per day, over a child's early lifetime spent in school structures, the dissemination functions of education become clearly evident. Sometimes teacher dissemination is direct, as in lectures in the classroom, but often it is indirect. Teachers indirectly cause dissemination by assigning books and other cultural components in libraries. Or by inspiring and encouraging intellectual curiosity in students who then pursue library work on their own, teachers disseminate culture. And of course by introducing the young to the written language, a teacher enables the child as a student and later as an adult a lifetime of access to the cultural storehouse.

Cultural expansion.   Although economic, political, and military structures engage in cultural expansion, they do so primarily in the technological sphere. Educational structures are involved in innovation not only in this area but in all spheres of the cultural storehouse. Innovation is primarily the function of higher education where the roles of researcher and scientist proliferate. But education contributes to innovation in more subtle ways. By encouraging flexibility, adaptability, and curiosity, teachers impart to students basic capacities necessary for innovation, whether as students in higher educational structures or later in military, political, and economic structures. Innovation always involves a myriad of personality traits other than knowledge, and education has profound consequences in imparting these in future incumbents.

Socialization.   With virtually every person in a society in a student role for at least seven or eight years (and usually more in postindustrial systems), much of personality system formation inevitably occurs in school structures. From an institutional perspective, schools instill two basic traits in the personality system: *skills* and *commitment.* Skills are those traits enabling participation in institutional statuses. The normative demands on most status positions require two types of skills, vocational and interpersonal. Vocational are trade skills or expertise necessary for carrying out the actual job requirements of status, usually an economic position. Interpersonal skills are those capacities allowing a person to "fit in" and "get along" in various institutional statuses. These involve mechanisms of neutrality and specificity as well as the capacity to schedule and pace work activities. In the industrial-bureaucratic structures of modern societies both skills—vocational and interpersonal—become necessary requisites for workers. Commitment is that personality trait involving the desire and willingness to enact roles in institutional statuses, particularly in the economy. People do not innately desire to play institutional roles; little is intrinsically satisfying about enacting them. Thus structures instilling in actors the desire—or at least willingness—to become incumbent in a position providing an income and living emerge in societies. This process of generating commitment is always problematic in modern societies, where alienation is a prominent personality trait. Socializing commitment and skills is increasingly becoming the responsibility of education. The family subsystem, by imparting basic values and beliefs, still has many consequences for imparting commitment. But education has virtually usurped the familial consequences for instilling skills.

Kinsmen cannot impart the vocational skills necessary for participation in the occupational sphere. Nor can family interaction lead to the acquisition of those interpersonal skills required by industrial and bureaucratic organizations. In socializing commitment and skills different school structures have a varying impact. Primary schools impart commitment, while allowing the young student to become accustomed to a formal organization with elements of neutrality, specificity, scheduling, pacing, and performance. Secondary and higher educational structures increase formalization and vocational training. And many peripheral schools have vocational training functions with the degree of formality varying. Thus, through participation in some or all of these school structures, appropriate commitment and skills are imparted to many—though not all—future adults. But it is clear that a significant portion of both secondary and higher educational incumbents all over the world are uncommitted or alienated from not only schools but also from economic, political, legal, and religious structures. And so it cannot be assumed that educational socialization is always "successful."

Social placement. Since schools socialize many of the skills and commitment affecting eventual participation in the wider society, they inevitably have social placement consequences. Because of this, counselor statuses evolve to facilitate allocating students not only to schools but also to the outside society. Utilizing a battery of tests—IQ, scholastic achievement, personality adjustment, and so forth—counselors label students at various stages as "gifted," "under-" or "overachievers," "problem cases," "adjusted," and a host of other descriptive titles. The actual jargon or euphemisms used by counselors vary from society to society but their use has the same consequence; students are placed into various schools and programs on the basis of how they are labeled by counselors. In turn these programs affect the kinds of skills and nature of commitment students acquire. And these latter ultimately determine where a student can become incumbent in the wider society.

Most modern educational systems have a series of national examinations about midway in a student's career. Performance on these examinations becomes the basis for allocating students to different types of schools—vocational, trade, technical, or university. How far in any one of these schools a student advances is determined by subsequent performance. As we will see, the United States does not formalize national examinations to the extent that other societies do, but examinations play an important part in allocating students within the institution of education and later in placing students in the broader society.

Social transformation. The significance of education in socialization and social placement has revealed its potential in generating social change and reform. If education socializes many personality traits crucial for success and systematically places students into the broader society, it can become a powerful instrument of social change. This fact is attested to by the "social revolutions" in China and Russia where new kinds of personality traits and processes for allocating people and distributing rewards emerged in a very short period of time. This occurred through an "educational revolution" in which the educational subsystem was dramatically modernized by the polity. In other systems the transformation consequences of education are not so far-reaching but are nonetheless profound. In the United States various peripheral educational structures — Head Start and Job Corps, for example — have been implemented to resolve economic inequality. The attempt to desegregate schools exemplifies another approach for using schools to eliminate racial inequality. Another example comes from American universities which have admitted minority students while providing counselors to assist these students' social and intellectual adjustment. A major difficulty in utilizing education for social transformation is that consensus over just what reforms and changes are desirable is difficult to establish. These issues inevitably become political and this further decreases the possibility for consensus. Even when there is consensus over what should be reformed, there is usually dissensus over how education should be utilized. Despite these difficulties the social transformation consequences of education will increase as societal planning becomes a prominent feature of modern societies.

WORLD TRENDS IN EDUCATION

162

In traditional societies, formal education is a comparatively recessive institution. But once modernization of education in the contemporary world is initiated it begins to reach the masses and have manifold and far-reaching consequences for society. As this transition takes place certain common trends and problems, which are explained in this section, become evident.

massification and democratization

With modernization the number of student statuses increases as education becomes "massified" (Clark, 1962). Massification occurs first at the primary level and then at the secondary level. And currently in extremely modern systems such as the United States, pressures for universal higher education are becoming evident (Coombs, 1968). Some of these pressures for massification are a partial reflection of modernization in other institutions, especially the economy. In many developing societies of the Third World, however, the pressures come from the populace, for education becomes the symbol of the good life and a better future. Should the polity ignore these demands of the populace it runs the risk of being overthrown, because polities in the developing world are unstable and have trouble legitimating themselves in the eyes of their people. Yet, as noted earlier, even without population pressures, polities often massify at least primary, and frequently secondary, education because it is perceived as the key to modernization. For whatever reason, massification in developing Third World societies is often premature, since the economy and other institutions are not sufficiently developed to absorb graduates. Graduates who are unemployed inevitably become frustrated, angry, and susceptible to revolutionary ideologies. Moreover, premature massification can also hurt the quality of education in impoverished societies, since classrooms soon become overcrowded, textbooks scarce, and, most important, qualified teachers rare (Coombs, 1968). This is compounded by the fact that the population in these systems tends to expand rapidly and hence create even more crowded conditions. Thus developing societies almost always face the problem of balancing quantity and quality, for large quantities of poorly educated incumbents in other institutional spheres, such as the economy and polity, ultimately retard long-range modernization. Even in highly modern and wealthy systems, maintaining educational quality with rapid increases in the quantity of students is difficult.

Massification of education implies democratization. Education in traditional systems is elitist, but with modernization it begins to be democratized and incorporate students from diverse social classes, races, and both sexes. Yet democratization is never easy, since in most societies the stratification system is rigid and discrimination against women, certain races, ethnic groups, and social classes is always prevalent. Thus in both developing and developed societies, democratization is never complete (Clark, 1962). Even in educational systems where all the young enter primary school, discrimination against certain classes of students occurs because unequal school facilities, instruction, and counseling result in privileged or elite groups of students going on to higher education, with less elite groups completing at most only secondary schooling (Cicourel and Kitsuse, 1963). Thus, one of the most difficult problems facing education in modernizing societies is complete democratization. To the extent that this cannot be achieved, systems waste potential talent while generating potential revolutionary subgroups, such as the Indios of Latin America, blacks in America, and disenfranchized tribes in Africa.

bureaucratization

With increases in size schools usually become bureaucratized. Problems of coordination, control, integration, and communication become too intense and severe for any alternative form of organization (Clark, 1962; Goslin, 1965). This trend forces student, teacher, administrative, and counselor roles to become organized in this way:

1 Statuses are specialized with duties and obligations clearly specified.
2 Performance and seniority become the major criteria for evaluating incumbents.
3 Role behavior is carried out neutrally and with impersonality.
4 Activity is organized into classrooms and offices where role behavior is coordinated and regulated. Within and between offices is a hierarchy of authority and supervision.
5 Incumbents often make a career of moving up within the bureaucracy.

Bureaucratization of education is similar to bureaucratization in the economy; and in many ways it is more extensive, since virtually every member of a society participates at some time in the educational bureaucracy. Furthermore, educational bureaucracies are charged with the delicate tasks of socializing the very young and placing people in the wider society. Processing and allocating people is usually more difficult than processing and distributing goods and services. This fact poses difficult problems for administrator, teacher, and counselor, for they are caught between the impersonal and specialized demands of the bureaucracy and the more personal and diffuse demands of students. This conflict is most intense at the primary level, since students have yet to become accustomed to participating in a formal bureaucracy.

Bureaucratization occurs not only within schools but between them. Schools become arranged in hierarchies from primary to higher levels with activities at one level coordinated with those at another level. Such a situation creates a tremendous administrative burden and this furthers bureaucratization.

centralization

Most developing systems have difficulties in establishing national goals and priorities among them. Even when national priorities are clear, coordinating resources, especially human, is difficult. One predominant system response to this problem is centralization of the educational subsystem so that national and educational priorities can be better coordinated. This means that the linkages between the governmental and educational bureaucracies are explicit (usually through a Ministry of Education or similar office). It also means that the educational bureaucracy is vastly expanded beyond what it is in more decentralized systems.

One principal reason for centralization of education is financial. Education is expensive and so are other structures contributing to goal attainment. Most systems cannot afford the luxury of having the educational subsystem producing graduates who fill positions not directly related to national priorities. This is especially true of developing systems where economic growth is the primary system goal. To have graduates with knowledge in the arts and humanities does not directly contribute to the goal of development. In Russia, for example, technical schools have long dominated the educational subsystem in order to meet the dual goals of economic growth and military supremacy. And so as it centralizes, the educational subsystem becomes more responsive to political priorities. In the United States extensive centralization has been unnecessary because enough money and a large student population have always existed to assure that a sufficient number of students graduated in areas considered essential to national priorities.

Large and centralized bureaucracies often subvert and sabotage their very reason for existence: efficiency in organizing a complex set of activities. They can become a labyrinth of offices and hierarchies of authority through which messages and policies have difficulty traveling. One result of this situation is that national priorities cannot be effectively translated into educational policy in local schools.

professionalism

In many spheres of modern societies professionalism is becoming a dominant force. Professionalism denotes at least these things (Corwin, 1965):

1 Role behavior requires extensive formal training.
2 Role performance requires a high degree of skill and expertise in a specialized area.
3 Role behavior displays a low degree of standardization with the professionals utilizing various alternative procedures for successful performance.
4 Role behavior involves decision making on the basis of training and expertise.

5 Role behavior is client oriented, involving aiding and assisting clients.

6 Role behavior is colleague oriented, with colleagues and colleagual associations possessing considerable sanctioning power.

Professional norms thus stress flexibility and utilization of expertise for the benefit of clients. Such norms are constantly reinforced and maintained through interaction with colleagues and membership in professional associations. Membership in these associations usually includes subscriptions to specialized professional journals and attendance at meetings and conventions. Professionalism is thus *cosmopolitan* for it includes a common sense of identity throughout a society with fellow professionals. This cosmopolitanism typically begins before actual participation in a professional status, since during the latter stages of formal education students become indoctrinated into the values, ideologies, vocabulary (jargon), practices, and techniques of their future profession.

Professionalism has many beneficial consequences. It keeps standards high. It regulates and adds predictability to role performance. It keeps members abreast of new developments in the profession. However, within bureaucracies professionalism can pose some problems. The normative demands of the bureaucracy and those of the profession can come into conflict. Within the educational subsystem organizational demands for instructing, grading, promoting, and allocating students can subvert teachers', counselors', and even administrators' professional commitments. Counselors must just process rather than guide, counsel, and treat students. Teachers must just manage and control rather than teach and inspire students in classes. Administrators must maintain peace and quiet instead of making and implementing new and imaginative policies. In well-financed educational structures the conflict between professional and bureaucratic norms is mitigated, because sufficient resources exist to allow for both. But when resources are limited, professionalism can appear an expensive luxury in structures where just meeting minimal bureaucratic requirements is financially difficult.

In Table 6–1 the inherent conflicts between professionalism and bureaucratization are summarized (Corwin, 1965:229–247; Havighurst and Neugarten, 1967): The normative demands of bureaucracies and professionalism delineated in Table 6–1 often generate role conflict, especially for the teacher and counselor in modern education. In lower education, the teacher can exercise some professionalism in the classroom but there are many bureaucratic constraints, including a standardized curriculum, incessant evaluations by administrators, and the necessity for implementing administra-

TABLE 6-1

BUREAUCRACIES	PROFESSIONS
1 Standardization of role behavior	1 Flexibility in role behavior
2 Low degree of autonomous decision making	2 High degree of decision making
3 Role behavior is oriented to organization	3 Role behavior is oriented to client
4 Role behavior conforms to administrative practices of organization	4 Role behavior conforms to the standards of colleagues and professional associations

tive policies. In higher education these constraints are mitigated and the conflict between teacher professionalism and bureaucratic demands is less severe. Counselors are constantly constrained by the bureaucratic demands for processing large numbers of students, keeping records, and maintaining calm. To evaluate individual achievement and ability becomes difficult at all levels of education, since the pressures for processing and keeping records for large numbers of students make intensive individual treatment impossible.

In educational structures there is another source of conflict arising from professionalism which revolves around the fact that three different sets of professional norms — those of counselor, teacher, and administrator — apply to a single client: the student. Each of these three professions inevitably sees the student from a somewhat different perspective. The counselor sees the student as one who needs guidance, the teacher as one who needs instruction and evaluation, and the administrator as one who needs to be labeled, categorized, and promoted. Furthermore, counselors, teachers, and administrators are likely to look at each other from different and sometimes divergent perspectives. Counselors can be viewed by teachers as outsiders who do not really know the students; administrators can perceive teachers as subverters of the order and counselors as hopelessly naive idealists; and teachers can see administrators as inefficient bureaucrats who are inhibiting instruction. With high degrees of professionalism these conflicts are more subtle, because most professional norms require courteous behavior toward other professionals. Yet whether subtle or not, professional conflict becomes a serious problem during modernization of education.

politicization

To the extent that governments finance and regulate education some degree of politicization is inevitable. Political intrusion into education is most visible in systems such as China, Russia, and Cuba, where political indoctrination in schools is a part of the curriculum. Yet as we will see in a more detailed analysis of American education, political pressures are easily discerned in even so decentralized an educational system as that in the United States. In fact the trend toward centralization of education throughout the contemporary world signals the increasing control of and influence on education by political processes in a society.

Another visible and often tumultuous source of politicization in modern societies is from students in higher education. Increasingly university students have become political activists, seeking to transform the structure of both higher education and the broader society. Such activism has often led to open and violent conflict between students on the one side and university administrators and police or military forces on the other. Just why this is occurring all over the world is not clear. Part of the answer may lie in the fact that students are increasingly questioning the validity of some of the most cherished beliefs, values, customs, dogmas, and ideologies of the cultural storehouse. These are usually the very cultural components held by the political and economic elite of a society. This means that as students question, they affront and perhaps confront the interests of the major sources of power in a society. However, often students do not question the basic beliefs and values of society's culture but the failure of political processes to realize and implement these values.

This critical attitude toward basic beliefs or a government's inability to realize them can be traced to several forces in modern and developing societies. First, education, especially higher education, expands and liberalizes people's outlook and viewpoint. It makes them more flexible, reflective, and willing to entertain alternatives. This means that socialization in higher education conflicts with the more narrow and parochial family socialization (Selvin and Hagstrom, 1960). The basic values, beliefs, traditions, and ideologies imparted in family socialization are examined more skeptically in the classroom and student subcultures of universities.

Second, students in a modern society such as the United States have been exposed to a comparatively free media system. From early ages children in the modern societies can acquire a world view extending considerably beyond that possible in previous generations. Students thus become cosmopolitan at an earlier age, with the result that they are less likely than previous generations to accept at face value the conventional wisdom of elders or the ideologies and beliefs of the cultural storehouse.

Third, and perhaps most important, students in higher education are segregated and detached from the main institutions of a society. Not only are they segregated but they are also physically concentrated; and coupled with considerable leisure time, communication of ideas can occur more readily than in the general population. These structural conditions, in addition to the liberalizing effect of instruction in the classroom, can result in the formation of student subcultures that are less accepting of the existing values and institutions in a society. For example, in Third World nations, student populations are the most likely to question the relevance of traditions, religious dogmas, and prescientific values for an industrializing but impoverished society. To illustrate further, students in modern industrial and postindustrial societies are, from their detached perspective, the most likely to question the appropriateness of commercial, acquisitive, materialistic, and nationalistic values, practices, and ideologies in an affluent society where human rights, complete social equality, and national and world planning are becoming imperative (Skolnick, 1969:84–85). And students in both types of societies can more easily than those involved in a society's institutions question the responsiveness of the polity to institutional changes in the economy, religion, family, law, and even education. Thus, under conditions of social change from either an agrarian to industrial or industrial to postindustrial economy (and all the other institutional changes associated with these transitions), questioning and protest by students are likely, given their previous socialization experiences and present structural location (Lipset, 1970). However, the purpose of these protests and the attendant ideology should vary, since the structural changes in developed and developing systems are different. In developing nations the rhetoric is likely to be quasi-communist or quasi-socialist, since the key questions revolve around the fundamental redistribution of wealth and power from the ascriptive elite to the emerging masses of workers. But in developed systems the central issues become extending power and wealth to all segments of the society, combating the giant centralized bureaucracies, and increasing (rather than establishing) the effectiveness of political opposition (Skolnick, 1969).

THE AMERICAN EDUCATIONAL SUBSYSTEM

massification of american education

Virtually everyone becomes a student in American society. Ninety-nine percent complete primary school, 75 percent secondary school, and 40 percent start some form of higher education. Less than 3 percent are illiterate. The reasons underlying these occurrences are various and include: (1) Early Protestant sects and denominations in the United States stressed education and literacy to enable people to read the Bible. Often these sects and denominations established schools to indoctrinate the young in their teachings. (2) Political democracy emerged early in the United States and with the extension of suffrage, education became desirable and necessary. (3) Mobility has always been a part of American life. People have been able to move horizontally across the nation and up and down the stratification subsystem. Education provides one of the major keys to the latter. (4) The United States during one period in its history was the immigration center of the world, with the result that masses of immigrants who wanted to become acculturated began attending schools. Such demands for education from the immigrant population forced the rapid extension of public education in the United States. (5) And with industrialization, pressures for a literate and skilled work force led to the expansion of public education. For at least these five reasons, then, massification of education began early and has been an integral part of the American social system.

democratization in american education

Complete democratization of education in the United States has not occurred. Even with almost universal primary and secondary education, not all citizens have access to quality education (Clark, 1962). This was most dramatically demonstrated in the old "separate but equal" schooling in the South, where separate was more typical than equal (Williams, 1970:321). "Separate and unequal" is also an appropriate assessment of education in many other regions of the country, for rural education is usually inferior to urban, and ghetto education always lags behind suburban. The variations in the quality of education in primary and secondary schools is perhaps greater in the United States than in any other modern society. Furthermore, ethnicity, race, and social class often have as much—if not more—to do with who goes on to higher education as does intelligence or ability. This is true in many modern systems, but because of the racial and ethnic heterogeneity of American society, inequities are more pronounced. Because the tests and grading system of American schools favor the white and middle-class students, equality of opportunity extends only to primary and secondary education. Although the trend is toward increasing democratization of higher education, white and middle-class students are overrepresented in these structures.

bureaucratization

As we know, massification forces bureaucratization. School bureaucracies in American education are localized and much smaller than their counterparts in other modern systems (Clark, 1962; Goslin, 1965). Lower public education bureaucracies usually encompass a district which is a territory roughly concomitant to city and county boundaries. These district bureaucracies, which usually include a board of education, supervise activities of specific primary and secondary schools as well as two-year community colleges. These district bureaucracies are connected to a state board of education, although actual control of schools—teachers' salaries, curriculum, facilities, and the majority of financing—is maintained by the district bureaucracy.

In the United States there are also many private primary and secondary schools. Depending upon their size they too become bureaucratized. Some churches maintain a national network of schools and these are coordinated and controlled by a national bureaucracy. Others are only statewide and are regulated by state bureaucracies. And there are many private school structures maintaining only a local school bureaucracy. While bureaucratization tends to occur in all types of school structures, it is not so pronounced as in public schools.

Recently the number of peripheral lower educational structures has increased in the United States. Most of these programs are financed and implemented by the federal government. Typically they are geared toward expanding educational opportunities to disadvantaged segments of the population. These programs have included the Job Corps, Operation Head Start, and various youth opportunities programs. Because they are financed and administered by the federal government to meet the needs of local populations, logistical problems, such as how federal money is to be dispersed to local areas, how is it to be administered, how local programs are to be evaluated by the government, and how local administering agencies are to be chosen or constructed become immense. Resolving these administrative problems arising from the distance between the federal funding agency and the local community has led to considerable bureaucratization. Often such bureaucratization has subverted the goals of these educational programs by creating rigidity in an area where considerable flexibility is required. A recent trend has been toward decentralizing the bureaucracy by allowing more local autonomy in the administration of these peripheral programs.

The bureaucratization of higher education is varied. About one-third of higher education is private (Williams, 1970:332–333). Bureaucratization of private schools is usually school specific, encompassing only one campus location. However, public higher education tends to be statewide, with a central bureaucracy coordinating a series of campus bureaucracies. States vary in how much control the statewide bureaucracy exerts over these campuses (Pierce, 1964).

Thus, bureaucratization of education in the United States is ubiquitous. Its extensiveness varies in terms of how large and how many school structures are involved and in terms of whether or not they are private or public, federal or local. But it is clear that virtually all educational roles, from administrator to student, are organized bureaucratically.

professionalization

The United States is professionalized in almost all institutional spheres. Actors are increasingly being socialized into a set of professional norms which are subsequently reinforced by professional associations. Perhaps more than in any other institution, education is professionalized. Administrators, teachers, and counselors belong to a variety of professional associations. At the lower educational level, the most encompassing of these is the National Educational Association. But more specific associations for administrators, teachers, and counselors are emerging at both the state and national level.

Higher education is even more professionalized than lower education. Each instructor and researcher is likely to belong to an association reflective of a specialty, such as the American Sociological Association, the American Political Science Association, the American Anthropological Association, and a host of similar specialized associations. Counselors have associations either related to psychiatry and social work or to educational testing and vocational counseling. Administrators have similar associations, though they tend to be less pervasive. This may result in part from the fact that administrators must remain oriented more to the local bureaucracy than instructors or counselors, since it is they who must administer its policies. Divided loyalties between a strong professional association and the needs of a local bureaucracy would be difficult to reconcile for administrators.

unionization

This is an incipient trend in the United States and it extends only to teachers—usually in lower education (Havighurst and Neugarten, 1967:502–593). In teacher unionization there is a curious paradox: teachers tend to define union activity as *unprofessional* and yet they increasingly must engage in it to maintain some degree of professionalism in their working conditions. As educated and skilled employees in a difficult and stressful job, teachers at lower educational levels have often been treated unprofessionally: low pay and little voice in those policies determining the conditions of their work. Yet traditional union activities such as walkouts, strikes, boycotts, and picket lines have been viewed as violating professional dignity. But as limited pay, coupled with rigid bureaucratization, has increasingly excluded teachers from control over their own activities, unionism has increased. Professionalism clashes with both bureaucratization and unionism; but in lower education it increasingly clashes more with the former and less with the latter. The result is teacher militancy.

In higher education unionization is low. This probably results from two facts: bureaucratization is less rigid in higher than in lower education; and professional norms are extremely powerful. Only when bureaucratic demands begin to prevent conformity to professional norms is unionization in higher education likely. It is no coincidence that where unionization has occurred, it has been at large state and city universities where bureaucratization tends to be greatest.

decentralization

Decentralization is uniquely American, for every other modern educational system in the world is centralized. This usually takes the form of a federal ministry of education which finances, coordinates, and controls most lower and higher education. But in the United States there is no national educational bureaucracy, national policy-making agency, or national evaluative procedures (Pierce, 1964). However, recently the federal polity in America has become involved in certain marginal areas of both public and parochial lower education. Federal expenditures for education have gone from less than 2 billion dollars in 1955 to nearly 9 billion dollars today. And the Federal Education Act of 1965 provides both parochial and public schools financial support for bus transportation, remedial programs, library facilities, cultural enrichment programs, and textbook loan programs (Williams, 1970:333). Yet even with these changes the federal government still has only a series of loosely connected agencies affecting state and local schools in few systematic ways. The actual coordination, control, and financing of education occurs at the state and local levels. However, this decentralized situation is more true of some educational structures than of others: There is heavy federal control of lower peripheral education, considerably less of higher education, and even less of lower public education.

DECENTRALIZATION AND PERIPHERAL EDUCATION

Federal regulation of peripheral education is extensive, with various federal agencies—Departments of Agriculture, Interior, and Health, Education, and Welfare—administering programs in job training, agricultural extension, youth opportunities, agricultural experiment stations, farm modernization, and the like. Although these programs are increasing they represent only a very small part of education in the United States. Furthermore, many peripheral structures — on-the-job training, secretarial schools, and so on — are completely autonomous structures with no administrative ties to the polity.

DECENTRALIZATION AND HIGHER EDUCATION

Higher educational structures display some degree of centralization. State college and university systems are centralized at the state level. And both private and public university systems have extensive financial — and hence administrative — ties to the federal polity, since many of the research, building, scholarship, and other financial resources required by higher education come from the federal government. Even with this extensive financial input the administrative ties between higher education and the federal government are often not clear or explicit. When a federal agency finances a research project which may include construction of elaborate facilities at a university, it has some influence over how these facilities are used. But it is difficult to tell how much influence, since aside from research reports and financial liaisons administrative ties between the federal polity and university are usually limited. The same is true of fellowship monies, construction loans, grants for computer facilities, library construction, and so on. There is considerable money from federal agencies flowing into higher education (approximately 25 percent of the total higher education budget), but there is no central administrative agency overseeing and coordinating this flow. Rather, specific agencies within various departments — Defense, Agriculture, State, and Health, Education, and Welfare — finance and administer monies for higher education. Just how this is done varies from agency to agency.

State higher education systems are centralized at the state level. A state board of regents or trustees establishes broad policies implemented through a central, statewide administration and the local administration of any campus. These policy-making powers vary in extensiveness from state to state. They can be confined to financial matters or extended to include every phase of administration. Even when the powers of the board of regents or trustees are great, considerable de facto local autonomy exists, because the typically large size of state universities gives local administrators considerable flexibility to juggle, hide, and selectively implement statewide policies.

Thus, unlike most modern societies, higher education in the United States is only partially centralized. Except at the state level there is no clear pattern of centralization. Instead there are administrative liaisons which come, go, and change over time. Compared to other systems it can appear chaotic and perhaps wasteful and inefficient, because the mechanisms for channeling educational structures toward national priorities are indirect. However, what may be considered wasteful and inefficient can also be viewed as flexible, comprehensive, and unconstrained. American higher education probably offers a greater variety of choices and alternatives to students than any other higher educational system in the world. This can probably occur only in a higher educational system not systematically and directly linked to national political agencies.

DECENTRALIZATION AND LOWER EDUCATION

More than any other modern system, lower education in the United States is administered at the local, community level. The federal and state polities frequently provide only a small proportion of financial resources for education. The majority of financing usually comes from the property taxes of community residents. Except in certain areas such as school integration, the federal government makes few policy decisions for lower education. Most decisions are left to the states, which in turn tend to delegate policy decisions to local school districts.

More specifically, lower education displays these structural features. Teachers and students in a classroom are in specific schools. Each local school belongs to a school district and is accountable to the district administration. The district administration is staffed with professional administrators who implement the policies set by the district school board composed of elected members. District administrators are in turn coordinated by the state department of education. Policy for this department is set in various ways, depending upon the state. There can be an elected or appointed state board of education, an elected or appointed state superintendent of schools, or both. The crucial feature of this state administration is that *it is always political*, since officials in key policy-making offices are elected and/or appointed by the dominant political party. The state administration is then loosely connected to the federal polity.

The political nature of the state and district departments of education assures that at all levels of lower education, public pressure greatly affects policy decisions. The most intense public pressure occurs at the community and local school level. Because local school districts rely on community tax monies and community approval of bond issues they must be responsive to public opinion. Such opinion exerts a continuing influence on educational decision making through the elected school board. Even at the school and classroom level public pressure exists, for the neighborhood parent-teachers association (PTA) is always a force to be reckoned with by teachers and administrators. Even families of individual students can apply pressure on the classroom teacher by forcing local school administrators (principal and vice-principal) to look into matters. In Table 6–2 the intensity of such public pressures at different educational levels is outlined.

175

TABLE 6-2

LEVELS OF SCHOOL BUREAUCRACY		TYPES OF PUBLIC PRESSURE
FEDERAL	Federal agencies ↑ (weak)	←---------- (weak)	National opinion as it affects national leaders
STATE	State Board of Education ↓ (strong)	←——————— (moderate)	State opinion as it affects board members and superintendent
DISTRICT	School district administration ↓ (very strong)	←————————— (very strong)	Broad community opinion as it affects board members and superintendent
	Local school administrators ↓ (very strong)	←————————— (strong)	Neighborhood public opinion as it affects school principals
NEIGHBORHOOD	Teachers in the classroom; counselors	←——————— (moderate)	Student's family grievances

The arrows at the top of Table 6–2 reveal only a weak influence on the state board of education by the federal government. About all that is required of states is that free public education be provided. This is insured by various general laws of the legal subsystem (Pierce, 1964). The Constitution of the United States contains no specific references to education but its "general welfare" clause ("We, the people . . . [will] provide for the common defense, *promote the general welfare*, and secure the blessings of liberty to ourselves. . . .") has come to legitimize the federal polity's right to force the states to provide free public education. Under the Fourteenth Amendment public education must be equal for all segments of the population.

Only when states violate these general laws can the federal polity intervene in lower education. The most dramatic case of such intervention is the forced racial desegregation of certain state school systems under the tenets of the Fourteenth Amendment. Aside from this influence the federal polity finances many special-education programs for teacher education, library and classroom construction, lunch programs, and subsidies for federally impacted and controlled areas. However, the array of federal agencies implementing these programs is without overall administration, planning, or coordination (Pierce, 1964:42).

With only these general and weak guidelines education is delegated to the individual states. It becomes their legal responsibility and state constitutions always carry provisions outlining the general profile of lower education. Traditionally the state has delegated much authority in policy matters to local districts. Thus while the school districts are created by the state, they operate at the local community level. However, the state still maintains certain key powers over the local districts (Pierce, 1964:42).

1. States maintain the power to set the general curriculum. Sometimes it is spelled out in detail, but more frequently only a few required courses (usually government and history) are set by the state with the rest becoming the responsibility of the local school board.

2. The state pays for part of education and so it has some control over the local school district's "purse strings." The range of support varies greatly from state to state. The average proportion of financial support is around 35 percent of the local district's total budget.

3. The state usually sets minimum standards for physical facilities, number of student hours in the classroom, school accreditation, and teacher certification.

4. The state also exerts some control over which textbooks are used in local schools. This is usually done by having a list of approved texts from which the school districts may select.

5. States provide for the welfare of local school employees with health and retirement programs.

6. And finally the state frequently has a statewide testing program. Intelligence, vocational, achievement, and other instruments used by counselors are dictated by the state board of education, and administered at specific times each year.

On the surface these state influences appear highly constraining, but in practice the local district board has tremendous autonomy from the state. It can add to most of these state requirements and/or selectively implement directives (often illegally). And of course the local community pays for the majority of the educational facilities in a district. With this local autonomy from the state, pressures on education from the local community, neighborhood, and family increase. What is striking about this pattern is that it is the reverse of the pattern in other modern societies where community forces have little influence on education. Rather, the central polity finances and sets policy for education. Decentralization of American lower education is thus one of its most unique features. The consequences of this fact for the role performance of administrators and teachers are extensive.

Administrators at the local district and school level are trapped in cross pressures from the community and neighborhood, the school board, state administration, teachers, and recently students. The professional school superintendent and his administrative staff are perhaps the most vulnerable. They must reconcile the demands of teachers for more pay, better working conditions, academic freedom, tenure, and smaller classes with those of the community for lower taxes and better education. Administrators must also be responsive to the community pressures and yet protect the teachers from community infringements upon professionalism. And district administrators must constantly reckon with the elected school board, whose views on how schools should be run always differ somewhat from those in the community. In addition to these pressures administrators must meet the general dictates of the state board of education. District administrators in other modern systems are protected from many of these pressures by the high degree of bureaucratic centralization evident in these societies. But in the United States such bureaucratic insulation rarely exists. Even in large school districts with an extensive and centralized administrative bureaucracy, professional administrators and the school board are continually confronted by community pressure groups. In heterogeneous communities these pressures often conflict and place school administrators in the difficult position of having to reconcile opposing demands from different segments of the community.

Like their counterparts at the district level, local school administrators must reconcile diverse and conflicting demands. In perhaps a more immediate, face-to-face manner local school administrators must confront teacher, student, district administrator, and parental pressures. Since local school bureaucratization is rarely extensive, its administrators cannot effectively hide and avoid such cross-pressures.

Teachers in American schools must be diplomatic, for they are extremely vulnerable to parental pressure. Since teachers, especially at the primary level, become parent surrogates for the young, the real parent is rarely a disinterested bystander. Parents always have advice for teachers, especially with respect to their child. Often these parental pressures for special treatment of children conflict with administrative demands for impartial testing and grading as well as for tranquility and movement to the next grade (regardless of whether the child is ready). And these kinds of administrative pressures conflict with the emerging professionalism of teachers. Teachers are to be client (student) oriented, bringing to bear their expertise for each client. Professionalism is further subverted by "parental expertise," where parents know what is right for their child. The subversion of professionalism by administrative and community forces is perhaps one of the reasons unionization has caught on in the United States. Under conditions where professionalism is strong and where it is constantly undermined by outside pressures unionization as a means of achieving professionalism is a likely response. In most modern societies teacher professionalism is protected from community pressures by the centralized bureaucracy. This fact may partially explain the differences in teacher union activity in the United States and other modern societies.

THE AMERICAN EDUCATION HIERARCHY

The American education subsystem is a vast hierarchy of primary and secondary schools, community colleges, technical schools, and state and private universities and colleges. From state to state the profile of this hierarchy differs, depending upon a myriad of circumstances. For example, just how rural or urban, how rich, and how much cultural, ethnic, and racial diversity exists will affect the pattern of education in a state. These and many other circumstances make education in the United States highly diverse. This diversity is amplified by the lack of a national educational program and the consequent control of education by the state and local community. The result of this situation is that school facilities and curricula, teachers' salaries and credentialing, and students' cultural backgrounds vary not only from state to state but from community to community. In fact, it is somewhat of a miracle that education displays a "national character" or consistency. This miracle probably occurs for several reasons: (1) The growing professionalism of school incumbents and their national organizations force upon states and schools certain common standards. (2) Through various national associations where communication of policies, methods, and techniques occurs, some consensus over educational programs is established. (3) The high rate of mobility among Americans generates a common and cosmopolitan outlook about what a good education system is. These mobile parents and students bring pressure for certain common educational facilities and programs.

These and other forces cutting down the diversity in American education allow us to draw a very general and somewhat unified picture of the educational hierarchy in the United States. Primary schools display six grades following a year of kindergarten in which children become accustomed to the school environment without intense demands for academic performance. Primary schools tend to be small, located within delimited residential areas. They are neighborhood schools. Upon completion of primary school, most students go on to a larger junior high school lasting two to three years. These junior high schools mitigate the severity of transition from the small, neighborhood elementary school to the larger, consolidated high school. Junior high schools pull students from several elementary schools and yet maintain some of the neighborhood atmosphere of the elementary school. High schools tend to draw students from several junior high schools and encompass a whole community or large sections of a metropolitan area. They are highly bureaucratized and represent the end of formal education for many students.

At the primary, junior high, and high school levels there are private and public systems existing side by side. Curriculum and standards of these schools are sufficiently similar so that students can move between the private and public systems. The public system is run by the state and community government while the private schools are run by a variety of organizations, such as churches, businesses, and foundations. Among states the lower educational system of primary, junior high, and high schools is somewhat similar, with movement from school to school within or between states less problematic than might be expected in light of the decentralized profile of American education.

At the end of high school a major status transition occurs. Students either go out into the work force or on to higher educational structures. However, this transition is being increasingly delayed through the proliferation of community and junior college structures. These junior colleges are usually administratively tied to a local school district and provide a general liberal arts and vocational program for high school graduates. These colleges can be either terminal or used as a transition to more extensive university and college structures.

Overlapping with community colleges are universities, colleges, and technical-vocational schools. Vocational schools tend to be a part of the peripheral educational system and hence vary considerably in size, curriculum, and extensiveness. This is also true with respect to college and university structures, where small private and public liberal arts colleges, technical and scientific universities, and large colleges and multiversities all comprise what is called higher education. Increasingly higher education is becoming dominated by the large private university and the even larger state college and university system. Small liberal arts colleges and highly prestigious scientific schools still persist but the state, in conjunction with the federal government, is assuming much of the higher education burden. Within higher education there are two major divisions: undergraduate and graduate schools. Most students leave for the work force after four years of undergraduate education, but many go on to graduate school to acquire special expertise.

passing through the american educational hierarchy

It is through this state and private hierarchy of primary schools, junior highs, high schools, community colleges, and universities that students pass. This passage is rarely smooth and without disturbance. Considerable student alienation and rebellion occurs from schools at all levels in the hierarchy. And it appears to be increasing. Passage is not completely democratic, for social class, race, and ethnicity all affect how far up the hierarchy students will go. To understand why this is so it is necessary to outline what happens to students who move through various school structures. Some of the important features of this passage are explored below.

THE CLASSROOM: SURVIVAL OF THE FITTEST

Teachers and students come together in the classroom and it is here that education is to take place. At the primary level, there is usually only one classroom for a student, but in secondary and higher education students move from classroom to classroom during the course of the day. There are two unique features of the American classroom: teacher-student relations tend to be more informal than in other modern societies; and individual achievement and competition in the classroom are much more intense than in other systems. Overall it appears that the American classroom is more hostile than in other systems because increases in informality are more than compensated for by the increased emphasis on *individual* achievement. In some systems, such as the Soviet, there is formality and competitiveness but emphasis is on *group* competition. In American systems, upon entering the first grade the apprehensive and nervous neophyte learns quickly that teachers are usually "nice guys" (or gals, as is more often the case) and that they expect performance and competitiveness. And so it will be all the way up the educational hierarchy. Those who do well will be praised and paraded while those who do poorly will become innocuous and perhaps alienated. By operating under the "star" system the American classroom makes life difficult for the majority of students who cannot or do not excel. As a means of protection from the rigors of competition, antiacademic student norms emerge and persist at all levels of the American educational hierarchy. At the primary level these norms emphasize peer solidarity in the face of teacher demands. This usually results in student prankishness and resistance to certain academic activities. At the secondary level—especially high school—norms of fun become dominant. Traditionally these have emphasized the importance of personal appearance, dress, looks, good reputation, athletics, parties, and a host of other nonacademic traits. The student role is one of disinterested involvement in class and having fun outside class (and often within). It is not clear why these norms dominate the American high school but they probably emerge as protection from the competitiveness of the American classroom. A second reaction of students to the competitive classroom is rebellion and alienation. These students have no involvement in the classroom, often disrupt school activities, and leave school as soon as (often before) the law will allow. Third there is the scholastic student, who can be successful in classroom competition. These students work hard, perform well in class, and get the best grades. But they are far outnumbered by the fun subculture of looks, dates, dances, sports, and drugs (Coleman, 1961). Fourth, cutting across all these student subcultures is a "drug culture," which has emerged in recent years. Just what effect this new subculture will have on American education is as yet unclear. But the emergence of this culture can perhaps be seen as a reaction against the competitiveness of the American classroom.

In higher education individual competition is stressed within a larger and more impersonal classroom situation. The traditional response to such a situation has been an emphasis on collegiate student norms, which are basically the college counterpart of high school fun norms. Another traditional response has been vocationalism, where students accept the college classroom as a necessary evil on the way to employment in the work force. Academic norms stressing intellectual involvement in the classroom have been the least prevalent of all, primarily because large, competitive classrooms are not conducive to such involvement. Over the last decade activist norms have come to guide a significant number of students. To a great extent these norms have emerged in response to many structural conditions lying outside higher education. Yet it is clear that higher education is often the target of student activism. Part of the reason for this probably resides in the aggravating effect of the college classroom on students concerned with larger sociopolitical issues. The competitiveness, size, impersonality, and perceived "irrelevance" of the classroom and broader university structure often leads students to seek change in the "corrupt" university environment.

Thus passage through the classroom in the American educational hierarchy generates a series of student responses. These responses become codified into norms and subcultures. Much of the turmoil, conflict, and confusion of American education derives from the tremendous competitive burden placed upon the young student. And this burden continues to increase and becomes coupled with increases in formality and impersonality as students move up to higher levels in the system. Most students survive but what appears to be a growing number are becoming disaffected from the rigors of the American classroom.

What kind of student survives in the classroom year after year? How is entrance into higher education decided? Who goes into vocational programs? Who drops out? Answers to these questions reveal the nature of the selection and allocation processes built into the American educational hierarchy.

In any modern society requiring expertise in most statuses education becomes the key to success. Just how far a student goes in the educational hierarchy is a reflection of noneducational influences as they affect individual performance in the classroom. The family, social class, and racial or ethnic origins of a student have a profound impact on classroom survival. This fact can be illustrated in a number of ways. For example, intelligence as measured by IQ tests is affected by many social forces having little relationship to innate ability (Rosenthal and Jacobson, 1968). Studies clearly reveal that students from lower classes and certain minority groups or types of families are discriminated against by IQ tests, for these tests are not value- or bias-free. Rather the IQ test reflects the biases of its middle-class constructors (university researchers). First, the test is written, which favors children from literate, middle-class homes. Second, it is a test requiring *performance*. Middle-class students are more accustomed to performing under time pressures than lower-class children. The whole concept of test taking assumes a kind of competitive spirit much more prevalent in middle-class children (Rosen, 1956). And third, the content of the actual test questions usually portrays a middle-class world. This can be illustrated with a typical question from an IQ test (Havighurst and Neugarten, 1967:78–79):

> A symphony is to a composer as a book is to what?
> ( ) paper ( ) sculptor ( ) author ( ) musician ( ) man

Middle-class children are more capable of answering such a question, for parents are more likely to have talked about symphonies, composers, books, and authors than working-class parents.

Students are given IQ tests at an early age in the American system — usually in the first or second grade. These tests are administered by counselors and used by teachers as a guide for teaching. The fact that teachers now have an "objective" measure of child's "innate ability" has profound consequences for what goes on in the classroom. Students become labeled by teachers as smart or stupid or average; and even by well-meaning teachers, these categories of students are treated differently. In both obvious and subtle ways students derive a message from the teacher about their ability. And these test scores follow the student from grade to grade. After years of such

183

labeling a student probably accepts his teacher's definition of ability and begins to adjust his or her life goals and aspirations in terms of such definitions (Rosenthal and Jacobson, 1968).

There are other noneducational factors affecting classroom performance. American schoolteachers tend to be middle class, with values, beliefs, and expectations typical of this class. When these teachers encounter poorly dressed lower-class students with an ethnic accent they are probably repulsed or at least shocked. If these lower-class students sit in the classroom side by side with comparatively well-spoken and well-dressed middle-class students, the teacher's social-class bias will favor — perhaps in very subtle but still powerful ways — the middle-class student who is more familiar and responsive. Furthermore the home environment of middle-class children supports school activities more than that of lower-class students. Middle-class parents read more, are more articulate, and encourage achievement and success more than lower-class parents. This means that the compatibility of school and home is greater for middle-class than lower-class students.

These and other kinds of influences work against high performance in the classroom for many students. These factors also make inevitable low scores on basic achievement and IQ tests administered by counselors. Yet these tests, coupled with these students' classroom grades, follow them up the educational hierarchy in a file maintained by counselors. But none of these indicators in the file necessarily reveals a student's true innate ability, especially those from the lower classes. Nevertheless, by secondary school, counselors begin to utilize the contents of each student's file to advise and track students into various programs — vocational, remedial, and college preparation (Cicourel and Kitsuse, 1963). With this channeling the life station of a student after secondary school is greatly determined. It is in this way that the educational hierarchy has social placement consequences for the broader society. Whether or not such channeling is "democratic" is difficult to determine precisely, although it appears that social placement in American schools reinforces as much as disintegrates social-class boundaries.

American education has a unique feature: "the second chance" (Clark, 1960). Counseling decisions are not final; students can change their curriculum; and even IQ and achievement tests are not completely determinant. Nor are poor grades in high school an insurmountable hurdle to higher education. Unlike other modern systems, there are few set policies about how students should be allocated to higher education on the basis of grades and tests. This partly results from the lack of a centralized and national educational bureaucracy which typically makes such policy decisions in other societies. Furthermore specific higher education structures have vastly different admissions criteria—some high, some low, and many in-between. This means that a student can become incumbent in some higher educational structure—if he has the money. Here again there is a built-in bias against the lower-class student. But recently, to correct for such financial difficulties, the community or junior college has become a prominent structure in the American hierarchy of education. In these public structures a student with a marginal academic record can acquire the first two years of a college education at a cost not much greater than that for high school. If the student performs well in the junior college he can move on to a full four-year college or university—assuming the financial difficulties can be overcome. Yet the same social forces operating against the lower-class student at the secondary level probably operate against him at the junior college level. The result is that lower-class drop-out rates are high; and even if the lower-class student completes two years, transferring to a four-year college may be difficult for both academic and financial reasons. But there is another, perhaps unintended, consequence of the junior college: failure to succeed becomes individualized. For the intelligent student who for a myriad of social reasons does not succeed in the junior college, failure becomes *personalized*. "I had the chance, but I blew it" might be a common sentiment. Junior colleges can "cool out" lower-class "marks" by making them individualize their failure rather than attribute it to inequities *built into* the educational hierarchy or to the wider stratification subsystem in American society.

In sum, it can be concluded that the middle-class student is the most educationally fit and most likely to survive the educational process. The competition in the American classroom all along the educational hierarchy is not so much a process of "natural selection" as "social-class selection." This means that American education is not fully democratic. It does not provide equal opportunity to do well. But these facts should not obscure this comparison: A far greater proportion of American students reach higher educational structures than in any other modern system. The screening, selecting, allocating, and sorting of students occurring in American education is not so final or definite as in many other systems where national examinations and grades channel and place students into various educational programs at the beginning of secondary school. American education is more flexible in channeling and hence is structured in a way allowing for a second chance.

the student revolt in the american educational hierarchy

Campus unrest has become widespread and has extended down to secondary schools. Since the middle 1960s demonstrations, protests, sit-ins, and physical violence have occurred on many college campuses. Not all or even most campuses have been subjected to violence, yet it is significant that unrest has tended to occur on "elite" campuses—both state and private—of the American educational hierarchy. Just why unrest has emerged in the last few years cannot be known for sure. In this section we will attempt to outline some of the contributing factors (Skolnick, 1969:79–124).

The current student revolution is incompatible with the conception of the university as a free forum of inquiry where academic issues are pondered with a certain degree of civility. Often the university is considered a community, "sharing common values and culture and standing apart from both internal political conflict and external political influence. . . ." (Skolnick, 1969:112). This conception of the university has long dominated American ideals of what a university should be. As we will see in the next chapter, universities have never been completely shielded by such an ivory tower. Economic, political, legal, and religious institutions have greatly influenced what goes on. In the United States most universities were originally affiliated with religious denominations—and many still are. With the Morrill Act of 1862, the land-grant college emerged in response to federal demands for higher education. Today giant corporations (Ridgeway, 1968), the Departments of State, Defense, and Health, Education, and Welfare, and numerous foundations influence research and teaching in the university. And recently in state higher educational systems the public and their elected officials have begun to exert direct control over not only financial but other administrative policies. In light of these facts it is somewhat remarkable, especially compared to other societies, that such a high degree of academic insulation and freedom has traditionally existed in American higher education. However, the complete ivory tower university never really existed. The university—especially today—is not a community sharing common values and interests. The perspective, interests, and values of university trustees differ greatly from those of faculty and students. Also, administrators and faculty are continually in conflict in the modern university. Faculty have become cosmopolitan, looking toward their profession rather than the university administration. This means that administrators concerned with the local organization and its efficiency now must confront faculty who are oriented to national and international professions—not to the local bureaucracy. The modern university is thus heterogeneous, rife with conflicts of interests, and constantly influenced by its institutional environment.

A new kind of student is coming into this mixture, which has made periodic explosions and disruptions perhaps inevitable. As outlined earlier, American lower education is massified with students from all social classes, ethnic, and racial backgrounds. Even though the majority of students from lower classes and certain ethnic and racial groups do not go on to higher education, some are able to overcome discriminatory practices and financial problems. Furthermore, as higher education attempts to democratize, many minority and lower-class students are admitted under special programs even though they do not meet entrance requirements. The values, perspectives, ideologies, and interests of these students differ greatly from those of the traditional white, middle-class student. Coming from poor, urban ghetto, and culturally divergent environments, these new students are unlikely to accept or understand the existing structure or ivory tower conception of the American university. Because they do not accept this conception they are likely to attempt to change the university in a direction compatible with their interests —eliminating certain injustices within the broader society. Such pursuits inevitably come into conflict with all those attempting to implement the noninvolvement of the university in partisan social affairs. Furthermore, white, middle-class students also differ from their counterparts of previous decades. Raised in front of the television set, where very early they saw adult dissensus and where they became aware of a myriad of social problems and ills, these cosmopolitan students are likely to suspect the ivory tower image of the university. Having visualized racial injustice and seen war on television, many students enter the university concerned with reform of society as a whole and in particular the "irrelevant" (as they see it) relation of the university to various society-wide problems. Furthermore, these students are also particularly aware of the impact of business, the military, and government on the university. Often they begin to perceive the "hypocrisy" of the administrative "foot-dragging" on social-problem issues in the name of the ivory tower image, while business, the military, and government encroach upon university research and funding. And the hypocrisy becomes the focal point of conflict between the administration attempting to maintain lucrative and often financially necessary ties to the outside and the students attempting to implement the ivory tower image, or more likely, to involve the university in social transformation programs. As the university administration resists these attempts, frequently in repressive ways, radical students can often enlist the support of moderates in both the faculty and student body. To the extent this occurs the now typical confrontation between the university administration and students (and a few faculty) occurs. The level of violence in such confrontation varies with the rigidity of the administration and the degree of radicalization of students. Usually, when confronted with large numbers of moderate students who have been drawn into the confrontation, the administration is less rigid. The smaller the number of students and the more rigid the administration, the more likely is violence. But frequently, with strong repressive violence by the administration, moderate students and faculty begin to support radicals, thus forcing the administration to be flexible. Yet one of the difficult and persisting problems facing college administrators is when and how to be either rigid or flexible. Both permissiveness and rigidity can encourage further violent dissent. As activism and protest increasingly become a life style or persistent subculture within the university community, these problems facing administrators revolving around how to react will increase. Because no effective formula for administrators to follow appears likely to emerge (outside of total repression) student protest and violence will persist well into the 1970s.

One of the consequences of student political activity has been for campus unrest to become a society-wide political issue. Increasingly this fact has resulted in direct federal and state intrusion into campus affairs by federal agencies of social control, such as the FBI and National Guard. Frequently local campus administrators are not consulted in such intrusions, with the result that confrontations can no longer be viewed as administration-student conflicts. With such direct political intrusion into American campuses the ivory tower conception of the university becomes even more remote—as either an ideal worth striving for or as an accomplished fact.

SUMMARY

Over the last 100 years, and more recently in some societies, education has emerged as a conspicuous social institution. In this chapter we have attempted to outline some of the structural features, societal consequences, and trends in this rapidly expanding institution.

First we delineated some of the consequences of education for the society in which it is an institution. These included: cultural preservation and storage; cultural dissemination and retrieval; socialization; social placement; cultural expansion; and social transformation. We then briefly examined the structure of education in primitive societies of the past and in parts of the contemporary world. Here we noted that the consequences of education in these societies were limited to cultural preservation and limited degrees of cultural dissemination. We next turned to a brief portrayal of how education originally expanded in historic societies of the past. In these societies educational development was slow and sporadic, although its consequences were expanded beyond those for primitive societies to include socialization and social placement. Turning to the contemporary Third World, we emphasized that educational development is often rapid since it becomes a major political goal in these modernizing societies. Under these conditions the social transformation consequences of education are prominent as the Third World attempts to alter radically its traditional profile. Finally, we examined education in modern industrial and postindustrial societies where education as a highly complex structure has far-reaching consequences for cultural preservation, dissemination, and expansion, as well as for socialization, social placement, and social transformation.

We next examined some of the ubiquitous trends accompanying educational development. These included: massification and democratization; bureaucratization; centralization; professionalism; and politicization. We can hypothesize that educational development in the long run and in all types of societies will evidence these trends.

Finally we offered a brief portrayal of the American educational subsystem. Like any modern system, American education reflected all the major trends in educational development except high degrees of centralization. However, in the long run it appears that the federal government may increase its control and regulation of American education. To the extent this occurs, education in the United States will lose its uniquely decentralized profile.

the
institutional
environment
of
EDUCATION   7

Educational development from a recessive to dominant institution is in many ways a response to change in other institutions. Alterations of the economy, polity, law, religion, and kinship greatly circumscribe the form of education in a society. In turn changes in education feed back and influence developments in these other institutions, as has been revealed with respect to the economy and kinship. Later we will examine the consequences of education for the polity, law, and religion. In this chapter attention will be drawn to some of the *one-way* lines of influence which flow from the institutions surrounding education. While the structure of education in a society is always a partial reflection of unique historical and contemporary forces, we will focus on those institutional influences on education that appear to be *common* to all societies as they undergo modernization.

ECONOMY AND EDUCATION

Frequently educational and economic development are seen as occurring together, with changes in the economy fostering changes in education and vice versa. However, such a correlation between economic and educational development cannot firmly establish a causal relationship nor can it sort out the details of a causal relationship should one exist, because unraveling causal relations among institutions poses one of the most difficult analytical problems facing sociologists. Our analysis must therefore be couched in very general terms: to the extent that the economy has an impact on education, it does so in those areas outlined in this section.

The economy of a society is dependent upon a constant influx of manpower and technology. Without these basic economic elements, economic subsistence in a society would be impossible. This fact leads us to speculate that the relationship between the economy and education may revolve around economic pressures for manpower and technology and the capacity of education to supply these necessary economic elements. While we cannot view economic pressures for these basic elements as the sole cause of educational development we can hypothesize that the more developed an economy, the more direct the pressure from the economy on education for skilled manpower and technology.

In hunting and gathering economies low levels of technology and human energy are involved in gathering, producing, distributing, and servicing. The economy depends upon a steady flow of strong bodies able to provide the energy necessary to perform basic economic tasks. Technology remains minimal. In this kind of situation considerable structural overlap between the economy and kinship is inevitable, since economic labor with only the limited skills that low technology will allow is most efficiently generated and organized within the family. Education is thus a recessive institution in the absence of strong economic pressures for skilled labor and technology.

In agrarian economies animal power begins to supplement human labor as a basic source of energy. Furthermore, new kinds of technology or knowledge about how to manipulate the environment emerge, including domesticating and herding animals, as well as seeding, planting, and harvesting crops. With a more stable relationship to the environment and the capacity to produce more commodities and goods evident in agrarian societies, distributive and service roles emerge to handle the increased volume of production ushered in with these new sources of energy and more advanced technology. Vendors, shopkeepers, craftsmen, and other commercial statuses now become an integral part of the economy, with the result that skills such as reading, writing, and accounting become increasingly required of workers. While the vast majority of workers remain illiterate and acquire no training outside kinship, economic pressures for literacy force some to receive training in schools. The emergent distributive and servicing roles of an agrarian economy can thus promote the expansion of primary and secondary schools. Furthermore, since formal education in agrarian societies is often dominated by the church, these economic pressures can also initiate the process of educational secularization.

With industrialization the economic pressures for formal education increase dramatically. Workers in the emerging factory system increasingly must be literate in order to be able to read plans and directions. Also, as the factory system expands, workers need specialized trade skills and a whole host of personality attributes such as the interpersonal styles of specificity and neutrality, which are more efficiently acquired in formal education structures. Furthermore, since work is now performed in factories, working adults are away from home with the result that their children can no longer learn work skills by parental tutelage (Clark, 1962). In this situation children often leave the home and master in schools those minimal work skills necessary for their participation in the economy. With further expansion of the factory system and the resulting increase in economic production, administrative, distributive, and service roles become more prominent (see Chapter 2). Frequently these are organized bureaucratically. Many involve professional training. And most of these new positions require not only literacy but also specialized and often high-level expertise in a wide variety of areas. The emergence of these statuses is both dependent upon and perhaps an impetus to the expansion of higher educational structures, for only in undergraduate, graduate, and professional schools can the expertise needed to fill these positions be acquired.

Economic conditions requiring expertise not only stimulate the expansion of higher education during industrialization, they also result in its secularization when dominated by religious interests. Furthermore the elitist and aristocratic profile of traditional education becomes altered toward more pragmatic and vocational concerns. However, rarely is such secularization nonproblematic. For example, the emergence of vocationally oriented universities during the industrialization of Europe and the United States was not automatic, for professional and vocational training was included in the curriculum only as a last resort. The University of Berlin in the nineteenth century was foremost a scholarly structure, with professional and "official classes" only a secondary concern. The modern British university as a professional school began with the foundation of the University of London (Halsey, 1967) but professional training was still largely a twentieth-century occurrence. And even to this day the nonvocational and elitist Cambridge and Oxford dominate the British higher education system. In the United States the Morrill Act creating land-grant colleges failed to integrate completely education with the economy. Even today at the undergraduate level professional and vocational training is still resisted in the name of a liberal arts education. More technical training has been added to the curriculum not by revision of the undergraduate curricula but by the extension of formal education into graduate school (Halsey, 1967). Societies currently undergoing industrialization usually fare somewhat better in this process, since there is less likely to be a long genteel or religious tradition dominating higher education.

Aside from these manpower requirements, the technological demands of industrializing economies can also stimulate the expansion of higher education. Industrialization relies on the constant infusion of technology; societies that are to keep pace with this demand often expand research and development facilities in higher education. For example, the graduate lab assistant, researcher, researcher-teacher, and researcher-consultant have become prevalent roles in higher education as the technological requisites of an industrializing economy have become built into the curriculum and research programs of colleges and universities.

All the pressures on education in industrial economies are intensified as the economy moves toward a postindustrial stage of development, because as machines displace labor from the factory system, requirements for skill and expertise escalate. Since machines can perform unskilled jobs, but not most highly skilled jobs as yet, the reliance of the economy on brainpower increases, resulting in the expansion of higher education to create the necessary brainpower (Drucker, 1959). Since brainpower is not always readily available, educational structures often open their doors to the masses in an attempt to meet the brainpower needs of the economy.[1] Just as the desire for a literate labor force during industrialization massifies lower education, the requirements for brainpower can massify higher education at the postindustrial stage. As higher education becomes perceived as necessary for participation in the economy, the whole educational system democratizes, because increasingly the disadvantaged have access to what has been (and to a great extent still is) the privilege of the advantaged.[2]

The technological requirements of a postindustrial economy are immense, but not just for knowledge about machines. Increasingly "human relations" technology is becoming necessary because the economic problems of a postindustrial economy are as much interpersonal as mechanical. Such interpersonal technology revolves around questions such as how employees are to be made happy, satisfied, and how large numbers of skilled workers are to be coordinated efficiently. Coupled with the ever-increasing demand for mechanical technology, these demands for interpersonal technology can promote further expansion of higher education. Aside from scientific and engineering structures, social science and business administration structures begin to proliferate as pressures from the economy for social science research escalate.

We can now visualize some of the economic forces involved in educational development. The economy is not the only institution influencing this process, however. As we will outline in later sections, education can initially evolve during early stages not so much in response to economic pressures, but in response to religious and political pressures. But with industrialization the economy begins to exert an increasingly profound influence on education, especially higher education. This is clearly evident in educational systems such as the Russian, where higher education is geared closely to the economy. Economic manpower and technological demands greatly influence the structure and curriculum of Russian higher education

---

[1] Coupled with such massification, there frequently is pressure to find talent early, sort it out from the not-so-talented, and render it special training (Clark, 1962). This trend points to the importance of counselors as gatekeepers in the educational process.
[2] Once higher education is perceived as necessary to incumbency in a modern economy an "educational ethic" appears to emerge in postindustrial societies. This ethic stresses the importance of higher education per se regardless of whether or not it will lead to better employment. In fact, modern societies can overeducate their populations to such an extent that the economy cannot absorb all graduates.

(DeWitt, 1961). In fact over 55 percent of all graduates are science and engineering students. As the Russian economy begins to approximate a postindustrial profile the increasing demands for interpersonal technology may lower that percentage (Halsey, 1967:411). Although we often tend to view the American higher educational system as an ivory tower that is insulated from the institutional environment, economic interests have long influenced what goes on: The trustees of American universities are likely to be business leaders; the university typically has extensive research contracts with industry; the major state and private universities are incorporated and own stock in major industrial organizations; university administrators frequently sit on the boards of directors of major economic organizations; large endowments for universities come from business leaders and philanthropic foundations of major corporations; and so on (Ridgeway, 1968). Much of this influence is invisible and subtle but nonetheless powerful. And much of such influence may be inevitable in light of the fact that business corporations in the economy have a vested interest in what occurs in higher education. Given the manpower and technological requirements of a modern economy, it is not surprising that the economy and higher education have become intimately interconnected in American society.

POLITY AND EDUCATION

Both historically and in the contemporary world educational and political development are correlated, although this correlation does not necessarily reveal a causal relationship. While many other forces influence educational development the polity by virtue of its hold on society-wide power and decision-making prerogatives has always exerted some control over educational processes in a society. Much educational development of the past and currently in the present is therefore a response to political decisions, policies, and imperatives.

In most traditional societies of the past (and in a few today), kinship and polity were fused. In these systems decision making occurred primarily in accordance with descent and authority norms. Yet over time in these historical societies certain kinship groups began to appropriate territory, with the result that differences in power between the kin groups in a society began to emerge. As the control of territories and the use of power became consolidated by only some kin groups, an emerging polity, which was to some extent distinguishable from kinship, became evident. Yet the separation was not complete, for political leaders were also kin leaders (in accordance with descent rules) of powerful kinship groupings. For these developing polities a whole series of administrative problems began to emerge as they expanded their territory: territory must be governed; lines of authority for carrying out the leaders' orders must be established; and a military system for conquering more territory and maintaining order must be administered. These kinds of administrative problems often resulted in bureaucratization but not in the form typical of modern societies, for recruitment to and promotion in the state bureaucracy were based as much on kinship criteria as on administrative expertise. Yet skill in writing, accounting, and other tasks was increasingly required as administrative problems intensified. In the long run this fact forced the polity to establish formal educational structures for kinsmen who would occupy crucial administrative posts. Such formal education was initially only a pupil-tutor relationship but it marked the beginnings of a secular educational subsystem. Later, as more kinsmen became literate, education expanded, perhaps to a classroom in a separate building called a school. As the polity continued to expand, ascriptive forms of recruitment into the governmental bureaucracy became inadequate, because the pool of available elite kinsmen who could perform the increasing number of administrative tasks became inadequate. Such a situation often required that actors from less elite kin groups had to be formally trained and inserted into at least the lower levels of the governmental bureaucracy (Parsons, 1955). This training of nonelites inevitably forced the expansion of lower education to accommodate these new students. This occurrence also marked the crude beginning of educational massification, although the vast majority of societal members were still trained within kinship structures in these historical societies.

These political pressures also had the consequence of secularizing education in traditional societies. The skills taught were for the administration of mundane rather than sacred tasks. And these skills were being imparted to an ever-increasing number of students —thus forcing educational development. In a political system where nonelites acquired skills in lower educational structures for administrative positions, elite students usually went on to higher education where they acquired a more comprehensive education in art, literature, music, religion, and other aspects of an aristocratic education. These elites in turn became the political leaders in the polity. It is probably out of this kind of tradition that the ivory tower conception of the university first emerged in Europe and later in the United States. Relatively undaunted by economic pressures, higher education was a mixture of broad liberal arts training for future political and religious elites.

Obviously the historical facts for any particular society of the past will deviate from the account of educational and political development offered in the above description. Yet in general the increasing administrative burden of a developing polity can be viewed as a major stimulus to the expansion and secularization of education. In many traditional systems in feudal Europe religious elites performed many of the administrative tasks of the state bureaucracy; but in the long run, domination of the secular state bureaucracy by religious practitioners proved impractical as the interests of the state and church began to come into conflict. A similar process of secularization of the polity and education appears to have occurred in other historical societies as the administrative burden of the polity increased.

With industrialization of the Old World or of the contemporary Third World, political pressures, in conjunction with economic realities, force rapid expansion and secularization of education. In European societies, and to a lesser extent in the United States, changes in education were resisted because of its elitist profile. However, in developing Third World nations in Africa, Latin America, and Asia the breakdown of elitist education has been more rapid, although far from complete. The polities of most Third World societies have as their principal goal rapid economic development, for within a comparatively few years these systems are attempting to move from an agrarian to industrial basis of economic organization. To do this rapidly political elites are aware of the pivotal function of education in supplying manpower and technology for the developing economy. Therefore political as well as economic imperatives force the rapid development of secular and mass education in these systems. However, we should recognize that political elites promote education for many noneconomic reasons: (1) Education has a certain prestige value and this is desirable in and of itself — regardless of its relationship to industrialization. (2) Providing education is a means of placating the restless urban masses of Third World nations. Extension of education becomes evidence that progress and the better life are ahead. (3) Education is also an effective political socialization structure where the political elite can indoctrinate the masses into acceptance of policies and ideologies. Since elites in developing countries often have difficulty in maintaining legitimacy, state-controlled education becomes a major tool of political survival. Thus once the importance of education for achieving various political goals such as economic development becomes recognized, it increasingly becomes a central concern of the polity. This fact helps account for the worldwide trend toward centralization of education, since centralization enables the political subsystem to control directly what goes on in schools. Such control allows for matching educational curricula, programs, and structures to major political goals and policies. The necessity for centralization is intensified in societies with limited resources, for they cannot afford to spend money on educational programs not directly related to political goals.

Centralization of education therefore occurs as a result of political pressures. With this conclusion we might pause and ask why American education has remained comparatively decentralized. One reason is that until very recently political demands have not been as significant in educational development as they are in Third World societies. The American political subsystem has remained comparatively stable and legitimate, with the result that it has been unnecessary to manipulate extensively educational socialization. More fundamental is the fact that lower and higher education initially emerged more in response to religious than either political or economic pressures. The sect and denominational school and college were evident long before state—to say nothing of federal—involvement in education occurred. One consequence of this is that mass lower education existed when the United States was still a predominately agrarian society. These historical circumstances run counter to either the European or Third World pattern, where mass education emerged with industrialism. Thus because the United States had a large and literate labor pool, extensive federal intervention in education was not necessary when industrialization did occur in the nineteenth century. Another consequence of a prematurely literate population was that it allowed for a viable political democracy at an agrarian and early industrial stage of development. As we will see in Chapters 10 and 11, political democratization typically does not occur—especially in the Third World—until advanced industrialism or postindustrialism (Parsons, 1955, 1964; Buck and Jacobson, 1968). Democracy requires literacy in order to be effective; and perhaps because of the relatively high level of literacy in the American population, the political democracy established after the American Revolution persisted. The significance of the American situation is that the polity's reliance on the population's literacy did not result in direct federal implementation of education. This was unnecessary and so education remained decentralized. But since the Constitution stated the need to separate church and state, gradually state schools began to replace religious schools. States were allowed to do this without federal intervention. These historical facts help account for the peculiarly decentralized profile of American education.

However, we should not lose sight of the fact that the American federal polity controls and regulates much of what goes on in education. Many local school districts are coming to rely heavily on federal funds, and by the polity's threatening to withdraw funds, control over local school boards can be exercised. This is well illustrated in the South over desegregation in certain states. Another source of federal involvement in American lower education concerns a host of special programs providing disadvantaged minorities with educational opportunity. These programs require federally financed special training for culturally disadvantaged students in order to increase their chances of performing well in the highly competitive educational hierarchy. Such programs are in line with the political goals of equal opportunity and democracy and they tend to be typical of many modern societies. In fact highly centralized educational systems tend to finance and administer such programs in a more systematic way than in the United States, since in this country programs are funded through a variety of federal agencies without any overall direction and coordination.

Perhaps more systematic and certainly more comprehensive is federal involvement in American higher education. As we know from the previous chapter, the federal polity finances about one-third of higher education. Such financing is selective and is increasingly revolving around types of research carried out in major universities. Research funds often come from the major federal funding agencies, such as the Agency for International Development, the National Science Foundation, the National Institute of Mental Health, as well as the Departments of Agriculture, Interior, State, Defense, and Health, Education, and Welfare. Thus the federal polity can exercise control over what kinds of research occur in higher education. By financing those projects or issuing research contracts considered by various federal agencies to be important, regulation occurs. Frequently what is considered important is often what is in line with major system goals, not with pure science. Because these research funds are not coordinated by any single agency or ministry of education, it is hard to know how extensive this control is. But control does appear to be extensive, indicating that even in a comparatively de-centralized educational system such as that in the United States the polity greatly circumscribes cultural expansion and innovation. While in more centralized educational systems control is more direct and encompassing, the less direct and visible control over education exercised by the American polity should not be under-emphasized.

In sum we can say that educational evolution is greatly affected by political development. This has been true historically and to the present day. Furthermore, even in highly modern societies such as the United States where national political influence on education has traditionally been low, the trend appears to be toward increasing control in areas considered crucial for achieving national goals and policies.

RELIGION AND EDUCATION

In traditional societies of the past and in primitive societies of the contemporary world education is intimately fused with religious life.

Religion—or the concern for the sacred, cosmos, and unknown—pervades virtually every aspect of societal functioning. Religious traditions and beliefs are the most important components of the cultural storehouse; and it appears that early in societal evolution the roles of shaman and priest emerged and had the consequence of preserving these sacred components. Since early human societies did not have a written language in their cultural inventory an extensive oral tradition became the means by which these entrusted priests preserved religious dogmas and rituals. These priests passed on their knowledge to students who were usually selected on the basis of kinship criteria. Analytically this religious tutelage can be considered formal education for priest-teachers systematically impart knowledge to a body of students. And it is probably in this context that the institution of education first evolved in human societies (Parsons, 1955).

With the development of a written language in more advanced historical societies, two things occurred: (1) Religions could become codified; and with codification, dogma became more complex and extensive. (2) Education of a new generation of priests now involved the imparting of literacy as well as the expanded religious belief systems. Under these conditions educational structures became more formal and extensive. Education in societies at this stage of development were thus elitist, training only the religious leaders. Later as political pressures for secular training increased (see above), education began to lose some of its elitist profile while becoming more secularized.

In almost all agrarian societies of the past and today in the Third World, education arrives at this juncture: dominated by religion with state pressures for massification and secularization. But often in the twentieth-century agrarian societies of the Third World, church education is already partially massified and reaches nonelite peasants in an attempt to proselytize. Missionary schools are thus common in Third World nations; but even under these conditions, education still reaches only a minority of the members of a society. Furthermore only primary and perhaps secondary schools are at all prevalent, for higher education is unnecessary for religious proselytizing in these societies. It is only under political and economic pressures that education massifies and begins to involve both extensive higher and lower education. When this occurs schools begin to secularize and become detached from their religious origins. Often this is facilitated when a developing system has had a history of colonialism where the colonial powers initiated secular lower education for certain groups. But even when this is not the case, actual industrialization and/or the political desire to develop assures the segregation of religion and education.

Replacing church with state schools has not always been easy. For example, at the turn of the century in England, long after industrialization was initiated, there were more church than state schools (Wilson, 1969:79). Rather than representing a comprehensive program of educational reform and change, state education in England emerged merely to fill the gaps in coverage by church education. But as industrialization continued to generate pressures for secular work skills and technology, state schools engaged in technical training began to replace church schools. And within secular schools the religious curricula increasingly diminished (Wilson, 1969:74). In higher education a similar process occurred, although the breakdown of the aristocratic and genteel profile of English colleges proved more difficult to change than their emphasis on religious training.

In the United States state lower and higher education expanded rapidly with advanced industrialism. Although a large portion of the nation's school system remained attached to religious denominations, secular education within religious schools increased and began to dominate the curriculum since secular work skills increasingly became necessary for participation in the wider society. In the Third World the polity is so extensively involved in education that secularization is occurring more rapidly, for at least two reasons: the state has the commitment and power to force secularization; and there is less of a legacy or tradition of church education, especially higher education. Segregation of church and school has therefore been less difficult than in England and other Old World societies.

In sum we can say that political and/or economic changes eventually lead to the segregation of education and religion in the Old and New Worlds. Even within those persisting religious schools secular curricula eventually came to dominate religious training. In Third World nations political more than economic forces cause the segregation of church and state schools. Once such segregation occurs education tends to become highly responsive to economic and political pressures. Thus educational development is often a process of segregating religion and education so that further societal development can occur in accordance with other institutional pressures. To the extent that this segregation does not occur in Third World nations, industrialization and overall modernization will be inhibited.

LAW AND EDUCATION

Law emerges as a conspicuous institution in societies as problems of coordination and control intensify. As economy, family, polity, education, and religion become increasingly separated and differentiated from each other, integrative problems of coordination become prevalent. One consequence of legal evolution is thus to mitigate some of the potential and actual conflicts among and within differentiating institutions. For example, law regularizes interchanges and linkages between education on the one hand and polity, religion, family, and economy on the other. In this way educational development is greatly facilitated, for without this intervention by law, education would remain in conflict with the family and religion while being completely dominated by the economy and polity.

legal system mediation between economy and education

In highly traditional societies economic activity is carried out within kinship. This situation points to the fact that labor is supplied to the economy by virtue of family procreation and socialization. With this structural fusion of economy with family, kinship rules have the consequence of assuring a labor supply for economic activity. For example, as we know from Chapter 5, residence rules can maintain a relatively constant labor pool, while descent and authority rules can coordinate economic labor.

With initial industrialization, work and home become separated in both time and space. Rather than the whole kin unit only a few kinsmen now work in the economy. This in itself poses integrative problems since getting a worker away from the home on time and on a regular schedule can often be problematic in industrializing societies, because workers often approach the new factory work place with agrarian skills, orientations, and attitudes. These integrative problems become compounded as pressures for a larger but skilled and literate work force increase. Under these conditions workers must undergo formal education to participate effectively in the economy. With further industrialization the period of formal education necessary for economic participation is extended. At some point in this process a severe problem develops, revolving around how sufficiently educated laborers for the economy are to be supplied. In response to these problems compulsory education laws, which force the young out of the home and into the school for designated periods of time, become evident in the legal system. In initially industrializing systems laws specify the necessity of primary education, while in more advanced industrial systems laws extend the period of required education through secondary school. With the onset of postindustrialism higher education becomes more and more necessary as economic demands for brainpower increase. While no system has compulsory higher education laws, most modern systems reveal a body of laws for educational assistance. These laws establish guidelines for assisting financially qualified students who desire higher education. The National Defense Education Act providing low-interest loans and scholarship funds is an American example of what is a common feature of legal systems in all modern societies. The overall consequence of these kinds of laws is that they integrate economic demands for manpower and the educational structures supplying that manpower. In Chapter 3 we referred to this process as one of the entrepreneurial functions of law. However, laws do not assure perfect or even near-perfect integration between education and economy—strains, conflicts, and tensions still exist. And many members of even the most advanced society do not acquire skills leading to efficient role performance in the economy. In highly modern societies structuring education to meet at least some of the demands of the economy represents a serious problem. To cope with this problem a considerable amount of educational legislation is increasingly necessary in these modern societies.

legal system mediation between kinship and education

With industrialization children leave the home for the school. Frequently compulsory education laws assure that they do so. One major consequence of these laws is that they smooth over what potentially could be a highly conflictual situation. Schools must perform much socialization, and after a few years of school socialization children possess verbal and intellectual skills approaching those of their parents. They also possess knowledge that perhaps surpasses that of their parents, especially in Third World nations. Children under these conditions are more questioning, enlightened, and sometimes precocious. This means that traditional patterns of authoritarianism and parental respect can become unviable. And tight and rigid familial socialization of the precocious child becomes increasingly difficult as the child passes up the educational hierarchy. Thus the family in modern societies must relinquish its traditional dominance of socialization to schools. In turn school socialization makes traditional child-training practices in the family inappropriate. The potential disruptiveness in this situation is partially mitigated by compulsory education laws and related enforcement agencies, for in modern societies penalties for violation of education laws are stiff and enforcement is rigorous. Under these conditions when there is no choice for parents or children, reconciliation and adjustment—rather than resistance—are likely. Parents and children come to accept the inevitability of dual socialization and thus adjust.

mediation of law between religion and education

As we know, during initial educational development education is often church controlled. Then with industrialization education is increasingly regulated by the polity. This sudden reversal in institutional influences on education could pose a severe conflict between education on the one hand and religion and polity on the other. But much of the conflict occurs between organized religion (or church) and the polity (or state) without involving education. For example, much of later European history revolved around the corrosion of the church's political power and the gradual consolidation of power in the hands of the state. Increasingly the political system was ruled by constitutional rather than "divine" right. This is another way of saying that political legitimation occurred through the legal rather than the religious subsystem. (This will be thoroughly discussed in later chapters on the polity and religion.) In the United States political legitimation was always a legal subsystem process regulated by the Constitution, which explicitly separated church and state. In Third World nations—even those with strong religious traditions—political power increasingly tends to rest in the hands of the military elite, which attempts to utilize law, though often unsuccessfully, for achieving legitimation. And in most societies this conflict between church and state is resolved in favor of the state at an agrarian stage of economic development.

The implications of these facts for educational development are that once industrialization and the consequent demands for mass and secular education are initiated, the state can assume control of education without generating too much educational turmoil. The state can do so because it is the legitimate source of power and the church is not in a position to resist. But assumption of educational control by the state usually occurs gradually and haphazardly in response to economic or political changes. As we know this was the case in England, where by 1900 most schools were still operated by the church. In the United States this was true to a lesser extent. And in the Third World nations the state rarely tolerates mass church education, usually because of the need to manipulate political socialization in schools.

In most systems the legal subsystem thus lays the groundwork for this potentially conflictual transition from church- to state-dominated education. Even though the legal subsystem has generally settled who has the right to control education, conflict still erupts. For example, the spectacular Scopes trial in 1925 over whether or not evolution could be taught in certain American schools was essentially a last-ditch attempt of organized religion in the South to exert some control in state schools (Moberg, 1962:331). And even today conflict persists in those societies where both state and church school systems exist. This conflict usually erupts over the issue of how much control the state can exert over church schools. In the United States, aside from the general guidelines in the Constitution separating church and state education, control over church schools occurs at the state level, where the state legal subsystem specifies general conditions of support, credentialing, accreditation, and in some instances the curriculum for church schools (Pierce, 1964). Thus even where church and state schools coexist, the legal subsystem has integrative consequences for coordinating schools in the dual system.

legal system mediation between polity and education

Ultimately the polity has the power to control educational processes in a society. This is often because the legal subsystem provides the polity with the right to exercise such power and control. In the United States the General Welfare Clause (Article I, Section 8) of the Constitution, the Fourteenth Amendment, and the Due Process Clause (Article V of the Bill of Rights) give the federal government considerable power in regulating education, even in a supposedly decentralized system (Pierce, 1964). In more centralized systems these powers are more direct.

However, there are certain constraints on political manipulation stemming not so much from law but from the structural features of modern education (Clark, 1962, 1964). Modern education is massified, centralized, and hence bureaucratized. This means it is a giant and complex hierarchy of administrative offices. This fact alone can keep political manipulation minimal, because the very size of the bureaucracy makes it somewhat autonomous. Political policies can be subverted or selectively implemented and the complexity of the bureaucracy keeps outside observers ignorant of the bureaucracy's internal functioning. Professionalism also impedes total regulation. As those who run the bureaucracy become recognized as expert professionals they become even more capable of insulating themselves from manipulation. Their professional prestige, aided by a forbidding jargon, can keep would-be political manipulators off guard and away. Yet these insulating conditions should not obscure the simple fact that when it wants to or must, the polity can more than any other institution control educational processes in a society. If for no other reason, financial support for education flows almost exclusively from the polity. Even in systems with dual private and public schools, the polity with its taxing, subsidizing, and research-contracting powers can easily manipulate private education. In the United States, by simply taxing church schools, withdrawing low-interest loan programs (for building and other facilities), and withdrawing in concert lucrative research contracts, the polity could cause financial disaster to private education. The fact that such a potential exists—and is recognized by administrators in private schools—can itself represent a source of political manipulation.

SUMMARY AND OVERVIEW

institutional pressures and trends in education

These institutional pressures from the economy, polity, religion, and law greatly affect the course of educational development. Without changes in this surrounding institutional network extensive educational development would be unlikely. Moreover, basic educational trends—massification, democratization, bureaucratization, and centralization—would not be explicable without attention to the institutional environment of education. With industrialization the pressures for mass literacy and other work skills can force the expansion of education to others than the elite. Sometimes the political subsystem encourages this process through the desire to develop economically, the need to politically socialize (or indoctrinate), or the need to mollify a restless population. Democratization of education can also be a reflection of economic and political processes. As the economy and polity increasingly rely on brainpower, educational opportunities become extended to all the population in order to assure an adequate supply of labor. Certain political policies causing massification can further democratization, since it is at the educationally disadvantaged (the lower classes and minorities) that indoctrination and pacification are usually aimed. Bureaucratization of education usually occurs in response to massification, since administrative problems begin to multiply. Bureaucratization can thus be seen as one kind of internal subsystem adjustment to increase in numbers of educational incumbents. Bureaucratization is thus only an indirect reflection of political and economic pressures. However, centralization is both an internal and external response. Increases in size per se can generate bureaucratic centralization but political policies requiring control of education in a society also cause centralization. Aside from political control and manipulation, rapidly implementing and expanding education in a developing society requires centralization, especially where financial resources are limited. With centralization, financing and other administrative processes can be more economical and geared to national priorities such as economic development.

Other major trends in education—professionalization, unionization, and politicization—bear more complex relationships to the institutional environment. This is one way of indicating that the impact of the institutional environment on these trends is not clear. Professionalization is partly an internal subsystem response to the need for trained and expert incumbents. But professionalization may also be a defense against extensive encroachment from the polity. This seems particularly true in the United States, where teachers possess an almost compulsive concern for their professional image, which is under constant exposure to community politics. Unionization is a difficult trend to analyze: it is not so widespread as other trends; and its sources stem from more specific and non-institutional pressures—economic exploitation and poor working conditions. However, some of the impetus to unionization may be generated by extensive political encroachment on teaching, especially when professionalism and bureaucratization prove to be ineffective insulation. Finally, politicization of students in higher education is partly a reaction to a new awareness of economic and political encroachment on education. Such encroachment can be considered "immoral," particularly when university administrators resist student pressures for university involvement in "moral" social problems (race relations, poverty, and war).

SUGGESTED READINGS

Wilbur B. Brookover and David Gottlieb, *A Sociology of Education*, 2d ed., New York: American Book Company, 1964.

Burton R. Clark, *Educating the Expert Society*, San Francisco: Chandler Publishing Company, 1962.

John F. Cramer and George S. Browne, *Comparative Education*, New York: Harcourt Brace Jovanovich, Inc., 1965.

David Goslin, *The School in Contemporary Society*, Glenview, Ill.: Scott, Foresman and Company, 1965.

Robert J, Havighurst and Bernice L. Neugarten, *Society and Education*, 3d ed., Boston: Allyn and Bacon, Inc., 1967.

I. N. Hunt and Don Adams, *Educational Patterns in Contemporary Societies*, New York: McGraw-Hill Book Company, 1964.

Patricia G. Sexton, *The American School*, Englewood Cliffs, N.J.: Prentice-Hall, Inc., 1967.

the
institutional
environment
of
EDUCATION

LAW 8

From inconspicuous origins in traditional societies law emerges as a dominant institution in modern societies. Such development is intimately connected to the more general process of societal modernization. As societies modernize, severe problems of coordination, control, organization, and syncronization emerge among system units. As these problems intensify, the institution of law expands and comes to have far-reaching consequences for a society.

BASIC ELEMENTS OF LEGAL SYSTEMS

There is tremendous variability in legal systems throughout the world's societies. However, all possess at least rudiments of these elements (Hoebel, 1954): explicit laws or rules of conduct; mechanisms for enforcing laws; mechanisms for mediating and adjudicating disputes in accordance with laws; and mechanisms for enacting new or changing old laws.

laws

Any legal system is composed of an interrelated body of rules or laws. These rules specify what is appropriate and inappropriate conduct in a variety of situations. The substance of most laws revolves around: (a) regulating and controlling *relationships* between system units—whether individuals, groups, clans, corporations, strata, or institutions; and (b) defining and regulating deviance among individual system units. In many traditional legal systems, rules or laws are unwritten or codified. And they are partially fused with custom, religious dogmas, kinship rules, and traditions. But in more modern societies laws are written and codified in elaborate codes and statutes, and they display considerable autonomy from religious dogma. Yet as we will see, all laws in both traditional and modern systems are intimately related to custom, tradition, and other cultural components (Ehrlich, 1936; Lowie, 1966; Gurvitch, l953).

enforcement of laws

In order to be an element of a legal system, rules must be enforced by *specifically designated statuses* (Lowie, 1966:156–175; Weber, 1954). In some societies, enforcement statuses and the norms attendant on them cluster into large administrative and police organizations. But frequently in traditional societies, enforcement statuses are not permanent but temporary and invoked only on certain occasions. An organized and permanent police force is not typical of many legal systems.

mediating disputes

Disputes, disagreements, and conflicts of interest are endemic to human societies. Even with explicit laws and their enforcement, there are always disagreements over how to interpret the laws, their relevance to a particular case, and how much punishment should be administered for violations (Parsons, 1962). Also, new conflicts not covered by existing laws frequently arise and need to be resolved. And frequently laws themselves conflict so that it is not clear how they apply to a particular dispute. These and many other sources of disputes require mediation. Early in the evolution of legal systems explicit agencies of mediation emerge (Schwartz and Miller, 1964). These are usually called courts or tribunals and are a feature of all legal systems. Courts resolve or adjudicate disputes by ascertaining pertinent information, invoking relevant laws, and then arriving at a decision settling the dispute (Bredemeier, 1962). Such settlements are then enforced by designated agencies or statuses. But often laws are outdated or irrelevant to a dispute. Laws can be — and frequently are — archaic, ambiguous, in conflict, or nonexistent. As we will see later, courts under these conditions establish new laws or precedents in rendering a decision. This is one mechanism for keeping laws abreast of actual sources of conflict in society (Friedmann, 1959:24 – 30).

enacting laws

Judicial precedent is not the only means for changing old or establishing new laws. All legal systems have specific statuses designated to *make* laws. This is usually referred to as the *legislative element* of a legal system (Lloyd, 1964; Davis, 1962; Sawer, 1965). Sometimes law making is invested in the head of a kinship system, council of elders, military despot, or legislature of elected officials. The exact structure of the legislative element can take a wide variety of forms, ranging from very simple to complex and from despotic to democratic.

In sum we can say that any legal system is composed of law, enforcement agencies, courts, and legislative bodies. The organization of these elements can be exceedingly complex, as in American society, or very rudimentary, as in most traditional systems. Despite their variability in the exact structure from society to society, the general consequences of legal systems for the broader society appear much the same.

LAW AND SOCIETY

Maintaining relationships among system parts, whether strata, groups, organizations, or institutions, is always problematic in social systems. Societies abound with conflicts, violence, strife, disjunctures, and disorder among individuals, groups, organizations, strata, communities, and institutions. To the extent that these cannot be mitigated and controlled, a society will remain disjointed and conflictual. However, perfect integration or coordination of parts in a society never occurs, for only *degrees* of integration are ever possible. Some societies are rife with tension and conflict; others appear stable and peaceful; but most are somewhere in-between. Many structures and processes in a society promote coordination, harmony, and integration. The principal *institutional* structure having these consequences is law.

STRUCTURAL COORDINATION

System units, whether individuals, interest groups, or corporations, must be minimally coordinated. Law has major consequences for establishing, maintaining, or reestablishing coordination. This is done in a variety of ways: (1) The legal subsystem specifies and enforces appropriate action in crucial areas of interaction among system units. Laws, courts, and enforcement as well as administrative agencies regularize interaction and give it predictability. (2) Law also provides procedures for settling disputes and conflicts when they arise. The legal subsystem enables an alternative to violence and vengeance by allowing disputing parties to settle their sources of conflict in courts. In this way law restores coordination when it breaks down. (3) Law checks deviance which could pose a serious breakdown in coordination and control. By specifying what is deviant and providing negative sanctions for such deviance the legal subsystem controls action in critical spheres. Such control facilitates coordination by increasing conformity and hence the predictability of social action.

LEGITIMIZING POWER AND INEQUITY

The legal subsystem legitimizes power. It gives certain system units the right to control other units. One of the major consequences of law in social systems is that it legitimizes the polity, bestowing on it the right to wield power, while giving its elites and those who influence them wealth and privilege. Sometimes such inequality is written into laws and enforced by courts and police. Frequently the legitimation is subtle: Police differentially enforce the same laws for the rich and poor; the wealthy have the knowledge and financial resources to effectively press their interests in courts; or administrative agencies in the legal system are usually established to facilitate the interests of the rich, not the poor. The overall consequences of this are that law often reinforces and perpetuates inequality or stratification.

CULTURAL PRESERVATION, CODIFICATION, AND INTEGRATION

As we know, every society has a cultural system—a storehouse of customs, traditions, values, lores, beliefs, technology, and dogmas. Much of this cultural inventory, especially basic values and beliefs, is reflected in the codes and statutes of a legal system (Weber, 1954). To the extent that this occurs, law preserves and codifies certain crucial components of the cultural storehouse. For example, basic American values of equality, justice, humanitarianism, and individualism are preserved and codified in the Constitution, as well as in a wide number of national and state codes and statutes. Similarly, in Russia basic values of collectivism are codified in the Soviet constitution and legal system. Or in a traditional society, basic customs, traditions, and religious dogmas are preserved in the laws of the legal subsystem (Durkheim, 1933; Weber, 1954).

But law does more than preserve and codify. It integrates values and other cultural components into concrete and specific structural situations. Law specifies in certain crucial situations just exactly how values, beliefs, customs, and traditions are to be realized in day-to-day interaction among system parts. However, the relationship between law and culture is more complex than this because in any rapidly changing society, culture changes. New values, beliefs, and ideologies emerge and often conflict with the old. Frequently the laws and courts of a legal system must reconcile changing values not only with each other but with concrete interaction situations that are affected by value conflict (Gurvitch, 1953). Not to reconcile these sources of cultural conflict results in social disorganization. Thus the legal system of a society resolves many—but never all—of the conflicts resulting from a lack of cultural integration, especially as it affects concrete relations among societal parts (Friedmann, 1959). For example, in the United States at the turn of this century the value of rugged individualism and laissez faire came into conflict with emerging values of collectivism and social welfare. The conflict was particularly acute in labor-management relations as labor sought to bargain collectively with management determined to preserve old laissez faire values. And this conflict between values was reflected in conflicts at the factory gates. In the long run a host of labor-management laws partially resolved this integrative crisis (Evan, 1962). Similarly, the conflict in American values of rugged individualism and laissez faire on one hand and humanitarianism on the other was resolved in the face of poverty and was mitigated with the emergence of a host of welfare laws at both the national and state levels. Similar examples of the integrative impact of law on culture and society can be found in all societies, especially those undergoing rapid cultural and social transformation.

defining the institution of law

In an institutional analysis of society we are concerned with the general organization of statuses, norms, and roles. With respect to law as an institution we are focusing on how certain statuses, norms, and roles cluster into basic elements of legal systems: laws, courts, enforcement, and law-enacting structures. We are also concerned with the general consequences of this clustering for the society in which it is located. With this in mind we can define *law as an institution* in this way:

> Law is that interrelated, pervasive, and relatively stable cluster of statuses, norms, and roles revolving around rules, rule making, rule enforcing, and rule mediating and interpreting in a society and having consequences for (1) structural coordination; (2) legitimation of power and inequity; and (3) cultural preservation, codification, and integration.

TYPES OF LEGAL SYSTEMS

There are as many different legal systems as there are societies. The intent of this section is to ignore much of this variability and see if general types of legal systems can be isolated. Although there are dangers involved, we will discuss three general types of legal systems: primitive; transitional; and modern. Naturally such broad categories do not do justice to the complexity of the real world, but they are necessary in an analytical discussion.

primitive legal systems

These are the most rudimentary of legal systems. They are typical of hunting and gathering and simple agrarian societies. But like all legal systems, they possess laws, enforcement statuses, courts, and law-enacting bodies. While these elements frequently blend into one another they are discernible in rudimentary form.

LAWS IN PRIMITIVE SOCIETIES

The laws of a primitive legal system are not written down or codified into extensive codes and statutes. They are permeated by custom, traditions, religious dogmas, and values. And they are often coexistent with kinship norms. Primitive laws are also comparatively undifferentiated. But there emerges in primitive systems some differentiation between *substantive* and *procedural* laws (Hoebel, 1954). Substantive laws consist of rights, duties, and prohibitions on system units. It is the content of law, specifying what is right, wrong, permissible, and unpermissible. On the other hand, procedural laws are rules concerning just how substantive law is to be administered, enforced, changed, and used in mediation of disputes. All further differentiation of types at later stages of legal evolution can be encompassed under these two general types of laws.

ENFORCEMENT OF LAWS IN PRIMITIVE SOCIETIES

When norms or rules are enforced by specific statuses they can be considered laws. This criterion enables us to distinguish legal rules from custom, religious dogma, kinship rules, and other general norms in a society. When one violates some dogmas, the gods will punish him. But when one violates a law, specific statuses are charged with enforcement. Those customs, dogmas, kinship rules, and other norms which are enforced constitute the laws of a primitive legal system. Enforcement in primitive legal systems is usually carried out by kinsmen of the aggrieved or deviant. When a violation of a law has occurred, specific kin statuses are charged with enforcement. Just which kin statuses are so charged can vary with the offender, the law violated, and the severity of the violation (Hoebel, 1954). Sometimes the wronged party in a dispute is both victim and policeman, carrying out punishments demanded by the law and/or courts. For example, at one time among the Australian aborigines an aggrieved "plaintiff" and his kin hurled spears at the "defendant" who was armed with a shield. When the defendant was wounded, the punishment was over (Sawer, 1965). Thus the crucial condition for a rule to be part of a legal system is that certain statuses have the right to enforce rules and administer punishments for their violation. As legal systems evolve, these statuses become permanent with specialized incumbents charged with enforcement. Such a development, as we will see, constitutes the emergence of a police force. But in small, poor, and cohesive societies such specialists are rarely needed. Rather, procedural rules designate who upon a given type of violation should engage in enforcement. The police force is thus invoked for specific occasions rather than constituting a standing, on-going cluster of roles.

COURTS IN PRIMITIVE LEGAL SYSTEMS

Courts are clusters of statuses settling disputes in accordance with laws. In primitive systems courts, like the police force, are temporarily invoked and then dispersed as disputes arise and are settled. Despite their temporary nature courts are composed of at least two clearly differentiated roles: judges who are to hear evidence and render decisions in accordance with laws; and disputing litigants who are to abide by the judge's decisions. Sometimes a third role can be discerned in such primitive courts: a representative or "lawyer" who is to plead the case for a litigant. As a legal system evolves these roles become clearly differentiated from one another. And many new positions become part of the court. But in primitive legal systems these three statuses frequently appear sufficient to maintain a high degree of societal integration and coordination.

To illustrate one such court in a primitive society we can turn to the Yurok Indians of California, whose courts possessed only the most rudimentary structure (Kroeber, 1924). A Yurok feeling cheated by another Yurok would engage the assistance of two nonkinsmen from another community. The other Yurok involved in the dispute would do the same. These assistants would then assume the status of judge, or as they were known to the Yurok, the status of "crosser." Procedural laws indicated just how these "crossers" were to behave. After hearing the evidence offered by the litigants and their pleas pertaining to substantive law, the "crossers" would render a decision in accordance with a rule of punishment known by all (Hoebel, 1954:24). Here is a primitive court, *analytically* very similar to those in modern systems. The litigants were their own lawyers (a right still possessed by litigants in many modern courts), but clear-cut judge statuses were invoked to interpret grievances in light of unwritten laws. Frequently the composition of courts is more stable than in the Yurok legal system. For example, a chief, his council of elders, and henchmen may constitute a stable court which can be invoked upon violation of laws or at the request of litigants. The tribal councils of American Indians (Hoebel, 1954) and the court of West African Ashanti were so structured.

LEGISLATURES IN PRIMITIVE LEGAL SYSTEMS

Legislatures are political bodies. They are clusters of statuses charged with law making that are parts of both the legal and political subsystems of a society. In highly traditional societies there are only a few statuses charged with law making, because there is no well-evolved political subsystem. The polity is composed of kin leaders (in accordance with descent and authority rules), councils of elders or chiefs, and perhaps various councils of kin and religious leaders. Law making in systems with only incipient polities often occurs by decree. For example, the chiefs of the Bantu-speaking Tswand of South Africa possessed considerable law-making authority. They could lay down edicts and declare old laws obsolete (Schapera, 1956). To illustrate this Hoebel (1954:278) relates that in 1934 a young married man died childless. According to kinship rules the young man's unmarried younger brother was supposed to take up with the widow and "seed" her children. However, he would not do it, with the result that his father took up sexual relations with the widow—substituting for the derelict son. But this did not sit well with his wife, who appealed to the district council (she is now litigant, the council is now a court of law) to have her husband stopped. The council ruled against her, saying that her husband's conduct was in accordance with "ancient right and custom" (i.e., laws). But the district chief overruled the council, declaring the custom obsolete. The chief thus assumed the status of legislator by declaring the old rule outdated. When the father refused to obey the chief's declaration, he was punished severely (clearly, the chief's edict was a law, because it was enforced).

Frequently court judges and political leaders are one and the same in highly traditional societies. And so a court decision can also involve law making. This is also true of modern legal systems where court decisions become precedents (or laws) guiding future court decisions. This, as we will see, is referred to as *common law* (i.e., court-enacted law) as distinct from *civil law* (legislative law enacted by political bodies). But in primitive systems such distinctions usually do not exist, because courts are political, with their decisions constituting legislation (whether or not these decisions are common law or civil law is a moot question in such societies). To illustrate the partial fusion of courts and legislatures in primitive legal systems, we can take a case from Llewellyn and Hoebel's (1941: 127–128) description of the Cheyenne Indians. To go on the warpath a Cheyenne warrior borrowed, without asking, the horse of another Cheyenne warrior. When the horse was not returned the aggrieved warrior went to a court (as a litigant) of "warrior chiefs." These chiefs sent for the culprit, who confessed, agreed to restitution, and even offered to make the aggrieved warrior his blood brother. The matter as a court action was then settled. But the chief then assumed the status of legislature, proclaiming: "Now we shall make a new rule. If any man takes another's goods [note: not just horses, but any goods] without asking, we shall go over and get them back for him. More than that, if the taker tries to keep them, we will give him a whipping." Thus new substantive and procedural laws were enacted by the chief, as both judge and political legislator.

There are always limits on just what laws can be legislated. To decree a law deviating too far from custom, dogma, or basic values would invite violation. Such laws would also be difficult to enforce. Laws are accepted as legitimate because they seem reasonable in the minds of men (Gluckman, 1963). They fit actual circumstances while not deviating too far from salient cultural components. Chiefs can change old laws for these same reasons but with an advantage not possessed by modern legislators. Since laws are unwritten, they are held in the human mind. This means that old and inappropriate laws can be forgotten or at least become hazy and vague (Lowie, 1966). The result of this is that the chief-legislator can stricke, rescind, or change old laws more easily than the modern legislator, since there are no hard and fast written codes to obstruct reinterpretation. Rather, only vague memories stand in the way and when the new appears reasonable, little resistance is offered. As we will see, getting old laws off the books in modern societies is rarely this easy (Lloyd, 1964:235–241).

The functions of law in primitive systems are the same as those in all social systems. They preserve important cultural components —especially as these components affect actual behavior and interaction in society. Law, court, enforcement, and legislative statuses also coordinate interaction among system units by settling disputes, checking deviance, and regularizing crucial exchanges. Primitive law also legitimizes what inequity exists in highly traditional societies. By codifying, preserving, and enforcing certain key kinship rules (usually descent and authority), religious rituals and dogmas, and the chief's right to enact laws, differences in power and privilege are preserved and made to seem appropriate (Carlston, 1962).

In sum we can say that primitive legal systems display at least the rudiments of explicit laws, courts, enforcement statuses, and legislators. Laws are neither written nor extensively codified. Courts contain at least litigant and judge statuses, although there may be no permanent judges. Some primitive legal systems have specifically designated elders and leaders as judges, while others invoke certain incumbents to mediate disputes. Enforcement rarely involves a standing police force; rather, designated actors—frequently the kin of the deviant or the aggrieved—administer sanctions to violators. Legislation is the prerogative of political leaders and is frequently fused with their positions as judges of court structures.

transitional legal systems

As we will see in the next chapter, legal system evolution from a primitive to transitional stage is a reflection of more general societal development (Diamond, 1951). Transitional legal systems are found in advanced agrarian and early industrial societies, where the economic, political, and educational subsystems are becoming clearly differentiated from kinship. Since society is more complex, relations among system units pose more serious integrative problems than in highly traditional societies. With increases in integrative problems the legal subsystem becomes more complex and extensive. This is reflected in clear-cut differentiation of basic legal elements —laws, courts, enforcement agencies, and legislative structures— from each other. It is further reflected in the increasing differentiation or complexity within each of these basic elements.

At a transitional stage of development most of the features of a modern legal system have emerged—although not to the degree evident in the modern systems of the United States, England, Russia, Sweden, and other developed societies. Some of these emergent features of transitional legal systems are outlined below.

Law always reflects culture. But with legal evolution law becomes more differentiated and distinct from traditions, customs, and religious dogma (Lloyd, 1964). The legal system still preserves and codifies basic values, but it is more secularized and more present-oriented than in primitive legal systems. Furthermore, in response to growing societal diversity, many different types of law emerge. With the emergence of a distinct polity or state, *public* and *private* law become evident. Public law concerns the relationships between system units and the state, while private law regulates relations among nonpolitical units. Accompanying this differentiation of laws, *criminal* law becomes distinguishable from *torts*. Criminal law denotes wrongs against the state, community, and public. Torts are laws pertaining to private wrongs of parties against each other rather than against the state or public. And as we see, the sources of laws also become diversified: some emerge out of court decisions or precedents and are known as *common* laws; others are enacted by the legislative bodies of the state and are referred to as *civil* laws. And all these laws are either *substantive* or *procedural*.

As the types of laws increase, laws become *systems* of rules. Laws bear ever-more systematic relationships to each other. They become hierarchically arranged with general laws encompassing more specific laws. But at the transitional stage such systems of laws are somewhat chaotic. Clear relationships have yet to evolve; hierarchies are only incipient, with many holes and gaps; laws contradict each other; and they are a curious mixture of national and local laws, frequently contradicting one another. Yet as laws begin to display a systematic character, they develop an autonomy and an internal logic of their own. This further divorces them from the weight of custom and religious dogma.

Much of this internal differentiation of law derives not only from the pressures of growing societal complexity, but also from the fact that law at the transitional stage is now written down, codified, and preserved in books. It now transcends the limitations of human intellect and memory, thus allowing for its rapid expansion and codification.

COURTS IN TRANSITIONAL LEGAL SYSTEMS
Courts apply laws to specific disputes. The growing differentiation of laws in transitional legal systems is reflected in the increased complexity of courts. At least five distinct types of statuses evolve and become permanent: judge; representative or lawyer; litigant; court officials and administrators; and jurors. The status of judge becomes institutionalized, requiring special training and expertise in applying

the increased body of laws. Judges are no longer invoked, but permanent with incumbents pursuing careers as judges. Lawyer roles also become institutionalized, requiring special training in law so as to represent and assist litigants in courts. Lawyers are bound not only by the procedural laws attendant on courts but also by a growing cluster of professional norms specifying appropriate conduct in and out of court. The status of litigant persists, being filled by violators of rules and disputing parties. But the procedural rules governing if, when, how, and in what way litigants are to conduct themselves in court become more clearly specified and constraining. As the court becomes more complex, applying an increasingly complex body of laws, administrative problems of coordination, control, and communication increase. These administrative problems are intensified as written records of court proceedings become common. These problems lead to the emergence of a host of administrative roles within the court and eventually court officials come to outnumber judges and lawyers. In the long run the proliferation of administrative duties leads to the incipient bureaucratization of the court. In some transitional systems the jury becomes institutionalized, with norms requiring jurors to assess the guilt of a litigant. Juries tend to become more typical of court cases involving violations of public and criminal laws rather than private or tort laws.

As the internal structure of courts becomes more differentiated, relationships and linkages among courts become more complex. As with laws, the courts of a transitional legal system begin to approximate a unified and coordinated system, although the relations among courts still display considerable ambiguity. There are a large number of local community and territorial courts, which often apply different laws and customs and are governed by somewhat different procedural rules. A few national courts emerge as the political organization of a society becomes more centralized. But these have only partial jurisdiction over local courts. No clear hierarchy of courts has evolved, primarily because political organization is not complete and the system of laws remains somewhat chaotic.

With the emergence of clearly differentiated, autonomous, and stable courts, legal development can accelerate for at least these reasons: (1) Laws enacted by the growing legislative body of the polity (see below) can be applied systematically to specific circumstances by professionals and experts. This means that laws enacted by the centralizing polity have institutional channels of application. (2) Where political legislation of laws is absent, an established court can enact laws by handing down common-law precedents. Such common laws tend to fit nicely the structural conditions in a society, since they emerge out of attempts to reconcile actual and concrete conflicts. But to the extent that courts remain local and common-law decisions reflect local conditions, the emerging body or system of laws from all courts can be a labyrinth of conflicting and overlapping rules. Such conflicts and overlaps can have positive consequences for unification of a legal system, since they force the polity and higher courts to assert their authority and resolve them. This whole process of resolving conflicts and ambiguities among common-law precedents can thus eventually lead to a more codified system of laws.

ENFORCEMENT IN TRANSITIONAL LEGAL SYSTEMS

In transitional legal systems explicit, stable, and somewhat autonomous police roles emerge. Enforcement is taken out of the hands of aggrieved litigants and kinsmen. Norms attendant on these emergent police statuses require enforcing court decisions and apprehending violators of laws. But such enforcement and apprehension are always selective, for the poor in all societies are more subject to police enforcement than the wealthy. And since the police are initiated and paid by the polity, the political elites are less subject than nonelites to police action. Selective enforcement can represent a form of law enactment. By enforcing some laws and not others or by enforcing them only with respect to certain groups or under certain circumstances, the police make laws. They partially determine what is and what is not a law. As we will see, such police legislation increases in more modern legal systems.

LEGISLATION IN TRANSITIONAL LEGAL SYSTEMS

As the political subsystem evolves, the legislative structures and processes in a legal system become more complex. Legislative statuses are more clearly differentiated from judicial (court) and enforcement (police) statuses. Legislating new laws or abolishing old ones is rarely a matter of simple decree. And the laws enacted are of many different types, ranging from constitutions to penal codes.

In transitional legal systems a relatively small cluster of statuses —whether organized in a forum, senate, or royal council—enact laws. This legislative body is usually dominated by the political elite and responsive to its demands. Initially the laws enacted by this body are situation specific—meeting the needs of the political elite and resolving particular disputes. But as political development increases and as conflicts between and inadequacies of common laws become evident, legislative enactment is more comprehensive, involving a group of laws pertaining to certain general problem areas. With enactment of these more comprehensive and systematic statutes and codes, a system of civil law begins to supplement common law.

Just what the ratio of civil to common law will be varies greatly from system to system. In France under Napoleon, civil law dominated common law, whereas in England just the opposite was and is the case. In fact to this day England does not have a systematic constitution. In Third World nations civil law is often imposed prematurely on undeveloped judicial and police structures. In these cases constitutions and national laws have little relevance and meaning for actual behavior in local areas.

The evolution of effective civil codes presupposes several things: a well-developed and established court system and police force; a pool of educated and quasi-professional legal counselors and judges; a history of common law; and some degree of political and national unity (and development) so that civil codes are viable. All of these conditions rarely exist in Third World nations, so the relationship between common and civil law remains ambiguous. But this ambiguous relationship between legislative (civil) or judge-made (common) law is endemic to transitional legal systems. It is only in more advanced legal systems that extensive civil-law and common-law statutes become integrated into a more or less consistent and viable system of laws.

The functions of transitional legal institutions are similar to those in primitive systems but more complex and perhaps less successful in resolving integrative problems. Laws preserve and codify culture but begin to display autonomy from religious dogmas, customs, and traditions. Structural differentiation is more complex and necessitates extensive court mediation, law enactment, and enforcement. Political development increases, resulting in large inequities in power and wealth. Civil laws, and their selective enforcement by police, legitimate many of these inequities.

As the economy, polity, religion, and education are no longer organized around and within kinship and local community, the coordination of individuals, groups, organizations, strata, and institutions becomes highly problematic. Many of the developments in the legal system at the transitional stage represent a response—frequently unsuccessful—of social systems to increased differentiation and complexity.

modern legal systems

Modern legal systems display all the structural features of transitional systems, but in more elaborate arrangements. Also, the arrangements tend to approximate more of a system than transitional law since more coordination among and between courts, police, and legislatures exists.

LAWS IN MODERN LEGAL SYSTEMS

Laws in modern legal systems are extensive networks of local and national statutes, private and public codes, crimes and torts, common and civil laws, and procedural and substantive rules. One of the most distinctive features of modern law is the proliferation of public and procedural laws, especially that type we can call *administrative* law. With expansion and then bureaucratization of both the polity and legal subsystem (see below), much law is designed to regulate and coordinate activity within and between bureaucracies as well as between individual incumbents on one hand and governmental and legal bureaucracies on the other. Another feature of law is the increasing proportion of civil over common law. With political development legislation becomes a more typical way of adjusting law to social conditions. Common law remains prevalent and actually increases in systems with premature or long histories of civil law. Yet as a codified system of law emerges, civil law dominates over common law in all modern societies.

Laws in modern legal subsystems constitute a more well-defined system than in transitional systems. There are clear hierarchies of laws, from constitutional codes to regional and local codes. And there is some degree of consistency in these hierarchies of laws, although many ambiguities remain. National, state and regional, and community laws are now less inconsistent, with fewer gaps and conflicts than in transitional systems. As law develops this kind of internal structure it becomes more autonomous and differentiated from culture. It still preserves basic values and ideologies and has many consequences for reconciling conflicts among cultural components. But law is more autonomous, possessing its own distinct logic. This autonomy is amplified as the practitioners of law—lawyers, judges, and police—become more professionalized, since professionalism inevitably generates its own norms, values, and traditions, which often deviate significantly from those of the broader society and culture.

COURTS IN MODERN LEGAL SYSTEMS

Modern courts reflect the complexity—and resulting integrative problems—of the wider society. With the high degree of differentiation of a modern society, there are many more disputes and more widespread deviance than in traditional societies. And since kinship, community, and religion no longer exert the pervasive influence and control typical in traditional societies the courts come to have profound consequences in mediating and mitigating conflicts, disputes, deviance, and other sources of malintegration.

The statuses of judge, lawyer, litigant, juror, and administrator which emerged in transitional systems become distinct and clearly differentiated from one another in modern legal systems. Furthermore, judge and lawyer roles become highly professionalized, with each respective actor licensed, sanctioned, and guided by professional organizations. They also become specialists, dealing only in certain types of cases (family, corporate, criminal, etc.). Such specialization is necessary as the volume of codified law in any particular area expands. Administrative statuses—clerks, bailiffs, stenographers, and public prosecutors—proliferate and specialize to such an extent that they become heavily bureaucratized. Such bureaucratization is inevitable, since modern courts must handle a tremendous volume of cases, creating vast administrative problems.

Just as the statuses within courts become increasingly differentiated and specialized, so do the courts themselves, with particular courts—like their incumbents—often mediating only certain kinds of disputes. This is especially likely at the local level in large communities. For example, in the United States courts can usually be distinguished in larger urban areas along at least domestic (family and divorce), criminal, and civil (or more accurately, torts) lines. Hierarchically there is a clear differentiation of courts from community to territorial and from territorial to national levels. Territorial and national courts usually reverse the trend toward specialization of courts at the local level, for they tend to hear all varieties of cases not fully resolved in local courts. Probably the distinctive feature of courts in modern societies is that they constitute a clear-cut system of community, regional, and national mediation and adjudication structures. The jurisdictions of each court are more clear (Parsons, 1962) and the hierarchy of control is less ambiguous than in transitional legal systems. Cases unresolved in lower courts are argued in higher courts, with these courts having the power to reverse lower court decisions.

One of the serious problems facing modern courts is case overload. Courts cannot properly handle the volume of cases needing mediation and adjudication. One of the consequences of this fact is that litigants—whether the public prosecutor and criminal, individual and individual, individual and corporation, or whoever—often settle out of court in order to avoid delays created by case overloads and backlogs. For example, criminals "cop pleas" and plead guilty to a lessor charge; corporations pay off; individuals settle out of court; and so on. Such proceedings further the normative obligations on lawyers, who must negotiate for a client out of court as often as plead and argue a case inside the court. Another problem endemic to modern courts is a result of bureaucratization. Bureaucratization tends to make the process of adjudication somewhat invisible. Behind the vast hierarchies of bureaucratic offices much hidden mediation occurs that never reaches courts, is recorded, carried out in accordance with procedural laws, or made public. Since modern legal systems usually attempt to implement justice, such proceedings can severely threaten its implementation. In fact administrative bureaucracies are often judge and jury without many of the procedural (and professional) safeguards required within a courtroom. But with extensive court backlogs this kind of "administrative mediation" is perhaps necessary in modern legal systems.

ENFORCEMENT IN MODERN LEGAL SYSTEMS

Enforcement of laws and court decisions in modern legal systems is performed by a clearly differentiated and organized police force. In most modern systems there are several different kinds of police forces with separate and yet somewhat overlapping jurisdictions. There is usually a community, district or regional, and a national police force. Each police force possesses its own internal organization which becomes increasingly bureaucratized. Between forces there are clear lines of communication, power, and control. These separate but integrated forces are a reflection of advances in the political subsystem from a transitional stage. Each force is under the control of different segments—community, regional, and national —of the polity and their integration manifests the degree of political unity typical of modern societies.

Police forces at all levels are heavily bureaucratized with many administrative statuses. This is a reflection of their size and the complexity of their function in modern legal systems. Because of such bureaucratization, police forces are guided by many procedural laws —especially those we labeled administrative laws. These laws regulate and control the way in which enforcement can occur. But since police bureaucracies are large they can hide many violations of these procedural laws. And because they can do this the police can maintain considerable autonomy from laws, courts, and even the political bodies supposedly regulating their activities. These facts always pose the problem of unequal or arbitrary enforcement of laws, denying rights of due process (and all modern systems, even totalitarian ones, have them), and concealment of illegal police action.

Enforcement of laws often is a more purely administrative process in modern societies. The administration of law becomes as important as actual police enforcement. This is evidenced by the growing number of regulatory agencies in modern societies. In the United States agencies such as the Federal Communications Commission, Federal Trade Commission, Federal Reserve Board, Federal Aviation Agency, and others oversee and regulate conformity to laws. These agencies cannot be considered a police force in the strict sense, but they do enforce laws—calling in police and courts if necessary (rarely is this done, however). Much law enforcement in modern societies is of this kind: administrative agencies interpreting laws for various system units, while constantly checking on these units' degree of conformity to laws. The emergence and proliferation of these strictly administrative units furthers the process of bureaucratization of law enforcement in modern legal systems.

LEGISLATION IN MODERN LEGAL SYSTEMS

In modern systems legislative bodies within the political subsystem increase in size and power. And they are responsible for a vast majority of law enactment in the legal subsystem. Just how free the legislatures (or assemblies, congresses, parliaments, or equivalent bodies) are to enact law differs greatly from society to society—under variations in these conditions: (a) How rigid and established is the constitution of the legal system? The more established the constitution—as in the United States, but not in England—the more constraint on law enactment. (b) How many and how powerful are the higher courts of the legal system? Do they have the power to interpret the constitutionality of laws? To the extent that they do, constraint on legislators is increased. (c) How extensive and effective are the enforcement agencies of the legal system? The more extensive and effective, the greater are the law-enacting powers of the legislature. (d) How extensive, professional, and integrated is the court system in a society? The more courts are an integrated and institutionalized mechanism for applying laws, the more effective law enactment can be. (e) How strong is custom and tradition in society? How much value and ideological consensus is there? The stronger custom and the more consensus over values and ideology, the greater is pressure on legislatures to enact laws not deviating too far from these cultural components. (f) How responsive to public opinion must the legislature be? Are legislatures elected in free elections? If they are, the more law enactment must reflect the fads and foibles of public opinion and sentiment. (g) And most important, how autonomous from the political rulers in a highly centralized polity is the legislature? To the extent that power lies with a small number of elites, the greater is the political constraint on legislatures. All of these conditions affect the legislative processes in modern societies. By establishing the weights and relative influence of each factor, predictions about exact legislative structures and processes could be made for each particular legal system.

Despite all the potential variability, several overall generalizations about legal legislation in modern systems can be made. Legislation is not piecemeal but comprehensive. Law enactment increasingly tends to cover large areas where disputes and integrative problems are evident (or at least perceived as problematic by legislators and political elites). This means that civil laws become a prominent part of the legal system, even where—as in England—a long tradition of common law exists. Once legislative enactment becomes prominent, a more consistent and stable body of laws emerges. While laws will always contradict and overlap each other in any legal system, comprehensive enactment tends to generate a more discernible system of laws than in transitional legal systems. And with the emergence of a stable legislature, comprehensive law enactment can become an effective mechanism of social change—of establishing new structures and relationships. This is especially true where an effective court and enforcement system exists to force and maintain the changes dictated by laws.

The functions or consequences of the legal system in modern societies are far reaching. Because of the high degree of differentiation and societal complexity, structural coordination is highly problematic. The legal system resolves many of the potentially destructive sources of structural disorganization in modern complex societies. Political development is advanced in modern societies. Tremendous power is concentrated in the polity and one of the major consequences of law is to make legitimate such concentration. This is usually done by a constitution and host of procedural laws outlining the ways in which power is to be used in a society. Because modern systems are constantly changing and in flux, new values as well as other cultural components inevitably come into conflict with the old. Modern legal systems resolve many of these conflicts, especially as they are reflected in actual structural disorganization. In the absence of a stable cultural storehouse, codified and enforced laws with clear-cut mechanisms for their alteration, adjustment, and mediation become a substitute for the lack of cultural integration and stability.

legal development: an overview
We have briefly outlined three types of legal systems: the primitive, transitional, and modern. All of these types can be found in the world's societies. Besides representing discrete types, these legal systems denote a series of developmental stages, although we should be careful not to stress unilineal evolution too much. Rather, all that can be inferred is that to the extent that legal change occurs in a society it will follow the pattern outlined above. What distinguishes legal systems from each other—whether as discrete types or stages in a developmental process—is the comparative degree of differentiation between basic legal elements and within these elements. From the primitive to transitional to modern, the once-fused elements of law, enforcement, mediation, and legislation increasingly become separated and somewhat autonomous (but of course integrated) from one another. And within the emerging body of laws,

court system, police force, and legislature there is growing size, complexity, and differentiation.

WORLD TRENDS IN LEGAL SYSTEMS

As societies modernize, religion, community, economy, and kinship can no longer organize all societal action. Societies become too large and heterogeneous to be organized in this way. To resolve the integrative problems inevitably accompanying differentiation, law becomes a dominant institution. In this process certain near-universal trends in the structuring of legal systems become evident.

bureaucratization

Because of the pivotal place of law in modern societies for coordinating action, the legal subsystem necessarily is large. Size inevitably generates administrative problems which are partially resolved through bureaucratization. We have pointed to the bureaucratization of enforcement and court structures in our previous discussion. We know that courts, police forces, and various administrative or regulatory agencies become heavily bureaucratized. Similarly, as legislatures increase in size, they too become vast administrative hierarchies. One consequence of this trend is that each bureaucracy of a modern legal system—courts, police, and legislatures—can achieve considerable autonomy from other elements because what occurs within each bureaucracy can be hidden and remain invisible. Such autonomy can protect and insulate the legal system—and its respective components—from excessive manipulation by either the public or political elite. Another consequence of bureaucratization and the resulting autonomy from supervision and control is that courts, police, and regulatory agencies can engage in de facto legislation—independent of the legislature and political elite. Within and behind the vast maze of bureaucratic offices in the courts, police, and regulatory agencies, differential and preferential enforcement—or lack of enforcement—of laws can be hidden. This amounts to law enactment, since laws are only laws when enforced. For example, the common process of "copping a plea" in American courts violates the spirit of American procedural law. By threatening delays, expense, and the risks of court trials, defendants can be coerced by court officials to plead guilty to a lesser charge. American police have been likely to treat violators of laws in an urban ghetto much differently from a white, middle-class violator of the same law in a suburban community. Such a practice amounts to police enactment of new substantive and procedural laws.

Similar processes occur behind the vast administrative bureaucracies of other modern legal systems. While bureaucratization is inevitable and necessary for the reasonably smooth functioning of a legal system, it grants legal structures autonomy, and in some cases license.

professionalization

Professionalization involves specialized training, regulation by professional associations, and the utilization of expertise for the welfare of clients. Professionalism in legal systems first emerges as courts become prominent and distinguishable elements. The most professionalized of court incumbents is the lawyer. By the Middle Ages lawyers' behavior involved three roles: *agent*, representing a client in court in various legal matters; *advocate*, pleading a case before a judge and perhaps jury of peers; and *jurisconsultant*, advising, teaching, consulting, and writing. The final criterion for professionalization is an active regulatory professional association. Lawyers in modern systems are usually regulated by such associations. Furthermore, because judges in most modern legal systems are lawyers, judge statuses can be considered quasi-professions in all respects except the formal regulatory capacity of the association. However, much informal regulation can still occur through judges' contacts with periodicals and members of the legal profession. Once the profession of law becomes established legislators in law-enacting bodies tend to be drawn from the profession. To the extent that this occurs, law-enacting structures become indirectly professionalized. Such professionalization of the legal system occurs for several reasons: (1) Modern legal systems are complex, with vast bodies of substantive and procedural laws. Such complexity necessitates considerable expertise and competence of courts and legislative incumbents. And this is usually achieved through extensive professional education. (2) Professionalism also stabilizes law—giving it a tradition that is passed from one generation of professionals to another. While the laws of a legal system constantly change, they are best changed by courts and legislatures in light of existing traditions and precedents. Professional and expert training assures some knowledge of these traditions and precedents. (3) Since so much legal activity occurs outside courts and legislatures in administrative hierarchies, considerable knowledge and expertise is required to carry out such administrative adjudication. Professional staffing of the bureaucracies and professional counseling of individuals negotiating within the bureaucracy thus become requisites for the smooth functioning of a modern legal system.

231

In all modern systems the legislative, court, and administrative statuses always possess a high proportion of professional participants. Recently the police in modern societies have also sought to professionalize with the result that specialized training and professional associations are becoming typical of the modern police force. Just how far this trend will go is unclear. Professionalization of the police probably increases its enforcement effectiveness, but for which client: the state or the violator? Since professional norms usually emphasize flexibility in the name of service for the client, it makes a great deal of difference just whom the police define as a client. If the client of the police is the state, then individual rights guaranteed under procedural law will be violated in service of this client. This is best illustrated in most totalitarian societies where a highly professionalized police force views the state as its client. On the other hand, if the violator is also defined as a client, then justice can probably prevail. But the former is more often the case than the latter with police professionalization in modern systems. Furthermore, in most societies powerful vested interests also become defined as clients of the police.

systematization and centralization

Law in modern societies is a subsystem, indicating a high degree of interrelatedness among its component parts. As legal systems modernize they come to constitute more of a system. There emerges a national system of codified laws which set general guidelines for state, regional, and local laws. While laws at each level display some autonomy from each other, they begin to approximate a reasonably consistent and coordinated system of rules. Courts also become systematized. The jurisdictions of local, state, regional, and national courts become clearly delimited. And they begin to form an explicit hierarchy of control and decision making. Enforcement structures similarly evolve clear boundaries of jurisdiction with a clear hierarchy of power and control.

Much of the systematization of the legal system is a reflection of political development and centralization. Until the exclusive use of force can be concentrated into a legitimate political structure, legal system development will remain somewhat disorganized at a national level. Nor can law become a system until clear legislative bodies emerge, for without a national legislature law remains tied to the scattered common-law precedents of local and regional courts or enactments of local legislatures. Once national legislative enactment of laws can occur and once there is a centralized source of force to back such enactment, then a comprehensive body of rules and courts to mediate them can develop and be effective. Conflicts, contradictions, anachronisms, and gaps in the law can be remedied by enactment of civil codes and statutes. These comprehensive codes and statutes help standardize both the procedures and substance of court and police actions into a more integrated whole. The reason for this lies in the fact that once mediation and enforcement agencies have a common set of procedural and substantive laws guiding their actions, consistency in enforcement and court processes across diverse regions can occur.

A major force promoting systematization and centralization of the legal system is the polity's use of law to effect social change. Law becomes the means for implementing the plans and programs of the polity. For example, in Russia legislative enactment drastically changed not only the structure of laws, but the courts, police, and administrative agencies. These changes were deliberately made to effect basic changes in conditions of production, commercial transactions, and the nature of legal ownership and contract (Friedmann, 1959). Law also radically changed the kinship structure by making marriage more of a legal contract, by creating egalitarianism among men and women in and out of the family, by removing much of the stigma of illegitimate children, and by the legislation of liberal abortion laws (Hazard, 1953; Berman, 1950). Utilizing legislation this way necessitates centralizing police, courts, and administrative agencies, because these must become integrated and centralized in order to enforce, administer, and mediate the new programs of the polity. To have courts, police, and other legal structures decentralized would make societal planning through legislation ineffective. Systems without this capacity to centralize and coordinate their legal subsystems cannot effect planned social change through legislation. However, there are many limitations on how much the legal system can be used as an agent of planned social change. These include: (1) How much do changes deviate from custom, tradition, and deeply held values? The more deviations, the greater will be resistance to planned change through law enactment (Lloyd, 1964:226–255). (2) How drastic are the structural rearrangements demanded by new laws? The more drastic, the greater resistance will be. (3) In what structural areas are changes legislated? It is probably easier to legislate change in the economic and educational spheres than in either the familial or religious spheres where values, traditions, and emotions run deep (Dror, 1968). And finally (4) how much force does the polity possess and how great is its capacity to apply that force? The more the polity has the sole possession of force and capacity to use it, the more it can overcome cultural and structural resistance to legislated changes.

In sum these trends — bureaucratization, professionalization, and systematization along centralized lines — appear ubiquitous. Some legal systems such as those in Continental Europe evidenced these trends early in the development. In others, such as in England, these trends became clear much later. Yet eventually as the integrative functions of law increase with general societal development, it can be expected that all legal systems will display a high degree of bureaucratization, professionalization, systematization, and centralization.

THE AMERICAN LEGAL SUBSYSTEM

Like any modern system of law, the American legal subsystem is a complex network of laws, courts, police, and legislatures. While these elements constitute an interrelated system, perfect syncronization and integration does not exist. As we will see, this results in part from the fact that there are multiple systems of laws, courts, police, and legislatures at the national, state, and local levels (Mayers, 1954). Much of this multiplicity—or duplicity—is the result of a historical legacy from colonial times. The American legal system was initially patterned after the English model, where to this day there is no formal constitution and where a strong common- (as opposed to civil) law tradition exists. This means that a system of law existed in each colony before a federal legal system was imposed after the American Revolution (Mayers, 1963:1–8). Buttressed by a strong states' rights ideology and values of individualism, the division between state and federal legal system elements has remained to the present day.

laws in the american legal system

The body of substantive and procedural statutes and codes in the United States is immense. Overriding *all* laws is the Constitution, which establishes the general profile of this body of law—but only very generally. At the federal level there is a body of specific federal codes. But in each state there is another body of state codes that are overridden by a state constitution. The relationship between these state and federal bodies of law is frequently unclear, ambiguous, and conflictual. However, state constitutions and codes cannot violate basic tenets of the Constitution. To add to the complexity of this picture are a host of local city and municipal charters, codes, and ordinances. These are only loosely integrated into, or even consistent with, state codes—although they tend to conform to the general articles of the state and federal constitutions.

Thus there can be considerable variability among federal, state, and local laws. And this raises a question as to why there is any consistency at all in the rules of the American legal subsystem. One reason for some degree of consistency is that law in America is highly professionalized, with lawyers, judges, and many legislators (who often are lawyers) holding common conceptions of law and a legal tradition. Also many legal organizations, most notably the American Law Institute, actively work toward the development of a uniform legal doctrine (Mayers, 1954:7–8). Furthermore, many state legislators or judges rendering landmark or precedent-setting decisions look around at what other kinds of enactment or decisions in similar areas have been made in other states (or at the federal level). And finally the Constitution sets general parameters circumscribing just what kinds of laws can exist. However, the lack of systematization in laws should be emphasized. Keeping state, local, and federal laws consistent remains a difficult — if not an impossible — task.

courts and tribunals in the american legal system

There are two general types of mediation structures in the American legal system: judicial courts; and administrative tribunals. The internal organization of these differs considerably.

JUDICIAL COURTS

These are the courts with which most Americans are familiar. They constitute a dual system of federal and state courts. Federal courts are not created by the Constitution. Rather, the Constitution merely empowers Congress with the right to establish courts if it sees fit (Mayers, 1954:5–39; 1963:10–11). And Congress has done so, with the result that there are several hundred federal courts scattered over the country. These federal courts constitute a hierarchy from local to appellate (appeal courts) and from appellate to the federal Supreme Court. Despite the seemingly systematic nature of federal courts, their jurisdiction is unclear. Usually they hear cases involving federal law but sometimes state courts also hear such cases. However, when a state court does adjudicate a case involving federal law, a federal court may review its decision. Frequently federal courts handle cases involving litigants from different states where different laws apply. Thus, while there are some boundaries of jurisdiction — interstate disputes and cases of federal law — these boundaries are not hard, fixed, or clear.

State courts are created by state constitutions. They also are organized in a hierarchy from local to appellate and from appellate to state supreme court. And like the federal courts, ultimate jurisdiction of the state court system frequently rests with the Supreme Court when an issue pertaining to federal law or the Constitution cannot be satisfactorily adjudicated in a lower federal or state supreme court.

The cases adjudicated or mediated within either the federal or state courts are of two general substantive types: *criminal* and *torts* (or civil cases). The procedural rules for each differ somewhat. Criminal cases involve the state as one of the litigants (in the person of the district attorney or Attorney General in federal courts), who prosecutes an accused defendant of crimes or wrongdoings against the state, people, or public. In these cases, not only is evidence gathered and presented in court but arrest and incarceration of the defendant by the state is often necessary. Because of this power of arrest and incarceration, a whole series of procedural laws protect the defendant not only in but outside the court—even before the defendant is brought to trial. Tort cases involve noncriminal disputes between two private parties, whether individuals or larger units. These cases usually involve issues of money, contract, foreclosure, and noncriminal harms. Because of this, somewhat different procedural rules govern proceedings in and out of court (Mayers, 1963: 12–43).

ADMINISTRATIVE TRIBUNALS

In order to meet system goals in a large and bureaucratized society, the polity is involved in extensive administration of policies which usually are codified in laws—but not always. Often to enforce these policies and laws the judicial court system is not utilized. Rather, a variegated array of administrative offices issue directory and prohibitive orders concerning a wide variety of activities. For example, these offices can forbid business activity, impose monetary penalties, deny the use of public facilities, withdraw licenses, and deny eligibility (Mayers, 1954:407). Because these offices apply, mediate, and often enforce laws in a wide variety of situations, they constitute a type of court or what we can call an administrative tribunal. The most prevalent jurisdiction of administrative tribunals is in the area of licensing at both the state and federal level. The law empowers administrative offices with the duties of granting licenses for certain activities such as selling liquor and running a television station. These administrative agencies are also empowered to revoke licenses for failure to conform to laws. What constitutes conformity is usually left up to a group of administrative investigators and judges. This makes such agencies a court, since they apply substantive laws, render decisions as to whether one has been violated, and then impose penalties. At the state level these administrative tribunals typically carry out these judicial operations in the field of licensing occupations, establishments, and businesses. At the federal level licensing and regulating has evolved in a wide variety of areas, including interstate businesses (Interstate Commerce Commission), agricultural business and exchanges (Department of Agriculture), commerce (Federal Trade Commission), air travel (Civil Aeronautics Board), communications (Federal Communications Commission), securities (Securities Exchange Commission), labor-management relations (National Labor Relations Board), banking (Federal Reserve Board), and a host of other government agencies. Each is a tribunal interpreting and enforcing rules as they relate to these and other activities (Mayers, 1954:403–498). Although the procedural rules governing these tribunals are typically not so exact as those governing the judiciary some procedural rules exist— sometimes written down but more frequently embodied in traditional practices. This naturally gives administrative tribunals considerably more latitude than the courts of the judiciary in adjudicating cases. Once an administrative tribunal has rendered a decision and penalty the administrative agency may enforce its decision by seeking a court order from the judiciary and the actual implied threat of force that goes along with such an order. Sometimes the courts overturn decisions reached by administrative tribunals, but rarely is this the case.

It is difficult to ascertain how much adjudication by administrative tribunals occurs in the American legal system, but it appears as though a great deal does occur and the amount appears to be increasing. There are both advantages and disadvantages to such a trend. On the one hand, adjudication of a wide sphere and volume of cases with administrative experts as judges and jury can occur, while on the other, the procedural safeguards in administrative tribunals are not so extensive or binding as those in judiciary courts. This means that adjudication can be a reflection of political imperatives rather than justice.

the structure of enforcement in the american legal system

The enforcement structure of the American legal system is a series of agencies with different but overlapping jurisdictions. Generally there are autonomous local community or city, county, and statewide police forces. At the national level the armed forces can be called upon to enforce laws and court decisions unenforceable by state, county, and city police. The national police, the Federal Bureau of Investigation, can enforce certain national laws when necessary. The jurisdictions of city, county, and state police vary considerably. Typically city police have jurisdiction within incorporated areas, county police or sheriffs within unincorporated areas of a county. However, the relationship of state police to either of these displays tremendous variation from state to state and within a state from city to city and county to county. In the American legal system the national police do not engage in day-to-day law enforcement. Rather, they are invoked only under unusual circumstances and are used only when state and local police are unwilling or unable to enforce laws and court decisions. Probably the most notable uses of the national police force in recent American history have been in riot control and in enforcing federal court decisions for school integration in the South.

the structure of law enactment in the american legal system

Each city, county, and state has law-enacting bodies — the city council, board of supervisors, and state legislature. At the national level, Congress is embodied with law-making powers. These multiple legislatures are a reflection of the complex, pluralistic, and decentralized political subsystem in the United States (see Chapter 10). Furthermore, law enactment occurs in other structures in the American legal system — most notably in the courts and police forces.

Common law is still a major source of law enactment in the United States. But more significantly the decisions of the Supreme Court represent a king of quasi-law enactment. By virtue of its powers to interpret the constitutionality of legislated laws as well as common-law precedents, the Supreme Court has a legislative prerogative. For example, when the doctrine of "separate but equal" was declared constitutional by an earlier Supreme Court, it had enacted a law. When this doctrine was declared unconstitutional, a new law had been enacted. It is not a question of any particular Supreme Court overstepping its prerogatives and powers, for law-enacting powers are invested in the structure of any body required to judge the constitutionality of laws and court decisions.

As noted earlier the police enact laws by determining which laws are to be enforced. Also, by differentially enforcing the same law the police can change the very substance of a currently enforced law. For example, to enforce or not enforce sex crimes amounts to legislating just what the sex laws are. Or to enforce a law with respect to blacks in a ghetto but not whites in the suburbs amounts to changing the substantive content of law. Such police enactment occurs frequently in the American legal system, although exact data are scarce (President's Commission on Law Enforcement and Administration of Justice, 1967). Although such police enactment of laws may be reflective of ideological biases, it is also a structural inevitability. In a complex legal system where there are volumes of laws (often conflicting, anachronistic, or irrelevant) and where the limited police force cannot possibly enforce all of them, selective and perhaps differentiated enforcement is inevitable (whether it is desirable or not is an entirely different question).

trends in the american legal system

On the basis of previous discussion it would be expected that the American legal system is highly bureaucratized, professionalized, and systematized. But it is not so centralized as many other modern legal systems, especially those in Continental and Eastern Europe. It maintains a multiple system of courts, police, and legislatures, as well as a varied and often conflicting body of state, local, and national laws.

This fact has far-reaching consequences for bureaucratization, professionalization, and complete systematization. No central legal bureaucracy exists to coordinate all legal activity. The Department of Justice in Washington, D.C., has only loose control over its counterparts at the state and local level. A high degree of bureaucracy exists in all legal structures but it remains localized rather than national. A similar situation exists with professional associations—most notably the American Bar Association. Although it is a national association the real power and control of professional activity rests with state bar associations, which are only loosely connected to a national association. National systematization can never be complete in a legal system so decentralized. But such a system potentially can remain flexible since it can be responsive to local and state conditions.

SUMMARY

In this chapter a brief outline of the profile of law in traditional and modern societies was presented. All societies were viewed as displaying certain basic legal elements, including laws, police, courts, and legislatures. The way these are organized into the institution of law was seen as varying tremendously. Yet in all societies the institution of law was considered to have certain general consequences for structural coordination, legitimizing power and inequity, and cultural preservation, codification, and integration. After these preliminaries, we turned to a description and comparison of primitive, transitional, and modern legal systems. Next certain general trends toward bureaucratization, professionalization, systematization, and centralization were briefly discussed. Finally the American legal subsystem was examined. Attention was focused on the structure of laws, courts, enforcement agencies, and legislative bodies. This structure was described as manifesting world trends toward bureaucratization, professionalization, and systemization, but within a pluralistic and in some ways decentralized form.

239

the
institutional
environment
of
LAW   9

Legal development can be viewed as one form of institutional adjustment to ubiquitous problems of control and coordination facing modernizing societies. While there appears to be some overall pattern of legal development the specifics are highly variable for any particular society because of many unique conditions, including geographical location, historical accidents, conquest, and current social forces. Obviously it is impossible to trace legal development from a primitive to modern profile for one society, since frequent changes of system boundaries and patterns of societal conquest inevitably obscure unilineal development. For example, the highly developed system of Roman law was imposed upon many primitive legal systems during the expansion of the Empire, with the result that a developmental jump occurred in these primitive legal systems. Or, as was the case in Soviet central Asia, the introduction of highly modern Soviet law into the more traditional areas along the Chinese border produced a legal system in central Asia with both distinctly primitive and modern elements (Massell, 1968). Yet in the long run changes of legal systems within a bounded area usually reveal certain general patterns during modernization. One of the reasons for this is that law tends to be responsive to alterations in its institutional environment. Modernization inevitably generates conflict, tensions, strains, and disjunctures which can force the modernization of law in a society. However, legal systems often remain rigid and unresponsive to the changes ushered in by modernization. In fact a legal system's incapacity to adjust to changing conditions can greatly impede modernization and result in a society's destruction. For this reason we will have to caution against overestimating the impact of changes in the institutional environment on legal development. To the extent that these changes force legal development, it is predicted that they do so in those areas delineated in this chapter.

ECONOMY AND LAW

In hunting and gathering and simple agrarian economies most economic activity is carried out in the family with kinship norms guiding and directing economic activity. Some of these kinship norms can be considered legal rules, for when violated they bring specified punishments administered by designated others in certain appropriate ways. Thus in hunting and gathering societies laws tend to be divided into substantive and procedural rules and enforced and mediated by invoked rather than standing courts and police. However, as soon as these primitive economies can generate an economic surplus of goods and commodities, exchange and market relations are likely to emerge and present a series of problems revolving around how exchanges of goods are to be regularized and how the good faith of both parties engaged in an exchange is to be assured. One of many alternative responses to such problems is the development of laws to regulate exchanges. The exact processes by which this occurs can be various. Sometimes through trial and error binding legal norms emerge in a subtle process of give and take between parties engaged in exchanges. At other times persistent conflicts revolving around exchange may be resolved by law only after a prolonged feud or war. Or as is frequently the case, tribal and village leaders in attempts to resolve disputes may legislate certain laws to regulate trade. While only a detailed historical account for a particular society can reveal just how the economy influenced the emergence of such trade laws, it is clear that once they emerge in a society they become powerful sources of social control. For example, among the Trobriand Islanders when a party failed to meet his economic obligations (such as defaulting a payment) the economic support of the whole community could be withheld from the defaulter. He would then be isolated, alone, and helpless—a very severe penalty. This situation marks what is perhaps the simplest kind of legal regulation of economic activities. There is no distinction between crimes and torts, for violation is an offense against the whole community and the community serves as both court and police (Durkheim, 1933).

Once exchanges of economic goods expand in volume and intensity, economic conditions can further legal development. The first step in such development is the distinction between criminal and tort laws—that is, laws regulating violation against the public or community (crimes) and those concerning disputes among individuals (torts). Torts, as distinct from crimes, apparently first emerged in the Egyptian legal system sometime before 4000 B.C. While the exact reasons for this can never be known, torts probably emerged in response to the extensive trading that occurred among the semi-nomadic groups of this society. In Mesopotamia somewhat later the Codes of Hammurabi dating from 2100 B.C. contained numerous sections dealing with commerce—deeds, sales, loans, deposits, bills of lading, agencies, and partnerships (Davis, 1962:81). Law apparently resolved many problems of coordination and control stemming from trade in the ancient crossroads of the world. In feudal Europe several thousand years later, when economic surplus began to be exchanged in the emerging markets, a similar body of torts developed. For a long time these torts, or "merchant laws" as they were known, remained outside the formal legal system. Only later, through a long series of common-law decisions in local courts, did they come to be incorporated into a formal legal system and become enforced by state police.

Thus under the impact of increased economic exchange, torts become clearly differentiated from crimes. And with this basic differentiation, courts, police, and eventually legislatures develop to codify and expand the growing body of torts. The emergence of these laws and structures to mediate, expand, and enforce them allows for increases in exchanges of goods and property. This in turn represents positive feedback to the productive sector of these trading economies — thus encouraging expanded economic activity. When more advanced industrial technology and capital become typical of these European economies, these torts governing marketing perhaps provided an initial stimulus to economic development by allowing for more extensive and easy distribution. And with a well-established body of rules, courts, police, and legislatures revolving around property, contract, and trade, torts could be more readily changed as they became inadequate to the increased production and distribution ushered in by industrialization. This relationship between the law and economy can be visualized by examining China — a society which was as developed technologically and culturally as feudal Europe but which did not industrialize until much later. One of the great mysteries of history is why China did not industrialize until only recently. Part of the explanation apparently lies in the Chinese legal system, which had extensive laws as well as court and police structures but not a codified body of torts. The Imperial Code of medieval China was a criminal code and did not concern matters of trade, commerce, transactions, exchanges, contract, and property. These matters were left to local customary law and did not become incorporated into the national legal system until recently. Without such torts a major block to economic development existed in China despite its advanced technology (Weber, 1954; Sawer, 1965:55–60; Lloyd, 1964:241–242; Davis, 1962:80–81).

The impact of the economy on law in traditional Third World societies is difficult to ascertain because much of the Western legal system has been imposed upon and/or absorbed by these societies as a result of colonization, conquest, and emulation prior to economic conditions necessitating an extensive tort system. The adoption of the Western legal model presents many problems, since inevitably it will conflict with local and customary laws, courts, and enforcement structures and processes. Tribal, village and territorial, and clan law must coexist with an imported, highly codified, and systematized legal system. This results in confusion and chaos, since each legal system subverts and contradicts the other. However, in the long run there can be advantages to such importation of foreign legal systems. With initial industrialization in traditional societies economic conditions begin to fit the imported legal system, with the result that there is less lag between the emergence of new economic conditions and the eventual reliance on a codified body of torts in the legal system. In this way much of the long, drawn-out process of changing old traditional laws through a myriad of common-law court precedents is eliminated, since courts can rely on the imported body of laws. To have an existing body of torts can thus greatly accelerate the process of economic development in Third World nations.

Modern industrial and postindustrial economies present many sources of malintegration. For example, problems of regulating, coordinating, and controlling exchanges within and among the myriad of gathering, producing, distributing, and servicing economic organizations are immense. The intensity of these problems is manifested in the vast legislative expansion of private law (torts), as well as the courts and police to adjudicate and enforce these laws. Thus the trend initiated with incipient trade and exchange in traditional economies expands exponentially with industrialization. In a highly complex economy where rapid and voluminous exchanges, transactions, and transfers of property are necessary, a modern body of laws rather than tradition or custom becomes the only viable means to avoid chaos and confusion in the economy as well as in the broader society.

One of the most prominent and problematic exchanges in an industrial or industrializing economy is between labor and the various economic organizations where labor is employed. Human effort must be exchanged for wages, but one of the problems in such exchanges is that labor usually views wages as insufficient for the amount of human effort expended. This sense of inequity is usually heightened when coupled with unsafe, unsanitary, and unpleasant working conditions. Frequently labor unionizes in an effort to increase its benefits in the exchange. This response usually leads to resistance by employing organizations with the result that conflict, violence, and strife become typical of labor's participation in an industrializing economy. As long as this situation persists, the functioning and perhaps survival of both individual laborers and the economy as a whole are greatly impaired. The conflict is usually resolved through labor-management legislation, where substantive and procedural laws, courts, enforcement, and administrative agencies are established to mitigate these problems. Societies not developing these legal mechanisms can inhibit economic growth, since there is no assurance or predictability of labor's integration into the economy. Resolving these labor-management problems is thus a major stimulus to expansion of substantive and procedural bodies of laws as well as court, legislative, administrative, and enforcement structures in a modern legal system.

Partially in response to resolving labor-management problems, but also as a response to more general problems of coordination between a modern economy and polity, the proliferation of administrative law, agencies, and tribunals accompanies societal development. Whether in a highly centralized state as in Russia or a comparatively decentralized state as in the United States, administrative laws, agencies, and tribunals come to regulate further general economic activity. This increasing extension of state control over the economy through administrative law occurs for at least two reasons: (1) Economic processes always have far-reaching consequences for the rest of a society (we documented this for the family and education). As the economy increases in size and complexity these consequences become even more extensive and come to have profound political ramifications which force the polity to begin regulating and controlling economic activity. In both socialistic and capitalistic systems this is done through the enactment of vast bodies of administrative law and the establishment of administrative tribunals. (2) Many of the goals and political policies of a society — whether modern or modernizing — hinge upon economic growth and development. This often results in a situation where political stability and legitimacy rest on what occurs in the economy. To synchronize economic processes to political goals thus requires extensive economic legislation as well as establishment of administrative agencies and tribunals to review and enforce such legislation.

In at least these ways, then, we can view the economy as having a significant impact on legal development. With the emergence of economic surplus, exchange occurs. Efforts to regularize these exchanges can eventually lead to the clear differentiation of torts from crimes. This differentiation in turn creates new and different procedural rules governing these two bodies of substantive law (sometimes referred to as public and private law). In turn creation of new bodies of law can force courts to reorganize and specialize in order to mediate and adjudicate many different types of cases governed by diverse substantive and procedural laws. Eventually such a situation creates more diverse and complex enforcement problems resulting in the growth of police and other enforcement agencies. As economic changes increase in volume and diversity new laws are enacted to encompass growing economic activity. Extensive law enactment further solidifies legislative processes as the most expedient means of adjusting laws to changing conditions in a society. As the consequences of the economy become inseparable from political processes a vast body of administrative law and accompanying enforcement and tribunal structures become a prominent feature of the legal system. These events increase the complexity of the substantive and procedural laws in a modern legal system, while greatly expanding the scope of court, enforcement, and legislative processes in a society.

POLITY AND LAW

Legal system development is intimately connected to political development. To understand the structure and function of legal systems therefore forces us to examine the impact of the polity on law. Additionally many of the trends toward bureaucratization, centralization, and systematization in legal systems are often an adjustment to political processes in a society.

Traditional polities display tremendous variability. In the most primitive society the polity is fused with kinship structures and in essence is composed of family heads (in accordance with descent and authority rules). In advanced traditional systems the polity is often clearly distinct and differentiated from kinship and embodied in a state with a vast administrative bureaucracy (Bohannan, 1964). In general we can usually locate primitive legal systems in societies where the state has only begun to evolve and differentiate from kinship. These facts pose the question of just what relationship an emerging polity—or state—has to legal development. For reasons not fully understood, particular kin groups in highly traditional societies often begin to engage in conquest and acquire territory. Once these kin groups begin to acquire property and territory, they gain power and possess the capacity to control and regulate other, less propertied kin groups. The possession of power and territory presents administrative problems of maintaining control, coordinating activities in territories, and in general just keeping track of subordinate groups. These administrative problems can lead to the crude beginnings of bureaucratization. When bureaucracies are small they are staffed by kinsmen. But as they grow with territorial conquests and expansion they come to be staffed by administrators from nonelite kin groups. This whole process of acquiring territory and power and the gradual proliferation of an administrative bureaucracy documents the emergence of a state—a locus of power and its administration and implementation within a delimited territory (Fried, 1968; Parsons, 1955). Such political processes have frequently occurred throughout recorded history. In many areas territorial boundaries have become stabilized and so we can speak of a nation-state. And frequently as competent or powerful administrators move up the bureaucratic hierarchy, they assume leadership positions regardless of kin affiliation. Over time leadership and elite classes or castes emerge, which are composed of kin groups much different from those originally engaged in territorial conquest. And with successive military *coups*, peasant revolutions, or colonization by foreign powers, the leaders of the state bureaucracy change—thus further removing the state from its initial kinship origins.

For our purposes what is important in this process is that the development of a political state generates problems of coordination and regulation, which can stimulate legal development. The emergence of public and private law as well as a clear differentiation between torts and crimes often occur in response to administrative attempts to establish clear guidelines between the state and other system units. The emergence of legislative bodies to enact laws governing new areas of friction among individuals and organizations or between the state and the broader society is a further indication of the polity's attempt to regulate and control activities and deviations within its territory. The centralization of police, military, and other instruments of force into the polity expands the capacity of the state to legislate and regulate relations. But the proliferation of state or national courts establishes a process of mediating and adjudicating disputes and conflicts which can mitigate the use of force by the polity.

In emerging states, laws, courts, police, and law enactment are not completely centralized, bureaucratized, or systematized because the state does not yet have control over many localities within its broad territories. Much local kin and customary law enforcement and adjudication still occurs. But as the state evolves and comes to have clear-cut goals and policies it begins to consolidate and regulate more closely activities in its territories. Frequently this is done by force, but eventually it occurs through the development of legal rules, courts, legislatures, and enforcement structures. This process took hundreds of years to occur in Europe after the fall of Rome. In Third World nations, even where diverse tribes and territories have been incorporated into one nation, it appears to be occurring more rapidly, although somewhat chaotically. Yet in all developing legal systems much of the impetus comes from political attempts at consolidation of territories and regulation and control within these territories.

In sum, then, political development has these effects on legal development: (1) With the emergence of a state some civil law enactment is possible. Without a state to govern the total society system-wide legislation is difficult since laws remain tied to local common-law precedents or local community leader enactments. (2) Political development also means that power—especially the capacity to use force and coercion—becomes consolidated and centralized. This occurrence allows for a national enforcement system to emerge, with the result that some teeth can be put into law enactment at the society-wide level. (3) With an emerging—but far from complete or systematic —body of civil law and with national enforcement structures, courts can begin to be coordinated into a national hierarchy, extending from the national to the local level. Such coordination initiates the long process of emancipating local courts from local precedents, traditions, and customs. Thus political development in traditional societies allows for but does not guarantee the beginning of legal systematization.

Modern polities, like their traditional counterparts, attempt to regulate and control activity within their territory. However, in modern societies the state administrative bureaucracy and the capacity to use power and force are more consolidated and centralized than they are in more traditional polities. Furthermore, the goals, policies, and priorities among them are more clearly articulated and established. To achieve these more clearly delineated goals the polity must regulate, control, and allocate system units in virtually all institutional spheres more precisely. One way to do this is through the application of the force possessed by the state. But such application is effective only in the short run, because in the long run the use of force is inflammatory and generates strains, tensions, resentment, and conflicts. Much more effective is the development of reasonable and acceptable laws, courts to mediate them, agencies to administer them, and—only as a last resort—force to back them up. Rarely is such an idyllic situation achieved, for polities in even the most stable modern systems resort to force and coercion. But in order to coordinate actions in the pursuit of political goals modern polities increasingly rely on law and many of the features of a modern legal system reflect this fact.

The emergence of legislatures to enact vast bodies of civil law becomes crucial as the polity tries to regulate, coordinate, and allocate activity. While a considerable number of common-law precedents are enacted in the judicial system, legislative or civil law becomes necessary to maintain political control and coordination. The centralization of police and the courts into an integrated system marks the increasing desire of the polity to have control over legal system structures and processes. Such centralization is particularly evident in the area of administrative law, where in a very direct way the administrative bureaucracy and tribunals of the state control, regulate, sanction, and adjudicate activities crucial to achieving political goals. These administrative laws are enacted by the political legislature, and administered, enforced, and adjudicated within the governmental, not judicial or legal, bureaucracy of a society. Such laws, agencies, and tribunals thus give the polity tremendous power over activities among individuals and organizations without constantly having to utilize physical force and coercion.

Because modern legal systems are well institutionalized and established they can be effective in mediating disputes and mitigating conflict. When effective, laws, courts, and enforcement procedures become perceived as legitimate and proper by the population of a society. Under these conditions the polity does not have to resort constantly to force and coercion. Rather, by controlling legal processes ranging from law enactment to enforcement and administration, the polity can also control and regulate activity in a society. One of the best ways to illustrate this political utilization of law is to examine cases where it fails. The colonial powers consistently encountered problems in Africa when they attempted to impose European legal traditions on the primitive and transitional legal systems of this continent. For example, the Kuba of the Congo possessed a primitive tribal and territorial legal system which persisted long after colonial law was introduced, because the Kuba system was more relevant and effective in regulating the traditional activities of the Congolese. In providing stability and regularity to action it became legitimate in the eyes of the Kuba tribesmen. Persistence of local laws can reach extreme proportions, as among the Tiv, where it was considered immoral of a tribesman to adjudicate a case in a government or state court (Bohannan, 1964:202–203). These kinds of considerations reveal that there are limits on just how far the state can go in using legal institutions for coordination and control. To legislate and attempt to enforce laws calling for radically new social relations will be resisted and frequently violated. For instance, the attempt by the postrevolutionary Russian polity to restructure through law basic family and community relations in its Mongolian territories proved a disastrous failure (Massell, 1968), since the laws bore little relation to existing structural arrangements. But these cultural and structural sources are only constraints not roadblocks to legislative initiative by the polity. The state through its monopoly on force—as well as control over at least educational socialization—can legislate social change. As in Russia, the simultaneous enactment of new laws, state indoctrination into a new Soviet culture, and the threat or use of force allowed the Soviet polity to restructure radically through law a whole new series of social relationships (in pursuit of the goals of socialism, military power, and economic development). In the southern United States laws and their enforcement have drastically changed many (although far from all) existing structural patterns of racial oppression and discrimination.

In sum we can conclude that as power becomes consolidated into the state, law becomes a major mechanism for the polity's regulation and control of system processes and relationships. While the state's capacity to utilize the legal system for goal attainment is always limited, it does possess considerable latitude in using law to implement policies. These facts help account for the emergence of a systematized and centralized legal system culminating in various governmental structures—federal laws, legislatures, courts, and police. The emergence of a vast body of public and administrative law (and tribunals) is perhaps the best indicator of this increasing state influence and control over the legal system.

RELIGION AND LAW

All societies exhibit religion or a set of beliefs and structures revolving around the cosmos, supernatural, and unknown. The relationship between religion and law is complex and variable. Religious beliefs underlie many basic legal postulates in both the most simple and complex societies. In traditional societies specific laws are intimately connected to religious beliefs (Hoebel, 1954; Diamond, 1951). However, in modern societies the connections between laws and religion become less direct and visible. In fact from one perspective, legal development can be viewed as a progressive separation of law from religion. Part of the reason for this occurrence lies in the fact that the emergence, persistence, and growth of legal systems are increasingly related to secular rather than sacred pressures and processes in a society. However, except perhaps in the Soviet Union and other countries where religious extinction was at one time promoted by the state, religious beliefs remain among the cultural components codified and preserved by a modern legal system.

In every primitive society the existence of spirit beings and supernatural powers is a basic assumption and condition of social life. These beings are seen as responding with favor or disfavor to the mundane and specific behaviors and acts of mortal men. This relationship between the supernatural and secular is usually codified into a series of religious postulates or dogmas which represent the wills and dictates of supernatural spirits, beings, and powers. The members of a society are then required to harmonize their actions with the dictates of these religious beings. Religion is thus a very powerful source of social control and regulation in primitive societies. In some primitive legal systems laws are intimately entangled with religious dogma but regardless of the extensiveness of these interrelations, law always displays some autonomy from religion. Many religious dictates when violated in a primitive society are sanctioned by the supernatural—not by men. Violating a taboo will bring misfortune. For example, among the Eskimos violating a religious taboo is usually viewed as the cause of bad luck or hardship. To eliminate such misfortune requires an Eskimo to consult a shaman who points out the violations and serves as an intermediary between the gods and the violator in order to relieve the hardship (Hoebel, 1954:261). This constantly reinforced association in the minds of men between violating taboo and bad luck maintains considerable order and control in Eskimo society. But when an Eskimo persistently violates a taboo specific members of the community punish him. In this latter instance legal sanctions rather than religious sanctions of guilt and fear are employed. Excessive sin is thus a crime and is punished by men rather than gods, although in such cases law clearly embodies certain religious dictums. However, many of the laws of even the Eskimo society bear little relationship to religion. Wife stealing and murder are wholly secular, for the legal rules concerning these crimes do not derive from religious dogmas nor do they overlap with the jurisdiction of the supernatural (Hoebel, 1954:261). Thus, while interrelated with religion, even the most primitive legal system is also autonomous and encompasses purely secular crimes. Legal and religious norms thus represent overlapping but separate mechanisms of control and integration in highly traditional societies.

In more advanced traditional societies where a transitional legal system is evident, the separation of law and religion increases. Much law codifies and represents religious dogmas, just as it does other cultural components such as custom, traditions, and values. But the emergence of an extensive body of torts and the growing centralization and systematization of courts, police, and legislatures point to the influence of other institutions on legal evolution. These other influences emanate primarily from the polity and economy (see above) and to a lesser extent from the family and education (see below). With the increasing commerce and exchange of a modernizing economy and with the emerging state, the law concerns the integration of increasingly secular relations within the economy and between individuals and the developing polity. Since integrative problems stem more from strains in concrete relations among men and organizations than from strains in relations between men and the supernatural, torts come to rival crimes as components of the legal system. Also crimes become increasingly redefined as violations of the public's and state's will.

With economic and political development, problems of coordination and control intensify. Private and public laws, as well as the power of courts, police, and legislatures to adjudicate, enforce, and enact laws, proliferate and become more clearly articulated into a centralized system. Laws reflect the purely secular problems, such as how individuals are to relate to the state, how labor is to become incumbent in the economy, how education is to operate, how family relations and divorce are to be regularized, how disputes between individuals and corporations are to be settled, and even how religion is to relate to the state, economy, family, and education. Such is inevitably the case, since modernization generates a myriad of secular integrative problems which religion in its nonsecular and sacred focus cannot resolve. To the extent that religion has consequences for these secular issues, they are indirect in the form of religious beliefs serving as underlying judicial postulates.

252

EDUCATION AND LAW

Primitive legal systems possess unwritten and uncodified laws. Courts and police are simple structures adjudicating and enforcing laws as disputes emerge. Legislation is a mixture of common-law decisions and fiats by political leaders (who are often the judges of courts). Education in such societies is elitist, encompassing religious and perhaps political socialization of privileged kinsmen. To the extent that political leaders socialized in the incipient educational subsystem become judges and legislators, education is involved in legal processes. But this involvement need not be extensive for the simplicity of the legal system does not require prolonged formal education.

However, in transitional legal systems the situation changes. Laws are written, codified, and stored, creating an extensive legal tradition. With a large body of written laws forming a legal tradition, formal education of judges, lawyers, administrators, and legislators becomes necessary if they are to be capable of comprehending the growing body of law as well as administering, adjudicating, maintaining, and perhaps adding to its contents. In applying the increasingly complex body of law to specific cases or in establishing common-law precedents judges must possess considerable legal training if decisions and precedents are to display some degree of consistency with existing laws and social conditions. Lawyers advising clients and advocating their cases in courts must also have considerable knowledge of substantive and procedural law. While this knowledge can be acquired informally and through experience, formal professional training of lawyers becomes necessary if the legal system is to develop further. Also, just as the administrative bureaucracies of a developing economy require expertise, so do the court and legislative bureaucracies of a transitional legal system. Without some degree of formal and secular training these officials can subvert the legal system by generating administrative chaos. Finally emergence of a consistent body of civil law (enacted law) is dependent not only upon a large number of educated and professional legislators but also upon extensive law schools and libraries which can guide and assist lawmakers. For example, the early emergence of French civil law under Napoleon can be party attributed to the well-developed French law schools and the legal scholars in them (Lloyd, 1964).

In order for a legal system to become modern an extensive legal profession must exist. Attached to higher education, professional schools preserving the legal tradition while socializing future incumbents of the legal system must exist, for several reasons: (1) The laws of a modern legal system are complex, requiring considerable expertise in applying them. Judges must therefore be well versed in many areas to adjudicate cases properly. (2) Similarly, lawyers must be capable of advising and pleading cases in accordance with a complex body of substantive and procedural laws as well as the proliferating body of administrative law. (3) Legislators must have access to legal advice in law enactment in order to preserve some consistency among laws. (4) Court officials and administrators must have legal training to record, store, and implement court proceedings. (5) Officials in administrative agencies and tribunals must be capable of applying and adjudicating a host of administrative laws, because without some degree of professional expertise in this vast legal network bureaucratization would generate more chaos than it resolves. Furthermore, systematization as well as centralization of laws, courts, legislatures, enforcement, and administrative agencies would be impossible without at least some formal training of participants in the legal system. Thus without formal education and professionalization there would be few of the common legal conceptions, practices, precepts, or traditions underlying and supporting these trends typical of modern legal systems.

Aside from facilitating the internal development of legal systems, education also has far-reaching consequences for generating diffuse commitment in the members of a society to law. If a legal system is to be effective people in a society must have some willingness to obey laws, adhere to court decisions, and accept law enforcement and enactment. Educational socialization through instruction in history, lore, civics, and government generates diffuse commitment to the traditions and values reflected in laws as well as specific structures of the legal system (Almond and Verba, 1963). Furthermore, formal education probably generates cognitive awareness of legal structures and processes. Such awareness perhaps helps maintain the legitimacy of the legal system by making it familiar and less intimidating to the members of a society. It might appear that this would be particularly essential for the smooth functioning of a modern legal system with its complex structures and procedures. However, this point should not be emphasized too much. While formal education increases people's awareness of legal processes, such awareness may not increase their commitment to the system (Murphy and Tanenhaus, 1968). One study of the American Supreme Court (one of the most visible elements of the legal system) showed that most people were ignorant of the functions of the Court at even the most elementary level. Educated respondents were somewhat more likely to be aware of the Court's functions in American society—but only a little. Furthermore, only a minority of respondents in this study could name specific cases or landmark decisions of the Court—including school integration, reapportionment, and criminals' civil liberties. Of those who could, most disagreed with the Court's decisions. Yet when asked about the legitimacy or right of the Court to do what it was doing (even if they were not sure just what that was), an overwhelming majority answered in the affirmative. And so here is ignorance of and disagreement with a highly prominent and visible legal structure coupled with a general and pervasive commitment to that structure.

And although formal education is somewhat involved in this process, it seems unessential in terms of conferring legitimacy to the Court—and probably the rest of the Ameican legal system. What appears crucial, then, is that diffuse commitment exists, even in the face of ignorance and dissention. Perhaps this unreflective commitment is necessary if the Supreme Court in the United States must interpret the most controversial cases, especially those involving deeply held values and beliefs. To have too much knowledge could perhaps undermine the existing commitment of Americans to the Supreme Court.

What this points to is that diffuse, vague, and imprecise commitment is perhaps more important in conferring legitimacy than knowledge or awareness of legal structures and processes. This fact raises questions about the involvement of education in generating commitment. One answer is provided by the Soviet Union: in Russia a great deal of stress is placed upon legal education in the schools. Students are instructed on the organization and processes of the legal system as well as on the ideology and values that it preserves and codifies. The courts are also directly involved in legal education, with judges giving lectures and their courts publishing pamphlets and texts (Berman, 1950). Out of these processes knowledge of and commitment to the law has emerged. This emphasis on legal education in Russia is understandable in light of how it has been used by the polity to restructure and organize Soviet society. On the other hand, in the United States formal education revolves around civics and government, focusing only indirectly and vaguely on the law. Emphasis is on the values and traditions underlying the American form of government—rather than on the legal system per se. Out of this socialization or indoctrination some degree of commitment emerges, but just how much cannot be ascertained.

KINSHIP AND LAW

In primitive societies kinship is a dominant institution, for other institutions are intimately fused with family activity. As societies develop, other institutions including law increasingly become separated and differentiated from kinship. The structure of a primitive legal system is thus greatly reflective of kinship organization in a traditional society, while modern legal systems display a more segmental relationship to kinship.

Laws in primitive legal systems are often coextensive with some kinship rules as well as religious dogmas, customs, and traditions. And courts, enforcement, and legislative statuses—when existent or invoked—are often staffed by kinsmen. Familial socialization thus inevitably involves legal socialization. To the extent that the young acquire knowledge of and commitment to kinship, they also absorb a great deal of knowledge about and commitment to legal structures and processes. Knowledge and commitment are often, but not always, the unconscious by-products of family socialization.

In more advanced traditional societies with a transitional legal system the impact of family on law is less direct. The legal system has become more complex and approximates an autonomous system of laws, courts, legislative bodies, and enforcement and administrative agencies. Incumbents of the legal system are no longer kinsmen, but semiprofessionals. Such professionalization is the result of the fact that the legal system has become too complex to be staffed exclusively by lay kinsmen or political leaders. Under these conditions family socialization in imparting the basic values and traditions which law preserves, codifies, and integrates generates only diffuse commitment to the legal system. To the extent that the autonomous legal system does not reflect these values, traditions, and other cultural components, family socialization will have few or perhaps negative consequences for instilling commitment. This frequently is the problem in Third World nations, where colonial powers or new provisional governments impose laws departing radically from existing traditions and values. These systems usually have difficulty in becoming legitimated since family socialization does not instill the necessary commitment.

The complexity of a modern legal system is overwhelming. Intimate knowledge of its structure and functioning is impossible for the layman. As the above study on the American Supreme Court reveals, a tremendous amount of ignorance and misunderstanding surrounds even the most highly visible elements of a modern legal system. Under these conditions general and vague commitment to law is more typical than knowledge and understanding. A great deal of this commitment comes from family socialization, where core personality traits are instilled in the members of even a modern society. And in societies such as the United States where legal socialization in the schools is atypical, the consequences of family socialization for the legitimation of law and legal processes are more profound than in societies, such as Russia, where formal educational indoctrination into law occurs.

Finally modern kinship structures also influence legal development by becoming one of the major clients of a modern legal system. Because families in modern kinship systems display high dissolution rates, they place a heavy caseload on courts, while causing the proliferation of specialized family courts and laws, as well as enforcement and administrative agencies. Just as the volume of economic exchange and commerce leads to legal development, so does the incessant dissolution of the modern conjugal family structure. American divorce laws, courts, and lawyers, or the more inclusive family laws and courts of the Russian legal system attest to these familial influences on the structure of modern law.

SUMMARY

In this chapter a brief outline of some institutional influences on legal system development has been presented. These influences have been documented at the most general level, since present and historical conditions in any particular society determine their exact nature. We initially examined the consequences of the economy on legal development. In this analysis emphasis was placed upon the consequences of economic exchange for initial legal development. With economic development these exchanges intensify and further influence legal evolution. Modernization of the economy also creates new problems in labor-management and government-economy relations. By trial and error or by design and purposive experiments with these problems, modernization of the legal system occurs.

Next we turned to an examination of the polity and law. Here we noted that the increasing consolidation of society-wide power and policy-making powers in the hands of the polity often results in legal modernization as governments attempt to control and regulate activities in a society. Many trends in legal systems can thus be considered a direct reflection of political development.

Religion and law were then analyzed and it was noted that religious beliefs almost always underlie basic legal postulates in a society. As societies become more complex and secular, however, the immediacy of religious beliefs to specific laws and legal processes declines dramatically. Turning next to the impact of education on law, we focused on the consequences of education for generating professional expertise needed for legal development and on its consequences for instilling commitment to law in the general population. Finally the influence of kinship on law was briefly delineated. In primitive societies kinship norms are often coextensive with many legal norms, while in modern societies a clearer separation of kinship and legal norms exists. Yet in both traditional and modern societies, family socialization was seen as a major source of diffuse commitment to law.

257

SUGGESTED READINGS

Harold Berman and William Greiner (eds.). *The Nature and Functions of Law*, 2d ed., New York: Brooklyn Foundation Press, 1966.

Abraham S. Blumberg, *Criminal Justice*, Chicago: Quadrangle Books, Inc., 1970.

F. James Davis et al, *Society and the Law: New Meanings for an Old Profession*, New York: The Free Press, 1962.

William Evan, *Law and Sociology,* New York: The Free Press, 1962.

Wolfgang Friedmann, *Law in a Changing Society*, Berkeley: University of California Press, 1959.

Charles G. Howard and Robert S. Summers, *Law: Its Nature, Functions and Limits*, Englewood Cliffs, N.J.: Prentice-Hall, Inc., 1965.

Dennis Lloyd, *The Idea of Law*, Baltimore: Penguin Books, Inc., 1964.

Lewis Mayers, *The American Legal System*, New York: Harper & Row Publishers, Incorporated, 1954.

Edwin Schur, *Law and Society*, New York: Random House, Inc., 1968.

Jerome Skolnick, *Justice Without Trial*, New York: John Wiley & Sons, Inc., 1966.

L. A. Wigmore, *A Panorama of the World's Legal Systems*, Washington, D.C.: Washington Law Book Company, 1936.

258

the
institutional
environment
of
LAW

POLTY 10

Power, influence, control, and manipulation are endemic to social life. These facets of human society are often subinstitutional as individuals, groups, and organizations attempt to control, manipulate, and influence each other. However, much political activity is institutionalized and concerns the more pervasive ways in which the capacity to manipulate and control is distributed and patterned across a whole society. Such institutionalization is usually sufficiently stable and coherent for us to isolate out a political subsystem — or polity — in a society. While the concrete profile of this subsystem can vary enormously, its consequences for virtually every aspect of human activity are rarely minor. We have already examined the massive impact of the polity on economy, kinship, education, and law in previous chapters. Now we turn our attention to describing in more detail the nature of political structures and processes in human societies.

BASIC ELEMENTS OF POLITICAL SUBSYSTEMS

leadership and decision making

In most societies decision making for the whole society eventually becomes concentrated into the hands of a few. However, in some very small, simple, and primitive societies leadership is less concentrated, with all members of the society engaging in some decision making (Fried, 1968). For example, among the Eskimos there is extreme intolerance in bestowing extensive decision-making prerogatives on leaders. Sometimes temporary leaders emerge in crisis situations to make decisions, but they soon recede back into the collective life of the society (Fried, 1968:84). Thus, sometimes in very simple societies, decision making does not become stabilized and the exclusive prerogative of a few key statuses, groups, or individuals (LaPiere, 1965: 178–179). But as soon as societies display any size or complexity, such primitive egalitarianism gives way to clear-cut leadership positions which are charged with making general decisions affecting the whole society. As we will see, there are tremendous differences in the organization of these political statuses.

262

power and authority

Why should the members of a society obey or abide by the decisions of incumbents in leadership positions? Frequently they do not. History is filled with accounts of followers disobeying and revolting against their leaders. But equally often decisions are obeyed and followed, since decision makers are usually endowed with *power*.

Power is simply the capacity of one system unit to realize its will over other system units, even in the face of resistance (Weber, 1946:77–78). Power can be of many types and rest on many bases, including: the ability to manipulate cultural symbols such as values, beliefs, morals, and dogmas and thereby achieve compliance; the ability to persuade and exhort acquiescence to one's wishes; and the capacity to control and regulate information so as to achieve compliance. While these and other capacities are bases of power, we can view power as ultimately resting on the possession and ability to use physical force. In most societies the possession of the means of physical coercion become monopolized by only a few decision-making statuses. However, such monopolization is rarely complete, for there are usually counter bases of power—especially coercion—in societies.

However, if decisions are obeyed only through the threat or use of force, then instability, conflict, and perpetual strife are likely. To paraphrase Edmund Burke, no nation is ruled which must be perpetually conquered. Rather, in order for decision-making statuses to be maintained or stabilized they must rest on *authority*. Authority can be viewed as a situation where leaders are perceived by the general population as having the legitimate right to make decisions governing a society.

Most political subsystems rely on both coercive power and authority to realize decisions. The more authority possessed by the polity the less the need to use force, and vice versa. For example, even in the face of recent waves of civil disturbance, high authority is possessed by the American polity and force is used less than in many Third World systems where only tenuous authority is possessed by the polity. However, in very simple and small traditional societies, this ratio between force and authority does not exist. Leadership and decision-making statuses possess little if any capacity to apply force and coercion to achieve compliance. Instead leaders possess only authority. For instance, in some tribes of African bushmen, leaders in the hunt possess decision-making prerogatives because they are perceived as being more skilled or as possessing more luck than followers. Yet these leaders have no sanctions at their disposal to enforce decisions and thus they lead only on the basis of authority (Fried, 1968:11–12; Thomas, 1959:182–184). But with societal development the capacity to coerce becomes increasingly monopolized and used by the polity when authority breaks down.

In sum we can say that both simple and complex political subsystems display certain basic elements: leadership and decision making; and power and/or authority. As we will see when we examine variations in the structure of polities, there are many differences both in the way decision making is organized and in the use of various bases of power.

POLITY AND SOCIETY

The political subsystem as a locus of power usually has a massive impact on other structures and processes in society. To document the details of the polity's consequences for the broader society is beyond the scope of our inquiry. But at the most general level we can visualize four major consequences of the polity in virtually all types of societies: establishing goals; mobilizing and allocating system resources; distributing valued resources; and social control.

establishing goals

Societies have goals or ends toward which system units, energy, and resources are mobilized. These goals can be extremely simple and involve attempts to insulate society from the vicissitudes of the natural environment. In other societies they can be elaborate and involve such things as quests for territory, prestige, development and progress, equality, outer space, and world dominance. Except for some very simple or primitive societies where decision-making roles are so transitory as to be virtually nonexistent, the polity establishes most system goals. In modern or modernizing societies this is revealed as political leaders—whether individual elites, military juntas, legislatures, or monarchs—mobilize and allocate a society's resources and people toward goals. Typical goals in these systems include economic development, national defense, prestige, world economic dominance, internal stability, and social equality. These and other goals are pursued because the polity has vast capacities of power—ranging from coercion and force to various forms of authority. In traditional societies, chiefs and councils of elders have similar decision-making powers. Perhaps in extremely traditional and primitive societies where the polity is somewhat ephemeral, the goal-establishment powers of decision makers are not so extensive. Tradition, custom, and environmental exigencies determine goals, and leaders arise as they display competence in meeting these exigencies (Fried, 1968; LaPiere, 1965). But once political leadership becomes stabilized the goal-establishment powers of the polity expand.

Systems usually have several or multiple goals. Since societies usually pursue more than one goal at a time, priorities among goals become established. This involves political decisions about which goals are most important and the resulting differential mobilization and allocation of system resources and units. These decisions about goal priorities are usually made by the political subsystem.

allocating and mobilizing

Sometimes system goals are not explicitly stated or formulated. One of the best ways to discover the goals of a society is to examine what

264

areas most resources of a society are allocated to and for what activities most system units are mobilized. Such an examination will reveal not only the kinds of goals pursued by a system but also the priorities among them. In fact, given frequent distortion in political rhetoric, this is probably a better way to discern a society's goals. If we observe, for example, that most of a society's resources and manpower are mobilized for and allocated to the expansion of the economy, then we can assume that the most important goal of that society revolves around economic development. Or if a society's resources and populace are mobilized and allocated toward just barely insulating the society from the natural environment, then we might hypothesize that a major goal of that society is economic survival and subsistence. If we discover, as in the United States, that the majority of tax revenues go into military activities, we can stipulate that national defense — and perhaps conquest — are major system goals.

Polities allocate not only natural resources but also cultural (such as technology), monetary, and human resources. Frequently before resources can be allocated to goals, certain system units must first be *mobilized*. For example, to allocate natural resources for military conquest often requires prior mobilization of the economy — and of people — to that end. To develop economically, polities often have to manipulate and mobilize the population ideologically to undergo the sacrifice and deprivation that will result from investments in capital goods (machines for production) instead of consumer goods and services.

Both mobilization and allocation are possible by virtue of the simple fact that polities have many bases of power — coercion, authority, control of media, and so forth. Once goal-attainment decisions are made, the polity can usually pursue them by virtue of its capacity to use these multiple types of power.

distributing valued resources

In mobilizing and allocating toward system goals the polity often becomes involved in distributing valued resources to system units — whether individuals, institutional spheres, or specific groups and organizations. These distributed resources can take many forms, including goods, money, prestige, esteem, privilege, services, power, rights, and freedom. Except in the simplest traditional society where the polity is only incipient, such distribution is rarely equal. The unequal distribution of valued resources ultimately becomes codified into a stratification system of social classes and sometimes castes. By virtue of the polity's monopolization of power it can grant power, privileges, and freedoms or take them away. It can distribute money through its taxing powers or it can distribute vital services such as utilities, transportation, health care, and education to some and not to others.

Sometimes this differential distribution is consciously and deliberately performed by elites in power. At other times it is an unintended consequence of mobilization and allocation in the pursuit of certain goals. For example, if economic development is a major system goal, then privilege, freedoms, money, services, and power are likely to be distributed to key statuses in the economy. Or if military conquest is a major system goal, the same would be true of key military statuses. However, whether intended or not, a major consequence of political allocation is to establish and reinforce the stratification system in a society. Once some individuals, groups, organizations, and institutional spheres have benefited from unequal distribution, they often become part of the polity. And once this occurs they have the power to maintain the unequal distribution of valued resources. It is in this sense that the political and stratification subsystems in a society inevitably overlap. Elites in one tend to become elites in the other.

social control

Establishing goal priorities and then mobilizing and allocating system resources for their achievement not only involves differentially distributing valued resources but also necessitates social control. This means that the polity must often regulate, manipulate, and force conformity. This can involve physical coercion, but equally often it involves ideological manipulation. Social control becomes particularly obvious when polities possess little legitimacy in the eyes of the population and when distribution of valued resources is grossly unequal. Under these conditions the polity must engage in considerable direct social control in order to establish and pursue system goals. For example, the ascendence to power of a military junta of tenuous legitimacy in a society usually results in massive efforts at social control— control of the mass media, educational indoctrination, mass jailings and executions, as well as other forms of suppression. Over time with growing legitimation of the polity, law can emerge as an effective institution and assumes many of these social control consequences. But even law enforcement ultimately rests on the capacity of the polity to supply the instruments of coercion and force.

defining polity as an institution

Like education and law, the polity is a developing institution. In simple and highly traditional societies a stable and autonomous polity is difficult to find empirically or even to isolate analytically. But as we will see the political subsystem develops rapidly with societal modernization into a pervasive and highly visible institution. We can therefore define the polity as an institution in this way:

> The polity is that increasingly interrelated, pervasive, and relatively stable clustering of statuses, general norms, and role behaviors which are involved in the acquisition and exercise of society-wide power and decision making and which have consequences for: (1) establishing system goals and priorities among them; (2) allocating and mobilizing resources; (3) distributing valued resources; and (4) maintaining social control.

POLITY IN DIFFERENT SOCIETIES

There is enormous variability in the structure and functioning of polities in different types of societies. They can vary with respect to size and pervasiveness, degree of monopolization of power, stability, extent of democratization, and goal-attainment effectiveness. For example, at even the most superficial level of analysis, it is obvious that the leaders of an Eskimo hunting party, the ruling junta of a military dictatorship, and the giant state bureaucracies of the United States and Russia represent political structures of an entirely different nature.

This range of diversity in the polities of the world's societies poses an anlytical problem of how to capture the essence of various types of polities, while at the same time comparing their similarities and differences. One way to cope with this problem is to isolate out key dimensions of all polities which can alert us to the ways that political roles are organized and enacted in societies. Five such dimensions are listed below.

1. *The locus of power and decision making in a society.* This dimension will force us to ask: What positions in a society are vested with power and decision-making prerogatives? How many of such statuses are there? How are they organized? How stable are they? How centralized? Answers to these questions will tell us where, as Weber put it, "the house of power" is located (Weber, 1946).

2. *The sphere of power and decision making.* What is the territory or sphere of control exercised by statuses invested with power and decision-making tasks? In other words, what is the jurisdiction of the political subsystem? Is it stable? Ambiguous? Large or small?

3. *The basis of power and decision making.* What kind of power does the polity possess? Why do some positions have decision-making powers for the total society? Is the polity legitimate? Or must it rely on naked force and coercion?

4. *The acquisition of power and decision-making prerogatives.* How do rulers come to rule? What are the mechanisms in a society by which

power holders and decision makers arise? Is power acquired democratically? Or through force? In other words, what are procedures and general norms governing leaders becoming incumbent in the polity?

5. *The exercise of power and decision-making prerogatives.* How are power and decisions administered? What kinds of structures exist to channel power and decision making? Is there a governmental bureaucracy? How much reliance is placed upon the military? Or more generally, in what ways are statuses organized to implement and enforce decisions in a society?

Answers to the questions posed for each of these five dimensions should facilitate our analysis of different kinds of polities. We are now ready to describe various types of polities in traditional and modern societies.

polities in traditional societies

For convenience, we can classify traditional polities as either *primitive* or *advanced*. Under primitive polities two distinct types are evident in the world's societies: egalitarian and kin-based polities. With respect to advanced traditional polities, we find two additional types: state-based polities and modernizing.

PRIMITIVE POLITIES

(*a*) *Primitive egalitarian polities.* These polities are most likely to exist in very simple societies with hunting and gathering economies. In these societies several kin groups wander over a territory as a band, seeking a subsistence living off the land (see Chapter 2). Sometimes these societies are called egalitarian because they often display no set, established, or stable rules of power and decision making (Fried, 1968). Leadership statuses seem to emerge and then disappear with each successive crisis and its resolution. Within each of the society's kin groupings, descent and authority rules specify authority and decision-making obligations for specific kinsmen. But across these kin groupings, norms tend to emphasize the inappropriateness of stable, society-wide power and decision-making status norms. In other primitive societies more permanent leadership statuses exist and are usually referred to as *headman* positions. However, the normative obligations attendant upon these statuses are extremely delimited. For example, among the !Kung Bushmen of Africa the headman's main duties revolve around directing migrations and some economic activity, while performing certain necessary religious ceremonies for the society's welfare (Fried, 1968:87). But these leaders possess no sanctioning power or capacity to use force. Even among the more sedentary and warlike Yanomano of northern Brazil, permanent leadership statuses exist but are invoked only in the face of a crisis or incident requiring a major decision. After the crisis or incident is over the leader goes back to work like the rest of the Yanomano villagers (Chagnon, 1968:96). Thus with respect to the *locus* of power and decision making in primitive polities, it often tends to be temporary, with no clear, distinct, or permanent power and decision-making statuses. Even with permanent political statuses actual leadership role behavior is invoked on only specific occasions. And in all primitive polities the power to coerce conformity to decisions is virtually nonexistent.

The *sphere* of power and decision making in these polities is also limited. It is usually confined to a very specific and limited number of activities affecting the whole society. Most decisions are made by the individuals or by kin leaders for their kin group. These primitive traditional societies display territoriality but the boundaries of territories are open and constantly penetrated by kin groups and bands from other societies. This means that the actual sphere of decision making is defined less in terms of geographical territories than in terms of social territory — of those kin groups in a band or village willing to take orders from a headman. The *basis* for a leader's power of decision making is thus authority rather than threats of physical coercion. Leaders tend to be obeyed as long as their leadershp proves effective. In fact leadership statuses are usually held by incumbents who display either luck or skill in spheres necessary to the survival of the society. To be defined as lucky or skillful usually means that leaders must work harder and longer than other members of a society. For example, village leaders among the Yanomano must set an example for others by being ambitious and producing large quantities of food for their families or for visitors they might entertain (Chagnon, 1968:95–96). *Noblesse oblige* is thus rare in primitive polities.

The process of *acquiring* power and leadership positions in a primitive society presents a somewhat ambiguous pattern. Skill, performance, luck, and expertise in crucial areas are the principal ways of gaining access to leadership statuses. But frequently age and birth order in one's family as well as authority and descent rules limit the pool of such potential society-wide leaders. Yet primitive polities come as close to being a pure democracy as any type of political subsystem in the world. Finally,

269

the *exercise* of power and decision-making prerogatives in primitive polities is simple: leaders give orders, and because of their authority (based on luck or skill), they are likely to be followed. If compliance is not forthcoming there is no administrative or military organization to force compliance. Sometimes society-wide leadership directives pass from headman to a kin-group leader who in turn directs his (or her) family's activities. But equally often kin leaders do not perform this mediating function. Family members do as necessity dictates; and if a headman's order seems reasonable and appropriate, they obey.

(b) *Kin-based polities.*   This type of polity is typical of simple agrarian (or horticultural) societies where a stable but tenuous relationship to the land exists and where the level of technology and capital formation is not conducive to a large economic surplus. In such societies the locus of power and decision making is rarely ambiguous. In most of these polities particular kin groups — usually clans — have assumed territory and hence power. The authority and descent rules of these dominant kin groups determine who the political elite are. These elites make decisions for others in the dominant kin group as well as for subordinate kin groupings. These elite leaders are usually called chiefs in smaller agrarian societies, while in more extensive, quasi-feudal agrarian societies they become kings. This points to the fact that the sphere of power and decision making in these traditional polities can vary greatly. In some there are limited territorial boundaries encompassing various kin groupings over which a chief or chiefs rule. In others territorial boundaries are sufficiently vast and fixed as to approximate a nation. In either case the polity maintains and defends its boundaries from outside encroachment. To do this both chiefs and kings begin to appropriate economic surplus of subordinate groups (usually through taxation) to finance the administrative and military organizations needed to maintain and control the territory or nation. Thus the sphere of power and decision making of the polity becomes more clearly articulated, geographically bounded, and compelling on subordinate incumbents.

The basis of the polity's power to make decisions is a mixture of tradition, religious sanctioning, and force. In small kin-based polities the power to make decisions is based more on tradition and religion than on force. Leaders are sanctioned by their ties with the gods and by the fact that custom and tradition have always dictated who should rule. But as the territorial sphere of the polity increases, force often becomes necessary to maintain control. This is especially true if the polity is expanding the boundaries of its influence through conquest of neighboring territories. This in turn forces the polity to appropriate surplus from conquered territories in order to maintain the military organization needed to enforce decisions. The acquisition of power and decision-making prerogatives in kin-based traditional polities is through hereditary succession in accordance with the authority and descent rules of the kinship subsystem. But this is not always the case. Succession often involves considerable violence and bloodshed as fellow kinsmen jockey for the right to rule. And sometimes high-level and ambitious administrators or military leaders from nonelite clans become involved in power struggles. However, such *coups* and usurption of power from elite kin groupings become much more frequent and typical in advanced traditional polities (see below).

The exercise of power and decision making involves both an administrative staff and military organization. The administrative staff is composed of kinsmen from elite kin groups, but as the tasks of administration increase, incumbents from nonelite kin groups begin to be recruited. Military organizations are usually led by members of elite kin groups, while the rank and file tend to be drawn from the nonelite kin groupings. Exceptional performance in military activities can often lead to promotion of nonelites into leadership positions in the military. The emergence of these kin-dominated military and administrative organizations marks the incipience of the state, which becomes the principal form of political organization in more advanced political subsystems.

ADVANCED TRADITIONAL POLITIES

State-based polities. These political subsystems are (and were) found in large agrarian societies where technology and capital allow for an economic surplus. Such societies display marked urban centers which encompass many thousands of residences (Lenski, 1966:198–199). The locus of power is in these urban centers and consolidated into a monarchy composed of a king and his top administrative and military officials. In highly centralized monarchies, the status of king is the ultimate source of power and decision making. Military and administrative organizations carry out and enforce decisions. However, decision making frequently is more decentralized, with multiple loci of power which are consolidated and coordinated by a monarch. This latter arrangement can be labeled a *feudal* polity and was typical of medieval Europe and China. Even today it is typical of parts of Southeast Asia and Latin America. The sphere of power and decision making in state-based polities is great and includes a large geographical territory and population. One of the major reasons for this is that these types of polities used to engage in warfare and conquest (Lenski, 1970:197–211). The result of such an emphasis on conquest is that the monarch possesses extensive powers of taxation and pillage of conquered territories. In turn these powers allow for further military conquest —thus extending the sphere of power and decision making. The basis of power is *force* and the capacity to bestow wealth, privilege, and some power to subordinates who might threaten the monarch's power. In feudal polities the latter capacity is especially important in keeping other loci of power (lords and tribal chiefs) in line. The masses of the population are usually apathetic, although ever-cognizant of the capacity of rulers to use force. Also the masses frequently bestow legitimacy on leadership statuses, especially when rulers come from traditionally powerful kin groupings. The acquisition of power displays considerably more latitude and variance than in primitive polities. Kinship rules—and the traditions and religious sanctions behind them—cease being the only or even major principle of rising to a power and decision-making position. Norms of hereditary succession become confounded by external conquests from outside the society and by power struggles within the government. Military and administrative leaders from nonelite kin groups often wrest power from leaders of traditional ruling kin groups. Or minor loci of power in feudal systems rebel and conquer the existing monarchy. One of the principal reasons for such anomie in acquiring power stems from the fact that the tax revenues, pillage, and booty of conquered territories in agrarian economies constitute an economic surplus which can provide great wealth, privilege, and hence power (Lenski, 1966:210–230). With these potential rewards at stake, struggles for power are probably inevitable.

The exercise of power and decision making in traditional state-based polities occurs through a clearly organized cluster of military and administrative statuses. This cluster of roles is sufficiently coherent and articulated to be considered a state. In its centralized form the state is composed of administrative and military positions which are organized bureaucratically. Furthermore, the bureaucracy is large and the administrative and military tasks sufficiently complex to necessitate high levels of expertise and skill of members. This fact means that norms begin to emphasize recruitment into and promotion within the bureaucracy on the basis of competence, expertise, skill, and performance (Parsons, 1966). However, much ascription still dominates, for kinsmen of elite kin groups remain in many high-level positions within the bureaucracy. The pressures for extensive bureaucratization come from the administrative and military problems involved in controlling large geographical territories. These are compounded by the fact that these territories are often conquered and subjected to exploitative taxation and other forms of political appropriation. In more decentralized or feudal forms of political organization bureaucratization is less extensive; and to the extent that it exists, ascriptive kin criteria tend to dominate recruitment to and promotion in the bureaucracy. For a highly centralized bureaucracy to develop there must be efficient transportation and communication facilities in order to coordinate and keep track of activities over the large territories of these societies. When these facilities are lacking, the exercise of power remains somewhat decentralized and feudal, with many smaller locuses of power and local bureaucracies dominated by elite kinsmen (Lenski, 1966:235–237).

(b) *Modernizing polities.* These polities are typical of societies initiating economic development and are thus most prevalent today in Third World nations. The locus of power and decision making exists in a few elite positions within a highly centralized state. Much of the state is composed of an extensive military organization under the control of elites. In fact elites often tend to be former military leaders. The sphere of power is extensive and embodies a clearly defined territory called a nation. Within its national borders the state has the power to intervene —often with force—into virtually all areas of the societal functioning. The basis of power and decision making is various and often tenuous. Frequently coercion is necessary, for rarely are elites considered legitimate by all or even by a majority of the population. Except for a few traditional monarchs in Southeast Asia and the Middle East, custom and tradition are weak sources of political legitimation. *Charisma*—or the exceptional qualities and abilities imputed to elites—is quite often a major source of political legitimation, as is the case with Castro in Cuba or the late Nasser of Egypt. This is especially likely after a violent overthrow of an existing set of elites (Weber, 1946).

Another major source of legitimation comes through ideological manipulation. Because the polity tends to control directly the mass media and educational structures in these societies, it attempts to indoctrinate the population into an ideology revolving around economic development, self-sufficiency, and national prestige. These appeals are particularly effective in firming up elites' power in societies with a long history of colonial rule and domination. The variable and often tenuous basis of power and decision making in these societies derives from the fact that the processes for acquiring power are unstable. Usually there are no clear-cut norms specifying how leaders ascend to elite positions. Sometimes kinship rules of hereditary succession operate, but increasingly these are suspended as military and administrative leaders wrest power from traditional ruling families. Some polities have written constitutions specifying election — or least selection — procedures but these norms rarely are followed, for winners in elections often never assume power. Thus the acquisition of power is governed by few rules and hence is very unstable. Power can be acquired violently through a popular revolution led by a charismatic leader. Or it can be acquired through a military *coup* in which high-level military leaders wrest power from an existing hereditary monarch, previous military *coup*, or charismatic leader. Even where an existing ruler maintains power for a considerable period of time his retirement or death usually generates a crisis of succession. Where there are no clear or binding rules of succession, a power struggle inevitably ensues.

The *exercise* of power and decision-making powers is through a highly centralized state bureaucracy and military organization. Even after a charismatic leader succeeds in overthrowing an existing elite, he often inherits and then reorganizes or establishes a new, highly centralized administration (Weber, 1946). Because of the far-reaching tasks and goals — including economic development — of such an administration, much recruitment to and promotion in both the military and administrative bureaucracy must be on the basis of expertise and performance (Parsons, 1966). In order to establish goals and to allocate and mobilize system units, facilities, and resources to their attainment as well as maintain order and social control, the polity must centralize and recruit at least some expert incumbents — both military and administrative — into the state bureaucracy. This transition is often easier after a revolution where leaders can engage in extensive "housecleaning" of the previous ascriptive bureaucracy. Where new elites must try to reform and slowly reorganize the government, the achievement of goals will be inhibited by the inefficiency inevitable with a heavily ascriptive and kin-based bureaucracy.

Concluding our discussion of traditional polities, we should emphasize one point: These four types of traditional political subsystems—egalitarian, kin based, state based, and modernizing—are very crude and encompass only part of the diversity in traditional polities of the present and the past. Also, while there is an implicit evolutionary sequence in these types, it should not be pushed too far. It would be difficult to find any one society which, as a clearly bounded nation, has gone through all these stages. The history of the world is too full of national conquests, colonization, and ever-changing national boundaries for this to be possible. However, as we see in a later section, this does not negate the fact that to the extent that a society has undergone development and to the extent that it has remained a bounded society, we can observe during development certain general transformations in the political subsystem. These transformations would be along the lines outlined above and below.

polities in modern societies

Modern polities are typical of societies with an industrial or post-industrial economy. They display not only a state but also another relatively stable clustering of statuses we can call *political parties*. Parties are organized to insert leaders into elite positions within the state (Williams, 1970:273). As such they are composed of a wide variety of positions, including elites already in the state, aspirants to elite positions, party organizers and officials, and rank-and-file members of the party drawn from the general population. Political parties first emerge in traditional modernizing systems and increasingly become the principal mechanism for inserting leaders into elite positions in the state of modern systems. However, the way in which political parties are organized varies tremendously from modern society to society. One way of cutting through this diversity is to compare political parties along these two dimensions: *membership* and *internal structure* (Duverger, 1954).

Rank-and-file membership in parties can be either direct or indirect. Indirect membership exists when party members are primarily participants in other organizations such as a labor or trade union. The trade union in turn is affiliated with a particular political party. Membership in the union thus makes one a member of the party, but by an indirect route. Such double membership usually results in a strong and cohesive political party, because union participation strengthens party participation and vice versa (Johnson, 1960:363). Direct membership involves voluntarily joining and participating in a party as an individual.

The internal structure of a party can vary with respect to: the nature of its constituent groups; the relationships among these groups; and the degree of centralization of the party structure. Generally parties are composed of predominantly one or the other of two types of groups, *caucuses* or *branches*. Caucuses are small groups whose membership is restricted to major contributors, spokesmen, and professional organizers of the party. Caucuses determine political strategy for putting members in power within their local sphere of influence, whereas at the national level, the leadership of each major caucus forms a decision-making body which maps strategy for inserting leaders into national elite positions. Between elections caucuses are often inactive. American political parties are good examples of parties composed of caucuses (see a later section for details). Parties composed of branches are more active all of the time. Leaders of local branches are constantly recruiting members and holding political meetings and rallies. The Socialist and Christian Democratic parties of Western European countries are good examples of parties composed of branches. A variant form of party is seen in the Communist parties in Eastern Europe and Russia. These parties are organized into *cells*. A cell is a small group of devoted members who engage in propaganda and other tasks. Cells exist at all levels of society with cell members usually working in the same general area and maintaining constant communication. Cells are not so large as Socialist party branches, for the membership tends to remain exclusive. Thus cells are like caucuses in that membership is restricted but like branches in that they are constantly active.

Turning to the relationships among these units, we find that there tend to be weak relations among caucuses, moderately strong relationships among branches, and extremely strong relationships among cells. Caucuses display loose articulation with one another. Informal contacts among members of different caucuses frequently occur, but there are few formal means for regularizing relations among caucuses. Only at election time do caucuses begin to display any degree of close articulation. Branches maintain both informal and formal contacts, reviewing various strategies for party activities. These relations intensify with the approach of an election. Cells maintain about the same degree of close articulation regardless of whether or not an election is approaching. Part of this is because elections are not contested the way they are in modern Western societies. With respect to the degree of centralization of political parties, caucuses centralize only at election time, branches maintain a more on-going emphasis on party centralization, and cells are always highly centralized into a clear-cut hierarchy of cells.

In sum, then, modern polities display a party system for placing leaders into the state. The membership and internal structure of these parties vary greatly. In addition to the internal organization of the parties themselves, modern polities also vary with respect to how many political parties exist in a society. In this respect we can generally distinguish one-party, two-party, and multiple-party political subsystems.

Despite differences in internal party organization and the number of parties, all modern polities are very similar in terms of the locus, sphere, and basis of power and decision making. The locus of power and decision making resides in a few stable statuses. Under these elite positions is a vast administrative and military bureaucracy. However, the organization of elite roles varies from polity to polity. In two- and multiple-party systems there is usually a division of power between a few key executive positions and a clustering of assembly or congressional statuses. In one-party systems executive positions dominate and have considerable power over assemblies and congresses. The spheres of power among modern polities are more or less equivalent. National boundaries are clearly demarcated and the polity possesses extensive decision-making prerogatives and power to back up decisions within these boundaries. The basis of power for all modern polities rests on authority with occasional use of physical coercion. Authority tends to rest on multiple bases: tradition, personal charisma of leaders, and most important, law. Leadership positions are heavily invested with legitimacy stemming from a well-developed legal subsystem to which the population is committed (more on this later). Propaganda, ideological manipulation, media control, and educational indoctrination are also prominent means for establishing political legitimacy. However, one-party systems tend to rely more heavily on media control, regulation, and censorship than do two- and multiple-party polities.

The most distinguishing feature among modern polities revolves around the acquisition of decision-making powers. The number of parties in a society as well as their form of internal organization greatly influence the way power is acquired. In all modern polities acquisition is regulated by laws and usually involves the participation of the population in elections. But the nature of elections differs among polities. One-party systems, as the label indicates, possess only a single dominant party through which leadership selection occurs. The party is dominated by the state and thus it usually serves as a tool for the state to mobilize mass sentiment for candidates selected by the leadership of the party and state. Under these conditions the party is highly centralized, organized into closely related cells or branches, and membership is usually direct and voluntary. Elections within the party are basically a ritual for reaffirming commitment to the party and state. Since major candidates who get on the ballot in one-party systems are automatically elected, considerable manipulation, competition, and sometimes coercion within the party occur before elections as party factions vie for power. Frequently, however, there are competitive elections for less elite positions in the state, with rivalry among candidates selected by different factions in the party and state leadership. Such a system for acquiring decision-making power is most evident in systems dominated by a strong Communist party, such as the Soviet Union and other Eastern European societies.

In two-party and multiple-party systems, political parties display considerably more autonomy from the state. They represent less of an extension of the state and more of a mediating structure between the general population and various interest groups on the one hand and the state on the other. Parties tend to be composed of either branch or caucus subunits with branch organization more typical of multiple-party and caucus organization of two-party systems. The size, degree of organization, and extent of centralization varies tremendously in both two- and multiple-party systems. Despite this variability, the election process is competitive and all parties usually insert elites into the assembly of the state. However, systems vary in the extent to which one party dominates the elite executive positions of the state. Finally the exercise of power and decision making in all modern polities occurs through a vast administrative hierarchy culminating in a few elite executive positions.

the consequences of traditional and modern polities for society

With political development and evolution, the functions of the polity expand. Primitive egalitarian polities are engaged in establishing goal priorities and allocating and mobilizing resources and people to their attainment. Since leadership can be temporary and rests solely on authority, the polity usually does not have extensive social control or distributive consequences for the society. With the development of a more stable kin-based polity, the functions of the polity expand greatly. Clear-cut leadership statuses, in addition to an incipient administrative and military organization, allow for the establishment of more elaborate goals and extensive allocation and mobilization of system resources, With the basis of power resting on both authority and the capacity to use force, the polity now begins to have many social control and distributive consequences for the total society (Lenski, 1966:237). And with the development of an increasingly nonascriptive state and its subsequent elaboration in more modern systems, the polity thus comes to have far-reaching consequences for establishing goals, arranging priorities among them, allocating and mobilizing resources for their attainment, distributing valued resources, and social control.

WORLD TRENDS IN POLITY

No single society has ever gone through complete political development from a primitive egalitarian to modern form of organization. The boundaries, shape, scope, and duration of societies have varied too much for this to have occurred. Conquests, defeats, colonization, national independence movements, and internal revolutions have changed and altered the boundaries of societies too often for long-term political evolution in one discrete system to be possible (Nisbet, 1969, 1970). In addition to these facts, colonialism, imperialism, and diffusion have often made political evolution in one system somewhat discontinuous. With colonization or imperialism modern state governments are often imposed upon primitive tribal regions with only egalitarian or kin-based polities. Under these conditions political development as a continuous process becomes obscured.

But these facts should not dissuade us from looking for general patterns of change in polities. Since societal modernization appears to be a worldwide trend, political development—whether continuous or disjointed—is occurring. Polities are increasingly approximating a modern form of organization. Whether the starting point for such development is a kin-based or traditional state polity is not important for our purposes here. Nor are we to be daunted by the fact that conquest, diffusion, and colonialism result in great leaps in political development. Rather, we are concerned with certain general trends in political development which emerge with societal modernization—whether rapid or slow, long or short range, continuous or discontinuous.

increasing size of polity

With modernization the polity increases in size. Primitive egalitarian polities are composed of only a few, usually temporary, personages. Kin-based polities display a larger clustering of political roles, organized into an ascriptive but incipient administrative and military organization. With the organization of power and decision-making statuses into a state bureaucracy and military organization the polity tends to increase in size. The emergence of a state reveals that society-wide power and decision making are now highly consolidated. In turn administrative consolidation enables the polity to regulate an increased number of structures and processes in a society. Such increased regulation furthers expansion of administrative and military organization in order to accommodate this expanded involvement in the broader society. When the polity seeks further involvement in regulating, controlling, distributing, mobilizing, and allocating system resources in the pursuit of diverse goals, the administrative and military bureaucracy begins to approach the vast proportions typical of all modern systems. Thus the expansion of the polity's size appears endemic to political development. This trend is true in both large and small societies. Political development always involves an ever-increasing proportion of the total status-norm network of a society revolving around society-wide decision making as well as its administration and enforcement.

bureaucratization

By now we should be aware that increases in size lead to bureaucratization. We have seen how this is true with the institutions of economy, education, and law. And so it is with the polity. The ever-increasing involvement of the polity in society-wide affairs and its resulting increase in size forces bureaucratization. However, initial bureaucratization in kin-based polities differs from that typical of a highly modern economic, educational, legal, or political system. It tends to be ascriptive, with kinship criteria determining just where one participates in the bureaucracy. But with further political development—whether through conquest, colonialism, or gradual evolution—bureaucratization becomes more rational, with recruitment and promotion increasingly based on a combination of expertise, performance, and seniority. This rationalization occurs primarily for reasons of scarcity and efficiency. As the polity expands in size, the pool of available—and qualified—kinsmen to fill positions in the polity becomes scarce, for the bureaucracy simply outgrows the number of elite kinsmen in a society. Equally significant in stimulating rationalization is the desire of leaders for increased efficiency. As the extensiveness and complexity of tasks performed by the governmental bureaucracy increase, the necessity for qualified and expert employees in the bureaucracy to carry out these tasks becomes evident.

These facts do not mean that rationalization of the state bureaucracy is automatic. Rarely is this the case. Ascription and political patronage usually persist long after the desire for rationalization has appeared. Yet as long as widespread ascription and patronage persist, political development, as well as broader societal modernization, will be greatly impeded for a lack of efficiency in the polity. This roadblock to development is particularly evident in most modernizing Third World polities today. Whether staffed by patrons of the ruling junta, a dictator, or by kinsmen of formerly dominant kin groups, such bureaucracies often remain inefficient. Even where colonial powers have installed and left a quasi-rational bureaucratic structure, it frequently becomes kin-ascriptive or dominated by patrons of the ruling postcolonial elite. For example, many of the post-colonial governments of African nations are staffed by elite kinsmen of formerly dominant tribes (Coleman, 1955; Southhall, 1961; Apter, 1955). In Latin American polities officials in the governmental bureaucracy are appointed on criteria of patronage as often as expertise. This is done to assure loyalty of administrators to elites who often hold only a tenuous grasp on power in these societies.

In highly modern systems some form of civil service usually exists. Civil service sets minimal and objective standards such as scores on examinations and educational requirements for participation in various administrative positions. Civil service usually cuts down on the amount of ascription and patronage in the governmental bureaucracy, but it frequently creates inefficiency by encouraging promotions within job classifications on the basis of seniority as much as on performance. Complete rationalization of governmental bureaucracy is thus impossible. Yet without some degree of rationalization the administrative bureaucracy represents negative feedback for effective and efficient functioning of the polity. In modernizing polities, such negative feedback inhibits further political development since the polity cannot efficiently establish and implement system goals.

the rise of nationalism

Political development inevitably involves the rise of nationalism. Although the notion of nationalism has many diverse connotations, we will emphasize only two of its many dimensions (Kornhauser, 1963): clearly demarcated geographical boundaries; and a sense of unity and identity among the population within these boundaries. In many traditional societies, geographical boundaries are vaguely delineated. Polities have clear decision-making powers only within a territory immediately surrounding centers of power. There are many marginal areas which only partially and sporadically fall under the polity's jurisdiction. The populations in these marginal areas rarely identify or share a common sense of identity, purpose, or heritage with the polity. In feudal political systems this is particularly evident, since political alliances come and go (thus making system boundaries rather fuzzy) and where the peoples of different regions have little cultural heritage in common. Such a situation existed during much of feudal Europe and exists today in post-colonial Africa and in parts of Southeast Asia. But one of the most conspicuous political forces in the world today is nationalism. State polities are attempting to solidify their boundaries and arouse through media and educational manipulation a common unity and purpose among heretofore culturally diverse tribes and/or feudal territories.

Much of this is necessary in order for the polity to legitimate itself and thus exercise decision-making prerogatives without extensive use of force. But once initiated, nationalism per se becomes a driving ideological and psychological force in a society. Mobilized by ideological pleas on the part of the polity for national unity, purpose, prestige, and betterment, the population's expectations and aspirations are raised (Davies, 1962; Coleman, 1955). This places a tremendous burden on the emerging state polity to fulfill the expectations raised by its ideological manipulation. Such a burden can force the polity to be judicious and to establish explicit goal priorities and carefully allocate system resources and units to their attainment. This in turn furthers administrative bureaucratization and increases the need for an effective military organization in the event that the population resists allocations and/or becomes disillusioned with the existing political elite.

Modernizing polities are thus in a difficult bind. Political development requires the firming of system boundaries and the cultural unification of a previously diverse population. This requirement often leads the polity to make promises about a better future as well as national glory and prestige. In turn the population's expectations and aspirations are raised and they begin to demand evidence of the polity's capacity to fulfill its promises. But such societies rarely can generate either the material (natural or monetary) or human resources (skills and other capacities) that would enable the polity to realize its promises. The polity can thus have generated the seeds of its destruction, for should the population become too disillusioned revolution is a likely outcome (Brinton, 1965; Davies, 1962). When revolutions are successful the new political elite faces the same dilemma as their predecessors, except more so: Expectations have probably increased, since revolutionary leaders usually offer even more extravagant promises of a better future to the population in gaining their support.

In the long run the overall effect of rising nationalism and the resulting rise in expectations is to create imperatives for a more efficient political subsystem. Frequently a series of revolutions and *coups* occurs before these imperatives are realized. But eventually the administrative bureaucracy is at least partially rationalized — frequently by purging and executing its previous participants who were installed for reasons of ascription or patronage. Concurrently similar rationalization of military organizations must occur in order to maintain control during governmental reorganization.

In modern societies nationalism is a less volatile and yet very powerful force. Geographical boundaries are clearly established and the population shares at least some national myths, values, beliefs, customs, traditions, and ideologies. And in times of crisis these cultural components can be used to mobilize public sentiment toward certain government policies.

In sum we can say that nationalism is necessary for political development in two senses: it serves as an underlying basis of political legitimation and stability; and it tends to force the polity to become organized efficiently. But nationalism can also generate during its initial emergence the potential for conflict and revolution. Therefore in the long run nationalism probably encourages political development and stabilization, whereas in the short run it usually generates tremendous political instability.

centralization of polity

Except for primitive egalitarian polities, where leadership roles are often temporary, political subsystems are centralized. The very existence of visible decision-making positions points to this fact. Furthermore the increasing monopolization of the capacity to use force by a few statuses also indicates the trend toward centralization. While some centralization of political roles appears endemic to the existence of a polity, modernization of a society results in a larger centralized polity. This trend is evident for several reasons: (1) Nationalism and the consequent rising expectations of the population generate imperatives not only for bureaucratization but also for centralization. When material and human resources are scarce, allocation and mobilization must be carefully controlled and regulated if achievement of system goals is to occur. (2) With rising expectations in the population and a high probability that the polity cannot fulfill all of its promises the development and use of extensive police and military organizations become necessary. Keeping these organizations under the control and supervision of decision-making elites is often problematic and results in a continual effort on the part of decision makers to centralize the instruments of force in a society. Without such centralization large military and police organizations frequently become detached from elites and undermine their power to make decisions and implement system goals. Often leaders of the expanding military become sufficiently detached from elites to assume through *coups* the decision-making positions in a society. Once established these military leaders attempt to consolidate and centralize police and military organizations.

In more modern societies these imperatives for consolidating the instruments of force and coercion persist. However, with clearly demarcated boundaries, a sense of national unity in the population, political stability, and authority as the basis of power, the polity can extend its decision-making powers into many diverse spheres within a society without the use of force. When this is possible long-range and society-wide planning with respect to health, education, welfare, economy, and family size becomes viable. To implement such goals requires an extensive and centralized administrative bureaucracy to mobilize, allocate, distribute, and regulate persons, organizations, and resources in their pursuit. Thus as the functions of the polity increase, so does bureaucratic centralization.

democratization

Democratization is more of an incipient trend than an accomplished fact. And perhaps it is only an apparent trend (Parsons, 1964; Lenski, 1970:355). Most generally we can view democracy as a situation where nonelites or the general population of a society have some influence on who ascends to positions of power and decision making and on the decisions rendered by elites once they are in power. Just how much and in what ways the general population influences decision making differs from society to society, since the degree and profile of democracy always varies. Most importantly we should be careful not to equate the particular form that democracy takes in the United States with the more general phenomenon of democracy itself. The former is a variant of the latter.

Much political development from a primitive egalitarian level involves *de*-democratization. With the emergence of kin-based and state-based polities, leaders assume power in accordance with kinship rules and/or through the use of force and coercion. Such leaders usually rule by decree and pay little attention to the general population—until the latter becomes restive. But with the onset of complete modernization a reversal occurs, with the masses increasingly influencing decision making. Such democratization can occur within one-party or multiple-party polities. In one-party systems democratization occurs as a by-product of the increasing mobilization of public sentiment by the polity. Frequently elites in modernizing societies establish a political party which is extended to large segments of the population as a means for mobilizing public sentiment and commitment to their decisions. Once the population is organized in this way it begins to exert pressure on elites for certain programs in line with the rising sense of nationalism and escalating expectations. Furthermore within the party, conflicts and factions among leaders develop and they begin to appeal to the public for support. Once this occurs, rank-and-file members come to have an influence in determining at least some of the policies of party leaders. Eventually such competition among factions within the party can become translated into competitive elections for certain low-ranking party officials. This appears to be the trend in one-party polities such as Russia (Brzezinski and Huntington, 1965).

284

In multiple-party systems of modernizing societies in the Third World, parties often are ideological, with extremely utopian goals and uncompromising rhetoric. Even though parties often have slates of candidates the dominant, more pragmatic party leadership usually controls (often through fraud and coercion) the elections to such an extent that they remain in power. And where the dominant party loses in elections, it frequently refuses to give up power. Thus stabilization of a multiple-party system represents a major problem in many developing polities. In many Latin American and Southeast Asian systems this failure to institutionalize the process of acquiring power frequently leads to violence, conflict, and revolutionary rumblings. More stable modernizing polities such as Mexico display a hybrid of the one-party and multiple-party systems. One party dominates but opposition parties are allowed. Elections are binding but there is never a chance for the opposition party to gain access to elite decision-making positions, since the dominant party commands the allegiance of most of the populace. But to maintain their allegiance the dominant party must remain minimally responsive to its members' expectations and desires, with the result that party members exert at least some influence on elite decision makers. The long-run trend, however, appears to favor the increasing possibility of candidates from the opposition party gaining access to positions of power. This probably indicates that Mexico is moving away from its pseudo–two-party system.

More generally we can remark that true multiple-party systems probably are not viable in modernizing societies, since parties tend to be too ideological and elites too unwilling to relinquish power. Also frequent changes in leaders—especially leaders with vastly different ideologies—can result in tremendous ambiguity in system goals. This in turn means waste and inefficiency (and corruption) in the mobilization and allocation of system resources as well as in the distribution of other valued resources. A one-party system where the population exerts an increasing interparty influence or a pseudo–multiple-party system in which the members of the dominant party have some influence on elites and where members of the opposition parties slowly begin to gain some influence are perhaps more viable paths to political democracy in modernizing systems. Under these conditions, with a continuity of leadership (albeit somewhat totalitarian), society-wide modernization can occur through the more efficient allocation and mobilization of system resources in pursuit of stable and clearly ranked goals. Out of such a situation competition between parties or within a single party can become institutionalized. Although usually preceded by a history of *coups* and revolutions political stability with some degree of democracy in the Third World nations has occurred most frequently under these conditions.

We often associate democracy with modern societies such as the United States, England, Australia, and Sweden where stable two-party or multiple-party systems exist. It is difficult to deny that these polities are democratic in that the masses exert considerable influence on just who becomes a decision maker and on what decisions are made. Perhaps at this point it can be asked if such multiple-party forms of democracy are the end stage of political development and if the sporadic attempts at democratization in Eastern Europe, Russia, Latin America, and Asia are in the long run heading toward the Western form of democracy. However, these often-posed questions assume that a fully developed single-party system cannot be as democratic as a multiple-party system — a debatable assumption which is rife with Western ethnocentrism. At present it is difficult to know if factions within one-party systems will in the long run become separate parties. And it is even more difficult to establish if a highly competitive one-party system is any less democratic than a multiple-party system. Thus the only end state about which it appears safe to hypothesize is that populations are exerting considerable influence on decision makers in modern polities in many alternative ways. As we will see in the next chapter, the reasons for this trend lie as much in the institutional environment of the polity as in the polity itself.

And finally we should emphasize that no society is as democratic as its political rhetoric may expound. Pure democracy is impossible, since every citizen could not possibly participate in and influence every decision of elite decision makers. Chaos would be the result of such an attempt (Lenski, 1970:354–355). Modern societies and their polities are too large and complex for the population to exert an influence on every or even very many decisions. In fact most decisions in all modern polities are made without the public's knowledge, awareness, or concern.

world trends in polities: an overview

As polities modernize they expand in size, with increasing numbers becoming participants in the administrative and military offices of the polity. Increases in size generate severe problems of coordination which are partially resolved through bureaucratization. At first recruitment to and promotion in governmental bureaucracies occurs through patronage and ascription. With increases in size and complexity, norms emphasizing skill, performance, and seniority come to dominate recruitment and promotion. With bureaucratization of power and decision-making statuses in a society a state can be said to exist. State polities usually attempt to generate nationalism through consolidating territorial boundaries and through ideological manipulation of the population. Nationalism results in greatly escalated demands from the population. These demands force further bureau-cratization and a high degree of centralization in the polity as it attempts to meet these demands and its own goal priorities through careful and efficient allocation and distribution of system resources. Population demands, expectations, and aspirations can also become translated into pressures for greater democracy. Though fraught with tremendous political and social instability, democratization appears to be the long-run result of such pressures.

THE AMERICAN POLITICAL SUBSYSTEM

The American polity is a vast and vague clustering of statuses, norms, and roles. At its core is a large multicentered, and highly bureau-cratized *state*. But surrounding and penetrating the state are other structures endemic to the American political system: *parties* and *interest groups*. The fluid, hidden, fluctuating, and incredibly complex relations between the state, parties, and interest groups on the one hand and the broader society on the other makes identifying the boundaries of the American political subsystem difficult. And if we note the tremendous overlap of the legal and political subsystems in American society, identifying the boundaries of the polity becomes even more difficult. Because of these facts our analysis of the polity in the United States will first focus on the core of the polity—the state—and then on those more peripheral structures influencing the state—law, parties, and interest groups.

the state in america

Like any modern polity the American state reflects basic world trends. It is large; and in fact it is the nation's largest employer (Karlen, 1968: 225–226). The state is highly bureaucratized, with a vast network of military and administrative offices (Mosher, 1965:163–211). It is democratized in that elites in the state's executive and assembly branches are elected. There is a strong sense of nationalism with clear geographical boundaries and a common political history and ideology. But unlike most modern societies, the state is somewhat decentralized. It is a federalist system with fifty territorially demarcated states dis-playing some autonomy from the national or federal state. As Wil-liams (1970:243) notes, "it is the United States, not the United State." Yet, as we will see, there is a clear trend toward centralization of power and decision making.

    Structurally, the core of the polity exists at three levels: the na-tional or federal government, state government, and local community government. Because each of these displays some autonomy from the others, a considerable amount of decentralization exists. Also few clear-cut norms exist to regulate the division of power and decision making among these levels. The Constitution of the legal subsystem in the United States grants only general powers to the federal government: regulating commerce, levying taxes, and protecting each territorial state from insurrection and domestic violence (Karlen, 1968: 316–317). Aside from granting only a few general rights, the Constitution imposes several limitations on the federal government (Karlen, 1968:317; Williams, 1970:245): the federal government cannot confer or take away from the individual states' functions, procedures, and territories; it must maintain equal representation of the states in the upper house (Senate) of the assembly (Congress); and it must leave to the states all residual powers not conferred on the United States by the Constitution ("The powers not delegated to the United States by the Constitution, nor prohibited by it to the states, are reserved to the states respectively, or to the people"—Tenth Amendment). In actual practice, however, the ambiguity of these legal norms has allowed over the years increasing regulation of the territorial states and local communities by the federal state.

THE FEDERAL STATE
The federal government can be divided into two branches: the executive and the assembly (or Congress). Sometimes a third is added—the judiciary—in discussions of the American polity. But for our analytical purposes the judiciary is a part of the legal subsystem of a society. Yet the overlap between the polity and legal subsystem is so great that we cannot ignore the impact of the judiciary on the polity. In fact many of the general norms attendant upon the status positions contained in the executive and assembly branches of the federal state can be viewed as inputs from the legal subsystem. The American polity is a government of laws, which means that the role behaviors of incumbents are to some extent circumscribed by written rules. But these laws represent only a general framework within which many more specific norms stemming from tradition, utility, and actual practice have emerged to guide conduct.

The executive branch.   The increasing powers of the chief executive— the President—are perhaps the best indicator of the trend toward centralization in the American polity. The Constitution left tremendous discretionary power to the President; and over time as imperatives for rapid, nationwide decisions have necessitated or as the personality of the chief executive has dictated, the Presidency has become the major locus of power and decision making in the polity. These powers have become codified into a series of norms giving the President these powers: power of appointment to and removal from major positions in the federal bureaucracy; power to direct major administrative branches of the government; power to establish and implement with wide discretion foreign policy; power to initiate the legislative program of each Congress; and power to direct and initiate in detail military action.

Under the President there exists a clustering of statuses known as the executive office of the President. These statuses are organized into offices such as the Bureau of the Budget, National Security Council, Council of Economic Advisors, Office of Emergency Planning, National Aeronautics and Space Administration, Office of Science and Technology, Office of Economic Opportunity, Civil Service Commission, and so on. The most important of these executive offices is the *Cabinet*, which represents the appointed (by the President) heads of each major department of the federal bureaucracy: State; Defense; Post Office; Health, Education, and Welfare; Justice; Commerce; and so forth. Since these departments are responsible for the administration or execution of programs related to national goals, the power of the President to appoint and then control the heads of these departments represents a high degree of centralization of power into his hands. Through vigorous, reserved, or selective implementation of congressionally initiated programs and laws, the President can control to a very large extent the goals of the society and the mobilization and allocation of system resources to those goals. With these executive powers he can also manipulate the distribution of valued resources as well as the nature and extent of social control.

But as the American doctrine of separation of powers would indicate, there are certain checks on the Chief Executive's powers. The Constitution and the Supreme Court in the legal system constrain the President's decisions and their implementation. And as we will see below, the powers invested in Congress also serve as a check. An equally important source of constraint is the sheer size and structure of the federal bureaucracy. The federal bureaucracy is huge and represents a labyrinth of specialized and professionalized offices within divisions, divisions within agencies, and agencies within departments. Except for the heads of each major department in the federal bureaucracy, recruitment to and promotion within the bureaucracy is based on expertise and seniority rather than on political affiliation. The rank and file of the bureaucracy thus becomes politically neutral, since they come into the bureaucracy in an apolitical capacity and reside in the bureaucracy over the tenure of different Presidents (Williams, 1970:260–261). And the pressures for expertise and loyalty to a profession rather than to a political party increase as the size and complexity of the bureaucracy and its tasks multiply. The overall effect of this trend is to mitigate the power of the Presidency. Programs channeled through the executive bureaucracy can become altered and selectively implemented. This means that the long-term senior professionals within agencies of major executive departments possess tremendous power to counterbalance that of the Chief Executive and his appointed Cabinet members.

The military is one of the departments under the Chief Executive's direct control. The President is empowered by the Constitution to be the Commander in Chief of the armed forces. This area deserves special attention for two reasons: it is the largest and utilizes a majority of the financial resources of the federal state; and it is in the military that the instruments of force backing up the President's decisions ultimately reside. It is here that the power and influence of long-term senior department professionals on the President is perhaps greatest. This fact has generated speculation that the United States is a militarized society, with national goals revolving around military programs. In terms of the allocation of system resources, clearly the major system goal of the United States is defense. Whether this indicates that the United States is a militarized society is an open issue, since the word *militarized* has ambiguous connotations. As Williams (1970: 266) notes, it can mean at least these things: large standing army in times of peace; decisive importance of military counsel and decisions in determining national goals; and increased influence of military activities upon domestic structures and processes. Utilizing these criteria, it is safe to say that the trend is toward a militarized society.

The Congress.   The other major branch of the federal government is Congress. As conceived by the framers of the Constitution, Congress was to serve as a check on the executive branch of the national state. It was empowered to legislate and declare major policies, programs, and goals of the nation. It was to engage in extensive executive activities in filling government posts and cooperate with the President in executing policies. It was to investigate the actions of governmental agencies. It was to have extensive administrative functions in establishing governmental agencies. It was to have far-reaching judicial functions in determining the structure of the courts, while being a quasi-court in the impeachment process (Karlen, 1968:112). *Normatively*, Congress still possesses these powers. But in reality it has abdicated many to the executive branch of the national state—

another indicator of its increasing centralization. Currently the executive branch of the state establishes system goals and programs, initiates major legislation, makes major appointments, and establishes principal agencies. But Congress still exerts considerable power and influence both formally and informally. It regulates the budget of administrative agencies; it can fail to pass programs initiated by the President; it can refuse to confirm appointments of the President; it can block organization and reorganization of administrative departments. Thus Congress has become more of a reactive than an active force in initiating the goals of American society.

The formal structure of Congress is simple; the informal structure is highly complex. Formally Congress is divided into two subassemblies—the House of Representatives and the Senate. Incumbents are elected by direct popular vote and serve two years in the House and six years in the Senate. National elections are staggered so that half of the House and about one-third of the Senate seats are contested every two years. Most members of Congress are affiliated with one of the two major political parties —Democratic and Republican—and utilize their party's organization in seeking election. Senators are elected on the basis of territory—two from each state of the Union. Representatives to the House are elected on the basis of territory and population distribution. One representative to the House is guaranteed each state, with the rest allocated on the basis of the population of the state. However, within a state rarely do congressional districts reflect actual population distribution. Until very recently most districts were gerrymandered in a way favoring the disproportionate election of Representatives from rural areas within the state. In 1964 the Supreme Court ruled for reapportioning of state districts to reflect better the actual population distribution with each state. But the rural bias built into the districting process has not been completely eliminated.

Within either the House or Senate legislation is brought before a general meeting of all representatives or senators to be discussed and voted on. To get to the floor of either the Senate or House legislation must pass through a committee. Committees are composed of representatives or senators who become specialists in the sphere of their committee. These committees can write and rewrite legislation. Appointment to committees is made by party leaders and the committees are chaired by the senior member (in terms of length of tenure in Congress) of the majority party. A majority vote within a committee is required to get a piece of legislation to the floor. Committee chairmen have considerable latitude in bringing to a vote or stalling legislation in their committee. Once legislation is out of committee, it is debated, amended, passed, rejected, or sometimes sent back to committee for further study. The general floor meetings of the House are presided over by the Speaker of the House, who is the leader of the majority party. The Senate is presided over by the Vice President, and in his absence, a member of the majority party is the *pro tempore* president of the Senate. Parties in both the House and Senate also have floor leaders who are the actual holders of power in Congress for their party. Rarely is the *pro tempore* Senate president the actual leader of his party, whereas the Speaker of the House frequently is. Between the House and Senate, the Senate has more power and prestige. This derives from the fact that senators have longer office tenure and the Senate must review and pass all legislation initiated in the House.

Although the formal structure of Congress is more complex than indicated above (Karlen, 1968:109–170), we can now review some of the informal structures and processes actually shaping decision making in Congress. The constituencies of senators and representatives greatly affect how they will vote on a piece of legislation. Senators tend to be somewhat less responsive to the fads of public opinion than representatives, since they have job security for six as opposed to two years. This means that representatives must be highly responsive to the interest groups and opinion of their local constituencies. Because districting favors rural areas, representatives must be, as an aggregate, most responsive to rural interests and opinions. On the other hand, senators can be somewhat more detached because they represent a whole state and interests across a state often cancel each other out. But all senators usually must be responsive to the opinion and interests of the large urban and industrial areas where the big blocs of votes reside.

The structure of the committee system also affects decision making in Congress. Since chairmen of committees in both the House and Senate are selected on the basis of seniority, senators and representatives from areas where interests and opinions remain stable over long periods of time are the most likely to be reelected and hence assume the chairmanship of major committees. Interests and opinions tend to remain most stable in rural areas where urbanism and industrialization do not generate reorganization of interests, opinions, and populations. The result is that major committees in both the House and Senate are chaired by incumbents oriented not only to rural but local interests and opinions. Since these chairmen have considerable power in determining what legislation gets out of committees onto the floor, they disproportionately influence political decision making of Congress in a direction toward rural and local goals as opposed to urban and national interests.

The degree of party unity and organization within the Senate and House also affects political decision making in Congress. Representatives must be more responsive to party pressures than senators because their shorter term makes them rely heavily on party organization in seeking frequent reelection. Senators are more likely to control the statewide caucus of their party than representatives, who are tied to local districts and party caucuses. These local caucuses are usually dominated by major interest groups of the district rather than the individual representative and his organization. For this reason, straight party voting is more likely in the House than in the Senate.

The judiciary.   The judiciary is usually considered the third branch of the national state. The federal courts—especially the Supreme Court—pose a check on executive and assembly activities by interpreting their constitutionality. In fact executive and legislative action usually involve a consideration of how the Supreme Court will interpret such action. The Court thus serves as an implicit check on the executive and assembly branches of the polity. Also since many federal laws—as well as the Constitution itself—prescribe at a general level the obligations of incumbents in the executive and legislative branches of the state, the legal subsystem further checks (whether or not it balances is a more ambiguous issue) the state's action. Of course the powers of the judiciary are limited by several facts: Congress enacts the laws of which the legal system is comprised; the President and Congress can appoint and remove (although the latter is an awkward procedure) the judges of the federal judiciary; Congress can amend the Constitution (although this is awkward and difficult).

We might add that for our analytical purposes the law and polity are considered separate but greatly overlapping institutions. Several facts support this contention. Once appointed, judges can display considerable autonomy from the polity. They become governed by traditional norms of the legal as opposed to political profession. Because of the difficulty in amending the Constitution and because of the life tenure of federal judges plus the difficulties involved in impeaching federal judges, the profile of the legal system can display even more autonomy from the polity. Once laws are enacted, they have a binding force independent of the legislature that enacted them. Moreover, what kinds of laws are legislated is affected by the likelihood of the Supreme Court's ruling on their constitutionality. For at least these reasons, then, the analytical emphasis on the institutional autonomy — but not isolation — of the legal subsystem from the polity will be maintained.

STATE AND LOCAL GOVERNMENT

State government.   The Constitution and its amendments are vague on just how the states are to be articulated with each other and the federal government. Only five general types of relationships are clearly specified (Karlen, 1968:312–319): (1) The territory and power of territorial states is inherent and cannot be taken away by the federal government (Tenth Amendment). (2) The territorial states cannot pass laws or structure themselves in violation of the Constitution. (3) The states have certain obligations to the federal government, including sending representatives to Congress, establishing districts for election of representatives to the House, maintaining order within their borders, establishing and maintaining a republican form of government, and participating in procedures to amend the federal Constitution. (4) The federal government has the right to regulate commerce and levy taxes, as well as "make all laws which shall be necessary . . . for carrying into execution the foregoing powers." (5) The states have certain obligations to one another, including accepting public laws, records, and judicial proceedings of other states, allowing citizens of other states access to jobs and courts, and obligations to settle disputes between states peacefully.

Other than these general provisions and restrictions, the states were left to form their own internal political organizations. On the whole, governments of the states resemble in general form the structure of the federal government. Each state has a written constitution; each displays a separation of powers with an executive and assembly branch (as well as judiciary); most assemblies are two-house legislatures; each state holds popular elections for governor and the assembly; and all have an extensive administrative bureaucracy under the state's executive. Yet states can deviate from the form of the federal government in a wide variety of ways, including the effective operation of two major political parties, power of the governor and other executives, division of powers between executive and assembly branches, term of office for executive and assembly incumbents, length of legislative sessions, basis of assembly representation, and allowance for voter referendums and recalls. The activities of these state governments has increased greatly with urbanism, industrialization, and the increasing complexity of the government's tasks. Most states now finance a major portion of education, highways, public welfare, health and hospital care, police and fire protection, sewers and sanitation, parks, transportation, correction, and social insurance programs within their boundaries.

Local governments. Local governments within a state exist at the discretion of the state. They are created and can be dissolved by the state government. In practice, however, local governments, whether counties, cities, townships, or villages, maintain considerable autonomy from state governments. The structural organization of local governments varies greatly, although two general types prevail (International City Managers Association, Municipal Yearbook, 1970): *mayor-council* and *council-manager*. In mayor-council governments, both the mayor, who becomes chief executive, and the council, which represents a "mini" assembly, are popularly elected. Council members, however, are frequently elected from and represent districts in a community. Norms usually require the mayor to bear the major responsibility for the community's administration. The council and the mayor are jointly to make policy. But the mayor usually has the most decision-making power, because he usually must prepare the annual budget and execute its provisions. Thus there is a trend toward the centralization of power into the executive branch of community government in mayor-council systems.

On the other hand, council-manager governments display a reverse pattern of decision making. This pattern tends to be typical of medium to moderately large communities, with Cincinnati the only city with a population over 500,000 that has adopted and retained it. Council-manager governments operate under norms dictating that the city council will serve as a representative policy-making body and a professional manager selected by the council will bring nonpartisan and professional expertise to the tasks of administration. Norms usually require the manager to appoint department heads, prepare the budget for the council, and give policy advice to the council. With the growth of this form of community government, extensive professionalization of city managing has occurred. A national organization along with publications, training facilities, and a code of behavior has emerged. Such professionalism, along with the appointive and advising powers of the manager, greatly increase his power. He can selectively advise the council on policies and/or selectively implement policies established by the council. Since the manager and his appointees will be guided by professional norms, they are likely to display a high degree of consensus over what advice should be given the council and in just what ways policies should be implemented. Thus even in community governments where formal decision-making powers reside with the representative council much de facto power becomes transferred to the professional executives of the community government.

CENTRALIZATION OF THE AMERICAN STATE

As conceived by the framers of the Constitution, the American state was a three-part hierarchy of federal, state, and local governments. Each was to display considerable autonomy from the others. But since 1789 the federal government has increasingly co-opted and incorporated state and local governments. This has occurred in a series of confrontations between state and federal governments with the federal government prevailing. From the Alien and Sedition Acts of 1798 to arguments over tariffs, and through the Civil War, the Great Depression, and the school desegregation decisions, decision-making powers have become increasingly consolidated into the federal state. Coupled with two world wars and a prolonged cold war, as well as rapid urbanization, industrialization, new means of communication and transportation, and visible and pervasive social problems, nationwide goal attainment has become both possible and imperative. As the functions of the federal government have increased, state and local governments have become subordinate to and financially dependent upon the federal government. Thus the core structure of the American polity—the state—is beginning to display the degree of centralization typical of all other modern polities. And this trend will continue as various social problems increasingly become nationwide and cut across individual communities and states. As we will see later, the capacity of the American state to respond rapidly and effectively to these nationwide problems is limited because of its internal organization. But to appreciate these limitations fully we must first turn to somewhat peripheral but important structures of the American polity—political parties and interest groups.

political parties in the united states

Numerically the vast majority of positions in the American state are nonpolitical. Most employees in the American state staff the giant bureaucracy attendant upon federal, state, and local executive and assembly branches of government. However, incumbents in elite positions—President, senator, representative, governor, state legislator, city councilman, mayor, county supervisor, and so on—are inserted into the state through an elective process. This fact has led to the emergence over time of two dominant party organizations—the Democrats and Republicans—which compete to win elections and thus insert their candidates into these elite positions. In principle these two parties are the vehicle for expressing public sentiment about system goals, priorities, and programs to meet these goals. In reality political parties in America shape, as much as they are shaped by, public sentiment. They also tend to be dominated by various special interest groups whose programs often differ from those desired by the public. Furthermore, at the state and local levels a truly competitive party system frequently does not exist; rather, one party consistently dominates elections. These facts are attributable to a wide variety of structural interconnections within each party; between parties; between parties and the state; and among interest groups, parties, and the state. Some of these interconnections are discussed below.

INTERNAL PARTY ORGANIZATION AND DECISION-MAKING PROCESSES IN THE AMERICAN STATE

American political parties are composed of a series of quasi-autonomous and decentralized caucuses. Caucuses exist at the local, state, and national levels. The degree of articulation and coordination among these various levels of caucuses is loose—even at election time. The general structural features of both major political parties include: (1) Each local city, township, and county usually has a party caucus composed of volunteer workers, major financial backers, political incumbents or aspirants, and in large cities paid professional organizers. Aside from relatively stable local caucuses, special organizations for particular candidates often emerge independent of either political party. At election time these independent organizations may or may not become incorporated into local party caucuses. (2) Each state has a statewide caucus composed of paid professionals, prominent political incumbents, large financial backers, and leaders of large and powerful local caucuses. State caucuses attempt to coordinate the activities of local caucuses, but often the local caucus—especially in large cities—is more powerful and remains independent of the statewide caucus. The political machines of large urban areas are typical examples of powerful local party organizations. (3) There is a national party organization (the national committee) for each party, composed of professional organizers, large financial contributors, prominent members of powerful local and state caucuses, and sometimes prominent political incumbents and aspirants. The actual membership of the national committee usually extends considerably beyond the formal list of members. In this way the influence of large financial backers and powerful politicians can remain hidden. The party controlling the Presidency usually has the President's staff imposed on top of the national committee (Potter and Hennessy, 1964). The national committee is supposed to coordinate state and local caucuses, map general campaign strategy, and hold a national nominating convention in late summer of presidential-election years to select candidates for the Presidency and Vice Presidency. Local and state caucuses send delegates to the national convention who in turn nominate these candidates. The selection of delegates to the national convention varies tremendously from state to state. Some states hold a presidential primary election with the supporters of the winning candidate becoming delegates; other states rely on the state and local party machinery to select delegates; and a few hold primaries specifically designed to select delegates pledged to vote for a particular candidate. But in all cases the dominant caucuses in a state, whether they be the statewide committee or powerful party machines in large cities, greatly influence the selection of delegates. (4) The processes of electing party candidates at the national, state, and local levels also vary greatly. At the national level the delegates to the convention select a candidate, but just how is unknown and there appear to be few clear-cut norms guiding delegates. A party with a first-term President utilizes the convention as a ritual to renominate the incumbent for a second term. A retiring President can usually handpick his aspiring successor—if he wishes—because he usually has control of the party machinery and can thus select delegates to the convention favorable to his choice. For the party out of power the selection process is more ambiguous. Aspiring candidates usually run in the various state primaries during the spring and summer before the national convention. In these primaries the winning candidate picks up delegates while establishing his degree of national popularity. But a candidate cannot gather enough delegates from state primaries to secure his party's nomination—even if he wins all the primaries in the states that hold them. This fact results in considerable backroom persuading of non-committed convention delegates by the candidate's staff and supporters. These informal conferences between delegates and the various candidates' campaign organizers continue on and off the convention floor. The candidate eventually gaining a majority of votes from convention delegates then becomes that party's nominee for Chief Executive. Should this candidate win in the actual election, he is indebted to those groups originally supporting his candidacy as well as to the backers and interests of those major blocks of delegates who wrung concessions from the candidate in giving him their votes at the convention. As Chief Executive, many of his decisions will reflect this indebtedness.

At the state level primary elections are held to determine each party's candidates for elite positions in the state and federal governments (senators and legislators). The norms governing these state primaries vary. Some states require a *closed* primary where voters must register as either a Democrat or Republican (or in a third party if there is one) and can vote at the polls only for a slate of candidates in their declared party. A dozen states have *open* primaries where voters can vote for candidates in either party—regardless of how they register. But they can vote for candidates of only one party. In states where one party dominates, primary elections are, in effect, the process for determining the eventual incumbent in the state. Various factions of the same dominant party enter their candidates in the primary, with the winner assured of eventual election. Whatever the process, just who becomes a candidate and how he or she becomes a candidate is an illusive process. Candidates who are wealthy, who have at least part of the party machinery behind them, and who can cultivate the financial backing of major interest groups are best prepared to undertake the increasingly high cost of running for and winning office. This inevitably means that most candidates will come from a higher social class than their public and will be more indebted to special interests than to their public. Once elected, their policy decisions will inevitably reflect these facts.

At the local community level party organization is vigorous; but curiously, candidates for local office sometimes bear little or no affiliation to a traditional political party. Rather, ad hoc organizations supporting candidates are as common as party organizations. Party caucuses at the local level tend to be more influential in campaigns in large urban areas than in smaller communities. In smaller communities local party organizations tend to concentrate their efforts on state elite (assemblymen, governor, etc.) and national elite (representatives, senators, and the President) positions. The backers of political organizations—whether party or ad hoc—usually represent certain community interests and thus the winner of an election must make decisions which favor these interests. Sometimes these decisions favoring a particular interest are subtle and at other times highly visible and blatant (Agger, Goldrich, and Swanson, 1964).

In sum we can conclude that political parties in America are loosely organized. This fact has far-reaching consequences for decision making of incumbents in the state at all levels—national, state, and local. At the national level the President becomes indebted to the coalition of state and local party caucuses—and the interests they represent—that secured first his nomination and then his election. Senators and representatives become indebted not so much to the national party caucus as to the coalition of local party caucuses—and the interests these reflect—that secured victory in both the primary and general elections. As long as a candidate must rely on these local party caucuses he is indebted to local interest groups supplying the leadership and financial backing of these caucuses. This is particularly true of representatives in the House who must utilize this local party organization every two years. At the state level elite incumbents become indebted to the coalitions of local and state caucuses which were most instrumental in their primary and general election victories. At the community level elected officials are indebted to the local ad hoc organizations, or party caucuses in larger cities, that secured their victory. At all levels of the state decision making is always a partial reflection of a candidate's indebtedness. How much of a reflection is impossible to determine, for influences often remain hidden and/or covered up with political rhetoric. But it is safe to generalize that decision making in the American polity can be only a very imperfect reflection of public sentiment and nonpolitical imperatives facing decision makers. Much decision making is influenced by special interest groups, as they control or at least influence the party organization upon which the incumbent is dependent. And because of the decentralized and quasi-autonomous nature of these party caucuses, decision makers — even at the national level — remain highly responsive to local interests.

Since there are so many different and conflicting local interests influencing many different elites, a broad representation of interests influences decision making. This has been offered as one explanation for the persistence of the two-party system in the United States, since many different interests have the ear of at least some decision-making elites. The decentralized party system thus provides a legitimate — and often effective — channel for small local interest groups to push their interests at a national (and, of course, state and local) level. But at the same time this influence of local interests makes society-wide decision making difficult, since national decision makers — especially in the House of Representatives — must remain oriented to the local interests dominating the local party caucuses they depend upon for reelection. In part this helps explain the difficulty of the American polity in establishing clear national goals and priorities among them. It also inhibits effective mobilization and allocation of system resources for attaining national goals, since such action inevitably conflicts with local (and, of course, national) interest groups which have at least some and frequently a great influence on elites' decisions.

A society with more centralized political parties might be more capable of establishing goals, their priorities, and allocating and mobilizing resources toward their achievement. This is certainly true of a one-party system where the party is an extension of the state and a mechanism for mobilizing public sentiment for goals established by elites. As long as American parties remain decentralized and continue to encompass widely diverse — and even conflicting — interests, the polity will face problems of arranging goal priorities and mobilizing resources. To centralize American parties into a strong national organization with a unified ideology and tight party organization of caucuses (or branches) would probably increase the number of political parties in the political subsystem. This is primarily because centralized parties have more difficulty in cutting across diverse public sentiments and interest groups than the decentralized "brokerage" parties that are current in the United States (Lenski, 1970). In multiple-party systems, unless one party dominates as do the Socialists in Sweden, national goal-attainment decisions also become difficult because no one party can ever gain a long-term majority in the assembly. National decision making is one of the major dilemmas facing modern political systems with either a two-party or multiple-party system. The centralized parties of multiple-party systems have difficulties in establishing coalitions, while the brokerage-type parties in two-party systems remain tied to local and diverse interests. As national planning increasingly becomes imperative in complex industrial societies, this dilemma will pose series of crises and aggravate many pressing social problems. In the United States the trend toward the increasing centralization of power in the executive branch of the state—especially the Presidency—is perhaps the current system solution to this potential crisis. Without a fundamental reorganization of the party system this kind of resolution appears inevitable.

interest groups in the united states

In any complex and differentiated society a diverse number of interests are inevitable. Different social units at different places in the society have different goals. In a large society like the United States the vast number of societal subsystems pursuing different goals generates a large number of diverse interest groups—big and small business, labor, religion, education, agriculture, manufacturing, and so on. Since political decisions at all levels of the state affect in varying degrees these interests, their presence at all points of political decision making is inevitable (Key, 1961; Holtzman, 1966; Monsen and Cannon, 1965; Ziegler, 1964). In the United States interest groups are so pervasive and influence so many aspects of political decision making that we can consider them as part of the American polity. Exactly how pervasive and how much influence interest groups exert on decision making can never be precisely determined, but the influence is great. We have already seen how they indirectly influence decision making through control of party caucuses on which decision makers are dependent. In this section we will examine the more direct influences on decision making of this vast clustering of statuses.

Many interest groupings are highly organized, with permanent offices staffed by paid professionals. These offices are most conspicuous in Washington, D.C., and state capitals. In some large urban centers they can also be found. The purpose of such highly organized interests is simple: to secure decisions promoting the goals of a particular segment of the society. This means applying pressure and attempting to influence decision makers—especially legislators, but also elites in executive positions. To do this interest groups often have former legislators or employees of legislators and executives on their staff to give them an inside advantage through informal contacts and knowledge of the decision-making processes. The tactics of interest groups—or *lobbies* as they are frequently called—are various, including: bribing, introducing legislation through a "front" legislator, appearing before legislative committees and arguing their case, mobilizing public support through publicity campaigns for their programs, and mobilizing other interest groups behind their goals (usually in exchange for their support on another issue). Traditionally such lobbying has come from nongovernmental segments of the society—business, agriculture, labor, religion, medicine, education, and so forth. But increasingly major executive departments of the federal government have established offices specifically designated to influence legislation in Congress. The most conspicuous of these executive lobbies is the Department of Defense with a vast organization devoted to pushing its goals—usually for more money. Other executive departments have somewhat less organized and effective lobbying organizations.

The institutionalization of these interest groups into the American polity allows diverse segments of the society to exert direct influence upon elite decision makers. However, the high degree of access of interest groups to decision makers inevitably means that a few of the most financially solvent and best organized lobbies can have a greater influence on political decision making at all levels of government than the general public. This can mean that the narrow interests of a few, rich and well-organized, can prevail over the not-so-rich and poorly organized public. The disproportionate influence of well-organized lobbies can also inhibit nationwide decision making, since the pressure of both local and narrow-interest national lobbies can deflect decision makers' attention away from national society-wide imperatives.

the american polity: an overview

The American political subsystem can be viewed as having several component subsystems: the state, political parties, and interest groupings. In turn each of these is composed of subsystems. The state is composed of federal, state, and local governments. Political parties are a poorly organized and decentralized clustering of caucuses, with the latter being a vague cluster of interests, the public, and political leaders. Interests are composed of large or small, organized or disorganized, and private or governmental groupings from many different sectors of the society. The interrelations among these principal subsystems of the polity—the state, parties, and interests, and all their constituent subsystems—is incredibly complex. In this section we have just been able to scratch the surface of these interrelations.

One conclusion to be drawn from our analysis is this: Decision making at all levels of government in the United States is profoundly inflluenced by a few highly organized and well-financed interest groups. Whether this points to a "power elite"—as some sociologists contend—cannot be precisely determined (Mills, 1956; Hunter, 1959; Domhoff, 1967). Do decision-making elites and the interests backing them have a compact or are they engaged in a unified conspiracy? This latter seems unlikely, considering the diversity of powerful interest groupings in the United States (Rose, 1967). However, to assert this does not negate the fact that a few interests exert a disproportionate amount of influence on political decision making. Such disproportionate influence appears an inevitable by-product of the structure of the American polity. As to whether or not this has led to the emergence of a power elite requires empirical answers to these questions (Williams, 1970:263): How much consensus exists among elites? Is there a unitary or pluralistic set of elites in America? How entrenched in decision-making positions are these elites? How accountable are they to the public? To these questions there are no clear-cut empirical answers. As we have noted, centralization is inevitable in modern polities, even in the United States where a decentralized polity was originally established and institutionalized in law. Have these central decision-making status norms become dominated by a few narrow interests? To this question answers are needed.

SUMMARY

In this chapter we have explored the general features of simple and complex political subsystems. We began by isolating out two basic elements of all polities: decision making and power. We then examined some of the general consequences of polities for the broader society: establishing goals, mobilizing and allocating resources, distributing valued resources, and social control.

Next we turned to the difficult task of classifying types of political subsystems. To do this we introduced five dimensions which would facilitate classification and comparison. These dimensions included the locus, sphere, basis, acquisition, and exercise of power and decision making in a society. Utilizing these dimensions we described four types of traditional polities: egalitarian, kin based, state based, and modernizing. We then described different types of modern polities in terms of variations in their party systems or in the way power is acquired. Here we noted differences among one-party, two-party, and multiple-party polities.

With political development we noted several conspicuous trends, including: increasing size of the polity; bureaucratization along rational lines; and the rise of nationalism, centralization, and democratization. It was hypothesized that to the extent that political development occurs in a society, these trends would become increasingly evident.

Finally analysis shifted to the American polity. In this section we outlined the general contours of the American state, political parties, and interest groupings, as well as relations among these subsystems of the American polity. We also emphasized how the organization of these subsystems greatly inhibits establishment of nationwide goals, priorities among them, and the allocation of resources to their attainment.

the
institutional
environment
of
POLTY 11

Despite the tremendous impact of the polity on other institutions, it can never be completely insulated from the influence of surrounding institutions. What occurs in the institutions of economy, kinship, law, education, and religion profoundly affects the structure, functioning, and development of the polity. Even when changes in these other institutions are actually initiated by the polity, they feed back and circumscribe subsequent actions of political leaders. However, equally important is the fact that the form and profile of the polity in any society is shaped by existent institutional conditions in the broader society. While the rise of exceptional leaders, foreign conquest, and colonialism can greatly alter political patterns in a society, such alterations are always limited and affected by the structure and functioning of indigenous institutions. Some of the more conspicuous paths or lines of influence are traced in this chapter.

ECONOMY AND POLITY

More than any other institution the economy shapes political processes in a society. This influence has been alluded to in previous discussions where we associated types of polities with various types of economies—hunting and gathering, agrarian, industrial, and postindustrial. It is not by chance that vast political democracies are difficult to find in the agrarian societies of the past or present. Nor would it be possible for an elaborate political bureaucracy to develop indigenously in a hunting and gathering society. Nor is it unexpected that totalitarianism appears to be lessening, despite recent events in Eastern Europe, as societies approach a postindustrial stage of economic development. All of these political facts and trends are in part attributable to the nature of the economic system in a society. Many of the answers to questions such as why totalitarianism or democracy prevails or why the polity is large or small are thus to be found in the relationship between the economy and polity.

the economy and polity in traditional societies

Earlier we associated primitive egalitarian polities with hunting and gathering economies. The reason for this association lay in the fact that the economy places limits on the type of polity that can exist in a society. In order for a separate and discrete political subsystem to evolve in a society, the economy must generate sufficient surplus to support autonomous political leaders. Most hunting and gathering economies do not possess the technology or capital base to generate such a surplus (Lenski, 1966:94–116). More importantly, in such small and simple societies there is little real social necessity for a stable and established polity. Goals and goal priorities are usually abundantly clear and revolve around securing sufficient insulation from the natural (and social) environment. Allocation and mobilization of people and resources tend to occur within the kinship system—as does distribution of valued resources. Leadership positions are specified by kinship norms.

Where a somewhat permanent tribal headman or chief exists in such societies, norms usually allow him to direct economic activity—especially with respect to societal migration over a territory. But norms also restrict the headman's power and rarely give him the right to use force. For example, among the Siriono of eastern Bolivia chiefs occupy leadership positions by virtue of their personal qualities and skills. To maintain their status they must perform the same everyday tasks—only much better—that everyone else must perform. Because of his proven abilities a chief is more likely than someone else to be followed or obeyed, but there is no obligation of tribal members to obey him nor are punishments forthcoming for the tribal member who does not obey his chief (Holmberg, 1950). An equally typical leadership pattern in hunting and gathering societies is the somewhat spontaneous emergence of leaders in times of crisis—particularly economic crises. Because technology and capital cannot generate a surplus, survival in these societies is always problematic and an economic crisis is likely with even minor changes in the natural environment. For example, diseased animals, drought, and other natural events can generate imperatives for society-wide leadership cutting across kin groups. Under these conditions temporary leaders emerge to establish goal priorities as well as to mobilize and allocate system resources to their attainment. Once the crisis is eliminated these leaders frequently recede into the background.

The noticeable lack of distinction and power possessed by political leaders in hunting and gathering economies can thus be traced to the fact that without large amounts of economic surplus, these societies cannot possibly support a privileged ruling elite or social class. While considerable prestige and esteem can be bestowed upon leaders who display exceptional skills, the economy of these societies does not allow for the support of a nonworking group of political leaders. Nor, given the often tenuous adjustment to the natural environment of hunting and gathering societies, could they afford the luxury of leaders without demonstrable skill and expertise in the everyday economic tasks necessary for survival. It is for this reason that an almost egalitarian political profile is evident in these societies. Leaders must be proven experts; they have little real coercive power to establish system goals and allocate resources; and they cannot in any extensive way disproportionately distribute subsistence goods (although they can receive other valued resources such as esteem and prestige).

In societies with a horticultural or full-blown agrarian economy a discrete political subsystem is more evident. As would be expected, one of the major reasons for this is attributable to the increased capacity of the economy to generate a surplus (Lenski, 1966:117–296). Knowledge about cultivating, planting, harvesting, and irrigating and other forms of agricultural technology as well as new forms of capital such as hoes, plows, water troughs, and dams push productivity of the economy to levels beyond mere subsistence. With an economic surplus it becomes economically possible to support a nonworking political elite. However, such an economic possibility should not be viewed as an economic inevitability. Yet once an economy can generate a surplus, a host of problems emerge: Who gets the surplus? How is it to be distributed? How are conflicts over the surplus to be mitigated? Toward what ends is the surplus to be utilized? And so on. Economic surplus can better insulate a system from its external environment, but it can also generate severe internal conflicts. While the exact process is varied and somewhat unclear, the initial existence of an economic surplus usually results in a kin-based political subsystem.

One path to a kin-based polity can be traced in this way: Headmen, because of their prestige and other qualities, come to have the right to collect and then redistribute economic surplus. Such a right often frees the headman from economic tasks, for he can now appropriate (see Chapter 3) from the economy enough surplus to support himself and his immediate kinsmen. Just why the headman would be given such a privilege can never be known for most horticultural and agrarian societies. Yet we can hypothesize that political appropriation and distribution represented in these systems a solution to the actual or potential internal disruption created by the existence of surplus. This solution in all likelihood was not rationally or consciously thought out, but rather it probably emerged in response to successive and escalating internal crises resulting from conflicts over surplus goods. The evidence suggests that initially powerful norms requiring headmen to be exceptionally generous in redistribution usually dominate. Lenski (1966:165) refers to this as the "redistributive ethic," which requires the headman, especially in African societies, to redistribute much of the surplus he appropriates. However, over time powers of appropriation can become translated into real political power and society-wide decision-making prerogatives. Again the exact processes are not known, but we can make some reasonable speculations. Appropriated surplus emancipates headmen and their immediate kinsmen from time- and energy-consuming economic tasks. Frequently headmen possess sufficient prestige which can enable them to distribute differentially the economic surplus of a society —at first to an expanding number of kinsmen and later to other favored members of the society. It is in this way that elite social classes emerge in agrarian societies (Lenski, 1966:154–168). Once elite social classes become stabilized, leadership status is assumed as much by hereditary succession as by demonstrable ability and skill. Such a transition marks the incipiency of a kin-based polity.

In terms of political development the differential distribution of surplus has far-reaching consequences. It allows for the accumulation of wealth into the hands of elites. In turn this wealth is often used to establish and support armies. With this capacity to use physical force differential distribution which cannot be justified by leaders' prestige or by religious dogma can be justified by force—or the threat of its use. Once coercive power becomes consolidated into the hands of a few kin statuses in a dominant kin grouping, elites can set goals for the total society and then mobilize and allocate system resources to their attainment. One society goal that has typically emerged is conquest of other systems in bordering territories. When successful, conquest increases the wealth—and hence power—of elites, while expanding the size of the population and territory of the society. With increases in the size and territory of the society, administrative and control problems intensify. This in turn leads to growing bureaucratization of both the army and administrative staff of elite kinsmen—thus marking the incipiency of a state.

In advanced agrarian societies with extensive agricultural technology and a sophisticated capital base, considerable economic surplus is produced. This means that extensive trade and commerce become possible, which in turn results in the emergence of large urban centers. Such increased surplus also results in increased appropriation by the polity, usually through such mechanisms as taxation, levies, and tariffs. Increased appropriation results in the expansion of the polity—both administratively and militarily. Expansion allows for more extensive system goals to be established while increasing the capacity of the polity to mobilize and allocate system resources to their attainment. Through differential appropriation the polity often begins to regulate how much capital is accumulated in which economic enterprises so as to facilitate the attainment of goals. Subsidy can also emerge as a means by which the polity begins to regulate capital accumulation. This closer regulation of capital accumulation expands the tasks and hence size of the polity's administrative bureaucracy. However, extensive regulation of capital accumulation does not occur until systems begin the process of industrialization.

It is with this expanded economic surplus in more advanced agrarian societies and the resulting expansion of the military and administrative bureaucracy that the transition from a kin-based to state-based polity can be said to occur. As the size of the military and administrative bureaucracy increases, recruitment to and promotion within these bureaucracies becomes less ascriptive because tasks increasingly require expertise. As nonelite kinsmen assume dominant decision-making positions in the bureaucracy, much political decision making becomes decreasingly the hereditary right and prerogative of kinsmen from elite kin groups. Eventually, whether through such a quiet administrative revolution, a military *coup*, or social-class revolution, the power and dominance of the original elite kin group is eliminated. In its place is a new ruling social class composed of a new elite kin grouping which may emerge and persist for some time. But in the long run administrative imperatives, coupled with the typical instability of traditional state-based polities, operate against domination of the polity by any particular kin grouping.

With industrialization profound structural reorganization of a society occurs—including the political subsystem. While in most Third World nations industrialization is consciously initiated and regulated by political elites, industrialization per se generates a series of pressures forcing political reorganization in a society. These pressures can become translated into a series of structural demands not only from the economy but also from other sectors of a society (Easton, 1965). As we will see a particular political regime must often accede to these demands if it is to retain power.

To industrialize, the polity must initiate extensive and expensive changes in the economy. As we know from Chapter 2, this involves great infusions of new technologies into the economy; the development of a machine-capital base; the socialization of new attributes such as motives, interpersonal styles, and trade skills in labor; and the development of new principles of entrepreneurship such as the factory system, bureaucracies, and law. To generate—or even initiate—these changes in a predominantly agrarian economy poses a difficult problem for the political elite. Establishing economic development as the principal system goal and then mobilizing, allocating, and distributing system resources toward the achievement of this goal can present seemingly insurmountable obstacles to the polity. The financial and human resources of an agrarian society are limited and usually inadequate to the task and the general population will have to undergo prolonged sacrifices in the short run to reap the long-run benefits of industrialization. This latter problem is intense when the population of a society is clustered into large urban centers, impoverished, restive, and when the polity maintains only tenuous legitimacy. To mobilize the public to accept the hardships involved in allocating and distributing resources into long-range economic development rather than immediate welfare programs, the polity often engages in extensive ideological manipulation of the impoverished public—especially the urban masses. Such manipulation usually revolves around an ideology of nationalism where national prestige, unity, betterment, and sacrifice for development are dominant components.

Nationalistic ideologies can thus represent attempts by the polity to unify culturally diverse urban masses, while mobilizing them to undergo hardship and further impoverishment without withdrawing legitimacy from the existing political regime. Such manipulation is necessary in agrarian systems attempting to undergo rapid economic development. But as noted previously, nationalistic ideologies usually raise the population's aspirations and expectations about the future state of affairs. Even though the populace may be willing to undergo some short-run sacrifices, these raised expectations eventually become translated into a series of demands for welfare, housing, education, and consumer goods. Frequently when these demands go unheeded a *coup* or society-wide revolution occurs. Usually after a long period of political instability these population demands eventually force reorganization of the polity. New agencies which would be unheard of in agrarian polities become incorporated in the state bureaucracy. These agencies revolve around public education, welfare, health, labor-management relations, and housing. They can be seen as representing new structures designed to distribute valued resources more equally and hence placate the masses. The emergence of these agencies is usually accompanied by attempts at land reform, which represent another means for redistributing valued resources more equally.

Compounding and often conflicting with population demands are economic realities. Industrialization requires mass education in order to socialize new attributes into labor and to generate new technologies; it requires tremendous financial investments in machine-based capital and factories; and it requires a certain amount of reorganization of work on a nonascriptive, performance basis in new structures such as factories and bureaucracies. These economic realities can force reorganization of the governmental bureaucracy so that efficient allocation of resources can occur. Also, since economic demands such as those for capital and capital goods can conflict with the demands of the public for welfare and consumer goods, improved efficiency in the allocation of the system's limited resources becomes necessary if a political regime is to survive. This results in further rationalization and centralization of the administrative bureaucracy in order to cope with these allocative and distributive problems. This same dilemma also forces the polity to expand its military and police forces to engage in social control in the event that such allocation and distribution fails to placate the public. This is a somewhat self-defeating process, since expenditures for the military deflect resources away from both the economy and public.

To summarize, then, we can visualize a complex set of relationships between the economy and modernizing polities. The establishment of economic development as a system goal places a series of extensive demands for resources on the polity. In order to allocate these resources to the economy the polity must instill a nationalistic ideology in the public to forego immediate gratifications for a better life later on. But this very ideology eventually sets up a series of demands for valued resources from the public. And so to remain in power a political regime must begin to distribute certain valued resources to the general population. In turn these attempts to placate the public divert investments away from crucial sectors of the economy upon which long-range economic development is contingent. Without long-range economic development and the resulting increase in consumer goods and the standard of living the polity will have difficulty in meeting the ever-escalating demands of the public. In this event, the polity will be perceived as ineffective and begin to lose the support of the population, which can become receptive to a new regime or the rhetoric of revolutionary leaders (Lipset, 1960:1–86).

These pressures on the polity can often force the reorganization of the state bureaucracy. Such reorganization marks a profound change in the distributive functions of the polity. In advanced agrarian systems the polity appropriates and then redistributes most of the society's valued resources to elites, resulting in a small ruling class possessing vast wealth while the rest of the population remains impoverished (Lenski, 1966:189–296). But with the rising expectations of the population accompanying industrial development and nationalism, redistribution of appropriated resources becomes more equitable. This coupled with the extensive allocation of surplus resources into sectors necessary for economic development (education, factories, machines, etc.) forces even greater changes in the redistribution process. Thus elites can no longer horde the surplus, since both population and economic demands for that surplus have greatly increased in industrializing systems. These increases in the equitable distribution of wealth, along with the necessity of the polity to remain constantly aware of public sentiment and demands, can mark the beginning of political democratization.

the economy and polity in modern societies

High levels of technology and machine capital as well as elaborate forms of entrepreneurship give modern economies a high degree of access to a wide variety of natural resources. In turn these can be rapidly converted into a myriad of standardized goods and commodities. Such productive capacity in industrial and postindustrial economies results in a tremendous economic surplus — whether measured in terms of luxury commodities, per capita income, gross national product, or corporate profits. The existence of this wealth allows the polity to establish a large number and wide variety of system-wide goals. By appropriating much of this surplus the polity has the capability of establishing and pursuing extensive and diverse goals at the same time. The result of this fact is that virtually all major system goals in modern societies depend upon the productive capacity of the economy. Goals such as military defense, conquering space, economic development, world economic dominance, and internal prosperity are directly dependent upon the continuance of this capacity. Other typical system goals such as equal employment opportunity, universal education, and eliminating poverty are indirectly dependent upon the productive capacity of the economy, since each of these latter goals requires extensive financing that can only be derived from the polity's ability to appropriate economic surplus and then allocate it to these programs. Furthermore, each of these latter goals is dependent upon the economy in another sense: The economy must be capable of absorbing graduates of schools; poverty can only be eliminated when the economy can employ at least some of the impoverished; and equal opportunity inevitably means equal access to employment in the economy and hence equal capacity to purchase the consumer goods of the economy. The dependence of goal attainment in modern societies on the economy becomes evident—especially in capitalistic economies—during periods of recession, depression, or inflation where, for example, the polity in the United States at the beginning of this decade cut back on the financing of many domestic programs and goals.

This dependence of system-goal attainment on the economy has resulted in close regulation and control of the economy by the polity. In Chapter 3 we reviewed some of the mechanisms employed by the polity to control capital accumulation—and hence productivity in modern economics. These included appropriation, tariffs, subsidy, and symbolic manipulation. The utilization of these mechanisms by the polity is extensive in all modern societies and reflects the dependence of system-goal attainment on economic structures and processes. This dependence manifests itself in an ever-increasing set of administrative linkages between the polity and economy. Sometimes these linkages are so great that all major industries are both owned and controlled by the state. In this situation we can speak of a nationalized or socialized economy. In other systems only some industries—perhaps railroads and utilities—are nationalized. Or, as is the case in the United States, few industries are nationalized and yet few go unregulated. In such capitalistic systems a myriad of administrative agencies regulate and control the economy. For example, in the United States general executive branches, such as the Departments of Commerce, Agriculture, Treasury, Interior, and Transportation, as well as specific agencies such as the Interstate Commerce Commission, Federal Reserve Board, Federal Aviation Administration, Internal Revenue Service, and the like control and regulate the economy. In this way the economy can be more precisely mobilized toward the achievement of system goals.

The necessary and extensive administrative linkages between the polity and economy in both capitalist and socialist systems greatly expand the size and scope of the state bureaucracy. Once system goals become dependent upon economic productivity, bureaucratization of the polity accelerates. This process is initiated in agrarian societies and accelerates exponentially with industrialization. The necessity for these administrative linkages between polity and economy also promotes centralization of the polity. As national or society-wide goals are pursued the regulation of the economy increasingly is directed from a few elite statuses. In extreme form this results in nationalization of industry by the polity, while in more mitigated form it results in regulation by administrative agencies directly under the authority of the chief executive, such as the President's Cabinet in the United States. However, even in mitigated form as in the United States, a kind of de facto nationalization in the midst of a quasi-capitalist economy can occur. Probably the best example of this can be seen in the aerospace and defense industries in the United States. These industries are highly dependent upon the federal government for their survival. In fact, by virtue of the polity's allocating vast resources to these industries for the attainment of certain system goals they initially emerged as large-scale industries. Even though these industries are private corporations owned by stockholders the government controls them to such an extent that real ownership is somewhat ambiguous, since without resources from the polity they would cease to exist. And often to keep these corporations in operation the polity must award noncompetitive contracts or simply bestow cash subsidies on them. Thus in any capitalist system the polity always becomes one of the chief buyers in the marketplace for many commodities generated by private corporations. As a big buyer the polity can exert considerable control over these supplying industries by simply threatening to take its business elsewhere.

In sum we can conclude that this web of mutual dependence between the economy and polity has the consequence of expanding and centralizing the state bureaucracy in order to mobilize the economy for system-goal achievement. By virtue of these administrative ties the polity also controls the allocation of system resources. And when equality becomes a major system goal the polity can use these same administrative controls to force more equitable distribution of system resources. In the United States such force has been exerted to a limited extent by the appropriation of surplus through a progressive income tax structure and then redistribution through welfare, educational, and job opportunity programs. In other systems, such as

Sweden, the polity has utilized its taxing powers to force even more equitable distribution of valued resources.

At this point we might ask why equality should become a dominant system goal. Part of the answer to this question lies in other structural conditions generated by a modern economy. A modern economy is a machine-based economy. Large concentrations of machine capital tend to be concentrated into strategic resource and market areas, with the result that labor also tends to become concentrated or urbanized in modern systems. Urbanization is accelerated by similar concentrations of the giant bureaucracies typical of industrial and postindustrial economies. Besides concentrating societal incumbents into urban and suburban centers, modern economies in requiring a host of new attributes of labor also force the polity to initiate mass education. Furthermore, work in modern economies tends to become scheduled with the trend toward ever-decreasing workdays for most workers in the economy. The result of all these forces is increased leisure time of educated and literate workers living in close proximity to one another. In turn such a situation provides an opportunity for political and quasi-political activity, since people have the time and opportunity to communicate common interests, grievances, and purposes. Except in the most oppressive systems this occurrence leads to the increased capacity of organized groups to formulate and address their wishes to political decision makers (Almond and Verba, 1963). In one-party systems this capacity becomes translated into grievance channels within the dominant party, whereas in two- and multiple-party systems it becomes manifested in diverse party platforms and interest-group lobbying. This increased access to decision-making elites stemming from conditions typical of modern economies has at least two consequences: it marks increased democratization of the polity; and it usually results in more equitable distribution by the polity of valued resources to previously disenfranchised elements in the population.

KINSHIP AND POLITY

One of the invariable consequences of kinship for the polity is *political socialization* (Dawson and Prewitt, 1969). Through such socialization, basic attachments, loyalties, and commitments to the political subsystem and its leaders are ultimately generated. Additionally it is through political socialization that the basics of the political culture of a society, such as political beliefs, symbols, values, myths, heroes, ideologies, and knowledge, are transmitted. Kinship can thus be critical in molding either personal commitment to or alienation from the polity, and in transmitting, creating, changing, or subverting the

the
institutional
environment
of
POLITY

cultural props holding up political institutions (Almond, 1956; Verba, 1965:516–518). These facts reveal that the level of legitimacy possessed by the polity as well as the degree of political stability and unity in a society are greatly dependent upon the nature of political socialization within kinship.

kinship and polity in traditional societies

There is considerable structural overlap between kinship and polity in highly traditional societies. In societies with an egalitarian form of polity, decision making occurs primarily within discrete kin groupings such as clans, lineages, and moieties. Sometimes permanent, society-wide decision-making statuses exist, but frequently leaders emerge only in times of crisis. Political socialization is thus difficult to separate from normal everyday family socialization. By virtue of acquiring family attachments and absorbing kinship norms, each new member of a society unconsciously acquires commitment to leaders (elder kinsmen) while internalizing into his personality those cultural components supporting the existing pattern of decision making.

In kin-based political systems where a particular kin group dominates other kin groupings, less structural overlap between the polity and kinship system is evident. While much decision making occurs within or is delegated to each particular kin group, many other society-wide decisions are made by elites in a dominant kin group. This means that the interests of most kin groups in a society sometimes must be subordinated to those of the dominant group. Under these conditions political socialization becomes crucial in instilling in the population sufficient loyalty and commitment to the dominant kin group so that such subordination can occur. Also with the emergence of a clear-cut and relatively stable decision-making elite, certain cultural components such as custom and tradition, lore, and religious dogma usually justify and legitimate the decision-making powers of elites. Internalization of this incipient political culture by members of a society makes even less problematic subordination of personal and kin-group interests to those of the dominant kin group. Thus only when a separate and distinguishable polity begins to arise and differentiate out from the broader kinship system of a society does observable political socialization emerge and legitimate the power differentials now evident in the society (Parsons, 1966).

With state-based polities there is fairly clear structural separation of the kinship and political subsystems. Particularly evident is a marked increase in the decision-making prerogatives of elites and their power to force compliance with decisions. In turn this power means that the consequences of political socialization for political stability or instability become great. Frequently family socialization results in only weak commitment to the existing state, with the result that the polity must rely heavily on force and coercion. At other times family socialization can lead to political apathy and ignorance of the ideologies, myths, and customs comprising the political culture of the state. When the state has engaged in conquest of diverse peoples and regions, family socialization can result in alienation from the existing polity and internalization of a deviant preconquest political culture. These facts point to a built-in source of political instability in societies. Once the state is clearly differentiated from the kinship system, family socialization rarely results in total commitment to the autonomous polity or internalization of its political culture. Since each family and kin group varies, political socialization and its consequences for supporting or subverting the existing polity and its culture also vary. This is especially true of both colonial and emerging states in the Third World where the polity is (was) either imposed upon the society from the outside or where the polity must incorporate diverse kin groups, tribes, and villages. Family socialization under these conditions results in a wide range of political loyalties from commitment, to apathy, to alienation. In either of these situations the capacity of the state to overcome the transmission by the family of a competing political culture remains limited. As we outlined in Chapter 5 and will explore further later, political systems facing these problems establish mass public education to counteract or at least neutralize through formal indoctrination any negative impact of family socialization.

In modernizing polities these problems are particularly intense. Kin groups and tribes from diverse cultural backgrounds are often consolidated into a territory with a state-based polity pursuing the goal of economic development. In Africa this situation is typical in the case of Uganda and Nigeria. In Uganda various tribes, linguistic groups, and kingdoms are consolidated into one nation (in the geographical sense). Culturally these groups comprising Uganda are diverse, while exhibiting a long history of intertribal warfare. In such a situation the short-run possibility of family socialization resulting in political commitment and cultural unification is remote (Dawson and Prewitt, 1969:34). Nigeria is perhaps a more vivid case, where the incapacity of the state to integrate the Ibo, Hausa, and Yoruba tribal nations has resulted in tremendous violence culminating in the recent revolution in Biafra. Thus the incapacity of the polity to generate commitment to a single central state polity and to develop a unified and nationwide political culture presents severe problems for many emergent nations of Africa. The seemingly arbitrary consolidation of former kin-based polities (tribal kingdoms) under a single state-based polity has created a situation where political socialization in the family can subvert the goals and programs of the state polity. And because family socialization is crucial for both commitment and cultural transmission and because it is not easily manipulated, influenced, and controlled by a central state, political socialization could continue to subvert political processes in these modernizing polities. Since the family, as we noted in earlier chapters on kinship, is a conservative institution changing only very slowly, this condition will persist for some time until family processes are altered.

In these newly independent societies of the Third World kin groupings—especially tribes—can undermine political development in other ways.[1] For example, even with extensive migration into urban areas in some African nations, tribal loyalty and cultural identity are often maintained (by virtue of family socialization). These tribal attachments can mitigate the severity of the transition from rural to urban centers by providing a continuity of kinship involvement. Fellow tribesmen can be looked to for assistance while providing a sense of psychological support (Kornhauser, 1963). But frequently, as in Nigeria, political parties reflect old tribal groupings with the result that the old animosities and hatreds among warring tribes become translated into very intense political competition and rivalry. Political stability in such an intense situation is unlikely, since a political party that wins an election also conquers an old tribal enemy. When political competition becomes viewed this way, establishing peaceful party competition as well as regularized and orderly acquisition of power becomes difficult. Furthermore, creating national instead of tribal consciousness and unity remains problematic.

In other Third World nations in Latin America and Asia, problems resulting from family socialization are not so intense as in many African societies. A state-based polity, while often very unstable, has existed for a longer period of time and national boundaries never encompassed so many diverse, well-established, and organized tribes and nations as in Africa. Moreover, colonialization in Latin America was more extensive and enduring, with the result that cultural unity in at least language and religion emerged early and provided a sense of national unity cutting across kin groupings. Yet the political legitimacy of particular political regimes in most of these systems is tenuous (except for a few monarchies), reflecting the fact that family socialization has not generated strong political commitment or transmitted a consistent political culture (Almond and Verba, 1963). Until this occurs, political instability will persist (LeVine, 1963; Geertz, 1963).

[1] This statement is not to deny that these tribes in not supporting the existing state are also preventing, in many cases, their exploitation and perhaps their extermination. Since most state-based polities in Third World nations are totalitarian (and this appears structurally almost inevitable), we do not wish to soft-pedal the often vicious and ruthless practices of elites in modernizing polities.

In sum, then, we can view kinship as having a profound impact on political structures, processes, and development. In primitive political systems (egalitarian and kin-based) the kinship system provides many of the structural parameters within which societal decision making occurs. As a distinct polity increasingly differentiates out from kinship in more advanced traditional systems, problems of political legitimation intensify. Increasingly, if political stability is to exist, family socialization must instill in the members of a society commitment to the polity, while at the same time transmitting a stable political culture of ideologies, symbols, values, beliefs, dogmas, myths, folk heroes, customs, and other cultural components associated with the polity. The fact that this does not occur in many Third World nations helps account for the political instability typical of these developing systems.

family and polity in modern societies

In modern societies considerable political stability is evident. This comparatively tranquil political scene derives from the fact that the polity is usually perceived by the population as both *effective* in achieving system goals and *legitimate* (Lipset, 1960, 1967). Effectiveness in achieving system goals and political legitimacy are obviously interrelated. A legitimate polity is likely to be perceived (or misperceived) by the population as effective; and as noted earlier, effectiveness is a crucial condition for legitimacy. Equally obvious is the influence of other institutions on whether or not a polity is perceived as effective and legitimate. With respect to the high degree of political legitimacy existent in modern systems, family socialization is critical. In turn socialization resulting in high degrees of legitimacy creates favorable perceptions of political effectiveness—thus furthering political stability. As in any system, family socialization as it affects the polity revolves around generating political commitment and indoctrination of the young into a political culture.

FAMILY AND POLITICAL COMMITMENT IN MODERN SYSTEMS

Political commitment concerns the attachments and loyalties of a society's members to the polity. The diffuse and specific commitments of family members—especially parents—greatly circumscribe what kinds of political commitments their offspring will have as adults (Hyman, 1959). Such is the case for at least these reasons: (a) The family is the first socialization structure encountered by the impressionable, plastic, and pliable newborn infant; (b) relations within the family are more emotionally intense—and hence powerful—than in other socializing structures in modern societies (e.g., peer groups and schools); (c) the duration of family relations over a long period

the
institutional
environment
of
POLITY

of a child's formative years makes them highly influential. As the family instills those enduring core traits comprising a personality system, it also imparts basic commitments to the political system. In modern systems these commitments revolve around political attitudes (Karlsson, 1958; Hyman, 1959:70–75), political interests (Dawson and Prewitt, 1969:114–115), and identification of and with the nation and political leaders (Greenstein, 1960; Hess and Easton, 1960). Frequently these kinds of commitments emerge prior to a child's entering school socialization structures (Hess and Easton, 1960). The impact of family socialization on a person's political commitments is perhaps best illustrated by studies demonstrating the similar party affiliations of parents and offspring in modern societies, such as the United States, with a two- or multiple-party system. When parents belong to the same party the offspring are likely to develop a similar party affiliation.[2] The chance of such similar party affiliation between parents and offspring increase with the stability over time of the parents' affiliation, with the activeness with which parents pursue their affiliation (voting, campaigning, debating), and with the intensity and duration of contacts between parents and children (McClosky and Dahlgren, 1959).

In sum, then, we can conclude that family socialization determines a broad spectrum of personality traits affecting people's political interests, affiliations, and identifications. All of these represent different aspects of what we have called political commitment, since each involves some degree of attachment of loyalty to both general and specific segments of the existing polity. While specific political regimes or leaders inevitably change, these broad and narrow commitments are critical in maintaining the more enduring core structure of the polity, the state. Without such commitment, both regimes and the overall form or structure of the polity change (whether by *coups* or society-wide revolutions).

FAMILY AND POLITICAL CULTURE IN MODERN SOCIETIES

Associated with modern polities is a stable and coherent political culture. For example, in the United States this culture includes among its components: folk heroes (Washington and Lincoln); myths (George Washington and the cherry tree); values (equality); ideology (freedom for all); symbols (the flag); and knowledge about political rights,

[2] With all the talk about the generation gap that emerged in the late 1960s and has spilled over into this decade, this may seem like an incredible statement. But recent data suggest that discontinuities within generations are probably as great, or greater, than those between generations. Furthermore, by all studies parents and their children are far more likely to be similar than dissimilar in terms of basic attitudes and political inclinations. For a nice summary of data see Lipset and Raab, 1970.

duties, and privileges (voting, freedom of speech, etc.). Political systems incapable of creating and transmitting such a coherent political culture often experience problems of legitimation. Furthermore, systems incapable of adding to, reinterpreting, and readjusting components of their political culture in accordance with social change will eventually create a crisis of legitimacy as the gap grows between cultural components and actual or perceived structural conditions. Thus political stability depends upon an enduring and yet flexible political culture transmitted from one generation to another. In modern systems much of this culture is transmitted with school structures (see below). However, family socialization is also involved in cultural transmission in at least two ways: the family imparts at least in crude form some of these cultural components to the young; and in generating commitment or lack of it parents determine how readily this culture can be transmitted to their children in other socialization structures such as schools. In modern systems family socialization usually facilitates and reinforces—though not always, as is the case today among many students in the United States—transmission of a system's political culture in school structures.

We can conclude that family socialization greatly affects political stability and development. To the extent that political socialization in the family does not generate political commitment or transmit a coherent political culture (or reinforce its transmission elsewhere in a society), achieving political legitimation will be problematic and hence so will political stability. Once the polity becomes clearly differentiated from the kinship system in a society the consequences of political socialization for either the stability and instability of the polity become evident. Except in a few stable monarchies (or highly developed kin-based polities) and in highly modern systems, family socialization appears to work against at least short-run political stability in the new independent Third World nations—especially those in Africa (Dawson and Prewitt, 1969:125).

EDUCATION AND POLITY

Educational development greatly accelerates with economic and political development (see Chapter 7). In turn changes in education feed back and affect both economic (see Chapter 3) and political processes in society. With respect to the polity this feedback can be indirect, as when educational structures supply necessary labor for the developing economy which in turn allows for the achievement of goals by the polity. Feedback can also be direct, as when school socialization results in the transmission of a coherent political culture, which bestows legitimacy on the polity. In this section we will explore such direct feedback of educational structures on different

the
institutional
environment
of
POLITY

types of polities—especially with respect to their development and stabilization.

education and polity in traditional societies

We know from discussion of the institutional environment of education in Chapter 6 that educational development initially occurred under certain religious conditions in traditional societies. With the further modernization of a system political processes circumscribe much of subsequent educational development. Conversely, educational processes profoundly affect political development. In traditional systems, especially in the Third World, educational structures become crucial in creating, promoting, and transmitting a coherent political culture to people from diverse social classes, regions, and kin groupings. Since family socialization in traditional societies can subvert the development of a society-wide political culture, emergent state-based and modernizing polities often massify the educational subsystem in order to counteract the effects of family socialization. Unlike the family, educational structures can be manipulated by the centralized polity. This fact means that the school frequently becomes the principal center of political indoctrination in a developing society. In traditional societies, where the polity utilizes the school for these purposes, we can document, following Dawson and Prewitt (1969:143–150), several ways in which the school subsystem has consequences for transmitting a political culture.

Classroom indoctrination. Built into the curriculum and textbooks of the school system in modernizing societies is an explicit goal of instilling one unified political culture. This involves the selective, partial, and biased presentation of history, myths, legends, and current events. Classroom indoctrination occurs in all schools but is most visible in societies where a state-based, modernizing polity is attempting to unify diverse populations and regions, while legitimating its right to possess society-wide decision-making prerogatives.

Classroom ritual. In all classrooms in all societies the ritual life supports a particular political culture. Saluting the flag, saying a pledge of allegiance, singing patriotic songs, honoring national heroes, celebrating important events, and exposing students to patriotic symbols, pictures, and sayings of leaders are typical examples of the political ritual life in school classrooms (Dawson and Prewitt, 1969:155). In systems attempting to create and transmit a unified political culture where none has existed before, the amount of time and resources devoted to classroom ritual will be great. Rituals can be effective in two ways: (a) Since they involve *actual behavior* with respect to selected cultural components, they can manifest and sometimes instill emotional commitment (Hess and Torney, 1967:100–112). Rituals can invoke emotion toward an existing polity even though the words and symbols involved in a ritual are not fully understood by the young student. (b) This is amplified by the fact that rituals —saluting the flag, pledging allegiance, and singing national songs—are usually done in a *group* context. This in turn makes them highly compelling in the minds of young students (Dawson and Prewitt, 1969:157). When effective, ritual can instill both commitment to and the tenets of a particular political culture. But frequently rituals become mere formalities external to individuals and unconnected to the polity. This is especially the case when family socialization does not reinforce the political culture enacted in a ritual.

Teacher charisma. Because the teacher is the first adult outside of kinship to whom the young are exposed for a long period of time, he takes on special significance in the mind of the student. Sometimes in rural schools of developing areas teachers become dominant community or village leaders and wield influence extending beyond the classroom. Because of the prestige of teachers in these areas they can exert tremendous influence on both students and their parents. Since these teachers are usually controlled by the polity they can have far-reaching consequences in imparting a particular political culture to both students and their parents. However, in the larger urban centers of developing systems where schools are more bureaucratized and where teachers are less prominent, teacher charisma declines.

Besides these specific influences of schools in traditional systems on transmitting a political culture, education can have more general and diffuse consequences for political processes. These latter consequences revolve around a growing political involvement and awareness on the part of the educated population in modernizing systems. For example, Almond and Verba (1963:175–185) in a comparative study of five nations note that the educated in traditional systems, compared to their noneducated counterparts, display more awareness of governmental processes, more concern with political campaigns, more insight into the impact of government on the individual, more opinions on political matters, more willingness to engage in political discussion, more desire to join organizations such as a political party, and more confidence in their capacity to influence the government. Thus in establishing mass public education for indoctrination purposes the polity also generates a politically knowledgeable and involved public. Such a situation can become translated into political activities through which the public begins to place demands upon the polity. In the long run this can lead to the formation of effective political parties or factions within a one-party system and mark the beginnings of political democratization (Lipset, 1960:27–82).

Finally we should note the feedback consequences of political control and manipulation of education on other trends in the polity —especially bureaucratization and centralization. As the modernizing polity initiates mass education the scope of the state bureaucracy is extended into an area—socialization—which remains outside the purview of kin-based and early state-based polities. This extension greatly increases the size of the administrative bureaucracy. It also increases the degree of centralization of the bureaucracy as political elites attempt to regulate the creation and transmission of a political culture.

education and polity in modern societies

In modern systems there is rarely a need to create a political culture. Political stability has existed for a sufficient period of time for a body of myths, traditions, heroes, lore, and ideologies to have emerged and become codified. This also reveals that there are comparatively few, if any, competing political cultures deviating very far from the dominant one. Under these conditions transmitting political commitment as well as salient cultural components presents less of a problem for modern than for modernizing polities. Commitment tends to emerge as a by-product of family socialization. Cultural transmission also begins with family socialization and is continued in schools. But once the family generates commitment and initiates transmission of a stable political culture, the polity need not regulate and control school political socialization to the extent typical of traditional modernizing systems. This is perhaps best illustrated in Russia where there appears to be a reemphasis on family socialization of a political culture and commitment and an increasing de-emphasis on intense political indoctrination in schools (Dawson and Prewitt, 1969:126). Since at least two generations of parents in the Soviet Union have passed through tightly controlled schools and apparently absorbed both commitment to and the culture of the Soviet state, family socialization is now more congruent with that desired by the state than during the early years after the revolution.

However, in the Soviet Union or any modern system, schools

are not structured so as to engage in neutral political socialization. Political socialization always occurs, especially at lower educational levels, but less deliberately and intensely. The cognitive as opposed to evaluative and emotional aspects of the political culture are given more emphasis in modern than in traditional schools. School textbooks and curricula are more likely to revolve around the objective (but never completely so) presentation of civics or knowledge of governmental structures and processes as well as knowledge about how good citizens participate in government (Coleman, 1965:220–226). But inevitably slipping in the backdoor in any curriculum are certain political ideologies, myths, values, beliefs, and the other components of the political culture. The ritual life of the classroom in schools of modern societies is likely to be minimal, routine, and considered boring by both teachers and students. Teachers as professionals (see Chapter 6) are more likely to attempt to remain objective, avoiding partisan issues such as conservatism or liberalism, party allegiances, and so on. However, many of the assumptions of the political culture are imparted—sometimes unconsciously. For example, in the United States assumptions revolving around the sanctity of the two-party system, free enterprise, basic freedoms, and other aspects of American political culture are transmitted by teachers—even those attempting to remain objective.

Thus even though political socialization in schools is comparatively low key, it is extremely effective. Much of the reason for this lies in the fact that school socialization on the whole reinforces rather than counteracts family socialization.

However, political socialization in schools (and/or the family) sometimes does not appear so effective in modern societies. This is demonstrated by increasing student activism in modern democratic societies, which often goes beyond and outside traditional or legitimate political channels for exerting political influence. Frequently the traditional channels of political involvement—political parties—have been eschewed by students in favor of mass and sometimes violent demonstrations as well as individual acts of sabotage. Ironically much of this activism may be a reflection of *over*-socialization of commitment to realize the ideals of a democratic political culture. The political culture of most Western democracies emphasizes equality, freedom, opportunity, and the capacity of each citizen to influence governmental policies. Under the impact of the mass media, increased levels of education and sophistication of students, and increased leisure of students in higher educational structures, they become aware of how the existing political structure rarely realizes the tenents and ideals of its political culture. Coupled with the intense commitment of students to these tenents, the perceived hypocrisy between what politically *is* and what *should be* in terms of the political culture becomes unbearable. While alienated students often lead demonstrations they are effective only when drawing masses of students committed to the political culture but frustrated by perceived governmental hypocrisy. Just what the consequences of mass student movements will be for modern polities is as yet unclear. But such a movement cannot really be considered the result of insufficient political socialization; rather, just the opposite appears to be the case.

Another related source of student unrest and disenchantment with the polity in modern societies such as the United States comes from educational (and family) socialization processes which over-idealize political processes. For example, a massive study of 12,000 American schoolchildren in the early 1960s by Hess and others (1960, 1967), revealed tremendously idealized student conceptions, even among adolescents, about how the American game of politics is played. Hess and Easton (1960) found that preadolescents perceived the President of the United States as a virtual god, with 72 percent indicating that he rarely makes mistakes and that he would care a lot about what they think. Furthermore, these preadolescents believed that all laws were fair, necessary, and that criminal prosecution was always the result of law breaking. Even among eighth graders Hess and Easton found that these adolescents perceived individual citizens as more influential in making policies than big companies, rich people, and churches. These same eighth graders also tended to underestimate greatly the amount of competition, conflict, and rivalry among parties and candidates in the political system. Emerging from these studies, then, is a picture of political unreality among young students. Adolescent students misperceived the amount of conflict as well as group and vested-interest influence inherent in the American political system. Some degree of idealization of political processes is probably necessary for people to develop diffuse commitment to the polity. But it may be that students during their early socialization are overprotected from political realities. Later, when confronted with these realities students who had bought the textbook portrayal of the American political system can become disillusioned and alienated. Since exposure to political realities through contact with the mass media and student subculture is inevitable in a comparatively democratic country such as the United States, overprotection and then rapid exposure can intensify feelings of disenchantment and outrage. To the extent that this process is built into the socialization of the young, we can expect considerable outrage among students to persist.[3]

[3] This statement is not intended to deny the fact that there may be a sound, realistic basis for such outrage. Nor do we intend to be cynical and maintain that striving for political ideals is the simple foolishness of the young. Rather we are attempting to

Whether leading to a mass student movement or to active participation of people in existing political processes, educational socialization in modern societies creates mass involvement of the population in political decision making. As Key (1961) and Lipset (1960) emphasize, education in modern systems generates a strong sense of duty to participate in political processes. And because education is massified in modern systems this sense of duty is widespread. Under these conditions, political democratization is an inevitable structural adjustment.

RELIGION AND POLITY

In traditional societies religion pervades virtually every segment of society, with the result that there is tremendous structural overlap of religion and polity. However, as the polity becomes increasingly differentiated from kinship, a more clear-cut segregation between religion and the emerging state-based polity also develops. Such segregation of church from the state marks one of the most conspicuous trends of societal development.

religion and polity in traditional societies

In very primitive societies with an egalitarian pattern of decision making, religious ritual and beliefs are interwoven with most major decisions in the society—when and where to hunt, when to move on, or when and where to plant. The communal hunting and agricultural rituals associated with major decisions of these simple societies reaffirm religious beliefs. In doing so, rituals are an effective way for mobilizing people into necessary behaviors, while alleviating much of the uncertainty and anxiety arising from these behaviors (Wallace, 1966:110–127). Sometimes these rituals are performed by special practitioners such as shamen, while other times kin leaders double as religious practitioners. Thus one of the major consequences of religion on political decision making in very simple societies is to mobilize the members of the society and to give legitimacy or sanctity to decision makers. Since decision makers in egalitarian systems rarely have the capacity to use physical force or coercion, invoking the gods and performing rituals reaffirming a belief system becomes an effective and often necessary means to decision making.

With the emergence of a kin-based polity the legitimating consequences of religion for decision making are even more extensive.

account for (obviously only partially) the apparent intensity of student alienation from the political system. What is important in this discussion is that built into the current structure of educational, familial, media, and peer-group socialization processes in American society are certain inherent sources of discontent.

Societies with kin-based polities display a clearly visible locus of power and decision making, for one kin grouping has decision-making power over other kin groupings in the society. To reconcile this difference in power requires legitimation if the polity is to persist. Religion often provides the necessary legitimation of these power differentials in societies with a kin-based polity (Parsons, 1966). This legitimating consequence of religion can take various forms, but usually involves: elite decision makers are considered gods or at least as having special powers of communication with the gods; decision makers are usually charged with preserving the religious dogma and traditions of a society and hence become the religious practitioners in a society. Because religion is a powerful and compelling force in traditional societies, the domination of religious roles by political elites enables them, if they wish, to legitimate tremendous inequality by making it seem the way of the gods. To rule by divine right thus represents a major basis of power in traditional societies.

In more advanced kin-based polities where an extensive administrative bureaucracy exists, *literate* religious practitioners often perform many of the administrative tasks requiring expertise in the political bureaucracy. In systems where both extensive political and religious bureaucracies exist, as was the case in feudal Europe and China, considerable overlap between the emerging secular state and ecclesiastical bureaucracy exists. But as both the state bureaucracy and church bureaucracy develop, a clear segregation between the institutions of polity and religion becomes evident (Wallace, 1966:261). Usually, but not always, religion still legitimates the right of elites in dominant kin groups to hold and wield power. But eventually a basic conflict between the more sacred concerns of religion and the secular focus of the emerging state becomes marked.[4] To the extent that the state and religious bureaucracies are separated and to the extent that the state comes to have a monopoly on society-wide power and decision making, the religious bureaucracy and its leaders become subordinate to the state and its elites. This separation of religion and polity becomes even more distinct as administrative and military officials in the state from nonelite families assume elite decision-making positions. Under these conditions the common kinship background of religious and political elites is completely severed.

With the development of a state-based polity a legitimacy vacuum is often created. Religious elites attempting to regain lost power

[4] This is not to deny the fact that churches have many secular concerns. For example, in feudal Europe the church held vast tracts of land and was vitally concerned with keeping and expanding its secular power. But ultimately the church must appeal to the sacred, cosmos, and ultimate which puts it at a disadvantage when confronting a secularized state bureaucracy.

and influence often withdraw religious support from the state. Or as is more often the case, the extensiveness of the state's secular tasks makes religious or sacred legitimation inadequate and/or inappropriate. Increasingly the extensive secular consequences of the polity become so alien and divorced from the sacred concerns of religion that new sources of political legitimation become necessary if political stability is to exist. Such new sources of legitimacy do not always immediately replace the fading capacity or willingness of religious practitioners to justify the extensive secular activities of the state. The existence of such a legitimacy vacuum helps account for the instability of state-based polities—especially those attempting rapid modernization. Modernization involves persistent state manipulation (mobilizing, allocating, distributing, controlling, etc.) of a society's people and resources. Legitimation of such manipulation is often difficult to establish.

Much of this necessary legitimation can come only with the creation, codification, and transmission of a civic culture (Almond and Verba, 1963). Such a political culture of predominately secular beliefs, values, ideologies, traditions, rights, duties, myths, and heroes, can give the polity the right to engage in extensive secular tasks. One author has referred to this civic culture as it emerged in the United States as a "civil religion" (Bellah, 1967). This term has double meaning in that it refers to both the development of a secular political culture and to its assumption of legitimating functions formerly performed by religion in more traditional societies. This civil religion revolves more around law, order, rights, and duties than around God, the ultimate, and the cosmos. To the extent that God is a component of this civil religion, individuals and government are required to carry out God's work in this world (Bellah, 1967:4–8). A more dramatic example of the emergence of a civil religion is found in postrevolutionary Russia where the new regime created, codified, and transmitted an entirely new political culture with all the trappings—ritual, beliefs, symbols, myths, saviors, and so forth —of more traditional religions (Wallace, 1966:262): the Communist Party became the ecclesia, Marx and Lenin emerged as the sacred figures, the tombs of leaders have become sacred places, the hammer and sickle became the sacred symbols, the works of Marx, Engels, and Lenin are now the sacred texts, and so on. In Russia the rapid emergence of a civil religion, or more precisely a civic culture, was dramatic and highly effective in legitimating in just two generations a new state-based and modernizing polity. In other modernizing societies nationalism represents an attempt by the polity to create a civic culture rapidly. And as we have seen, rarely does such a political culture fill successfully in the short run the legitimacy vacuum created by the emergence and expansion of the state and the decline of religion. It seems unlikely that most modernizing polities can shift from a religious to a secular basis of legitimation without an interim period of tenuous legitimacy and stability (Demerath and Hammond, 1969). Securing new sources of secular political legitimation while establishing some degree of institutional integration between the polity and religion often presents a major source of tension, strain, and conflict in modernizing social systems.

religion and polity in modern socieites

We can properly ask on the basis of trends evident in traditional societies whether or not religion in modern societies exerts any influence on political structures and processes. In general the polity in modern systems exercises tremendous control and influence over organized religion (see Chapter 13). But is the reverse true? Does the religion greatly affect political processes? For the most part religion in Western societies does bestow very diffuse and weak legitimacy on the polity. Religious beliefs, rituals, and symbols are frequently incorporated into the predominantly secular political culture of modern societies. However, in other modern societies, especially those with a Communist political culture, little if any religion is so incorporated. Yet where religious symbols are a part of the political culture political legitimacy does not rest to any great extent upon their incorporation.

Even in modern systems that supposedly have religious political parties, the religiosity of such parties is minimal. For example, it would be difficult to determine just what goals and programs of the Christian Democratic party in West Germany are specifically Christian or for that matter religious, since economic or bread-and-butter issues tend to dominate the party platform (Wilson, 1969:80). In Italy and France, where Catholicism and the Catholic Church were traditionally allied to the ruling elite, such established state religions led to the emergence of anticlerical political parties (Glock and Stark, 1965:203). But recent trends indicate an increasing irrelevance of religion for both clerical and these anticlerical political parties. The segregation of religion from the polity has increased to the extent that religious issues are relatively marginal and do not generate very much, if any, political debate or controversy (Wilson, 1969: 80–81). In fact religious issues (except perhaps in a few places such as Ireland) are sufficiently noncontroversial that, for example, the traditionally antireligious Socialist party in the Netherlands has frequently since the mid-1960s favored legislation promoted by churches in order to secure a few extra votes. Another example of this comes in the Labor party in England, which has in recent years supported legislation allowing for financial support of church schools, including Catholic schools (as recently as 1906, radical party members went to jail rather than pay taxes that might support Catholic schools).

To the degree that religion exerts other than a diffuse legitimating impact on modern polities, it is an indirect influence. Alford (1963) in summarizing data for several modern systems notes that political parties are usually disproportionately composed of members of a particular religious denomination. For example, in the United States white Protestants are more likely to be members of the Republican party and Catholics and Jews members of the Democratic party than would be predicted from their respective ratios in the population. But such a correlation is greatly confounded—and any religious influence mitigated—by the disproportionate social class and ethnic composition of the Democratic and Republican parties in the United States. Yet in all likelihood religion exerts a small but indeterminate and variable influence on political processes in the United States through such disproportionate party composition. A similar situation probably exists in other modern systems where political party membership and religious affiliation display some degree of positive correlation (Yinger, 1970:449–456).

Despite these indirect influences on the polity one conclusion is inescapable: Religion in modern societies does not have the massive consequences for the polity evident in more traditional systems. Religion has become increasingly segregated from political processes in modern societies.

LAW AND POLITY

The relationship between law and polity is exceedingly complex. One reason for this is that even in modern societies, there is tremendous structural overlap between the two institutions. Law-enacting bodies or legislatures are usually at the core of the political and the legal subsystems. Law-enforcing agencies or police and military are the ultimate sanction for both the polity and law. Administrative tribunals and to some extent judicial courts also overlap into the political structure of a society. These facts pose the question as to whether or not law and polity are really analytically and empirically distinct or separate institutions. For our purposes here law and polity are indeed separate institutions—both analytically and empirically. However, many authors would disagree with this separation, calling it arbitrary and an injustice to what exists in the real world. Yet we can justify our emphasis in at least these ways: (1) Rarely are courts in modern systems completely or even to a great degree manipulated by political elites. This is especially true of the judiciary, where judges are oriented to a legal profession, body of laws, and legal tradition — all of which display considerable autonomy from the polity. This is particularly evident as in the United States where a supreme tribunal or court can pass on the legality of actions on the part of both private citizens and *government*.[5] (2) Even though legislatures of the polity (and legal systems) enact laws, once enacted they become autonomous from the polity. In fact they can feed back and circumscribe the political action of legislatures. (3) Most modern legal systems have a body of both common and civil laws comprising a powerful legal tradition which exerts considerable influence on all levels of the state, while circumscribing future law enactment by political legislatures. (4) Most such bodies of law — and the legal tradition surrounding them — have at their pinnacle a written constitution as in the United States or as in England an unwritten but powerful and binding set of traditional postulates. These constitutions or traditional legal postulates set definite limits on the decision-making powers of the polity (for example, in the United States, the Constitution separates and hence circumscribes the power of both executives and legislators, while constraining the kinds of political decisions that can be made by elites). (5) The extensive professionalization and bureaucratization of prominent legal elements, such as courts, police, administrative agencies, and lawyers, give the legal system considerable autonomy from political manipulation — even where direct administrative ties to the polity exist on paper and even with centralization of the legal system. (6) And finally the structural overlap of law and polity in modern systems does not blur their separate structure, nor does it negate the different consequences of each for system survival. Were structural overlap of two institutions grounds for considering them as one, then in socialist systems there would be no economy since the polity regulates so much economic activity in these societies. Rather, structural overlap points to a main focus of this book — institutional interdependence. Sometimes interdependence and mutual influence are great, as illustrated in the relationship between the economy and polity in socialist systems or law and polity in virtually any modern system.

We have dwelt on this point for a good reason: Law has very profound consequences for the polity which might be obscured or underemphasized if we were to consider law as merely one component of the polity. Below we will see some of the reasons as to why this is so.

---

[5] This statement should not be interpreted to imply that political manipulation of the courts does not occur or is not continually attempted. The famous court-packing attempts of President Roosevelt during the Depression or President Nixon's politicization of the Supreme Court in 1970 attest to this fact.

law and polity in traditional societies

As polities modernize, the decision-making powers of elites are extended into virtually all spheres of societal functioning. From an initial form of temporary crisis leadership typical of egalitarian systems, polities come to possess far-reaching decision-making prerogatives and the power to enforce decisions. This increased power, control, and regulation of system processes inevitably creates strains, tensions, and potential disintegration. To mitigate these strains usually requires some independent sources of legitimacy that are separate and distinct from the governmental agencies responsible for the on-going political intrusion. In egalitarian kin-based and incipient state-based polities, the institution of religion has these legitimating consequences. But with expanded political activity into most areas of social life, new sources of legitimacy begin to emerge. Law represents one such source.

As we emphasized in earlier sections political stability in modernizing societies rests on the creation and transmission of a stable and secular political culture (civic culture or civil religion). Because law codifies, systematizes, and stabilizes cultural components (see Chapter 8) it can have major consequences for both the creation and stability of a civic culture. Law enactment can both create new cultural components or codify an emerging secular political culture. When such creation and codification specifies rights, duties, obligations, and privileges of both the public and state, it can potentially—though not necessarily—generate political legitimation. Such potential can become realized under two conditions: (1) Codification embodies important cultural traditions, while creation does not deviate too far from the demands of the population. (2) Effective political socialization of the codified culture can occur for at least part of one generation. Under these conditions political legitimation is greatly facilitated through legal development and the consequent unification of cultural components and their translation into rights and duties. As these rights and duties become traditionalized and hence binding on both the polity and public, political legitimation by law becomes even more probable. However, rarely do modernizing systems succeed completely in creating, transmitting, and then stabilizing a legal tradition.

A second way in which law can legitimate the polity is through an effective and responsive court system. When courts can impartially (or at least approximately so) mediate through a body of law the grievances and conflicts of the public, they can serve as buffers between political elites and the public. To the extent that the courts and the laws they apply are perceived as fair and just by litigants, then courts can cool litigants off and deflect their aggravations away from the state. As long as the public feels that they can effectively address some grievances through the court system, the legal system can have legitimating consequences for the polity. However, in most modernizing societies, courts are not perceived by the public as either fair or as an effective channel for adjudicating injustices, usually for good reasons: unprofessional and incompetent judges and lawyers; partial and biased application of laws; discrimination against the impoverished and poor, and so on. Until favorable public perception is created through political socialization in schools and basic reorganization of the courts, political legitimation of the polity by law will remain tenuous.

In sum, then, political modernization is greatly dependent upon the capacity of the legal system to codify a civic culture and provide channels for redressing grievances. In the wake of a legitimacy vacuum stemming partly from the typical segregation of church and state, a lack of development in the legal system can result in a series of political crises as factions within the polity or segments of the general population forceably assume power. Such is frequently the case in Third World societies and marks their inability in the short run to generate an independent, institutional source, such as law, of political legitimation. Until this is possible, political modernization will be stymied.

law and polity in modern societies

In modern societies the legal subsystem is well developed and codifies a stable and coherent political culture. As in the United States, the basic tenets of this culture are embodied in the written Constitution. Or as in England, where no formal constitution exists, the political culture is codified into a series of common-law precedents and legal postulates of a well-established legal tradition. The result of either situation is that laws and courts regulate processes within the polity while specifying the rights and duties of citizens and decision makers. A well-developed legal system thus circumscribes the polity by making it a government of laws rather than men. Decision makers are bound by specific and general laws that circumscribe the processes by which political decisions are made and power wielded. Many of these laws remain unwritten but nonetheless binding and compelling. Such laws usually prevent political leaders from the arbitrary wielding of power, because to violate flagrantly basic laws could result in a withdrawal of political legitimacy.[6] These laws embody a political culture which has been transmitted through political

[6] However, frequently leaders violate the law, especially when public opinion is with them. Perhaps the best recent example in the United States is the question of the constitutionality of the Vietnam war. The war's constitutionality was left vague and in question so long as public opinion supported it. But as the war became unpopular, con-

336

socialization in schools and the family. Even when a political culture is created by the polity it cannot be violated or suspended without some risk once a new generation has absorbed and internalized its ideals, especially when these ideals are codified in law. To do so would be to undermine the polity's basis of legitimacy.

A modern court system also promotes political legitimacy by allowing citizen grievances—even against the state—to be leveled with at least some possibility of unbiased adjudication. To the extent that courts appear autonomous from the state, they can serve as an effective mechanism for deflecting grievances away from the state and thus insulating decision makers from the public.

SUMMARY

In this chapter we have examined some of the institutional influences of economy, family, education, religion, and law on the polity. As we have seen in previous chapters, emphasis was placed upon the one-way influence of each institution on our focal institution—in this case, the polity. The influence of the polity on economy, kinship, education, and law has been analyzed in earlier chapters. The impact of the polity on the last institution to be analyzed in this book —religion—will be examined in Chapter 13.

We began our analysis in this chapter by focusing on how the economy influences political structures, processes, functions, and development. We noted that as the economy becomes capable of generating a surplus, the capacity of a society to support an autonomous political subsystem increases. With a surplus, problems of what to do with it emerge in a society. Although the exact processes are unclear, initial political development probably occurred as leaders sought solutions to this problem. Increasingly, as economic surplus and the size of the political subsystem increase, the polity comes to have many consequences for mobilization, allocation, distribution of system resources, and social control.

We next turned to analyzing the influence of the family on the polity. In traditional societies the family serves as the structural locus of much political decision making, while socializing political commitment and culture. As the polity becomes structurally differentiated from the kinship, effective political socialization becomes a principal condition of political stability. Until such socialization can generate some degree of political commitment in the population the polity will maintain only tenuous legitimacy. In modern societies this condition of political stability is usually met as the family imparts diffuse

siderable attention was addressed to just this issue with the result that the legitimacy of political regimes "violating" the Constitution became questionable in the minds of large segments of the population.

commitment and perhaps the rudiments of a coherent political culture to the young.

Analysis then shifted to ascertaining the consequences of educational structures on the polity — especially with respect to political socialization. Here we noted the significance of school structures in transmitting a coherent political culture on political stability. We also examined how the growing number of linkages between educational structures and the polity can expand and centralize the state bureaucracy. And finally we noted the general impact of mass education on political democratization.

Next we focused on the relationship between religion and the polity, where emphasis was placed on the growing differentiation and segregation of religion from the polity — especially with respect to religion's legitimating consequences. In this vein we described the decreasing consequences of religion on the polity during political development. Finally we reviewed the impact of law on the polity. We emphasized that as the capacity of religion to legitimate a developing polity decreases, law increasingly assumes this function although not without generating considerable tension, strain, and political instability.

SUGGESTED READINGS

Gabriel Almond and Sidney Verba, *The Civic Culture*, Princeton, N.J.: Princeton University Press, 1963.

James S. Coleman (ed.), *Education and Political Development,* Princeton, N.J.: Princeton University Press, 1965.

Richard E. Dawson and Kenneth Prewitt, *Political Socialization*, Boston: Little, Brown and Company, 1969.

David Easton, *A Systems Analysis of Political Life*, New York: John Wiley & Sons, Inc., 1965.

Clifford Geertz (ed.), *Old Societies and New States: The Quest for Modernity in Asia and Africa*, New York: The Free Press, 1963.

Gerhard Lenski, *Power and Privilege*, New York: McGraw-Hill Book Company, 1966.

Robin M. Williams, Jr., "Political Institutions of the United States," in *American Society*, 3d ed., New York: Alfred A. Knopf, Inc., 1970.

338

the

institutional

environment

of

POLITY

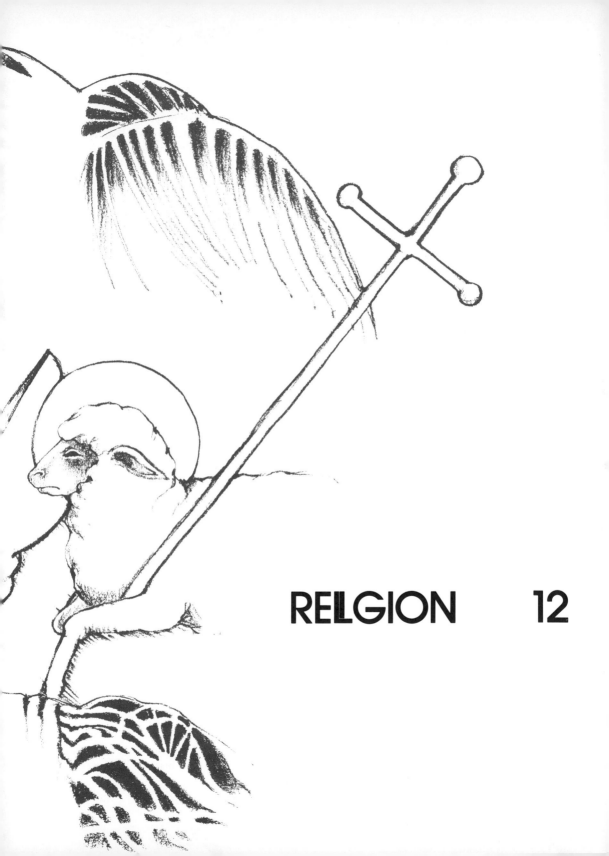

RELGION 12

The earliest human societies apparently evidenced some form of religion (Parsons, 1966). In fact the history of all societies that have ever existed reveals the pervasive influence of religion on man's activities. Even in the face of active political policies against religion in some modern societies, religion still appears to exert at least some influence on people's lives. Yet it has become apparent to most observers that even in societies displaying toleration and freedom, the impact of traditional religious forms on on-going social life has been decreasing with societal modernization. Whether this trend marks the death of religion or its transformation into a new form remains unclear.

Whether a dominant institution in traditional societies or a rapidly changing force in modern systems, religion must be viewed as one of the most enduring and conspicuous institutions in human societies. For this reason we explore in this chapter its changing structure and consequences in different types of societies.

BASIC ELEMENTS OF RELIGION

the sacred and supernatural

All religions involve a notion of the sacred. The sacred is a quality imputed by men to objects and events around them. The sacred represents highly intense, emotional, moral, and nonempirical ideas that men have about things and events which lie outside their ordinary understanding and control (Williams, 1970:356). Much of the power and influence exerted by religion in a society derives from its capacity to define for worshippers what is sacred. Because the sacred carries with it intense emotions, this capacity gives religion tremendous influence in mobilizing and controlling human action in a society.

Although there are some notable exceptions, religions usually contain assumptions about the supernatural.[1] The supernatural is a realm—usually vague and ill-defined—lying outside the everyday world. This other world is conceived as being occupied by forces, beings, spirits, and powers which in some way alter, circumscribe, and influence this world's happenings and occurrences. Sometimes the supernatural is a series of forces—all seeing and all knowing. The *mana* of many traditional societies is such a force that can change, alter, intervene in the world, and bestow power to objects, but which itself is not an object—only a vague and diffuse source of power underlying natural events. But frequently the supernatural is conceived

[1] In a few religions, especially in their early forms, the existence of a supernatural realm is not a necessary element. This appears to have been the case with classical Buddhism and Confucianism (Williams, 1970:355).

of as a set of personified beings—gods and deities. And sometimes the supernatural is seen as a spirit having the form of animals and other living creatures (Swanson, 1960:8). Whatever its form, the supernatural is viewed by the members of a society as underlying and influencing the natural.

The sacred and the supernatural cannot always be considered the same thing. Many events and objects are considered sacred because supernatural forces or beings are considered to have influenced them. Yet sacred qualities can be imputed to objects and events without necessarily invoking the influence of the supernatural. This situation obviously must exist for religions in which a clear conception of a supernatural realm does not exist.

ritual

Ritual is a kind of role behavior. It is behavior that addresses the supernatural. Such behavior is highly circumscribed by norms directing precisely when, where, and how this behavior is to occur. Rituals are thus *stereotyped* ways of behaving with respect to the supernatural (Goode, 1951:38–50). The content of ritual varies tremendously and can involve at least these forms of behavior (Wallace, 1966:52–70): prayer, music, dancing, singing, exhortation, reciting a code, taking drugs, eating, drinking, making sacrifices, and congregating. Rituals can be long or short and involve only some or all the behaviors listed above. They can involve merely going to church on Sunday or bowing to Mecca each morning, or they can include elaborate sequences of stereotyped behavior. Basically there are two types of rituals: *calendrical* and *noncalendrical*. Calendrical rituals are enacted on a regular schedule, such as at day or night, at the waxing and waning of the moon, at the beginning or ending of seasons, at eclipses and positions of planets and stars, or on the birthdays of supernatural beings. Noncalendrical rituals are performed sporadically, on special occasions, or in times of crises. Other noncalendrical rituals such as the puberty rites or *rites de passage* of many societies do follow somewhat of a cycle and do occur at certain more or less determined times in the life of each incumbent. But the time, place, and period of the ritual is not precisely set by the calendar. Whether calendrical or noncalendrical, ritual serves to link the natural and supernatural worlds. Much of what is observable about a religion is seen in ritual activities (Wallace, 1966:71; Goode, 1951:48–52).

343

beliefs

Beliefs give significance and justification to rituals. They define the meaning of rituals (Goode, 1951) while rationalizing their performance (Wallace, 1966). Religious beliefs are part of the culture of a society and usually contain two components: *a cosmology* and *values.*

COSMOLOGY

A cosmology is a system of beliefs concerning the nature of the universe, including the natural and supernatural. A cosmology usually includes a *pantheon* or group of supernatural beings and/or forces which in varying degrees affect and alter social processes in the natural world. In most religions the beings and forces in the pantheon are listed in terms of a hierarchy of their power and influence — from the most powerful god, to lesser gods, to mortals who are god-like. A cosmology also contains a body of myths about the historical happenings leading to the current hierarchical ordering of supernatural beings. These myths usually describe the origin, career, and interaction of gods with ordinary or only quasi-sacred mortals. In some societies these myths are codified into basic texts — the Old Testament, the New Testament, and the Koran being prominent examples. Furthermore, cosmologies usually include *substantive beliefs* about planes of existence lying outside the natural world — heaven, hell, nirvana, and other realms in the supernatural.

VALUES

Religious values guiding, justifying, and sanctioning ritual are usually very similar to those more secular values of a society's culture that regulate everyday activity. These values indicate what is right and wrong, proper and improper, and good or bad. Frequently religious values are codified into a religious code, such as the Ten Commandments in Christianity, the Ethics of Confucius in Confucianism, or the Noble Eight-Fold Path in Buddhism. Such values provide a highly general and overarching framework within which many secular values and specific norms in a society operate.

cult structures

A cult is the social structural unit where rituals made meaningful and justified by supernatural beliefs are enacted. The cult is therefore the most fundamental unit of the *institution* of religion in any society. As we will see, the structure of cults can vary from a world-wide church (such as the Catholic Church) with a vast bureaucracy to a small and exclusive group of tribesmen engaged in a common ritual addressed to the supernatural. Analysis of religious development and evolution as well as contemporary comparisons among religions must revolve around the structure of cults.[2] At the most

[2]Sociologists have made a wide variety of typologies pertaining to the organization of religious status norms. Probably the most influential typology was Weber's two polar types of religious organization: the church and sect. These were developed in more detail by Weber's student Ernst Troeltsch (1931), who viewed a *church* as a large, conservative, elite-based ascriptive and dominant religious organization. At the polar extreme to a church was a *sect*, which was viewed as a small, voluntary, quasi-rebellious

general analytical level we can outline these elements inherent in all cults: a set of common beliefs about the sacred and/or supernatural; a common set of rituals designed to appeal to the supernatural; and a membership or community of worshippers who share the cult's beliefs about the sacred and supernatural and who engage in its rituals. Thus it is at the cult level of social organization that beliefs and rituals about the sacred and supernatural become integrated.

Frequently in the sociological literature cults are considered as small, unstable, charismatically led religious groupings which deviate from the more established and larger church religions in a society. For example, religious groupings such as the Spiritualists, Bahai, Black Muslims, I Am, the Theosophical Society, the Father Divine Peace Mission Movement, and the early days of the Christian Science Movement are what sociologists usually label as cults. But in our terms, cult structure or cult refers to *any* religious grouping— no matter how large or small—that displays a concern for the supernatural and/or sacred, common beliefs, and common rituals. The term *cult structure* is thus a generic term referring to any form of religious organization (Wallace, 1966:84–101).

Religion in any society is a conglomeration of cults. Different cults in a society often hold similar beliefs and engage in similar rituals, but frequently they display divergent beliefs and rituals. In all except the most primitive societies, there is a variety of cult structures manifesting somewhat dissimilar beliefs and rituals. Structurally cults vary tremendously with respect to at least these things: size; degree of bureaucratization; existence of professional clergy; reliance on lay clergy; degree of centralization; stability of membership; and exclusiveness of membership. When we later examine religion in different types of societies, the structural diversity of cults will become more apparent.

In sum, then, the basic elements of any religion involve a concern for the sacred and/or supernatural. The supernatural is a realm lying beyond everyday, mundane activities and is composed of beings and/or forces that are viewed as influencing on-going social action

religious order. Numerous amplifications of this typology have been made in recent decades (Yinger, 1970; Pfautz, 1955; Becker, 1950). Generally, sociological typologies of religious organization include, from least to most organized: cult, sect, established sect, church, denomination, ecclesia (Salisbury, 1964:96–97; Moberg, 1962:73–99; Johnson, 1960:419–439). While useful in analyzing religion in modern societies, these distinctions do not allow us to grasp either the subtleties or complexity of traditional religious organization. For this reason we have abandoned a sociological classification in favor of a more anthropological one (Wallace, 1966). This classification will allow us to put in a comparative perspective modern religious organization. Thus, as noted above, cult structure is a generic term encompassing all *specific* forms of religious organization, whether a cult (in the sociological sense), sect, established sect, church, denomination, or ecclesia.

in a society. Religion usually involves certain stereotyped behaviors which link the natural and the supernatural worlds. Such rituals are made meaningful by beliefs. The most basic kind of structural unit within which groups of men and women act religiously is the cult. The structure of cults varies enormously.

RELIGION AND SOCIETY

Ascertaining just what the consequences of religion are for the broader society has been one of the most persistent topics in the history of sociology. Religion has been variously viewed as the "opiate of the masses" (Marx and Engels, 1848); a stimulus to economic development (Weber, 1904); the basis of group and societal solidarity (Durkheim, 1912); a means for explaining the unknown and mysterious (Tylor, 1871); and a mechanism for reducing anxiety and unpredictability (Malinowski, 1925). From the pioneering work of each of these classical sociologists and anthropologists, it has become clear that religion has multiple and varied consequences for a society. Furthermore, depending upon the society, religion can have few, manifold, or narrow consequences. At the most general level we can visualize four major consequences of religion for societies: reinforcing institutional norms; regulating socialization and social placement; legitimating inequality; and alleviating anxiety and tension.

reinforcing institutional norms

Religious rituals and values frequently reinforce concrete norms guiding role behavior within the economic, familial, and political institutional spheres (Swanson, 1960; O'Dea, 1966, 1970; Goode, 1951; Durkheim, 1912). Values give institutional norms special—perhaps sacred—significance and thus increase the probability of conformity. Religious rituals, particularly in traditional societies, frequently permeate and circumscribe crucial behaviors (Wallace, 1966:216–246). For example, among the Tikopia of the South Seas, religious beliefs and rituals guided and hence reinforced certain crucial economic activities (Goode, 1951). The Tikopia were a small, island society where fishing was one major economic activity (Firth, 1936). Religious rituals among the Tikopia permeated much of this fishing activity. For instance, religious rituals assured adequate preparation of fishing canoes for often dangerous expeditions into the sea. Overhauling and caring for canoes was viewed by the Tikopian native as an extension of his ritual obligation to the deities to secure food offerings. When work was performed as much for the gods as for human subsistence, the speed, energy, harmony, and coordination among workers increased greatly (Firth, 1936:90–95; Goode, 1951: 107–109). Similar consequences of religion were evident in reinforc-

346

ing and maintaining the Tikopian kinship system. For example, the patrilineal descent system of the Tikopians was reinforced by the fact that the dwelling of the oldest male ancestor was maintained as a temple for rituals to gods and ancestors (Goode, 1951:200). Patriarchal authority norms were reinforced by the exclusion of young women from certain religious rituals.

In other more modern societies, the reinforcing consequences of rituals for institutional processes decline. But religious beliefs—especially values—are frequently the cultural underpinnings of many specific institutional norms. This becomes abundantly clear when the religious code of the dominant religious cult in a modern society is compared to the basic legal postulates and statutes of that society's legal system. By virtue of the fact that law codifies many basic cultural—especially religious—values (see Chapter 8), it mediates between religion and other institutional spheres. Thus by an indirect route, religion even in modern societies has some consequences for reinforcing institutional norms.

regulating social reproduction and placement

In those societies where religion reinforces kinship norms, religion has profound consequences for regulating socialization and the eventual social placement of the young in the broader society. More specifically we can note that religious rituals in many societies guide first the birth of a child and then mark with sacred significance his or her passage through adolescence, adulthood, and marriage. The religious rituals surrounding these status transitions of societal incumbents are usually referred to as *rites de passage*. They regularize socialization and growth, while impressing upon their recipient the new normative rights and obligations attached to a new status. To exceed these rights or not live up to the obligations becomes difficult when sanctioned by the supernatural. In this way religion helps assure commitment on the part of maturing actors entering new adult status positions. In traditional systems the religious rituals are extremely elaborate and of great significance to the members of a society, whereas in modern systems their impact tends to decline.

legitimating inequality

Societies with any degree of differentiation display inequalities with respect to wealth, prestige, power, and privilege. In societies displaying stability such inequality tends to be minimally legitimated. In the last chapter we noted how religion in traditional societies has far-reaching consequences for legitimating political activity. However, this was only a partial picture of how religion legitimates inequality.

Frequently the broader stratification subsystem of a society is also maintained by religious beliefs. This reached its peak in traditional India where the Hindu cosmology revolving around Karma and reincarnation became a justification for a rigid caste system of stratification. Those born orthodox Hindus (i.e., Brahmans) were entitled to elite caste positions, since the gods in controlling their reincarnation had placed them in an elite family. As Hinduism spread across India, non-Hindus were absorbed into inferior caste positions. This was justified, since the non-Hindu tribes were ritually impure and ignorant of basic Brahman beliefs. Although rarely as extreme as in precolonial India, religion in most traditional systems legitimates not only the institution of the polity but the broader stratification system in a society.

In modern systems religious beliefs and rituals have fewer consequences for legitimating inequality. However, religious consequences in this area are not completely eliminated. For example, among Protestant countries, such as the United States, the traditional Calvinist ethic of hard work as the path to success and ultimately salvation persists in somewhat altered form and has consequences for legitimating social inequality. To put it crudely: "Those who do not work hard do not deserve to be in higher social classes." With this value premise the inability to reach a higher social class is seen as the result of an individual's failure to work hard enough. The religious antecedents for this kind of value frequently used to legitimate inequality in the United States and other Protestant societies are hard to deny.

Thus religion in all societies has consequences for social integration and control, whether through reinforcing institutional norms or legitimating inequality. This means that religion is more than something that is believed; it is lived. It constantly affects the degree of integration and coordination existent in a society (Goode, 1951: 222–223). But this fact should not obscure the potentially *dis*integrative consequences of religion for a society: New, emergent religious cults in a society can become a revolutionary collectivity. The sacralization of institutional norms can generate rigidity in behavior, which can become a liability when changes in the social and physical environment of a society require flexibility (O'Dea, 1966). Religion can legitimate in the short run a ruthless political regime or oppressive stratification system, which in the long run can create divisive and disintegrative strains in society.

alleviating anxiety and tension

In even the most modern society and certainly in all traditional societies tremendous uncertainty, fear of the unknown, powerlessness, unpredictability, and anxiety exist. Indeed these conditions

348

appear endemic to social life. Religious beliefs in providing a cosmology of the sacred and supernatural frequently have the consequence of alleviating or mitigating these multiple sources of tension. By providing an interpretation of the universe and by prescribing ritual behavior religion provides both answers and solutions to the collective tensions of the members of a society. In traditional societies where economic uncertainty is a constant condition of social life, these consequences of religion are extensive. In modern systems where many economic uncertainties have been eliminated, the alleviating consequences of religion are less far-reaching. But among many segments of the population in modern societies—the poor, disenfranchised, the aged, and alienated—religion still provides an interpretation and answer to their fears and uncertainty. For example, many of the fundamentalist movements and small, sectlike cults emerging in industrialized and urbanized societies appeal to those who for various reasons cannot adjust to a modern social structure (Loftland and Stark, 1965; Glock, 1964).

defining religion as an institution

As an *institution* we are concerned with how certain statuses, norms, and roles concerning the sacred and/or supernatural become organized. In this vein we can define religion as an institution in this manner:

> Religion is that interrelated, pervasive, general, and relatively stable clustering of statuses revolving around beliefs and rituals pertaining to the sacred and/or supernatural and organized into cult structures which have consequences for reinforcing norms, legitimating inequality, guiding socialization and social placement, and managing variable sources of tension and anxiety in a society.

It should be emphasized in this definition that both the structure and consequences of religion can vary. Some religions have manifold consequences for the society in which they are located, while others have very few. Some religions are vast, society-wide or even worldwide bureaucracies; others are a loose conglomeration of small cults. It is to such variability in the profile of religions that we now turn.

349

RELIGION IN DIFFERENT TYPES OF SOCIETIES

Because of their diversity, classifying religions into distinct types is both difficult and dangerous. If social life fell into neat and distinct categories our job as sociologists would be easy. Unfortunately the real world is far too complex for this to be true. And yet if we are going to begin the long and perhaps always incomplete task of understanding society, it is necessary to begin classifying social phenomena. And so it is with religions. In this section we undertake a hazardous task: pushing and shoving religions into just a few ideal types. Naturally the types of religions to be presented can be only a partial reflection of the real world; any taxonomy can only be approximate. Fortunately we are presented with a wealth of empirical data on religion as well as two highly sophisticated attempts to do just what we are proposing in this section (Bellah, 1964; Wallace, 1966). We will draw heavily from Bellah's and Wallace's classifications in an attempt to do justice to our topic. Also in the taxonomy to be presented there is an *intended* developmental or evolutionary emphasis. To the extent that religions change and undergo development, it is postulated that they develop in a *predictable direction* from one type to another.

To classify religions into types, we need to select some common dimensions that can serve as a basis or point of reference for both comparing religions and recording their development. We have selected two such dimensions: (1) the nature of religious beliefs about the supernatural evident in a society; and (2) the nature and organization of religious cults in a society.

(*1*) *Religious beliefs.*   This dimension or element of religion will force us to examine both the cosmology and values contained within the religious beliefs of a society. As we will discover, religions appear to display distinct — and classifiable — differences with respect to their cosmologies (including their pantheon and myths) and their values (including their moral code).

(*2*) *Cult structures and organization.*   The actual profile or structure of religion in a society is revealed by how rituals — justified and rationalized by beliefs — are organized into cults. And so if we are to examine variations in religion as an institution, we must also include as a basic dimension the nature of cult structures and how they become organized or clustered into the religious subsystem of a society.

religion in traditional societies

Traditional religions shade and blend into each other. Despite the overlap of traditional types of religion, we will attempt to distinguish four in terms of their belief systems and cult structures and organization. The four types to be discussed are labeled: primitive shamanic; traditional communal; traditional ecclesiastic; and premodern. Even though the lines separating one from the other are somewhat arbitrary, we will assume that these represent not only distinct religious types, but also visible stages in religious evolution and development.

Although some authors have identified an even more primitive type of religion (Bellah, 1964:361–364), the *primitive shamanic* is for our purposes the first distinct and unambiguous type of traditional religion.

Belief system.   In primitive shamanic religions, a well-articulated value system has not emerged. Rather, religious conduct tends to be circumscribed by certain rituals within which religious values remain somewhat vague and implicit. However, the cosmology of primitive religions displays some degree of definition and complexity (Bellah, 1964:364–366). Supernatural beings are objectified and viewed as clearly distinct from the natural world. Some of these beings willfully control and influence the worldly activities of men. Usually gods have specified and delimited spheres of influence. The relationships among gods are the source of considerable speculation and there emerges an incipient hierarchy or pantheon of relations among gods. Religious *myths* delineating the history of gods are as of yet not elaborately developed. This form of belief system can be illustrated by briefly noting the salient features of the Eskimo belief system. The Eskimo pantheon is composed of a varied mixture of lesser beings which are personified as the souls of preeminent humans and animals. Also, there are various minor and local spirits regulating the behavior of individuals. Usually particular kin groups have a set of ancestral souls and spirits with which they must reckon. Frequently some myths surround the emergence and persistence of these minor and local beings and spirits. Higher up in the pantheon are two primary gods—the Keeper of Sea Animals and the Spirit of the Air. But the mythology, division of powers, and the hierarchy of control among these higher, society-wide gods remain somewhat vague and blurred. Thus the Eskimo religious belief system marks a clear-cut distinction between at least some aspects of the natural and supernatural. Yet the internal differentiation of the cosmology into a complex and clear pantheon accompanied by supporting myths has only been initiated in such a primitive shamanic religion. And the distinction between secular and sacred values is not so clear as in more developed religious subsystems.

Cult structure and organization.   The fairly clear differentiation between the natural and supernatural in primitive shamanic religions results in a set of rituals through which gods and men interact. The locus of such rituals is the *cult structure*. Yet cult structures in primitive shamanic religions are loosely organized

351

(Bellah, 1964:363). Following Wallace (1966:83–90), we can distinguish two general types of cult structures within primitive shamanic religions: individualistic cults and shamanic cults (from which we derived the label for this type of religion). In *individualistic cults*, there is no categorical distinction between religious specialists and laymen. Members of the cult engage in appropriate rituals addressed to the supernatural without a religious specialist as an intermediary. *Shamanic cults* display a more differentiated structure with part-time religious practitioners serving as intermediaries between laymen and the supernatural. These intermediaries assume this status on the basis of family ascription, specialized training, and inspirational experience with the supernatural. General norms require that for a fee they act as magicians, witch doctors, medicine men, mediums, spiritualists, astrologers, and diviners. Depending upon the society, nature of religious beliefs, and needs of the client, shamans can usually perform at least several of these services. It is thus with shamanic cults that the first religious division of labor emerges in a society. The shaman is a religious specialist who is clearly differentiated from his lay clients. Both individualistic and shamanic cults in primitive societies are loosely organized. They are not clearly bounded, with membership varying considerably. In fact shamanic cults display a transient clientele. Also, there is little sense of religious community pervading either individualistic or shamanic cults. While certain beliefs and rituals are common to members, there is little mutual identification and solidarity among these members in primitive systems. Furthermore, there are few if any calendrical rituals required of cult members. Rituals are performed when needed. And quite often there is no stable locus of religious activity, such as a temple. When there is a temple it frequently doubles as the tribal or village meetinghouse.

Eskimo cult structure and organization reflect most of these conditions. Generally there are two individualistic cults and one shamanic cult organizing religious belief and ritual (Wallace, 1966:89). One of the individualistic cults is referred to as the Spirit Helper Cult. It is within this cult that individuals relate to the particular spirits, souls, and beings of their locale or of their kin grouping. Societal incumbents inherit patrilineally certain Spirit Helpers, who are seen as guiding and helping individuals in their daily activities. They are appealed to by wearing little statuettes of walrus tusks, bags of pebbles, and remains of shellfish. To secure help from the spirits individuals must also observe certain taboos, especially with respect to *not* killing the creatures being represented in this ancillary appeal. What is important about this cult is that there are no regularly scheduled rituals and each individual addresses and seeks the help of his ancestral and/or local spirits by himself. The second individualistic cult—the Game Animal Cult—has a more clearly established set of ritual norms. And these norms tend to cut across both local kin groups and communities. Certain society-wide taboos exist, ostensibly to inhibit behavior that would offend major game animals. For example, the flesh of land and sea animals is never to be cooked together, since to do so would bring illness and starvation (Wallace, 1966:90). These and other norms are believed to prevent giving offense to the souls and spirits—the Keepers—who control and regulate the supply of game upon which the Eskimos depend for survival. Because of this, violations of ritual norms must be openly confessed; and if violations persist on the part of one individual, he is banished from the community. In this way the community averts disaster. Thus the Game Animal Cult of the Eskimos displays a more clear-cut structure than the Spirit Helper Cult. It is society wide, has clear-cut ritual norms, and violation of ritual norms brings sanction from the community. But actual ritual behavior is still enacted by individuals without the assistance of an intermediary (hence, it remains an individualistic cult). The most complex cults among the Eskimos are shamanic. Shamans are seen as having a special ability to get the attention of a Spirit Helper. Thus, for a fee the shaman will call upon Spirit Helpers to assist a client. For clients suffering ill health or fortune, the shaman discovers from his Spirit Helper which supernatural being has been offended, which taboo has been broken, or which ritual has not been performed by the client. Once diagnosed, the shaman undergoes a spiritual trip to rectify the illness or misfortune. In the shamanic cult of coastal villages there is one quasi-calendrical ritual ceremony performed by the shaman: his annual spiritual trip to the ocean's bottom to persuade and entice Sedna—the Sea Goddess and Keeper of Sea Animals—to release from her domain a sufficient number of animals so that the communities and villages can survive for the ensuing year.

In conclusion, then, we can visualize primitive shamanic religions—as exemplified by the Eskimo and other small and simple societies—as the most basic religious type. The religious belief system, while distinguishing the sacred and profane as well as the supernatural and natural, does not display a clearly differentiated and systematized cosmology and value system. Structurally, cult organization displays at most a clear differentiation between two religious statuses: shaman and layman. And yet much religious activity occurs within individualistic cults.

TRADITIONAL COMMUNAL RELIGIONS

Somewhat more developed than primitive shamanic are traditional communal religions (Wallace, 1966:86–87). What distinguishes communal from shamanic religions is not an increase in complexity of the belief system. Rather, the principal difference is in the complexity of the cult structures and their organization. Below, utilizing the religion of the Trobriand Islanders (Malinowski, 1955), we will briefly delineate this type of religion.

Belief system. The cosmology of communal religions is only slightly more complicated than that in primitive shamanic religions. The pantheon is a loosely structured conglomerate of supernatural deities and spirits. However, the mythology surrounding these deities tends to be more elaborate than that of primitive religions. For example, among the Trobriand Islanders there are a series of ancestral spirits whose genealogy is well known. But the hierarchy of relations and power among these spirits still remains somewhat vague and ambiguous. The values of the belief system of communal religions are not clearly articulated or systematized. They remain implicit and are not codified into a moral code.

Cult structure and organization. The cult structure and its organization is considerably more complex in communal than in primitive shamanic religions. In addition to individualistic and shamanic cults there are cults which can be termed *communal* (Wallace, 1966:87). These cults usually display a threefold division of labor: lay participants; lay organizers, sponsors, and performers; and religious specialists (shamans, magicians, etc.). The rituals performed in these communal cults tend to be *calendrical,* with laymen organizing and often performing at least some of the prescribed rituals. Frequently this organization of lay personnel begins to approximate a bureaucratic structure with regular technical and supervisory assignments for laymen. Yet no full-time priesthood or elaborate religious hierarchy can be said to exist (Wallace, 1966:87). Communal cults vary in size from very small to very large, encompassing the whole community. Membership also varies and usually revolves around special social categories such as age and sex or around special groups like secret societies or kinship groupings.

As Wallace (1966:91–92) documents or as Malinowski's (1955) more extensive ethnography reveals, the Trobriand Islanders display two such communal cults: the Technological Magic Cult and the Cult of the Spirits of the Dead. In the Technological Magic Cult certain ancestral spirit beings control economic activity. Ritual deference must be paid to these spirits with respect to the main types of economic activity among the Trobriand Islanders: gardening and canoeing or fishing. No intermediary or spiritual helper is required to communicate with these ancestral spirits. But communal participation in the rituals is nevertheless supervised by magicians. These economic rituals occur on a fairly regular calendrical schedule each year. The second communal cult structure of the Trobriand Islanders—the Spirits of the Dead—relies less on magicians and intermediaries than the Technological Magic Cult. Ceremonies and rituals are organized and run principally by laymen. There is one major calendrical ritual held at the end of the harvest involving a prolonged period of food display, consumption, dancing, and sex. Aside from these two communal cults, the religion of the Trobriand Islanders is organized into shamanic cults with professional magicians and sorcerers causing and/or curing misfortune and illness for clients. Also, there are various individualistic cults requiring individual ritual activity with respect to matters such as love, protection from evil, lesser spirits, flying witches, and so on.

Communal religions thus display a level of structural organization beyond that evidenced in primitive shamanic religions. Cult structures are more varied and begin to evidence bureaucratic organization. The belief system is only slightly more elaborate than that among primitive religions, although the mythology tends to be more extensive. But within communal religions are the seeds of belief and cult structure and organization which become conspicuous features of traditional ecclesiastic religions.

TRADITIONAL ECCLESIASTIC RELIGIONS

Traditional ecclesiastic religions display a marked increase in the complexity of both the belief system and cult structure. In examining this type of religion we will utilize the extensive ethnographic data on the Dahomey of West Africa (Herskovits and Herskovits, 1933; Herskovits, 1938) during its political independence. It should be emphasized that Dahomean religion is just a recent example of a traditional ecclesiastic religion. The religions of ancient Greece, Egypt, Rome, and to some extent Babylonia displayed a similar profile. Finally we will draw heavily from both Goode's (1951) and Wallace's (1966) secondary analysis of Dahomean religion.

Belief System. The most notable difference between the belief system of traditional ecclesiastic and communal religions is the extensiveness and complexity of the cosmology. With traditional ecclesiastic religions, there is an elaborate pantheon or group of pantheons as well as a relatively clear hierarchical ordering of the supernatural beings in terms of power and influence. Also there is usually a creator god—a supernatural being who created both the natural and supernatural. The mythology of the cosmology is well developed and includes episodes in the lives of gods, fraternal jealousies, sexual relations, and competition among various supernatural deities. In some traditional ecclesiastical religions values begin to be codified into a religious code of rights and wrongs. Equally frequently, however, religious values remain tied to and fused with ritual activity.

The Dahomean religion displays such a belief system. There is a female Sky God—Mawu or Mawu-Lisa (Lisa being the son of Mawu and yet often fused with her). However, depending upon the mythology, Mawu can also be a male. Mawu or Mawu-Lisa is usually believed to have divided the universe and world, for Mawu is the creator of all things. Actually other myths reveal that other gods have created certain things and so there is some ambiguity over just which god is the Creator—although in most cases Mawu ultimately holds the formula for the creation of man, matter, and other gods. Although the mythologies surrounding Mawu or Mawu-Lisa are somewhat ambiguous, Mawu is almost always viewed as dividing the supernatural into three giant subpantheons pertaining to the Sky, Thunder, and Earth. With respect to these subpantheons there are a host of deities with an elaborate mythology surrounding each. A fourth pantheon revolving around sea gods also exists, but its relationship to Mawu is more ambiguous. Thus the Dahomean pantheon is extremely complex, containing not only ambiguous but sometimes conflicting mythologies. Yet despite these ambiguities there are incipient hierarchies of power and influence extending from Mawu or Mawu-Lisa down to the gods of the various subpantheons. Also, though somewhat clouded, there is a creation myth with respect to Mawu as well as some other gods in the subpantheon.

Cult structure and organization. We have labeled religions such as the Dahomean ecclesiastic because this label denotes a new revolutionary form of cult structure: the ecclesiastical. Ecclesiastic cults—unlike previously discussed cults—display a professional clergy which is organized into a bureaucracy. These clergy differ from shamans in that they are not private and individual entrepreneurs and from lay officials of communal cults in that they are formally appointed or elected as more or less full-time religious specialists (or priests). Relations among these priests usually become somewhat hierarchical in terms of prestige and power. These religious specialists of ecclesiastic cults also perform exclusively certain calendrical and noncalendrical rituals, with laymen increasingly becoming passive respondents rather than active participants and managers (Wallace, 1966:88). Such rituals are performed in established and enduring temple structures. Furthermore these religious specialists begin to exert tremendous nonreligious influence and perhaps authority in secular (as well as sacred) activities. The emergence of an ecclesiastic cult structure marks a major stage in religious evolution, since subsequent development of national or worldwide religions is dependent upon the existence of a bureaucratized cult structure.

Although the Dahomean religion never spread far beyond West Africa, it displays the incipient structural features of premodern and widespread religions such as Islam, Christianity, Hinduism, Buddhism, and the like (see below). The Dahomean religion has numerous individualistic cults where incumbents established ritual relations with various minor deities. The religious subsystem of the Dahomeans also evidences a shamanic cult—the Divination Cult—whose professional diviners discover the proper ritual for certain crucial activities (harvesting, marketing, etc.) as well as illness and misfortune. Various quasi-communal cults—the Ancestral Cults—organized around kinship groupings are also in evidence, with kin members organizing certain ritual activities—especially around death. But the distinguishing feature of the Dahomean religion is the evidence of an ecclesiastical cult. Each major pantheon in the belief system—Sky, Thunder, Earth, Sea—has a separate religious order or cult structure. Each of these cults has its own temple, professional clergy, and hierarchy of religious specialists. They thus represent different churches with related and yet separate cosmologies. Of interest in light of the last chapter is the Sky Cult, which is a kind of state church that was legitimated and was supported by the traditional monarchy of Dahomey.

PREMODERN RELIGIONS

Premodern is a label encompassing many of the dominant religions of the world since medieval times: Christianity, Hinduism, Buddhism, traditional Judaism, Confucianism, and Islam. Since these religions tend to cut across more than one society, it is difficult to make a blanket portrayal of any one as premodern or modern. Depending upon the modernity of the society in which they are located, their degree of modernity will vary. Yet they have tended to be the dominant religions of many traditional societies initiating economic development—in feudal Europe, at the turn of the twentieth century, and in the Third World today. Much of this is a result of the fact that through colonialism, war, conquest, and missionary proselytizing, they have become the principal religions of many developing areas. Frequently these religions have been imposed upon—and to some extent amalgamated with—a more traditional indigenous religion with the result that each society in which they are found has a somewhat unique variant of the main religious strain. Furthermore, these dominant premodern religions often bear common origins, with one being a revolt or break with another: Christianity from Judaism, Buddhism from Hinduism, and Islam from both Judaism and Christianity, and so forth. These facts probably help account for some of their common features. But this is not the whole story. As we will see in the next chapter when we examine the influence of other institutions on religion, many structural conditions per se promoted many of the similarities among these religions.

Belief system. The cosmology of premodern religions is greatly attenuated compared to that of traditional ecclesiastic religions. The pantheon becomes particularly truncated with a clear tendency toward monotheism—one all-encompassing god or supernatural force (Wallace, 1966:94–101). The hierarchy of the pantheon tends to be explicit, with power flowing from the all-powerful god or force down to lesser supernatural entities (Bellah, 1964:366). For example, Islam, Catholicism, Judaism, and Confucianism evidence clear tendencies toward monotheism (Allah, God and the Trinity, God, and Tao respectively being the all-powerful beings and/or forces of the supernatural realm). Hinduism evidences a more ambiguous pantheon, as does its offshoot Buddhism. Philosophical Hinduism (Wallace, 1966:94) is clearly monotheistic with its all-encompassing supernatural being or force, the "One." However, Sanskritic Hinduism maintains an elaborate pantheon of gods, including Siva, Krishna, Ram, Vishnu, and Lakshimi. The pantheon of Buddhism is similarly structured with the world being guided by a series of Buddhas (or "Enlightened Ones"). Compared to traditional ecclesiastic religions, the mythology of the pantheon of premodern religions is also truncated. Bellah (1964:366) has called this the process of "de-mythologization," since little myth surrounds the creation of the all-powerful god and his court of relatives. Thus the increasingly elaborate accounts of the jealousies, conflicts, rivalries, and genealogies typical of religious evolution up to this point suddenly decline at the premodern stage. For example, the myths revolving around Krishna and Vishnu, the historical sequences of Buddhas, the interaction of God and Moses, God and Jesus, Allah, the angel Gabriel,

Mohammed, and so on are sparse indeed compared to the myths of the Dahomeon and other traditional religions.

As Bellah (1964) emphasizes, one of the most distinctive features of premodern religions is the emergence of a series of *substantive beliefs* concerning the supernatural realm and the possibility for mortal men upon death to participate in this realm. These beliefs emphasize for the first time to men the possibility of understanding the fundamental nature of both natural and supernatural reality (Bellah, 1964:367). For instance, Hinduism emphasizes the possibility of not only a better reincarnation in one's next life but also holds out the possibility of becoming a god. Christianity offers salvation in heaven after death. Islam provides for the attainment of paradise after death, and so on. Also, it should be noted that premodern religious beliefs provide places for the unworthy—hell, a poor reincarnation, and so forth. Previous traditional religions have offered the chance for man to maintain only a peace and harmony with the supernatural realm, but premodern religious beliefs provide for the possibility of actually *becoming a part* of that realm. Under these conditions religious *values* become explicit, since it is conformity to these values which increases the possibility of salvation after death in the supernatural realm. These values become codified into a religious code spelling out appropriate behaviors for the members of a society: the Ten Commandments, the sayings of Confucius, the Noble Eightfold Path among Buddhists. What is significant about these religious codes is that they specify more than just stereotyped ritual behavior; they also place upon actors a set of diffuse obligations guiding everyday, nonritual conduct. Yet these codes tend to emphasize worldly resignation and retreatism. In conforming to religious law in order to secure salvation, worshippers must turn away and withdraw from the natural world even in the midst of worldly activity. To secure salvation requires one to be uncontaminated by natural events and to be suspended in waiting in this world.

In sum, then, the cosmology of premodern religions is greatly altered. It tends toward monotheism; it has a truncated pantheon and attendant mythology; and it contains substantive beliefs about the supernatural and salvation. Equally noticeable in premodern religions is the emergence of a codified value system controlling both ritual and nonritual behavior and encouraging a kind of world retreatism.

Cult structure and organization. The structural trends evident in traditional ecclesiastic religions are greatly magnified and accelerated in premodern religions. Ecclesiastic cult structures come to dominate over shamanic, communal, and individualistic cults. Usually one large ecclesiastic bureaucracy with an extensive hierarchy of religious specialists becomes dominant: Catholicism in medieval Europe and in many of the Third World nations of Latin America, Hinduism in India, Confucianism in pre-Communist China, Islam in the Middle East, and so on. The specialists within this bureaucracy claim a monopoly on religious expertise and the right to perform major calendrical and noncalendrical rituals. They become permanent residents in large and elaborate temple structures and devote all their time to operating the church bureaucracy. The extensiveness of this dominant ecclesiastic cult and its bureaucracy is so great that it begins to generate a religious elite with tremendous power and influence. Conflicts between religious and political elites become frequent: "whether Israelite prophet and King, Islamic ulama and sultan, Christian pope and emperor, or Confucian scholar official (mandarin) and ruler. . . ." (Bellah, 1964:368). The church and state bureaucracies thus become clearly differentiated with the result that the legitimating functions of religion for the polity are no longer automatic and nonproblematic. Sometimes religious beliefs and the organization of a religious cult become the stimulus and locus for rebellious social movements. Because of their well-articulated and codified belief system and their high degree of bureaucratic organization, premodern religions can *potentially* become a major source of social change. Thus cult structures in premodern religions, because of their capacity to be bureaucratized and thus engage in effective social action, often become a dynamic force in a society. As long as cult structures remained loosely organized in a communal or only incipient ecclesiastic form, they lacked the organizational resources to generate major social change in the face of a well-organized kin- or state-based polity. However, as we emphasized in the previous chapter, premodern religion usually—though not always—historically performed and performs today a conservative, legitimating function for the polity and other institutional structures in a society.

However, within the institution of religion, considerable change can occur as lesser cult structures become ecclesiastically organized and begin to challenge the beliefs and organization of the dominant ecclesiastic cult. Religious evolution has documented this process again and again, whether it be Catholicism revolting from Judaism, Protestantism from Catholicism, or Buddhism from Hinduism. With further modernization this results in the emergence of several dominant ecclesiastic cults (e.g., Catholicism and Protestantism in Europe) as well as subcults within these larger cults (e.g., the Protestant denominations). Thus at their most advanced stage, premodern religions display several large ecclesiastic cult structures dominating religious ritual and activity in a society. But they also evidence other forms of cult structures: communal, shamanic, and individualistic. For example, in India where Philosophical Hinduism dominates, religion in many rural village cults is organized into communal cults and utilizes Sanskritic Hinduism and pre-Hindu beliefs and rituals. In these same villages can also be found various ancestral cults which represent a similar amalgamation of Sanskritic and pre-Hindu beliefs and rituals. Furthermore there are shamanic cults of holy men (gurus, curers, etc.) who perform necessary ritual activities for clients. And finally there are various individualistic cults where ritual activity revolves around seeking harmony with various personal guardian spirits. Thus premodern religions display considerable structural heterogeneity. There are many different types of cult structures (ecclesiastic, communal, shamanic, and individualistic) and their size and relative influence varies tremendously. Premodern religions are a conglomeration of various cult structures having similar but always somewhat divergent belief systems. The interplay—conflict, assimilation, accommodation, and conquest—among these various cults frequently makes premodern religions highly dynamic. However when one large ecclesiastic cult dominates, a premodern religion will remain comparatively static—unless disrupted by nonreligious institutional influence (see next chapter). At any rate it is from this form of organization that modern religions appeared to have evolved.

religion in modern societies

In modern religions a curious reversal of developmental and historical trends occurs. Some of these are foreshadowed in certain features of premodern religions. But many occur as a reaction or revolution against the beliefs and structure of premodern religions, and still others as the consequence of modernization in other institutions. Yet religious modernization should not be viewed as ubiquitous. In reality most of the world's religions remain at a premodern stage, even in the face of massive modernization of the institutional environment (economy, polity, kinship, education, etc.). Thus discussion in this section concerns only those religions which have developed beyond the premodern stage. For convenience we distinguish between early modern religions and modern religions.

The Protestant Reformation marks the early emergence of modern religion. Until recently — and even now the matter is ambiguous — the great premodern religions of Islam, Buddhism, Hinduism, and Confucianism resisted such modernization. Early reform movements within these religions did not have the widespread appeal or far-reaching consequences of the Protestant Reformation (Bellah, 1964). Today, under massive pressure from other modernizing institutions in a society, these stable premodern religions are initiating modernization. To the extent that they do, we can predict changes in the belief system and cult structure delineated below.

Belief system. The cosmology of early modern religions becomes even more attenuated than that of premodern religions. The trend toward monotheism is more evident and the cast of supporting gods and deities decreases. Myths become comparatively unimportant and are deemphasized. More revolutionary than these extensions of trends evident in premodern religions is the emergence of a new set of substantive beliefs about the supernatural and men's relation to it. A clear separation of the natural and supernatural realms is maintained, but the premodern emphasis on the hierarchies within either of these realms is eliminated. God and men stand in direct relation to each other and mediating religious specialists (priests) are essentially excess baggage. Such substantive beliefs result in a reorganization of religious values which still stress the importance of salvation, but through a new route. Religious values now emphasize the importance of *individual* faith and commitment to God, rather than ritual performance or conformity to strict ethical codes. Values also emphasize the necessity for God's work to be done in this world. The world, in Bellah's (1964:369) words, becomes "a valid arena in which to work out the divine command."

Cult structure and organization. What distinguished the Protestant Reformation from reform movements in other premodern religions was that this new emphasis on individualism and deemphasis of ritual and priestly mediation between God and men became *institutionalized into strong ecclesiastic cult structures.* These structures were and are bureaucratized, with a hierarchy of religious specialists and with requirements of religious orthodoxy for lay members. Yet typical features of premodern ecclesiastic cults, such as compulsory membership, high authoritarianism, ritual emphasis, and *elaborate* hierarchy, were not evident in these early Protestant cult structures (Calvinism, Methodism, Pietism, Baptism, etc.). Thus a curious accommodation between new religious beliefs within a somewhat watered-down form of ecclesiastic cult occurred during early modernization. And this appears to be inevitable during early modernization of premodern religions (Wilson, 1969:21–108). The failure of other premodern religions to modernize lay not in a lack of a reform movement similar to that of the Protestant Reformation, but in the incapacity to institutionalize this reform into an ecclesiastic cult structure (Bellah, 1964:369). Yet early modern cult structures were not loosely structured or entirely permissive. On the contrary, the early Protestant cults required much orthodoxy and the conformity to church rules. And this requirement of conformity extended beyond the church doors into everyday life. But within these cults, the de-emphasis of ritual, the decreasing role of the clergy as intermediaries, and the emphasis on individual relations between God and men generated a whole series of contradictions between tightly organized ecclesiastic cults and a loosely organized belief system. With further modernization these contradictions become increasingly evident to both the clergy and laity. The result, as we will see below, is a loosening of religious orthodoxy and cult structure as well as a further individualization of the religious belief system.

MODERN RELIGION

Modern religions are most typical of a few Western societies with a Protestant tradition. Societies dominated by one of the large premodern religions do not display this modern religious type; and in societies which do, it exists alongside premodern and early modern forms of religion. Modern religions are thus neither widespread nor necessarily dominant in societies where they exist. Yet they appear to be the vanguard of the future and hence are discussed here as a distinct type.

Belief system. Modern religion is marked by the destruction of a coherent cosmology. Beliefs about the supernatural, mythologies, and substantive beliefs increasingly become unsystematic. Perhaps the most dramatic manifestation of the de-cosmologicalization of religion is reflected in considerable ambiguity over whether or not there is a god or a clearly distinguishable supernatural. A recent study of college students in the United States (Goldsen et al., 1960) revealed this ambiguity when only 49 percent of students feeling a need for religion accepted the notion of a deity as an important component of a religious system. Bellah (1964:370–371) has referred to this process as the breakdown of the basic dualism that has been central to all religions through history and throughout most of the world today. The belief in forces beyond man's control remains in modern religions but the clear-cut differentiation between the sacred and profane or supernatural and natural diminishes. Substantive beliefs begin to emphasize individualistic or personal interpretations of the nonempirical and sacred. Emphasis is placed upon a searching for truths fitting in with one's actual conditions of living. To the extent that salvation remains a tenet within the belief system, it is likely to emphasize multiple and personal paths to life in another world. These paths to salvation always will involve adjustment and happiness in this world. These alterations of the cosmology are reflected in a new, emerging set of religious values. Moral codes become completely obliterated and are replaced by values directing worshippers to seek adjustment, happiness, and self-realization with others and the world around them (Bellah, 1964:373; Berger, 1966). This was documented some time ago in the United States by the previously cited study on American college students (Goldsen et al, 1960). In this study students were most likely to characterize as necessary for a religious value or ethical system an emphasis on personal adjustment and development, closeness with your fellowmen, an anchor for family life and children, and intellectual clarity about the fundamental problems of living. Thus in modern religious belief systems the elaborate cosmology typical of traditional ecclesiastical religions has crumbled, while the explicit and rigid moral code of premodern religions has become loose and highly flexible, emphasizing adjustment to the secular rather than to the sacred or supernatural.

Cult structure and organization. With this flexible and individualistic form of religious belief system cult structures in modern societies are altered. However the tight cult structures of premodern and early modern religions still persist and usually outnumber the more loosely structured modern cults. These modern cults thus stand alongside older forms, although in the long run the trend is toward these new cults replacing or forcing modifications in the old. Yet in the near future modern structures embracing the more flexible belief system of modern religions will remain ecclesiastical. However, these structures remain somewhat fluid, adjusting themselves to the needs of their clients. (The reverse tends to be true in premodern and early modern cults.) There are many subunits and organizations within any cult which cater to diverse groups of clients, such as the old, young, conservative, liberal, ghetto resident, college student, and suburbanite. As the needs of clients change, the form of the lower organizational units of the ecclesia which service the membership will also change, for cults—churches, denominations, sects, and the like —come to provide more of a place or location where each individual works out his own solutions to ultimate questions about the cosmos and supernatural rather than a rigid orthodox structure where these solutions are prefabricated in the form of an established belief system and ritual pattern (Bellah, 1964:373; Lenski, 1963:59–60). This is increasingly the trend, especially among Protestant cults (denominations) in modern Western societies (Berger, 1967:369–372; Lenski, 1963:59). Thus modern church cult structures are a curious hybrid or cross between an ecclesiastic cult structure at their top and a more flexible, almost individualistic structure at their bottom or membership level.

modern religion: an overview

Modern religions appear to have emerged with the Protestant Reformation against traditional Catholicism. These early modern Christian religions—such as Calvinism, Methodism, Pietism, Baptism—joined a more individualistic and flexible belief system with a rigid ecclesiastic cult structure. Thus with the Reformation, Christianity as a world religion was broken into a number of different ecclesiastical cults (in other words, the large Protestant denominations). In turn each of these original cults had reform movements resulting in new ecclesiastical cults (denominations and small sects). The conglomeration of these large and small Protestant ecclesiastical cults (whether denominations, sects, or some other unit of organization) represented the first early modern religions (Wilson, 1969:21–181). Other premodern religions such as Hinduism, Buddhism, or Islam are only currently undergoing the transformation that Christianity underwent several hundred years ago (Bellah, 1964:371–372; 1966).

Modern religion represents a further transformation of early modern religious cults. Cults increasingly provide a permissive environment within which a variety of religious answers to questions of the ultimate and supernatural are sought by the membership itself. Professional clergy within a cult bureaucracy are still prominent but norms increasingly de-emphasize their ritual duties in favor of their consultant obligations for those seeking personal solutions to religious questions.

the consequences of religion for traditional and modern societies

In traditional societies religion has far-reaching consequences for society. It pervades virtually every aspect of social life. Religion re-

365

inforces major institutional norms in the economic, familial, political, legal, and educational spheres. Religion mobilizes sentiments and sacredizes institutional norms crucial to system survival. For example, ritual activity among the Tikopians—as noted above—assures that certain economic tasks revolving around the preparation of canoes for fishing are performed. Religion also has profound consequences for legitimating inequality—whether with respect to the stratification or political subsystem of a society. Religion provides for continuity of socialization by sacredizing crucial kinship norms and by clearly demarcating crucial status transitions from birth, to puberty, to marriage, and to death. And finally religion provides an explanation and interpretation as well as ritual recourse to the manifold tensions, frustrations, anxieties, and uncertainties of human existence in traditional societies.

With modernization this pervasive impact of religion on social life begins to decline. Religious rituals and beliefs reinforce crucial institutional norms in only the most indirect way—perhaps by providing the cultural or value premises of the legal system. This results from the fact that religious symbols and beliefs become incapable of furnishing overarching unity to the highly complex, differentiated, and secular activities of modern institutions (Berger, 1967:357). Political legitimation is increasingly the function of law and a civic culture (see previous chapter). With respect to family and kinship, religion ceases to circumscribe kinship norms as law increasingly specifies the minimal conditions for family activity (see Chapter 9). Emerging educational structures assume many of the *rites de passage* functions of religion as they certify (with diplomas) major status transitions of the young. All that remains for religion in modern systems are a few consequences for alleviating anxiety and tension. In modern societies there is much emotional as opposed to economic deprivation that can generate fears and anxiety (Glock, 1964; Berger, 1967). Furthermore people in modern societies have considerable leisure to ponder many personal-philosophical questions about self-realization, the purpose and meaning of life, what it's all about, where I am going, and so on. The highly flexible belief systems and cult structures of modern religions offer a place for personal answers and solutions to such questions. But so do other structures in modern societies—encounter groups, psychoanalysis, and psychiatry. Thus, even with respect to the anxiety reduction, other structures evolve to cope with the uncertainties posed by not only modern leisure but also by the tensions and pressures of modern life. Yet the leisure sphere and all the anxieties it is likely to generate (as contradictory as this may seem) are just emerging in modern societies and promise to grow. This sphere remains remarkably *under*-institutionalized, with the result that there are no clear-cut norms guiding people's role behavior (Berger, 1967:370). Some authors have hypothesized that it is in this area that religion can reexert much of the influence it has lost in other institutional spheres. The structural transformation of religion in modern societies toward a more flexible profile is perhaps an indication of this shift in the focus of religion (Berger, 1967: 369–370; Luckman, 1963).

WORLD TRENDS IN RELIGION

Much religious development and change are obscured by a number of facts: political and religious conquest, the instability of system boundaries, and the diffusion of premodern and early modern religious beliefs into societies with more traditional religions. Tracing historically religious development is thus a complex task—convoluted, altered, and distorted by many forces. Yet to the extent that we can observe religious change, there appear certain unambiguous alterations in the belief system of religions from a primitive to modern form. But this does not mean that every religion has undergone, or will undergo, these changes. Nor does this mean that changes must be smooth and continuous. Often change is abrupt and sudden, resulting in profound discontinuities from one stage to another.

changes in religious beliefs

Perhaps the most unambiguous trend in religious development can be seen in the alteration of religious cosmologies during modernization. If we compare primitive, traditional, communal, and traditional ecclesiastical religions, there appears to be an increasing codification and complexity of the cosmology. The number of deities in the pantheon, their degree of definition, the myths relating them and accounting for their emergence, and substantive beliefs about levels or planes in the supernatural realms all become more clearly articulated and codified into a comparatively unambiguous hierarchy of gods and supernatural forces. With the emergence of premodern religious forms the number of deities decreases as a tendency towards monotheism becomes evident. However, relations among supernatural beings as well as planes of supernatural existence remain clearly articulated. With emergence of early modern religions, these trends in cosmological development decelerate and begin to be reversed: mythology becomes attenuated; the size of the pantheon decreases; and the various hierarchical levels within the supernatural realm are eliminated. With further modernization there is a nearly complete destruction of the cosmology as beliefs come to emphasize personal interpretations and relationships with the supernatural.

367

Religious values display a similar curvilinear trend. From a primitive to premodern stage religious values become increasingly more explicit, culminating in the strict moral code of most premodern religions. This code persists with early modernization—although in a somewhat less compelling form. With modernization a rigid moral code disappears as values stress a more flexible relationship between men and the supernatural.

patterns of religious bureaucratization

Religious development entails an increasing bureaucratization up to the early modern stage. Primitive shamanic religions display only individualistic and shamanic cult structures. Traditional communal religions evidence communal cults with some degree of a division of labor among the lay membership. Traditional ecclesiastical religions reveal cults with a clear bureaucratic structure: division of labor between laity and specialized clergy as well as a hierarchy of control among the clergy itself. Premodern religions display an even more elaborate and extensive church bureaucracy with a high degree of centralization of its religious specialists. This is exemplified in the Catholic Church, which has a world bureaucracy with the Pope at its head. But early modern religions begin to decentralize their bureaucracies. Smaller, geographically dispersed, and local bureaucracies begin to evidence only loose administrative ties to a central staff of clergy. Strict and extensive relationships of authority among units within the religious bureaucracy decline. Only certain *episcopal* bureaucracies maintain tight links of local religious specialists to the upper administrative hierarchy (Wallace, 1966:84). More frequently the *presbyterian* form of cult structure exists in early modern religions. In these structures local religious specialists are responsible only to a presbytery or body of fellow peers (a kind of professional association). Also common in early modern religions is the *congregational* form of cult structure, where the church membership selects and controls the conduct of their clergy. With further modernization these patterns of bureaucratic decentralization become even more evident. Furthermore, at the local level bureaucracy becomes at best a poor description of the relations among religious specialists as they attempt to display increased flexibility with respect to new religious beliefs and the needs of their clientele.

compartmentalization and segregation

We have already noted the changing and decreasing consequences of religion for modernizing societies. The reasons for this lay in the structure of modernizing institutions surrounding religion. With economic development, rational and secular activity is required of workers. Religious beliefs concerning the supernatural are simply irrelevant to rationalized economic activity. Furthermore, religious ritual is unnecessary to assure that certain economic tasks are performed, since the rules and schedule of a modern industrial-bureaucratic economy assure their performance. In the political sphere the emergence of a large, secular state bureaucracy engaged in complex goal-attainment processes precludes the influence of practitioners concerned with the supernatural. Were this not so the secular administration of the polity would be undermined. Educational structures providing technology and incumbents for a modern economy cannot be overly concerned with the supernatural or economic development would be greatly impeded. As institutions become clearly differentiated from one another, integrative problems in a society increase. In response to these problems law displaces religion as the dominant coordinating and integrating institution in a society. Since problems of coordination among institutions are basically secular and ever changing, legal subsystems are far more able to provide both a secular *and* flexible response (law enactment) to these constantly changing problems of coordination. These institutional changes during modernization have the consequence of segregating religion from most institutional processes in modern society. As institutional processes become rationalized and secularized, religious beliefs concerning the supernatural and sacred become irrelevant. Compared to the diffuse intrusion of religion into virtually all aspects of social life in traditional societies, religion thus becomes compartmentalized in modern societies. In the next chapter, when we examine the institutional environment of religion, we will explore such segregation and compartmentalization in more detail.

secularization

To speak of a trend toward secularization of religion represents a contradiction in terms. Religion revolves around the nonsecular — the ultimate, the cosmos, the supernatural, and the sacred. And so our heading for this section is an overstatement, but it does point to a *directional* trend. Religion in modern societies is increasingly concerned with secular activities. To a great extent this has always been so, since religious beliefs and rituals in traditional societies have had consequences for economic, political, educational, and familial structures and processes. But in traditional societies, whether calendrical, noncalendrical, or magical, religious rituals have always made direct and strong appeals for the intervention of supernatural forces into everyday affairs. Modern religions decreasingly make such appeals. While operating on a supernatural or sacred set of premises, the actual role behavior of modern clergy in a myriad of secular activities such as social work, the leisure sphere, criminal corrections, youth programs, athletic leagues, marriage counseling, draft counseling, and group therapy frequently make little or no reference (much less an appeal) to the supernatural. Since the supernatural realm in modern religions has no clear-cut or elaborate cosmology or strict moral code, this is to be expected. And when beliefs begin to emphasize the importance of each individual establishing his personal relationship with the ultimate conditions of life, direct and strong appeals of clergy for divine intervention become inappropriate. To the extent that this occurs, we speak of a trend toward secularization of religious role behavior. But should such behavior completely lose sight of its supernatural or sacred premise, it would cease to be religious. And if all cult structures become organized solely for secular activities, then the institution of religion would no longer exist. Whether or not this is the long-run fate of religion is of course an unanswerable question.

THE AMERICAN RELIGIOUS SUBSYSTEM

Religion in the United States is a vast conglomeration of large and small cult structures — sects, temples, churches, denominations, national, and world organizations. The belief system and cult organization of American religion is thus diverse, although we can distinguish three general religious subsystems: Catholicism, Protestantism, and Judaism. However, with the possible exception of Catholicism these religious subsystems themselves manifest tremendous heterogeneity of belief and cult organization. Contained within this diversity are worldwide trends toward de-systematization of beliefs, de-bureaucratization of cults, compartmentalization, and secularization. Trends toward bureaucratization, systematization, active proselytization, and sacrilization are also evident in American society. Thus American religion does not constitute a unified clustering of cults and beliefs. Despite similar cultural and historical origins as well as the Christian profile (Jews constitute less than 10 percent of the religious population) of American religion, it displays premodern, early modern, and modern forms.

The diversity of American religious beliefs and cult structures derives from a number of historical occurrences (Williams, 1970: 374–391). (1) A wide diversity of *small* Protestant religious groupings originally settled the United States in what was — from the settlers' point of view — a religious vacuum. There was no indigenous and pervasive religious belief system or cult structure to dominate over these original cults. (2) The smallness of these cults made it difficult for any one cult structure to dominate. Even though most evidenced some degree of bureaucratization and were engaged in active proselytizing, no one ecclesiastic cult structure came to dominate *all* the original colonies. (3) The nature of the belief systems of these Protestant cults, which emphasized a personal relation between man and God, made establishing a society-wide and uniform belief system—and hence cult structure—difficult. Even though each cult demanded strict conformity to its doctrine, the sheer diversity of these doctrines allowed each potential religious client a choice of religious membership. The availability of similar (i.e., all Protestant) but somewhat dissimilar cults and beliefs precluded the possibility of any nationwide unification under one cult and common belief system. (4) And since no particular ecclesiastic cult structure could become dominant and form an alliance with the polity, religious freedom became institutionalized in law with the doctrine of separation of church and state. (5) Once institutionalized, other non-Protestant cults could emerge and exist without prosecution by the state—although community intolerance and prejudice against new religious cults often resulted in persecution. Under these conditions diversity of beliefs and cult structures became inevitable not only between but within the dominant religious subsystems of Protestantism, Catholicism, and Judaism. Below we briefly examine some of the diversity within and among these religious subsystems.

american protestantism

There are some 250 Protestant cults (denominations) in the United States. While most of these display an ecclesiastical structure, some approach a communal form of organization. Also most Protestant cults are small, with twenty-one cults containing more than 90 percent of all Protestants (Williams, 1970:377). Whether large or small, there is enormous diversity among these cult structures (denomina-ations) and their belief systems. With respect to their belief systems, we can classify them as modern or liberal, conservative, and neo-orthodox (Salisbury, 1964).

Liberal or modern Protestant beliefs. Liberal Protestantism is the closest approximation to the type of belief system that we earlier labeled modern (Hordern, 1957; Dewart, 1966; Stark and Glock, 1968:212–216). The distinction between the supernatural and natural is somewhat blurred in liberal Protestantism, for while God is is still worshipped, his realm (Kingdom of God) is broadly defined to include both the natural and supernatural without a necessarily clear line between the two. The *immanence* of God is stressed (Dillenberger and Welch, 1959:218–220). He is seen as working through nature, for there are no strong beliefs concerning a divine suspension of natural events—such as miracles. Thus the religious pantheon is virtually obliterated, except for a common belief in a supernatural. This is underscored by the de-emphasis of liberal Protestant doctrine on the Trinity. The mythology of liberal Protestantism is attenuated, with only minor attention paid to the myths such as the Virgin Mary and the physical resurrection of Jesus. The life and acts of Jesus are placed as much in a humanitarian as in a holy and sacred context. Mythology emphasizes the *worldly* humanitarianism of Jesus. This means that the Bible is not necessarily interpreted literally. Nor is it viewed as the last word or supreme authority. Rather, each individual is to reconcile *his* beliefs about God and the supernatural with the doctrines of the Bible. This necessarily means that prominent Biblical doctrines of heaven, hell, salvation, and immortality become personal matters of belief (or disbelief) for the individual worshipper. Thus liberal Protestantism represents a very flexible body of beliefs that requires a tremendous amount of individual interpretation. What is doctrine and not doctrine, what is religion and not religion, and what is sacred and profane become individual matters to be reconciled with each individual's existential experiences.

Conservative Protestant beliefs. In contrast to liberal Protestantism there exists a conservative or fundamentalistic belief system. In this body of beliefs, there is a clear distinction between natural and supernatural. The pantheon (the Trinity and saints) of the Bible is maintained. The mythology of the Bible—the virgin birth, the resurrection, and so forth—is literally interpreted; and there is a strong belief in divine intrusion into natural events. This is best evidenced by the belief that there is to be a second coming of Jesus, that Jesus will then judge the good and the bad, that he will again rule the world, and that eventually the final battle between God and Satan will occur (Salisbury, 1964:122). Thus conservative Protestantism represents a highly inflexible (though varying from cult to cult) belief system. Biblical orthodoxy is maintained and individual interpretative license is not granted, as is the case with liberal Protestantism.

Neoorthodox Protestant beliefs. Neoorthodoxy represents a reaction to liberal Protestantism. It reaffirms—much like conservatism—basic doctrines of the New and Old Testaments, while reemphasizing the doctrines of Calvin and Luther. There is a belief in a clear separation of natural and supernatural (the majesty of

God), in the doctrine of divine intervention, and in the necessity of salvation by grace. But the extreme orthodoxy of conservative Protestantism is not evident in neoorthodox Protestantism. Within the framework of God's constant intervention into world affairs and in salvation through grace, considerable latitude among individual beliefs is allowed—although far from that allowed in liberal Protestantism.

These various forms of Protestant beliefs are actualized within a wide variety of ecclesiastic cult structures. In these structures rituals reaffirming beliefs are enacted. The vast majority of these cult structures (or Protestant denominations) are dominated by liberal beliefs. Yet even with certain common beliefs, the structural organization of major Protestant cults varies. Three patterns are evident: episcopal, presbyterian, and congregational. Episcopal cults (denominations) are hierarchically organized but in American Protestant cults, authority is divided between the clergy and laity. The Episcopal and Methodist Churches in the Unites States best reflect this pattern of organization with a lay-clergy (vestry, rector, bishop, etc.) hierarchy of control from a local to a national level. The Presbyterian Church in the United States represents the presbyterian pattern of cult organization, with a body of clergy and elected laymen forming a presbytery which has jurisdiction in the selection and ordination of ministers for a group of local churches. The cluster or conglomeration of cults along a congregational pattern encompasses the largest number of Protestant worshippers. This form of cult organization is best exemplified in the Baptist, Unitarian, and Congregationalist Churches in the United States. In these cults the local church membership (or congregation) has considerable authority to hire and fire ministers, hold property, and modify church rituals. Despite this autonomy, however, there are state, regional, and national associations which constantly exert pressure on local congregations—thus preventing them from becoming too deviant and arbitrary. What is significant about all these forms of cult organization—the episcopal, presbyterian, and congregational—is that there is considerable local and lay control over church activities. This means that beliefs and rituals can be altered (within certain limits) to suit the needs of the local membership.

373

american catholicism

American Catholicism is part of the worldwide Catholic Church. It represents the most extreme form of the episcopal cult organization to be found in the United States. The basic unit of the Catholic Church is the parish, which is presided over by an appointed priest and which encompasses all those within a specified territory. A group of contiguous parishes constitutes a diocese, which is administered by a bishop who is appointed by the Pope in Rome. Every few years bishops must report to the Pope on the state of affairs in their diocese. Cardinals are also appointed by the Pope but do not have territorial jurisdiction. Rather they have the important role of advising the Pope, as well as selecting his successor. Thus American Catholicism is just one branch of a large and centralized bureaucracy culminating with the Pope in Rome. Within this structure norms require that certain ritual and other behaviors occur at the parish level. These include the Sacraments (Baptism, Holy Eucharist, Penance, Confirmation, Matrimony, Holy Orders, Annointing of the Sick) and the six Precepts (attendance at church, communion, confession, fasting and feasting, financial support of the Church, and compliance with marriage laws). While many Protestant cults also require similar behaviors, the degree of obligation to participate and the extensiveness of church rituals are considerably less than in the Catholic Church.

The extensiveness of the Catholic ecclesia and ritual activity is correspondingly evident in its belief system. There is a clear division between the natural and supernatural as well as a hierarchy of beings (God, the Trinity, saints, etc.) and places (heaven, hell, and various intermediate levels). There is a strong emphasis on life after death and on the pursuit of salvation for various sins, and the text of the Bible is accepted literally. There is also heavy emphasis on conformity to the Ten Commandments as well as on an extensive body of rules established by the Pope(s) for guiding everyday conduct (from requiring works of charity to directives against certain forms of birth control).

Thus American Catholicism represents a close approximation of a premodern religion. The pantheon is attenuated and yet explicit; values are codified into a moral code; mythology is truncated but still evident; substantive beliefs point to a clear and elaborate conception of the supernatural and to salvation; and cult structure is ecclesiastic. But as we will examine later, Catholicism in the United States is being affected by certain trends toward modernization.

374

american judaism
Although there is a tremendous diversity of beliefs in Judaism, we can identify at least these general tenets.

(1) *The nature of the supernatural:* one God who created the world and all the universe.

(2) *The pantheon:* contains only God, although He will eventually send a Messiah to enlighten and change the evils of this world.

(3) *Substantive beliefs:* involve notions of life in the supernatural after death for those who have been good, but no unambiguous planes of supernatural existence. Immortality and reunion with God is possible for the very good. Each *individual* must reckon with the supernatural.

(4) *Myths:* Moses going to Mt. Sinai and receiving the word of God as embodied in the Torah (the first five books of the Old Testament). Extensive documentation of the creation of the earth up to the death of Moses.

(5) *Values:* codified into an elaborate set of ethics—the Torah, the Talmud, the Creeds of Maimonides, and so on. Values stress brotherhood, learning, justice, and humility. Strong emphasis is placed on the importance of activity in this world in order to reveal the will of God. Values and ethics are concretized through 613 precepts concerning prayer, diet, dress, everyday behavior, and the like.

The cult structure and organization of American Judaism is highly decentralized—perhaps more so than with Protestantism. Each local temple displays considerable autonomy from other temples and belongs to one of three national organizations: Union of Orthodox Jewish Congregations (Orthodox), United Synagogue of America (Conservative), and Union of American Hebrew Congregations (Reform). But within all of these national organizations are nationwide lay groups for the young, old, male, and female that cut across local temples or synagogues. Within local temples a very elaborate set of ritual activities is required, although their extensiveness and the involvement of the congregation vary considerably. In general ritual involvement and extensiveness vary in terms of the national affiliation of the local temple. Ritual activity is most extensive in temples associated with the Union of Orthodox Jewish Congregations, next most with the United Synagogue of America, and least with the Union of American Hebrew Congregations. These variations in ritual activity are in turn a reflection of differences in the specific belief systems of these organizations. Orthodox Judaism stresses strict interpretation and conformity to the Torah, the Talmud, and the 613 precepts. Reform Judaism emphasizes the flexibility of beliefs and the need to change them as modern conditions dictate. Conservative Judaism emphasizes retention of basic ethics and creeds, while allowing extensive secular activity and involvement. In recent years Reform and Conservative Judaism have converged, resulting in emphasis of certain rituals and beliefs behind them while liberalizing and making less manditory conformity to the 613 precepts. Myths have become less extensive and the belief in the coming of a Messiah has become reinstated into the notion of a Messaic Age resulting from man's hard work and enlightenment through secular learning. Coupled with the decentralized cult structure and with the fact that Jewish beliefs have always emphasized the personal relationship between the supernatural and man, contemporary American Judaism comes close to approximating a modern religion.

trends in american religion

Since the United States is a highly modern society religion should display many of the world trends toward modernization outlined above, especially in light of the fact that Protestantism is the dominant religion. But as we will note, there are strong fundamentalistic trends within American Protestantism. Coupled with traditional forms of Catholicism, many cults and beliefs in American religion evidence features of more traditional religious types. Thus the United States displays a high degree of religious pluralism. This makes unambiguous statements about religious trends difficult, although there appears to be at least a modal direction to religion in America.

BELIEF SYSTEMS OF AMERICAN RELIGION

It is clear that liberal Protestantism and Reform Judaism evidence very flexible and unsystematic belief systems. The cosmology is minimal, with one God (vaguely defined), a few myths and a skeptical attitude toward even these, and very ambiguous substantive beliefs about planes of natural and supernatural existence. Values stress brotherhood and coming to terms with the conditions of this world. Moral codes, ethics, and precepts are deemphasized in the name of personal adjustment to this world and the supernatural. In contrast to these flexible beliefs are the systematic belief systems of fundamentalist or conservative Protestantism, Orthodox Judaism, and Catholicism. In all these belief systems, there is a clear—albeit somewhat different—cosmology with a clear-cut and hierarchical supernatural, monotheistic pantheon, and a variety of Biblical myths which are interpreted literally. Since around 50 million worshippers belong to cult structures with such systematic beliefs, it remains to be seen if these belief systems will become increasingly flexible or less appealing to church clients.

PATTERNS OF BUREAUCRATIZATION IN AMERICAN RELIGION

Historically American Protestantism (and Protestantism in general) and Judaism have been composed of relatively autonomous, small and local ecclesiastic cults. Bureaucratization has been concentrated at the local cult level and not at the national level. While the major Protestant denominations are national in scope, the local church has always had considerable autonomy—even those organized on an episcopal basis (Salisbury, 1964:101–156); Moberg, 1962). Local Jewish temples and synagogues have always had tremendous administrative autonomy from their national organization. Compared to premodern religions or even contemporary American Catholicism, Protestantism and Judaism represent a high degree of de-bureaucratization. However, a recent trend toward consolidation of Protestant cults into larger cult structures perhaps marks the beginnings of increased bureaucratization. For example, the merger of diverse cults (Congregational Christian, Evangelical, and Reformed Churches, etc.) into the United Church of Christ represents one such consolidation (Williams, 1970:379). The consolidation of smaller ethnic Lutheran cults into either the Lutheran Church of America or the American Lutheran Church marks a similar trend toward centralization. The result of these consolidations is to create a national bureaucracy and to incorporate smaller cults into larger and more complex cults. Whether or not the formation of such a national bureaucracy will completely undermine the autonomy of the local church is unclear. However, a rigid and extensive cult structure approaching that of Catholicism is unlikely for at least three reasons: (1) Oftentimes consolidation of Protestant sects and denominations involves the merger of cults with diverse structures and belief systems. Under these conditions complete unification of cults into a tight and highly centralized national bureaucracy is unlikely. (2) The nature of the Protestant belief system emphasizing individual spiritual independence would prohibit extensive bureaucratization, with professional clergy regulating all religious and ritual activity. (3) The Protestant tradition of local church autonomy is strong enough to impede complete consolidation of cult structures into a centralized and national bureaucracy. (4) As the established and dominant cults centralize and bureaucratize, many other small, loosely structured cults appear to be proliferating in the contemporary United States. These include: the quasi-religious profile of some drug subcultures, the revival of astrology, various Zen movements, the Eastern religious profile of many communes, the reemerging witchcraft cult, and the quasi-religious elements of the sensitivity group movement. While these proliferating cult structures incorporate only a small proportion of the religious population, their existence is enough to assure the maintenance of a de-bureaucratized religious tradition in the United States.

COMPARTMENTALIZATION AND SEGREGATION OF AMERICAN RELIGION

Religion in the United States, as in any modern system, is segregated from the economic and political spheres. Norms of the factory system and giant bureaucracies organize economic activity. With respect to the polity, religion has only a weak and indirect consequence for political processes. Religion and political party membership may be slightly correlated, but this is confounded by social-class variables (Williams, 1970:403; Yinger, 1970:416–456). Religion may have diffuse legitimating consequences for the polity, but these are minor in comparison to the consequences of law in this sphere.

Despite the massification of public (state) education, church schools and church-affiliated schools are still prominent in the United States educational subsystem. The most conspicuous linkage between religion and education is found in the Catholic parochial school system. While most of the curriculum in these schools is secular, imparting religious beliefs and rituals is still a major goal of these parochial schools. Since approximately two-thirds of Catholic children of elementary-school age and nearly one-half of those of secondary-school age attend a parochial school, the impact of religion on education remains significant—even in a highly modern society such as the United States. Jewish and Protestant education is less extensive than that of Catholicism. Conservative or fundamentalist Protestant cults and Orthodox Jewish organizations are the most likely to engage in formal education. However, the proportion of Protestant or Jewish children in religious schools is small, especially compared to the proportion of Catholic children.

The vast majority of American youth thus attend public schools where religious instruction is virtually nonexistent. Recently there has been a trend toward *objective* instruction about religion in schools, but this trend is only incipient. Thus religion remains segregated from most school structures in the United States. And even where churches directly control education, religious instruction tends to be segregated in time and perhaps in space from the regular, secular curriculum. Furthermore, since the state regulates and sets minimal standards for instruction in religious schools, religious instruction is forced to remain segregated from most of the curriculum. Therefore while religious teachings still permeate part of the educational subsystem, they remain somewhat segregated from many educational processes in both public and private church schools. Add to this the fact that higher education retains little affiliation with religion (except for certain small colleges and a few large universities), and the segregation of religion from education in the United States becomes even more evident.

The impact of religion on family processes is highly conspicuous in the United States, especially with respect to Catholicism and Judaism. These religions regulate many family patterns, including sex, birth control, number of children, the way children are raised, mate selection, and marriage. Except for fundamentalist cults, Protestantism exerts considerably less influence on family structure and processes in the United States. It is difficult to ascertain just how much religion influences family processes, since the lines of influence are often indirect, diffuse, and subtle. But the trend appears to be away from direct or indirect religious influence on family processes. Even though most children are baptized and most marriages are performed by religious officials, sex relations, the number of children in family, socialization, and mate selection are decreasingly influenced —in any far-reaching way—by the church (Salisbury, 1964:398–429; Berger, 1967:372–379).

But these facts reveal only a trend. Religion still exerts a considerable though decreasing influence on family processes (Lenski, 1963). In fact some commentators have argued that as religion increasingly becomes segregated from other institutional spheres, it attempts to expand its influence within the familial sphere (Berger, 1967:372). But it does so with a different emphasis. Rather than attempting to regulate and control family activities modern religion, it is asserted, attempts to occupy and guide the increased leisure time of modern families. American churches and synagogues are becoming vast and predominantly secular recreation centers attempting to satisfy the leisure needs of a diverse clientele—the young and old, married and unmarried, male and female. To the extent that this occurs, a shift in focus away from God, salvation, the supernatural, and scripture is inevitable. Although Orthodox Jewish, fundamentalist Protestant, and some Catholic cults have resisted this form of secularization, recreation appears to be increasingly the modal focus of American churches (Berger, 1963).

SECULARIZATION OF AMERICAN RELIGION

Aside from the increased emphasis on leisure time, there is further evidence of a trend toward secularization of American religion. Contrary to European trends (Wilson, 1969), secularization of American religion has not involved widespread antireligious attitudes or mass disaffection of church members (Williams, 1970:383–384). Rather there has been a slow and subtle but nevertheless profound shift in emphasis of most cult structures away from concern with salvation and reconciliation with the supernatural toward a concern with more secular and natural concerns: justice, self-realization, brotherhood, humanitarianism, civil rights, and fellowship. Specifically, American churches and synagogues now engage in such secular activities as recreation, welfare, community-action work, marriage and youth counseling, and individual and group psychotherapy (Berger, 1967). This emphasis represents an inherent potential in much Judeo-Christian religious dogma (O'Dea, 1966:86–90). But contrary to premodern and early modern religions, this secular focus and the emerging belief system surrounding it makes scant reference to God, the supernatural, salvation, divine intervention, and supernatural sanctions. This a reflection of the fact that the line between the supernatural and natural in modern religions becomes ambiguous and a matter for personal interpretation. Secular activities are pursued in the name of ethics and values that are not clearly attached to a transcendental entity or God. In many respects such deemphasis on the supernatural source of ethics has created a theological crisis in religion, which has resulted in a search for new foundations for modern theism (Williams, 1970:384; Dewart, 1966).

american religion: an overview

Religion in the United States is a vast conglomeration of large (denominations) and small (sects) cult structures. Whether large or small, most are ecclesiastic in that there is a division of religious labor and a bureaucratic form of organization. Most religious cults can be viewed as roughly clustering into one of three religious subsystems: Catholicism, Protestantism, or Judaism. However, there are many small cults dominated by other belief systems such as Buddhism, Islam, and Hinduism. Within each major religious subsystem — especially Protestantism and Judaism — there are a diversity of cult structures with divergent and flexible beliefs.

The Catholic religious subsystem is perhaps the closest approximation to a premodern religious system in the United States. Fundamentalistic (conservative) Protestantism and Orthodox Judaism also approximate a premodern and sometimes an early modern religious profile. Liberal Protestantism and Reform Judaism come close to displaying what we termed a modern profile. The very fact that many different types of religious subsystems from premodern to modern can exist within a highly developed society points to dangers inherent in our labels denoting religious types. If a religion labeled premodern can exist in a modern society without posing major problems, should we not also call it modern? In answer we should point out that we have not wanted to *evaluate* or pass judgment on religious types, but only to indicate that when change of a religion does occur, *it will occur in a predictable direction.* Our labels only represent signposts marking this direction. They do not imply that widely divergent types of religions could not exist within the same society. The fact that such religious pluralism exists with the United States attests to this. It also reveals, it can be argued, the high degree of segregation and compartmentalization of religion from the mainstream of social life in modern societies. Such religious pluralism is perhaps only possible when religions remain segregated and compartmentalized from economic, political, and legal institutions. Where this is not so, religious pluralism is likely to generate severe integrative strains and tensions in a society.

Finally we should note that American religion reveals trends toward de-systematization of beliefs (except for fundamentalist revivals), both de-bureaucratization *and* bureaucratization (denominational consolidation), segregation and compartmentalization, and secularization. With the exception of bureaucratization, where the trend is ambiguous, de-systematization, segregation, and secularization are likely to continue, to the extent that religions undergo any change in the United States.

SUMMARY

In this chapter we have too briefly covered an immensely complex topic—religion. We began by isolating out basic elements of all religion: the sacred, the supernatural, beliefs, rituals, and cult structures. Then we analyzed some of the consequences of religion for the broader society. These included: legitimating inequality, reinforcing institutional norms, regulating socialization and social placement, and alleviating anxiety. Later we noted that with modernization, religions come to have primary consequences only for alleviating anxiety.

A large portion of the chapter was spent documenting different types of religions in terms of their belief system and cult structures. From most traditional to most modern, we labeled these types: primitive shamanic, traditional communal, traditional ecclesiastic, premodern, early modern, and modern. It should be emphasized again that the labels for these types are not intended to be evaluative. Rather, they connote that to the extent that religions change, they are likely to do so in the direction implied by the ordering of these religions into types. However, such change is not inevitable nor is it necessarily continuous. Next we outlined several apparent trends of religious development. Again it should be noted that these are not inevitable; rather, they represent probable alterations in beliefs and cults given some degree of religious change.

Finally we examined the American religious subsystem, noting that it is composed of these constituent subsystems: Protestantism, Catholicism, and Judaism, as well as smaller sectlike cults. In examining these subsystems it became evident that religious pluralism is the most characteristic feature of American religion.

381

the
institutional
environment
of
RELIGION 13

Religious change and development do not occur in a social vacuum, for many of the trends documented in the previous chapter are adjustments to institutional processes that are external to religion. Much like kinship, religion is a conservative institution which undergoes alteration only under the impact of powerful social forces. Trends toward increasing de-systematization of beliefs, secularization, segregation, and compartmentalization of religion are therefore explicable only in terms of radical changes in the institutional environment. It is to this environment and its impact on religion that we now turn our attention.

ECONOMY AND RELIGION

The most critical variable in documenting the influence of the economy on religion is *technology*—or secular knowledge about how to manipulate the environment. Ultimately the level of technology affects the level of capital, the principles of economic organization, and the degree of access to natural resources possessed by a society (see Chapter 2). In turn the level of all these economic elements has far-reaching consequences for all institutions in a society. This we have already documented for kinship, education, law, and polity. Now we explore the impact of technology and the resulting organization of the economy on religion in traditional and modern societies.

economy and religion in traditional societies

Highly traditional economies exhibit low levels of technology. One result of this situation is low insulation from the vicissitudes of the natural environment which generates economic uncertainty and unpredictability. In such a technology vacuum, religious rituals assume a dominant place in economic activity, for by appealing to the supernatural to intervene through ritual activity much of the anxiety surrounding economic behavior is mitigated. For example, Malinowski (1955) noted that among the Trobriand Islanders, who engaged in dangerous deep-sea fishing, extensive magic (a form of ritual) was used to prevent disaster, with the result that much of the uncertainty and stress accompanying this dangerous economic activity was alleviated. Even though technology may have risen to a level eliminating the objective uncertainty of deep-sea fishing for the Trobriand Islanders, religious rituals persisted. This reveals that once initiated these religious rituals become *institutionalized*, even though the original conditions generating them have been eliminated or greatly altered (O'Dea, 1966:10). In fact the rituals may have actually increased the level of anxiety associated with economic tasks among the Trobriand Islanders (Radcliff-Brown, 1938). For us the crucial point is that in the absence of technology religion adds a sense of certainty and predictability and that this continues to be the case for a time once religious rituals become institutionalized.

Even in more advanced agrarian societies with an extensive technology religious rituals have similar consequences. For example, among the Dahomeans, who display certain features of a stable agrarian economy with a complex market structure, religious rituals are intimately involved in cultivation, harvesting, marketing, weaving, woodcarving, and ironworking (Goode, 1951:88–89). Through rituals, appeals to deities are made in order to assure success of parties engaged in the various kinds of tasks of the Dahomeans. This is true despite the fact that considerable technology is utilized in all phases of the Dahomean economy. However, with the emergence of an advanced agrarian economy, the prevalence of religious rituals in economic processes declines. The accumulation of technology, which is concerned with the *secular*, displaces religious beliefs and rituals, which are concerned with the *sacred*. Religion increasingly becomes segregated from technology (Wallace, 1966:257–259), particularly when secular services such as insurance and banking can alleviate much of the uncertainty in advanced agrarian economies.

Yet such initial segregation of religion from advanced agrarian economies should not be viewed as resulting in the decline of religion in society. The contrary appears to be the case, because with increased technology sufficient economic surplus exists to support elaborate ecclesiastic cult structures with an extensive professional clergy. Thus economic development has two seemingly contradictory consequences for religion. On the one hand, it increasingly excludes religious influence from the economy, while on the other hand, it provides the necessary economic surplus to support extensive ecclesiastic cult structures. With these elaborate cult structures of traditional ecclesiastic and premodern religions, systematization of religious beliefs and proliferation of the religious division of labor occurs. Without an extensive economic surplus, only shamanic and communal cult structures with shamans practicing magic are possible. But once economic development accelerates, technological expansion forces major alterations of religious beliefs and cult structures.

385

economy and religion in modern societies

Modern economies generate vast technologies which penetrate virtually every sphere of social life. Technological expansion becomes institutionalized into *science*. Scientific knowledge increasingly challenges religious beliefs, since the former relies upon "demonstrable proofs, perceptible by any normal human" (Wallace, 1966:261). Religion, on the other hand, is essentially nonempirical and relies upon faith and belief in the sacred and/or supernatural. As knowledge of the natural increases it inevitably must confront beliefs about the supernatural. Such confrontations are always won by science in the long run. And as the norms of science become codified into a quasi-belief system stressing the secular, religious beliefs concerning the supernatural become increasingly attenuated. God(s), pantheons, substantive beliefs about the supernatural, and rigid moral codes become displaced by a highly flexible belief system which includes at most a blurred distinction between natural and supernatural. Modern religions in attempting to reconcile beliefs to ever-expanding levels of technology begin to emphasize secular ethics and leave the working out of man's relation to the nonempirical to the *individual* (Wallace, 1966:382–384). Liberal Protestantism and Reform Judaism are the most conspicuous examples of such reconciliation (Salisbury, 1964). However, the very technology forcing the alteration of traditional religious beliefs ultimately supplies the vast economic surplus sustaining complex religious structures and organizations. Thus, despite the economy's consequences for the erosion of traditional religious beliefs, it can provide the surplus capable of supporting a vast religious bureaucracy, but at a price: de-systematization of beliefs, secularization, and segregation from most institutional spheres utilizing technology.

POLITY AND RELIGION

polity and religion in traditional societies

In highly traditional societies where stable leadership positions have emerged, political and religious role behaviors overlap. Those who perform religious rituals are also those who engage in societal decision making. For example, among the Tikopia, village and clan chiefs represented a link between secular and sacred activities. The chief, in Firth's words (1939), "is the bridge between kinship structure, the political organization, *the ritual*, and economic system. . . ." Chiefs represent the mouthpiece of gods with the supreme deity—Te Atria i Kafika—being the deity of the supreme chief of the island, Ari ki Kafika, and with local village and clan chiefs representing lesser gods (Goode, 1951:159). Thus chiefs are responsible for ritual activities in virtually all major spheres of social action.

Even in more advanced traditional societies where an elaborate kin-based or clear state-based political subsystem is differentiated from the rest of society, considerable structural overlap between religion and polity persists. Elite political positions are rationalized and legitimated as divine, while literate priests perform many of the administrative tasks of the state bureaucracy. Such a system was particularly evident in medieval China, where the Emperor was worshipped as a god, while state administrators (mandarins) were religious specialists and experts. A similar situation existed in much of feudal Europe, with the literate clergy performing many necessary administrative tasks for the polity. But despite such overlap between state and ecclesiastical bureaucracies, there is an inevitable source of strain and competition between the secular concerns of the state and sacred concerns of the church. Increasingly, as the state bureaucracy becomes involved in the secular tasks of allocating resources toward the attainment of goals, it must begin to usurp religious influence in the economy, family, education, and other spheres. And as the size of the state bureaucracy increases, this conflict between state and church intensifies.

Yet premodern religions are crucial in maintaining the legitimacy of the state-based polity. Even though the church bureaucracy and its specialists are increasingly segregated from the state bureaucracy, religion serves as the major source of legitimation for the polity (see Chapter 11). However, with further modernization new bases of political legitimation such as law and a civic culture are established and encouraged by the modernizing state. It is at this juncture that religion and the polity can come into conflict, with religious leaders withdrawing legitimacy and/or encouraging popular revolts. The state with its secularized administrative and military organizations is usually in a much better position to endure in such a conflict, although political instability may exist and persist for some time. Even with political instability the church rarely is able to assume any degree of political power. Rather, the church increasingly becomes segregated from or subordinate to the political subsystem.

polity and religion in modern societies

Modern societies exhibit a highly bureaucratized state. Religion in these systems no longer serves as either a principal legitimating or decision-making force. Incumbents are recruited to and promoted in the state bureaucracy on the basis of secular expertise. And the pervasive influence of the polity into a wide variety of spheres — the economic, familial, educational, and legal — reaches a level equal to that of religion in more traditional societies. With the ascendence of the polity in modern societies religion must accommodate itself with the state, rather than vice versa. Three patterns of accommodation are evident (Vernon, 1962:252–253):

1 The polity supports one group of cult structures over others.
2 The polity supports religion in general but displays no preferences.
3 The polity rejects religion and actively discriminates against all religions.

The first form of religious accommodation is most evident in societies with a state church such as the Catholic Church in France and the Church of England. In these cases the state endorses and supports the religious activities of these churches. In other modern societies the state church is less formally acknowledged but still given preferential treatment. This pattern exists with the Lutheran Church in Sweden and Norway as well as with Judaism in Israel. During early periods of development much religious tolerance and pluralism tend to become predominant in modern societies, although one church can maintain its favored position.

The second form of accommodation is the separation of church and state pattern most evident in the United States. This pattern was not intended (Williams, 1970:376), for the various cult structures originally established in the United States were hardly tolerant. For example, the Puritans came to America to set up a theocracy similar to that established by Calvin in Geneva, with church members holding secular authority (Vernon, 1962:255). Furthermore, religious persecution and killings were common in colonial America with, for instance, Quakers being put to death by Protestants. But the sheer diversity of religious groupings in the United States eventually resulted in the separation of church and state doctrine and in growing religious tolerance. Yet such tolerance, it should be emphasized, grew slowly out of a long period of religious conflict and persecution.

The third pattern of religious accommodation involves the polity's attempt to eliminate religion or at least greatly attenuate it. This pattern was most evident in postrevolutionary Russia where atheism was encouraged by the state. State persecution of all religion reached its peak during the late 1920s and early 1930s when church property was confiscated and a seven-day workweek was established to discourage traditional sabbath services, with days off adjusted to fall conveniently during midweek (Vernon, 1962:260). But since the early 1940s a more tolerant attitude of the Russian polity toward religion has been evident.

All these patterns of accommodation display a trend—the growing toleration of religion by the state and/or religious pluralism. This trend may not result in the complete separation of state and church or active state encouragement of religion, but it clearly reveals a growing tolerance of religion. One reason for increases in religious toleration results from the state's clear supremacy in modern societies. Religion no longer represents a threat because it has become so completely segregated from other institutional spheres or subordinated to the state in those spheres where both exert an influence. In a modern society it is hard to visualize an area of life where the state bureaucracy does not exert some and usually a great influence. The administrative linkages of the state to the economy, education, law, religion, and family are so vast as to make the question of competition between church and state simply nonexistent. Such a situation is the culmination of a long developmental trend: the emergence, proliferation, and eventual supremacy of the state bureaucracy. Just as technology is the single most important key to understanding the segregation of religion from the economy, political bureaucratization is the most important force in understanding the segregation of the church from the political life of a society.

LAW AND RELIGION

In Chapter 9 we pointed to the interaction between law and religion. We outlined processes leading to the increasing displacement of religion by law as the major integrating and coordinating institution in modern societies. In this section we will simply repeat this statement by noting a few important stages in this process. In traditional societies law often codifies and reinforces existing religious beliefs. Law and religion thus overlap. But as these institutions differentiate out from one another with modernization, many specific and secular problems of coordination, control, legitimation, and syncronization emerge. These problems become intensified with further internal differentiation of societal subsystems such as the economy and polity. Religious beliefs and rituals directed toward the supernatural are simply inadequate to provide the basis for integration and coordination in a highly differentiated and differentiating social system. Integrative problems are too specific, secular, variable, and ever expanding. Courts enacting common-law precedents in response to specific sources of malintegration or legislatures enacting bodies of civil laws represent more rapid, efficient, and relevant solutions to these problems of coordination than do religious beliefs which are always difficult to change. While religious values codified into moral codes may underlie and reinforce a myriad of specific secular laws, the church's codes, dogmas, and rituals cease to have in modern societies the massive consequences for social control and coordination they have in traditional systems. Such a decrease marks the increasing compartmentalization of religion in modern societies. Thus legal evolution might be viewed as a process of institutional invasion and succession of an emerging legal subsystem into a sphere which at one time was dominated—but never monopolized—by religion. Once law is firmly established it comes to have far-reaching consequences in regulating economic activity (entrepreneurship), political legitimation, reinforcing crucial socialization norms within kinship, controlling education and *rites de passage* in them (e.g., compulsory education laws), relations among individuals, and relations between individuals and the state.

We should not, however, view law as completely displacing religion as a force of social control and integration. For many segments of the population in modern societies religious beliefs and rituals are perhaps more salient than the laws, codes, and statutes of the legal system. Furthermore, some commentators have noted the increasingly religious profile in terms of ideologies, beliefs, symbols, and spokesmen of several conspicuous social movements, such as the civil rights and peace movements in the United States. These movements reveal that religion or at least a kind of religiosity has considerable power to unite and integrate masses in the population of a modern society. And frequently the goals of these movements — such as the abolition-of-the-draft movement in the United States — confront and call into question legal structures and processes in modern societies. Yet these sporadic movements which have at least nominally religious overtones cannot be viewed as a major source of societal integration or control; and when compared to the pervasive and paninstitutional influence of religion in traditional societies, the institutional segregation of religion in modern societies becomes abundantly clear.

EDUCATION AND RELIGION

The intimate relationship between education and religion in traditional societies has already been examined in Chapters 6 and 7. In all probability the first formal educational structures with clear-cut teacher and student roles were religious and involved the imparting of crucial religious beliefs. Education in highly traditional societies thus stores — and hence preserves — the pantheon, myths, substantive beliefs, values, and rituals of traditional religions by allowing for their dissemination from one generation of elite religious practitioners such as shamans, diviners, witch doctors, and priests to another. While much of such storage and dissemination occurs within kinship, formal education becomes evident as cult structures require professional religious specialists.

In more advanced and modernizing traditional societies, new structural conditions can cause drastic alterations in the profile of education. These conditions include: First, the emerging state polity must secure a new, nonreligious basis of legitimation. This involves the creation, storage, and transmission of a secular political culture. Second, skilled workers are required for performing the expanding administrative tasks of the state bureaucracy. And third, as the economy modernizes, demands for a mass and skilled labor force increase, as do those for rapid technological expansion. These structural pressures initiate both secularization and massification of education. Rather than storing religious beliefs and then disseminating them to religious elites, educational structures begin to store and disseminate secular cultural components such as technology and a political culture, while imparting to the masses crucial work skills.

With further modernization educational structures come to have far-reaching consequences for storage and dissemination not only of vast secular culture but also for cultural expansion and innovation, social placement, and social transformation (see Chapter 6). These expanded consequences are a direct result of intensified pressures for technology, political indoctrination, and a skilled work force. As the culture of a society becomes secularized, school curricula in storing and disseminating culture also become almost totally secular. As a massive and skilled work force is needed to staff the giant secular bureaucracies of the economy, polity, education, religion, and a host of professions, the schools in a society become secularized and massified. They also become critical in screening, sorting, allocating, and eventually inserting people into positions in the broader society. And as political legitimation becomes increasingly the result of a secular political culture, the state increasingly assumes control of school structures in order to assure proper indoctrination into a civic culture.

These trends culminate in modern societies where education is secular, mass, state controlled, and crucial for socialization, social placement, and cultural storage, expansion, and dissemination. These trends result in the further segregation and compartmentalization of religious beliefs and rituals in a modern society. With a largely secular curriculum and with state control of schools, religion becomes highly segregated from a sphere it dominated in traditional systems. Even in church schools the state controls the curriculum (through certification and accreditation powers), with the result that religious education becomes compartmentalized from a predominantly secular curriculum. And the fact that secular skills are the only skills widely marketable in a modern society further pressures religious schools to secularize. Thus as education becomes a pivotal institution in a society, it either displaces religious education or forces it to become increasingly secular. As this occurs, maintaining traditional beliefs and ritual patterns becomes difficult. Notions of God, the supernatural, salvation, myths, pantheons, and substantive beliefs must be adjusted to the predominantly secular training occurring in schools. If traditional religious beliefs and rituals are maintained, then they become clearly segregated in time and space from secular educational activities. In either case the overall impact of religion in people's daily lives has been decreased.

KINSHIP AND RELIGION

In traditional societies religion and kinship are closely interconnected. Frequently kin leaders are also religious elites and much ritual activity is performed by family members—especially in systems with no developed ecclesiastic cults. Thus kin groups provide the structural locus as well as ritual leaders necessary for engaging in religious activity. In such systems kinship also provides for the transmission and continuity of religious beliefs and rituals from one generation to another. In systems without formal instruction by designated and specialized religious teachers, this becomes a crucial consequence of kinship in maintaining the religious subsystem. Sometimes the influence of kinship structures on religion is subtle, as illustrated by Goode's (1951:218) observation that the hierarchical structure of traditional kinship systems (authority and descent rules) can have the consequences of reinforcing the emerging hierarchy of the natural and supernatural, the pantheon, and cult structure where specialized religious roles are just becoming evident.

Even in more advanced traditional systems where ecclesiastic cults dominate and where many religious rituals are performed outside kinship in temples by religious specialists, kinship socialization not only generates a committed membership, but also reinforces those rituals performed in temples. Often this is done through the performance of minor rituals—such as praying—by kinship leaders. Perhaps the most vital consequence of kinship on a religion displaying ecclesiastic cults and religious specialists is financial: Members of kin groups donate the economic surplus needed to support nonworking religious specialists. Even where religious cults own considerable property, the rank-and-file membership is always largely responsible for supporting a separate and autonomous religious subsystem. Usually the very act of giving such support is ritualized and rationalized by beliefs so that donating surplus reinforces commitment to a particular religious system.

In modern societies where massive institutional and cultural changes have forced drastic changes in the profile of religion, it would be expected that the interconnections between religion and kinship would also be altered. Family socialization and minor ritual activity still generate some commitment to and partially reinforce religious beliefs, but probably not to the extent revealed in traditional societies. A reflection of this fact is the greatly altered relationship between churches and their clientele. Increasingly, as the broader society becomes secularized and as the members of a society have vast amounts of leisure time, churches are no longer guaranteed a clientele. In traditional societies where little leisure exists and where religion and family are closely interconnected, membership is virtually automatic. But with modernization, organized religion confronts a competitive market situation (Berger, 1967). It must compete with a myriad of secular, leisure-time enterprises. And it operates under the handicap of a long legacy of religious beliefs and ritual practices that are irrelevant to much of the everyday life of people in modern societies. Furthermore organized religion must now appeal to a diversity of interests and needs not only between but within families. Coupled with this is the fact that most of these diverse family needs and interests are secular. Such a situation has forced many changes in religious beliefs, rituals, and cult organization. These changes are necessary by virtue of the fact that the family and its leisure time represent one of the last remaining institutional spheres in which religion is still capable of exerting a pervasive influence.

The de-systematization of belief systems in religions is largely a response to the secular interests and needs of the modern family. Rigid distinctions between the natural and supernatural as well as elaborate pantheons, myths, and moral codes become unmarketable in the secular, leisure-time sphere of the modern family. With the abandonment of the extensive belief systems of premodern religions, religious ritual activity becomes curtailed and churches begin to become involved in a wide variety of secular activities, such as recreation, community work, and counseling. All of these are designed to meet the needs of clientele of different ages, sex, marital status, and ideological persuasion. Not unlike a conglomerate business corporation, modern religious cults diversify their product in the ever-expanding and diverse family leisure time market (Berger, 1963; 1967:374–375). As the degree of competitiveness in this market increases, de-systematization of church beliefs will accelerate.

RELIGION IN THE FUTURE

In closing this chapter it is appropriate to ask: if trends toward de-systematization and secularization of religion continue, will modern religion really be religion? Will concern with the sacred and supernatural cease to be the basic postulate of churches? Will churches become just another secular, leisure-time enterprise? If segregation and compartmentalization of religion from all but a few family activities occur, will religion cease to be sufficiently pervasive and relevant to system-survival problems to be considered an institution? The answers to such questions in the short run are certainly negative; but in the long run we may have to radically change our definition of religion.

Most likely the profile of future religions will lack beliefs about the supernatural. Beliefs about the supernatural will probably continue to erode with the increasing accumulation of secular knowledge.

The supernatural may in Wallace's words (1966) become an "interest-ing historical memory." Since we have viewed a concern for the super-natural as a basic element of premodern and modern religion, religion will certainly be altered. But the elaborate ecclesiastical cult structures and residual beliefs that have relevance to secular activities will prob-ably persist. And they will not represent empty hulks and skeletons of the past. Rather, cult structures will likely contain and promote beliefs about personal adjustment, societal and world goals, and the utilization of science and technology to the host of desirables. Such desirable goals will revolve around the elimination of major world social problems: population control, ecological disruption, intergroup conflict, mental illness, poverty, hunger, and the like. These secular activities mark only the incipiency of a growing trend. In this process conceptions of the supernatural will give way to a nontheistic theology (Wallace, 1966:267) — one without gods and intervening forces. Yet myths about secular heroes, pantheons of great men, and a secular code will in all likelihood replace the supernatural cosmologies of current religions. To reinforce a secular belief system, rituals per-formed by a quasi-clergy in temples will persist and notions of the sacred will remain. Such rituals will reaffirm the tenets and goals of the belief system while distinguishing the sacred from the profane.

Such a portrayal of future religion is naturally guesswork. Yet in the current trends of de-systematization and secularization, the incipient form of future religion is perhaps revealed. As to whether or not a secular belief system and secular involvement of cult struc-tures into many spheres will reverse current trends of segregation and compartmentalization is an open question. It seems likely, however, that such a reversal is indeed probable — especially if the secular belief system of future religions, coupled with notions of the sacred, is held as fervently and as deeply as current cosmic belief systems about the supernatural.

SUGGESTED READINGS

Peter Berger, "Religious Institutions," in N. J. Smelser (ed.), *Sociology*, New York: John Wiley & Sons, Inc., 1967.

N. J. Demerath, and Philip E. Hammond, *Religion in Social Context: Tradition and Transition*, New York: Random House, Inc., 1969.

William J. Goode, *Religion among the Primitives*, Glencoe, Ill.: The Free Press, 1951.

William G. McLoughlin and Robert N. Bellah (eds.), *Religion in Amer-ica*, Boston: Beacon Press, 1968.

David O. Moberg, *The Church as a Social Institution*, Englewood Cliffs, N.J.: Prentice-Hall, Inc., 1962.

Thomas F. O'Dea, *The Sociology of Religion*, Englewood Cliffs, N.J.: Prentice-Hall, Inc., 1966.

——, *Sociology and the Study of Religion*, New York: Basic Books, Inc., Publishers, 1970.

Rodney Stark and Charles Y. Glock, *American Piety: The Nature of Religious Commitment*, Berkeley: University of California Press, 1968.

Guy E. Swanson, *The Birth of the Gods; The Origins of Primitive Beliefs*, Ann Arbor: The University of Michigan Press, 1967.

Anthony F. C. Wallace, *Religion, An Anthropological View*, New York: Random House, Inc., 1966.

Bryan Wilson, *Religion in Secular Society*, Baltimore: Penguin Books, Inc., 1969.

the
institutional
environment
of
RELIGION

Abrahamson, M.: "Correlates of Political Complexity," *American Sociological Review*, 34, 1969, pp. 690–701.

Agger, R. E., D. Goldrich, and B. E. Swanson: *The Rulers and the Ruled*, (New York, John Wiley & Sons, Inc., 1964).

Alford, R.: *Party and Society*, (Chicago, Rand McNally & Company, 1963).

Allott, A.: *Essays in African Law*, [London, Butterworth & Co. (Publishers), Ltd., 1960].

Almond, G.: "Comparative Political Systems," *Journal of Politics*, 18, 1956, pp. 391–409.

—— and S. Verba: *The Civic Culture*, (Princeton, N.J., Princeton University Press, 1963).

Apter, D. E.: *The Gold Coast in Transition*, (Princeton, N.J., Princeton University Press, 1955).

Atkinson, J. W. (ed.): *Motives in Fantasy, Action and Society*, (Princeton, N.J., D. Van Nostrand Company, Inc., 1958).

Auerbach, C. A., L. Garrison, W. Hurst, and S. Mermin: *The Legal Process*, (San Francisco, Chandler Publishing Company, 1961).

Bazelon, D. T.: *The Paper Economy*, (New York, Random House, Inc., 1959).

Becker, H.: *Through Values to Social Interpretation*, (Durham, N.C., Duke University Press, 1950).

Beer, S. H.: "The Analysis of Political Systems," in S. Beer and A. B. Olam (eds.), *Patterns of Government*, (New York, Random House, Inc., 1962).

Bell, N. W., and S. F. Vogel: *A Modern Introduction to the Family*, (New York, The Free Press, 1968).

Bellah, R. N.: "Ienaga Saburo and the Search for Meaning in Modern Japan," in M. Jansen (ed.), *Japanese Attitudes Toward Modernization*, (Princeton, N.J., Princeton University Press, 1966).

——: "Civil Religion in America," *Daedalus*, 96, 1967, pp. 1–27.

——: "Religious Evolution," *American Sociological Review*, 29, 1964, pp. 358–374.

Belshaw, C. S.: *Traditional Exchange and Modern Markets*, (Englewood Cliffs, N.J., Prentice-Hall, Inc., 1965).

Berger, P.: "A Market Model for the Analysis of Ecumenicity," *Social Research*, 5, 1963, pp. 21–34.

Berman, H.: *Justice in the U.S.S.R.*, (New York, Vintage Books, Random House, Inc., 1950).

bibliography

—— and W. Greiner: *The Nature and Functions of Law*, 2d ed., (New York, Brooklyn Foundation Press, 1966).

Bertalanffy, C.: "General Systems Theory," *General Systems Yearbook*, 1, 1956, pp. 1–16.

Bertrand, A. L.: "A Structural Analysis of Differential Patterns of Social Relations: A Role Theory Perspective for Rural Sociology," *Rural Sociology*, 33, 1968, pp. 411–423.

Bidwell, C.: "The School as a Formal Organization," in J. G. March (ed.), *Handbook of Social Organization*, (Chicago, Rand McNally & Company, 1965).

Blau, P.: *Bureaucracy in Modern Society*, (New York, Random House, Inc., 1956).

—— and O. D. Duncan: *The American Occupational Structure*, (New York, John Wiley & Sons, Inc., 1967).

Blisten, D. R.: *The World of the Family*, (New York, Random House, Inc., 1963).

Blood, R. O., and R. L. Hamblin: "The Effects of Wives' Employment on the Family Power," in N. W. Bell and E. F. Vogel (eds.), *A Modern Introduction to the Family*, (New York, The Free Press, 1960).

Bohannan, P.: *Africa and Africans*, (Garden City, N.Y., American Museum Science Books, 1964).

Bohannan, P. T., and K. Hickleberry: "Institutions of Divorce, Family and Law," *Law and Society Review*, 2, 1967, pp. 81–102.

Bouquet, A. C.: *Comparative Religion*, (Baltimore, Penguin Books, Inc., 1941).

Bredemeier, H. C.: "Law as an Integrative Institution," in W. Evan (ed.), *Law and Sociology, Exploratory Essays*, (New York, The Free Press, 1962).

Brinton, C.: *The Anatomy of Revolution*, (New York, Random House, Inc., 1965).

Bronfenbrenner, U.: "Soviet Methods of Character Education," in R. J. Havighurst (ed.), *Comparative Perspectives on Education*, (Boston, Little, Brown and Company, 1968).

Brzezinski, Z., and S. Huntington: *Political Power: USA/USSR*, (New York, The Viking Press, Inc., 1965).

Buck, G. L., and A. L. Jacobson: "Social Evolution and Structural-Functional Analysis: An Empirical Test," *American Sociological Review*, 33, 1968, pp. 343–355.

Buckley, W.: *Sociology and Modern Systems Theory*, (Englewood Cliffs, N.J., Prentice-Hall, Inc., 1967).

Callahan, R. E.: *Education and the Cult of Efficiency*, (Chicago, The University of Chicago Press, 1962).

Carlston, K. S.: *Law and Organization in World Society*, (Urbana, The University of Illinois Press, 1962).

Cavan, R. S.: *The American Family*, (New York, Thomas Y. Crowell Company, 1969).

Chagnon, N. A.: *Yanomanö: The Fierce People*, (New York, Holt, Rinehart and Winston, Inc., 1968).

Chin, R.: "The Utility of Systems Models and Developmental Models for Practitioners," in Bennis, Benne, and Chin (eds.), *The Planning of Change*, (New York, Holt, Rinehart and Winston, Inc., 1964).

Chinoy, E.: *Society, An Introduction to Sociology*, 2d ed., (New York, Random House, Inc., 1967).

Cicourel, A. V., and J. I. Kitsuse: *The Educational Decision-Makers*, (Indianapolis, The Bobbs-Merrill Company, Inc., 1963).

Clark, B. R.: "Sociology of Education," in E. L. Favis (ed.), *Handbook of Modern Sociology*, (Chicago, Rand McNally & Company, 1964).

——: *Educating the Expert Society*, (San Francisco, Chandler Publishing Company, 1962).

——: *The Open Door College: A Case Study*, (New York, McGraw-Hill Book Company, 1960).

—— and M. A. Trow: "The Organizational Context," in T. M. Newcomb and E. K. Wilson (eds.), *College Peer Groups*, (Chicago, Aldine Publishing Company, 1966).

Clark, C.: *The Economics of 1960*, (London, Macmillan & Co., Ltd., 1942).

Cole, C.: *The Economic Fabric of Society*, (New York, Harcourt Brace Jovanovich, Inc., 1969).

Coleman, J. S.: *The Adolescent Society*, (New York, The Free Press, 1961).

—— (ed.): *Education and Political Development*, (Princeton, N.J., Princeton University Press, 1965).

——: "Current Political Movements in Africa," *The Annals*, 298, 1955, pp. 201–212.

Coombs, P. H.: *The World Educational Crisis: A Systems Analysis*, (New York, Oxford University Press, 1968).

Corwin, R. G.: *A Sociology of Education*, (New York, Appleton-Century-Crofts, Inc., 1965).

Coser, L. (ed.): *Political Sociology*, (New York, Harper & Row, Publishers, Incorporated, 1965).

Cranner, J. F., and G. S. Browne: *Comparative Education*, (New York, Harcourt Brace Jovanovich, Inc., 1965).

Dahl, R. A.: *Who Governs?*, (New Haven, Conn., Yale University Press, 1961).

Dahrendorf, R.: "Out of Utopia: Toward a Reorientation of Sociological Analysis," *American Journal of Sociology*, 74, 1958, pp. 115–127.

Davies, J. C.: "The Family's Role in Political Socialization," *The Annals of the American Academy of Political and Social Science,* CCCLXI, 1965.

——: "Toward a Theory of Revolution," *American Sociological Review,* 27, 1962, pp. 5–19.

Davis, F. J. et al.: *Society and the Law,* (New York, The Free Press, 1962).

Davis, K.: *Human Society,* (New York, the Macmillan Company, 1949)

Davis, K. D.: "The Sociology of Parent-Youth Conflict," *American Sociological Review,* 5, 1940, pp. 480–492.

Dawson, R. E., and K. Prewitt: *Political Socialization,* (Boston, Little, Brown and Company, 1969).

Demerath, N. J., and P. E. Hammond: *Religion in Social Context,* (New York, Random House, Inc., 1969).

Dewart, L.: *The Future of Belief: Theism in a World Come of Age,* (New York, Herder and Herder, Inc., 1966).

DeWitt, N.: *Education and Professional Employment in the U.S.S.R.,* (Washington, D.C., National Science Foundation, 1961).

Diamond, A. S.: *The Evolution of Law and Order,* (London, C. A. Watts and Co., Ltd., 1951).

Dillenberger, J., and C. Welch: *Protestant Christianity,* (New York, Charles Scribner's Sons, 1959).

Domhoff, G. W.: *Who Rules America,* (Englewood Cliffs, N.J., Prentice-Hall, Inc., 1967).

Dror, Y.: "Law and Social Change," in R. J. Simon (ed.), *The Sociology of Law,* (San Francisco, Chandler Publishing Company, 1968).

Drucker, P.: *Landmarks of Tomorrow,* (New York, Harper & Row, Publishers, Incorporated, 1959).

Duncan, O. D.: "Social Organization and the Eco-system," in R. E. Faris (ed.), *Handbook of Modern Sociology,* (Chicago, Rand McNally & Company, 1964).

Durkheim, E.: *The Division of Labor in Society,* (New York, The Macmillan Company, 1933).

——: *The Elementary Forms of Religious Life, a Study in Religious Sociology,* J. W. Swain (trans.), (London, George Allen and Unwin, Ltd., 1912).

Duverger, M.: *Political Parties: Their Organization and Activity in the Modern State,* B. North and R. North (trans.), (New York, John Wiley & Sons, Inc., 1954).

Dynes, R. D., A. C. Clarke, S. Dinitz, and I. Ishino: *Social Problems,* (New York, Oxford University Press, 1964).

Easton, D.: *A Systems Analysis of Political Life,* (New York, John Wiley & Sons, Inc., 1965).

Ehrlich, E.: *Fundamental Principles of the Sociology of Law*, (Cambridge, Mass., Harvard University Press, 1936).

Eisenstadt, S. I.: "Social Institutions," *International Encyclopedia of the Social Sciences*, vol. 14, (New York, The Macmillan Company, 1968).

Eisenstadt, S. N.: *From Generation to Generation*, (New York, The Free Press, 1956).

Eschleman, J. F.: *Perspectives in Marriage and the Family*, (Boston, Allyn and Bacon, Inc., 1969).

Evan, W. M.: *Law and Sociology*, (New York, The Free Press, 1962).

Farber, F.: *Family: Organization and Interaction*, (San Francisco, Chandler Publishing Company, 1964).

Firth, R.: "Family in Tikopia," in M. F. Nimkoff (ed.), *Comparative Family Systems*, (Boston, Houghton Mifflin Company, 1965).

——: *Primitive Polynesian Economy*, (London, Routledge & Kegan Paul, Ltd., 1939).

——: *We, the Tikopia*, (New York, American Book Company, 1936).

Fried, M. H.: *The Evolution of Political Society*, (New York, Random House, Inc., 1967).

Friedmann, W.: *Law in a Changing Society*, (Berkeley, University of California Press, 1959).

Furstenberg, F. F.: "Industrialization and the American Family," *American Sociological Review*, 31, 1968, pp. 326–337.

Geertz, C. (ed.): *Old Societies and New States: The Quest for Modernity in Asia and Africa*, (New York, The Free Press, 1963).

Glaser, N.: *American Judaism*, (Chicago, The University of Chicago Press, 1957).

Glock, C. Y.: "The Role of Deprivation in the Origin and Evolution of Religious Groups," in R. Lee and M. Marty (eds.), *Religion and Social Conflict*, (New York, Oxford University Press, 1964).

—— and R. Stark: *Religion and Society in Tension*, (Chicago, Rand McNally & Company, 1965).

Gluckman, M.: *Order and Rebellion in Tribal Africa*, (New York, the Macmillan Company, 1963).

Goldschmidt, W.: *Man's Way: A Preface to the Understanding of Human Society*, (New York, Holt, Rinehart & Winston, Inc, 1959).

Goldsen, R. K. et al.: *What College Students Think*, (Princeton, N.J., D. Van Nostrand Company, Inc., 1960).

Goldstein, J., and J. Katz: *The Family and the Law*, (New York, The Free Press, 1965).

Goode, W. J.: *The Family*, (Englewood Cliffs, N.J., Prentice-Hall, Inc., 1964).

——: *Religion Among the Primitives*, (New York, The Free Press, 1951).

——: *World Revolution and Family Patterns*, (New York, The Free Press, 1963).

Goslin, D. A.: *The School in Contemporary Society*, (Glenview, Ill., Scott, Foresman and Company, 1965).

Greenstein, F. I.: "The Benevolent Leader: Children's Images of Political Authority," *American Political Science Review*, LIV, 1960, pp. 934–943.

Gurvitch, G.: *Sociology of Law*, (London, Routledge & Kegan Paul, Ltd., 1953).

Haire, M.: "Biological Models and Empirical History of the Growth of Organizations," in M. Haire (ed.), *Modern Organization Theory*, (New York, John Wiley & Sons, Inc., 1959).

Hall, A. D., and R. C. Fagen: "Definition of System," *General Systems Yearbook*, 1, 1956, pp. 19–28.

Halsey, A. H.: "The Sociology of Education," in N. J. Smelser (ed.), *Sociology*, (New York, John Wiley & Sons, Inc., 1967).

——, J. Floud, and C. A. Anderson (eds.): *Education, Economy, and Society*, (New York, The Free Press, 1961).

Harrington, M.: *The Retail Clerks*, (New York, John Wiley & Sons, Inc., 1962).

Havighurst, R. J., and B. L. Neugarten: *Society and Education*, 3d ed., (Boston, Allyn and Bacon, Inc., 1967).

Hazard, J. W.: *Law and Social Change in the U.S.S.R.*, (Toronto, The Carswell Co., 1953).

Herskovits, M. J.: *Dahomey*, (Locust Valley, N.Y., J. J. Augustin, Publisher, 1938).

—— and F. S.: "An Outline of Dahomean Religious Belief," *Memoirs of the American Anthropological Association*, 41, 1933.

Hess, R. D., and D. Easton: "The Child's Changing Image of the President," *Public Opinion Quarterly*, XXIV, 1960, pp. 632–644.

—— and J. V. Torney: *The Development of Political Attitudes in Children*, (Chicago, Aldine Publishing Company, 1967).

Hirsch, W., *Scientists in American Society*, (New York, Random House, Inc., 1966).

Hoebel, E. A.: *The Law of Primitive Man*, (New York, Atheneum Publishers, 1954).

Holmberg, A.: *Nomads of the Long Bow: The Siriono of Eastern Bolivia*, (Smithsonian Institution, Institute of Social Anthropology, publication no. 10, 1950).

Holtzman, A.: *Interest Groups and Lobbying*, (New York, The Macmillan Company, 1966).

Homans, G. C.: "Bringing Men Back In," *American Sociological Review*, 29, 1964, pp. 809–818.

Hordern, W.: *A Layman's Guide to Protestant Theology*, (New York, The Macmillan Company, 1957).

Hoselitz, B. F., and W. E. Moore: *Industrialization and Society*, (New York, Unesco, 1963).

Howard, C. G., and R. Summers: *Law: Its Nature, Functions and Limits*, (Englewood Cliffs, N. J., Prentice-Hall, Inc., 1965).

Hunter, F.: *Top Leadership, U.S.A.*, (Chapel Hill, N. C., University of North Carolina Press, 1959).

Hyman, H. H.: *Political Socialization*, (New York, The Free Press, 1959).

Johnson, H. M.: *Sociology: A Systematic Introduction*, (New York, Harcourt Brace Jovanovich, Inc., 1960).

Kampin, F.: *Legal History: Law and Social Change*, (Englewood Cliffs, N.J., Prentice-Hall, Inc., 1963).

Karlen, H. M.: *The Pattern of American Government*, (New York, Glencoe Press, The Macmillan Company, 1968).

Karlsson, G.: "Political Attitudes Among Male Swedish Youth," *Acta Sociologica*, 3, 1958, pp. 220–241.

Kerr, C.: *The Uses of the University*, (Cambridge, Mass., Harvard University Press, 1963).

Key, V. O., Jr.: *Politics, Parties, and Pressure Groups*, 3d ed., (New York, Thomas Y. Crowell Company, 1952).

——: *Public Opinion and American Democracy*, (New York, Alfred A. Knopf, Inc., 1961).

Kirkpatrick, C.: "Ethical Inconsistencies in Marriage," *International Journal of Ethics*, 46, 1935, pp. 444–460.

Kluckhohn, C.: "The Study of Culture," in D. Lerner and H. Lasswell (eds.), *The Policy Sciences*, (Stanford, Calif., Stanford University Press, 1951).

——: "Variations in the Human Family," in N. Bell and E. Vogel (eds.), *A Modern Introduction to the Family*, (New York, The Free Press, 1960).

Kornhauser, W.: "Political Man," in L. Broom and P. Selznick, *Sociology*, (New York, Harper & Row, Publishers, Incorporated, 1963).

Kroeber, A. L.: *The Nature of Culture*, (Chicago, The University of Chicago Press, 1952).

——: "Diffusionism," in the *Encyclopedia of the Social Sciences*, III, (New York, The Macmillan Company, 1937).

——: "Yurok Law," *22d International Congress of Americanists*, 1924.

LaPiere, R. T.: *Social Change*, (New York, McGraw-Hill Book Company, 1965).

Lenski, G.: *Human Societies*, (New York, McGraw-Hill Book Company, 1970).

——: *Power and Privilege*, (New York, McGraw-Hill Book Company, 1966).

——: *The Religious Factor: A Sociologist's Inquiry*, (Garden City, N.Y., Anchor Books, Doubleday & Company, Inc., 1963).

Lessa, W., and E. Vogt (eds.): *Reader in Comparative Religion*, (Evanston, Ill., Row, Peterson & Company, 1958).

LeVine, R.: "Political Socialization and Cultural Change," in C. Geertz (ed.), *Old Societies and New States,* (New York, The Free Press, 1963).

Lipset, S. M.: "Political Sociology," in N. J. Smelser (ed.), *Sociology,* (New York, John Wiley & Sons, Inc., 1967).

———: *Political Man,* (New York, Doubleday and Company, 1960).

——— and E. Raab: "The Non-Generation Gap," *Commentary,* 50, 1970, pp. 35–39.

Litwak, E.: "Geographic Mobility and Extended Family Cohesion," *American Sociological Review,* 25, 1960, pp. 385–394.

Llewellyn, K. N., and E. A. Hoebel: *The Cheyenne Way,* (Norman, The University of Oklahoma Press, 1941).

Lloyd, D.: *The Idea of Law,* (Baltimore, Penguin Books, Inc., 1964).

Loftland, J., and R. Stark: "Becoming a World-Saver: A Theory of Conversion to a Deviant Perspective," *American Sociological Review,* 30, 1965, pp. 862–874.

Long, N. E.: *The Polity,* (Chicago, Rand McNally & Company, 1962).

Lowi, T. J.: *The End of Liberalism,* (New York, W. W. Norton & Co., Inc., 1969).

Lowie, R. H.: *Social Organization,* (New York, Holt, Rinehart and Winston, Inc., 1966).

———: *Primitive Religion,* (New York, Boni and Liveright, 1948).

Luckman, T.: "On Religion in Modern Society," *Journal for the Scientific Study of Religion,* Spring, 1963.

Machlup, F.: *The Production and Distribution of Knowledge in the United States,* (Princeton, N.J., Princeton University Press, 1962).

Madsen, K. B.: *Theories of Motivation,* (Cleveland, Howard Allen, Inc., 1964).

Malinowski, B.: *Magic, Science, and Religion,* (Garden City, N.Y., Doubleday and Company, 1955). Originally published in 1925.

Mann, F. C., and R. L. Hoffman: *Man and Automation,* (New Haven, Conn., The Technology Project, Yale University, 1956).

Martin, T. W.: "Social Institutions: A Reformation of the Concept," *Pacific Sociological Review,* 2, 1968, pp. 100–109.

Marx, K., and F. Engels: "Manifesto of the Communist Party," in L. S. Feuer (ed.), *Marx and Engels, Basic Writings on Politics and Philosophy,* (Garden City, N.Y., Anchor Books, Doubleday and Company, 1959). Originally published in 1848.

Massell, G. J.: "Law as an Instrument of Revolutionary Change in a Traditional Milieu: The Case of Soviet Central Asia," *Law and Society Review,* 2, 1968, pp. 179–228.

Mayers, L.: *The Machinery of Justice: An Introduction to Legal Structure and Process,* (Englewood Cliffs, N.J., Prentice-Hall, Inc., 1963).

———: *The American Legal System,* (New York, Harper & Row, Publishers, Incorporated, 1954).

McClelland, D. C., J. W. Atkinson, T. H. Clark, and H. Lowell: *The Achievement Motive*, (New York, Appleton-Century-Crofts, Inc., 1953).

McClosky, H., and H. E. Dahlgren: "Primary Group Influence on Party Loyalty," *American Political Science Review*, LIII, 1959, pp. 757–776.

McIntyre, J.: "The Structural-Functional Approach to Family Study," in F. I. Nye and F. M. Berardo (eds.), *Emerging Conceptual Frameworks in Family Analysis*, (New York, The Macmillan Company, 1966).

Meier, R.: *Science and Economic Development: New Patterns of Living*, (New York, John Wiley & Sons, Inc., 1956).

Merton, R. K.: *Social Theory and Social Structure*, (Glencoe, Ill., The Free Press, 1957).

Miller, D. R., and G. E. Swanson: *The Changing American Parent*, (New York, John Wiley & Sons, Inc., 1958).

Mills, C. W.: *The Power Elite*, (New York, Oxford University Press, 1956).

——: *White Collar*, (New York, Oxford University Press, 1951).

Mitchell, W. C.: *Sociological Analysis and Politics*, (Englewood Cliffs, N.J., Prentice-Hall, Inc., 1967).

Moberg, D. O.: *The Church as a Social Institution*, (Englewood Cliffs, N.J., Prentice-Hall, Inc., 1962).

Monsen, R. J., Jr., and M. W. Cannon: *The Makers of Public Policy, American Power Groups and Their Ideologies*, (New York, McGraw-Hill Book Company, 1965).

Moore, W. E.: "Economic and Professional Institutions," in N. J. Smelser (ed.), *Sociology*, (New York, John Wiley & Sons, Inc., 1967).

——: *Order and Change: Essays in Comparative Sociology*, (New York, John Wiley & Sons, Inc., 1967).

——: *The Conduct of the Corporation*, (New York, Random House, Inc., 1962).

——: *Economy and Society*, (New York, Random House, Inc., 1955).

——: *Industrialization and Labor*, (Ithaca, N.Y., Cornell University Press, 1951).

——: "Social Aspects of Economic Development," in E. L. Faris (ed.), *Handbook of Modern Sociology*, (Chicago, Rand McNally & Company, 1964).

Mosher, F. C.: "Features and Problems of the Federal Civil Service," in W. S. Sayer (ed.), *The Federal Government Service*, (Englewood Cliffs, N.J., Prentice-Hall, Inc., 1965).

Murdock, G. P.: *Social Structure*, (New York, The Macmillan Company, 1949).

Murphy, W., and J. Tanenhaus: "Public Opinion and the United States Supreme Court," *Law and Society*, 2, 1968, pp. 357–384.

Nash, M.: *Primitive and Peasant Economic Systems*, (San Francisco, Chandler Publishing Company, 1966).

Niebuhr, R.: *The Social Sources of Denominationalism*, (Cleveland, World Publishing Company, 1957).

Nimkoff, M. F. (ed.): *Comparative Family Systems*, (Boston, Houghton Mifflin Company, 1965).

Nisbet, R. A.: *The Social Bond*, (New York, Alfred A. Knopf, Inc., 1970).

—— : *Social Change and History*, (New York, Oxford University Press, 1969).

Norbeck, E.: *Religion in Primitive Society*, (New York, Harper & Row, Publishers, Incorporated, 1961).

Pfautz, H. W.: "The Sociology of Secularization: Religious Groups," *American Journal of Sociology*, 61, 1955, pp. 121–128.

Phillips, B. S.: *Sociology: Social Structure and Change*, (London, Macmillan & Co., Ltd., 1969).

O'Dea, T. F.: *Sociology and the Study of Religion*, (New York, Basic Books, Inc., Publishers, 1970).

—— : *The Sociology of Religion*, (Englewood Cliffs, N.J., Prentice-Hall, Inc. 1966).

Ogburn, W. F., and M. F. Nimkoff: *Technology and the Changing Family*, (Boston, Houghton Mifflin Company, 1955).

Parsons, T.: *Societies: Evolutionary and Comparative Perspectives*, (Englewood Cliffs, N.J., Prentice-Hall, Inc. 1966).

—— : "Evolutionary Universals in Society," *American Sociological Review*, 29, 1964, pp. 339–357.

—— : "Family Structure and the Socialization of the Child," in T. Parsons and R. F. Bales (eds.), *Family, Socialization and Interaction Process*, (New York, The Free Press, 1955).

—— : "The Kinship System of the Contemporary United States," in T. Parsons, *Essays in Sociological Theory*, (New York, The Free Press, 1954).

—— : "The Law and Social Control," in W. Evan (ed.), *Law and Sociology, Exploratory Essays*, (New York, The Free Press, 1962).

—— : *The Social System*, (New York, The Free Press, 1951).

—— : "The Theoretical Development of the Sociology of Religion," in T. Parsons, *Essays in Sociological Theory*, (New York, The Free Press, 1949).

—— and R. F. Bales (eds.), *Family Socialization and Interaction Process*, (New York, The Free Press, 1955).

—— and E. A. Shils (eds.), *Toward a General Theory of Action*, (New York, Harper & Row, Publishers, Incorporated, 1951).

—— and N. J. Smelser: *Economy and Society*, (New York, The Free Press, 1956).

Pierce, T. M.: *Federal, State, and Local Government in Education*, (Washington, D.C., Center for Applied Research in Education, 1964).

Potter, C. P., and B. C. Hennessy: *Politics Without Power*, (New York, Atherton Press, Inc., 1964).

Pound, R.: *Law and Morals*, (Chapel Hill, N. C., University of North Carolina Press, 1924).

The President's Commission on Law Enforcement and Administration of Justice: *Task Force Report: The Police*, (Washington, D.C., Government Printing Office, 1967).

Presthus, R.: *The Organizational Society*, (New York, Random House, Inc., 1962).

Pye, L. W., and S. Verba (eds.): *Political Culture and Political Development*, (Princeton, N.J., Princeton University Press, 1965).

Queen, S. A., and R. W. Habenstein: *The Family in Various Cultures*, (Philadelphia, J. B. Lippincott Company, 1967).

Radcliff-Brown, A. R.: *Taboo*, (Cambridge, Cambridge University Press, 1938).

Reagan, M. D.: *The Managed Economy*, (London, Oxford University Press, 1963).

Ridgeway, J.: *The Closed Corporation: American Universities in Crisis*, (New York: Ballantine Books, Inc., 1968).

Rose, A. M.: *The Power Structure*, (New York, Oxford University Press, 1967).

Rosen, B. C.: "The Achievement Syndrome: A Psychocultural Dimension of Social Stratification," *American Sociological Review*, 21, 1956, pp. 203–211.

—— and R. D'Andre: "The Psychosocial Origins of Achievement Motivation," *Sociometry*, 22, 1959, pp. 67–74.

Rosenthal, R., and L. Jacobson: *Pygmalion in the Classroom*, (New York, Holt, Rinehart and Winston, Inc., 1968).

Rudolf, L.: *The Modernity of Tradition*, (Chicago, The University of Chicago Press, 1967).

Salisbury, W. S.: *Religion in American Culture*, (Homewood, Ill., The Dorsey Press, 1964).

Sawer, G.: *Law in Society*, (London, Oxford at Clarendon Press, 1965).

Schapera, I.: *Government and Politics in Tribal Societies*, (London, C. A. Watts and Co., Ltd., 1956).

Schumpeter, J. A.: *Capitalism, Socialism, and Democracy*, 3d ed., (New York, Harper & Row, Publishers, Incorporated, 1950).

—— : *The Theory of Economic Development*, (Cambridge, Mass., Harvard University Press, 1934).

Schur, E.: *Law and Society*, (New York, Random House, Inc., 1968).

Schwartz, R. D., and J. C. Miller: "Legal Evolution and Societal Complexity," *American Journal of Sociology*, 70, 1964, pp. 159–169.

Selvin, H. C., and W. O. Hagstrom: "Determinants of Support for Civil Liberties," *The British Journal of Sociology*, 25, 1960, pp. 51–73.

Service, E. R.: *The Hunters*, Englewood Cliffs, N.J., Prentice-Hall, Inc., 1966).

Sewell, W. H.: "Social Class, Parental Encouragement, and Educational Aspirations," *American Sociological Review*, 33, 1968, pp. 191–209.

—— and U. P. Shah: "Socioeconomic Status, Intelligence, and Attainment of Higher Education," *Sociology of Education*, 40, 1968, pp. 1–23.

—— and A. M. Orenstein: "Community Residence and Occupational Choice," *American Journal of Sociology*, 70, 1965, pp. 551–563.

Sharp, L.: "Steel Axes for Stone Age Australians," in E. H. Spicer (ed.), *Human Problems in Technological Change; A Casebook*, (New York, The Russell Sage Foundation, 1952).

Simon, R. J. (ed.): *The Sociology of Law*, (San Francisco, Chandler Publishing Company, 1968).

Skolnick, J. H.: *The Politics of Protest*, (New York, Simon & Schuster, Inc., 1969).

——: *Justice Without Trial*, (New York, John Wiley & Sons, Inc., 1966).

Smelser, N. J.: "Toward a Theory of Modernization," in A. Etzioni and E. Etzioni (eds.), *Social Change*, (New York, Basic Books, Inc., Publishers, 1964).

Southall, A. (ed.): *Social Change in Modern Africa*, (London, Oxford University Press, 1961).

Spier, R. F. G.: *From the Hand of Man: Primitive Preindustrial Technologies*, (Boston, Houghton Mifflin Company, 1970).

Spiro, M. E.: *Kibbutz, Venture in Utopia*, (Cambridge, Mass., Harvard University Press, 1956).

Stark, R., and C. Glock: *American Piety: The Nature of Religious Commitment*, (Berkeley, University of California Press, 1968).

Stephens, W. N.: *The Family in Cross-Cultural Perspective*, (New York, Holt, Rinehart and Winston, Inc., 1963).

——: "Family and Kinship," in N. J. Smelser (ed.), *Sociology*, (New York, John Wiley & Sons, Inc., 1967).

Stone, J.: *The Province and Function of Law*, (Cambridge, Mass., Harvard University Press, 1950).

Swanson, G. E.: *The Birth of the Gods*, (Ann Arbor, The University of Michigan Press, 1960).

Taft, H., *Legal Miscellanies*, (New York, The Macmillan Company, 1941).

Theobold, R.: *Free Men and Free Markets*, (New York, Crown Publishers, Inc., 1963).

Thibault, J. W., and H. H. Kelly: *The Social Psychology of Groups*, (New York, John Wiley & Sons, Inc., 1959).

Thomas, E. M.: *The Harmless People*, (New York, Alfred A. Knopf, Inc., 1959).

Thut, I. N., and D. Adams: *Educational Patterns in Contemporary Societies*, (New York, McGraw-Hill Book Company, 1964).

Troeltsch, E.: *The Social Teachings of Christian Churches*, O. Wyon (trans.), (New York, The Macmillan Company, 1931).

T'ung, T. C.: *Law and Society in Traditional China*, (Paris, Mouton, 1961).

Tylor, E. B.: *Primitive Culture, Researches into the Development of Mythology, Philosophy, Religion, Language, Art and Custom*, vol. 2, (New York, Harper & Row, Publishers, Incorporated, 1948). Originally published in 1871.

Verba, S.: "Comparative Political Culture," in L. Pye and S. Verba (eds.), *Political Culture and Political Development*, (Princeton, N.J., Princeton University Press, 1965).

Vernon, G. M.: *Sociology of Religion*, (New York, McGraw-Hill Book Company, 1962).

Wade, H. W. R.: *Administrative Law*, (Oxford, Clarendon Press, 1961).

Wallace, A. F. C.: *Religion, An Anthropological View*, (New York, Random House, Inc., 1966).

Warriner, C. K.: *The Emergence of Society*, (Homewood, Ill., The Dorsey Press, 1970).

Weber, M.: *On Law in Economy and Society*, (New York, Clarion Press, 1954).

——: *The Sociology of Religion*, E. Fischoff (trans.), (Boston, Beacon Press, 1963).

——: *From Max Weber*, (New York, Oxford University Press, 1946).

——: *The Protestant Ethic and the Spirit of Capitalism*, (London, Allen and Unwin, 1930). Originally published in 1904.

Wegner, E. L., and W. H. Sewell: "Selection and Context as Factors Affecting the Probability of Graduation from College," *American Sociological Review*, 75, 1970, pp. 665–679.

Wiener, N.: *The Human Use of Human Beings: Cybernetics and Society*, (Garden City, N.Y., Doubleday and Company, 1950).

Wigmore, L. A.: *A Panorama of the World's Legal Systems*, (Washington, D.C., Washington Law Book Co., 1936).

Williams, R. M., Jr.: *American Society*, 3d ed., (New York, Alfred A. Knopf, Inc., 1970).

——: *American Society*, 2d ed., (New York, Alfred A. Knopf, Inc., 1960).

Wilson, B.: *Religion in Secular Society*, (Baltimore, Penguin Books, Inc., 1969).

409

Winterbottom, M.: "The Relation of Need for Achievement to Learning Experiences in Independence and Mastery," in J. W. Atkinson (ed.), *Motives in Fantasy, Action, Society,* (Princeton, N.J., D. Van Nostrand Company, Inc., 1958).

Winthrop, H.: "Sociological and Ideological Assumptions Underlying Cybernation," *American Journal of Economics and Sociology,* 25, 1966, pp. 113–126.

——: "Some Psychological and Economic Assumptions Underlying Automation," *American Journal of Economics and Sociology,* 17, 1958, pp. 399–412.

Yinger, M. J.: *The Scientific Study of Religion,* (London, Macmillan & Co., Ltd., 1970).

Ziegler, H.: *Interest Groups in American Society,* (Englewood Cliffs, N.J., Prentice-Hall, Inc., 1964).

410

author index

subject index

419